THINKING

DIFFERENTLY

Becoming Digital Nations

Digital Society – Digital Economy – Digital Governance

REIMAGINING

Countries for the Digital Era

Mohammad J. Sear

“Visionaries imagine and create new realities by challenging and disregarding the status quo...”

Mohammad J. Sear

First Edition
Author: Mohammad J. Sear
Editor: LinkedCopy
Design: Publishing Spot
Publisher: Mohammad J. Sear

ISBNs:

- Ebook: 978-969-619-219-0
- Paperback: 978-969-639-267-5
- Hardcover: 978-969-639-268-2

Author's Website: https://mjmsear.com/

Printed in USA

PREFACE

We are living in an unprecedented period, one that is commonly referred to as The Digital Era.

If there are three things I would like you to take away from this book, then these are:

“REIMAGE to TRANSFORM”

“UNLEAR to LEARN”

And finally be “PURPOSE DRIVEN”.

This book is my way of getting all of us to think differently about digital, and is intended to be the first in a series that I plan writing about this subject.

This first book on the one hand will act as the mechanism for laying out my overall perspective on how countries need to think differently by elevating and broadening their horizon, and reimagine the country for the Digital Era. In essence, transform to become a Digital Nation comprising a digital society, economy and governance.

This book will then delve deeper into the digital governance element, as for me this is the foundational element of a digital nation and one that enables the other two. I shall do so by looking into the approach and progress that 198 countries around the world have made in this area.

In addition to sharing where each country stands in this area I will be also sharing the patterns that emerge in different regions around the world, the common problems they face, and the creative solutions they’re coming up with. My goal is to show just how diverse digital is around the world, with each country finding its own way forward.

I see this book as part of a bigger effort to share knowledge and ideas.

It's meant for everyone—whether you're a citizen, an expert, a decision-maker shaping these changes, or just someone interested in what's happening.

I believe that this information should be easy for everyone to understand because digital and digital transformation affects all of us, even if we don't always notice it.

But why is the reimagining governance so important?

I believe it's because it offers a way to tackle some of the biggest social and economic challenges we face. For an example it is a chance for us to rethink how government works—not just to make things faster or more efficient, but to REALLY improve how it serves people.

I think it's also a way to build a new kind of governance that respects and builds on the traditions and values of each country, rather than wiping them away. By reimagining governance for the digital era, countries can keep what's important from the past while also creating a better future that's more transparent, inclusive, and responsive. Obviously, there are some big global trends right now—especially the push for more digital services, leveraging Artificial Intelligence (AI) and the focus on tackling climate change. These aren't just popular topics; they're really changing how countries make decisions and how they interact with each other.

I think it's clear that the technologies driving these changes, part of what's often called the fourth industrial revolution, are playing a huge role. We're seeing the Internet of Things (IoT) connecting devices everywhere, governments putting more services online, and new technologies like blockchain and cloud storage changing how information is handled. These advancements are not just making things easier; they're influencing how countries prioritise their goals and solve their problems.

Which indexes have I used?

In writing elements of this book, I've relied heavily on the EGDI index, which stands for the E-Government Development Index. This index, along with other international publications from organisations like the OECD, the UN, and the World Bank, forms the backbone of my research.

However, as I said, EGDI was my main source for several reasons. One of the main reasons is that it covers *almost* every country, providing a comprehensive overview of global digitalisation efforts. (Most reports don't include this many countries.) The EGDI is updated every two years, which means it's not just a static snapshot but a dynamic tool that reflects the ongoing changes in digital governance. By tracking these updates, we can see how countries are progressing—or, in some cases, where they might be falling behind. It's this ability to capture change over time that makes the EGDI particularly useful for a book like this, where the goal is to understand not just where countries are now, but how they've been moving forward (or not) in their digital journeys.

Now, while the EGDI is incredibly useful, it's important to note that it's not the most detailed index out there. It provides a broad overview, but it doesn't dive deeply into the specifics of each country's situation. That's why I felt there was a need to put all my research into a book. There's a lot of information out there about digital governance, but there's value in bringing it all together in one place, especially when we're looking at something as broad and complex as global digital. My goal with this book is to provide a comprehensive resource that looks at digital efforts worldwide, drawing on the wide perspective that the EGDI offers.

How many countries are analysed?

In my research, I've analysed 198 countries. This includes every country listed in the EGDI plus more (even those that might not be officially recognised or are in conflict over their status, like Palestine or Israel, or even isolated from the rest of the world.) For example the

EGDI report analyses 193 countries. I think it's crucial to include these cases because they are part of the global story. Their experiences and efforts in digital, despite the unique challenges they face, contribute to our overall understanding of digital in governance in a world that is far from simple or straightforward.

The EGDI's broad scope and regular updates make it an excellent starting point for this kind of research. It's not perfect—no index is—but I believe it's the best tool we have for getting a general idea of where the world stands on digital in governance. And that's exactly what this book aims to do: provide a global overview, highlighting the different paths countries are taking towards digital, how they're addressing the challenges that come with it, and what this means for the future of governance.

How is the book structured?

The first chapter lays out my overall perspective on why countries need to reimagine themselves for the digital era and the three elements of a digital nation - digital society, digital economy and digital governance, and delves a bit deeper into reimaging governance elements.

The book will then take us on a journey to explore the digital approaches adopted and progress made by 198 countries around the world. I decided to divide this study into 6 continents: Africa, (South & North) America, Asia, Europe, and Oceania. I believe this division is essential for a few reasons, and I'd like to share why it's so helpful for both the structure of the book and the reader's understanding.

It's important to recognise that each continent has its own unique set of challenges, opportunities, and historical contexts that influence how digital is approached. Grouping countries by continents, I'm able to focus on these regional characteristics more closely, offering a clearer picture of the similarities and differences within each region. This approach makes it easier for readers to understand the broader trends and patterns that might not be as evident if the analysis were done otherwise.

For instance, countries within the same continent often face similar challenges, whether they're related to infrastructure, political stability, or economic development. By grouping them together, we can better understand how these shared challenges influence their approach to digital in governance. Moreover, this division helps highlight regional trends that might not be as obvious if we were to look at the world as a whole. For example, Africa, as a continent, faces unique challenges in terms of infrastructure and access to technology, but it's also home to some of the most innovative digital solutions. After that, I went deeper to look at every country within that region. This method allows for a thorough understanding of both the regional dynamics and the specific circumstances of each country. It's a way of zooming in and out to give you both the big picture and the smaller achievements or challenges for each.

One of the key questions I wanted to explore was whether there's a correlation between being in a particular continent and the level of development of digital in government. I believe there is a connection, though it's not always straightforward. For example, geography plays a role—countries in regions with better access to technology and resources tend to advance more quickly. However, it's also clear that political will, economic stability, and cultural factors can be just as important, if not more so. In some cases, countries in less developed regions are actually leapfrogging ahead by adopting innovative approaches and technologies that allow them to bypass some of the traditional stages of development.

In terms of what I've covered, my analysis looks at the initiatives each country has taken in digital governance. This includes everything from e-government services and digital infrastructure to policies aimed at increasing citizen engagement through technology. I've also looked at how these initiatives are progressing—what's working, what's not, and what lessons can be learned. In the end, digital governance is a vast and complex field, but by looking at it through the lens of the EGDI and other key resources, I hope to shed light on the global trends, challenges, and opportunities that are shaping the future of governance. And I hope this book serves as a useful resource for anyone interested in digital in countries around the world, particularly in the area of governance.

About the Author

Mohammad J. Sear is a digital era futurist and thought leader, and is focused on bringing purpose to the benefits of the digital era for nations. He likes to think of himself as a Chief Disruption Officer.

He has obtained leadership training from the Harvard Kennedy School of Government, USA and holds an MBA from the University of Leicester, UK. After a successful 12+ years career in the UK government during the premiership of Margaret Thatcher, John Major and Tony Blair Mohammad moved to the private sector and has now for 20+ years been advising government, public and private sector organizations in the UK, Middle East, Africa, Australasia and South Asia on strategic challenges and digital transformation.

He is currently leading the Digital Government & Public Sector and Start-up practices across the Middle East and North Africa for a global consultancy firm, and in the past for a 3 year period he was also a Digital Government, Public Sector and Innovation lecturer at the Paris School of International Affairs, Sciences Po, France.

He is a catalytic public sector changemaker and champion of diversity & inclusion, and passionate about transforming government. Being a change agent with a bias towards action he has enabled governments to become more citizen-centric and achieve operational breakthroughs by harnessing conventional and digital capabilities, as well as leveraging the power of design thinking, agile, behavioral science, emerging technologies such as artificial intelligence.

He is sought after by senior leaders' in government, public and private sectors for his futuristic and strategic thinking, and surgical advisory capabilities.

As a thought-leader and author of publications in the areas of digital nations, society, economy and governance, citizen centricity, customer experience, service design & delivery, emerging technologies

Mohammad is frequently requested to speak, moderate or be a panel member at top tier global events on topics including but not limited to: digital nations, emerging technologies, future of governance, humanizing technology, exponential digital transformation in countries, cross sector collaboration, citizen-centered governance, and design thinking in public policy. Some of the articles he has authored include:

- Digital is great but exclusion isn't – make data work for driving better digital inclusion published in **Harvard Business Review**
- Holistic Digital Government published in the **MIT Technology Review**
- Want To Make Citizens Happy - Put Experience First published in **Forbes Middle East**

And others such as "Bringing Purpose to Digital in Government", "How Digital is Changing the Way We Listen to Customers", "How Can GCC Governments Sustainably Deliver Better Citizen Experiences", "What is the Cure for a Better Patient Experience in the GCC", "Application of the Global Star Rating System for Public Services".

Moving from insights to execution Mohammad has designed transformational initiatives in several areas such as GovTech and Innovation Labs, digital product accelerators, digital government transformation, digital government service models and national citizen experience measurement strategies.

CHAPTER 1

Reimagining Nations for the Digital Era

We are living in an unprecedented period, one that is commonly referred to as The Digital Era.

What is actually the Digital Era?

"The Digital Era is defined as the present time, in which many things are done by computers and large amounts of information are available because of computer technology, and in which new business models have emerged" – Cambridge Dictionary.

In my opinion this requires us to make a paradigm shift in our thinking and approach – REIMANGINING - if we want our world to take full advantage of the immense benefit the digital era has to offer.

We need to think differently and centre our thinking on what we are truly solving for rather than blindly applying technology on top of what already exists. We need to realise that the digital era in addition to technology is as much if not more about new business models and new operating models.

We must question why something exists, the reason behind why we want to solve a particular challenge or why we want to explore a certain opportunity. In other words, understanding and defining the purpose behind these endeavours is paramount. We need to unlearn to learn to recognise the true power and benefits of the digital era.

Only then must we begin our journey of exploration.

So, firstly, what I am proposing is that instead of us taking the conventional approach that most around the world seem to be taking - Digital Government - that for me is answering the narrow question of "How will IT help the GOVERNMENT operate?" we flip it to – Government in the Digital Era - and therefore break away from looking at digital through a narrow technology lens and open our minds to answering a much bigger and broader question of "How should our GOVERNMENT evolve to operate in the Digital Era?"

Secondly, we must elevate our thinking from focusing on just Government in the Digital Era to the whole Country in the Digital Era.

In other words, How should our COUNTRY evolve to operate and thrive in the Digital Era?

I believe countries that don't take this approach stand to be left behind, and remain or become the developing nations of tomorrow regardless of where they stand today. Why do I believe this?

The Digital Era has ushered in a new playing field, and one where, as mentioned earlier, any developing country now has the opportunity to become a developed country in this digital world or any developed country be relegated to a developing nation.

This is because our world has changed significantly, as the web has and is becoming the playground for everything and our future world is going to be characterised by hyper-digital connectivity amongst both humans and devices, and all indicators are pointing to a continued shift of our day-to-day life activities from the physical to this online digital world.

In October 2024 there are approx. 5.52 billion internet users and around 5.22 billion social media users, and the social media users are growing at approx. 8%. Online users spent an average of 6.36 hrs time using the internet (in the second quarter of 2024) – according to Statista.com.

Digital advertising is surpassing traditional media advertising, and it stood at $442.6 billion in 2024 that denotes 58.8% of global advertising spend – according to Dentsu.com.

Salesforce and Publicis Sapient have published research that shows 87% of shoppers today start their product search journey to online.

The global digital education market size to be valued at USD 77.23 billion by 2028 and is expected to grow at a compound annual growth rate (CAGR) of 30.5% from 2021 to 2028 - according to grandviewreseaerch.com.

The digital healthcare market will be approx. $946 billion by 2030, up from $288,9 billion in 2024 at a CAGR of 21.6% - according to grandviewreseaerch.com.

The mobile payment systems market size was valued at USD 2.98 Trillion in 2023 and is projected to reach USD 27.85 Trillion by 2030, growing at a CAGR of 28.15% during the forecasted period 2024 to 2030 – according to verifiedmarketreports.com

The global video-on-demand market size is expected to reach $328.8 billion by 2030, rising at a market growth of 13.1% CAGR during the forecast period – according to kbvresearch.com

Finally, it is worth mentioning that according to a report published by the World Bank in 2022 the digital economy makes up more than 15% of the global GDP and has grown 2.5 times faster over the previous ten years than the GDP of the physical world. Also, a report published by Forrester says that the digital economy will be around $16.5 by 2028, which constitutes approx. 17% of the world economy. It also said that according to The World Economic Forum, more than 65% of value creation over the next 10 years will come from digitally enabled platforms.

Digital has both changed the playing field and rules of the game. It has and is continuing to democratise access to information, knowledge, tools and more that previously were available to only a privileged few. And digital platforms such as YouTube, Instagram and TikTok are creating economic opportunities for anyone to become a celebrity, influencer or an entrepreneur.

The Digital Era is both an opportunity and a threat for countries. Those who embrace the ambition of becoming a true Digital Native Country will lead the pack, but on the other hand, those who see digital as just a technology play will find themselves at the bottom.

In my opinion, The DIGITAL ECONOMY has become the new BATTLEGROUND. This is backed by the facts and figures shared above and due to the phenomena that digital businesses are by their very nature global businesses from DAY 1 as they operate in a digital world that is, for all intents and purposes, borderless. Now, I am NOT saying that each digital business will be a global business. Rather, it has all the potential to become one.

And most importantly, Generation Z or Gen Z (born between 1995 and 2009) and Generation Alpha or Gen Alpha born between 2010 and 2024 and other generations to come will make up the majority of the world population.

In 2024, Gen Z in 2024 represented 32% of the global population – according to qureos.com. And Gen Alpha population will reach more than 2 billion by the end of 2024 – according to McGrindle.com.

Why does this matter?

It matters because Gen Z is considered to be the first digital native population, and Gen Alpha not only fall into this category but also is a Generative AI native. Therefore, Gen Z and Alpha are and will continue to be the main drivers that will push countries to become Digital Nations.

So, in my humble opinion, countries stand at the crossroads of whether to go right or left.

On the right is the journey towards becoming a true Digital Native Country - one that will be an innovator, a trendsetter, a world leader and a high-value producer, and where its efforts are focused on producing high-value digital products and services and its people earn higher incomes and have a higher quality of life.

Whilst the left will take us on a course that will keep us as one of the countries in the world that exist at the bottom of the pack, and is a low-value low-cost producer nation where people earn lower income and live a lower quality of life.

So what does becoming a Digital Native Country actually mean?

In my view, this is more about a mindset that requires taking a radical step and reimagining a country for the Digital Era from the ground upwards.

Let's imagine that we bought an island and were creating a new country for the very first time that didn't exist before – a truly greenfield country -

This country would be considered a Digital Native Country as it was born in the digital era that we are living in today. We would have the benefit of deciding how to govern and administer the country or how the economy, society, and infrastructure, amongst other things that exist in a country, will be structured.

As in this greenfield country, we will have no legacy governance, economy, operating or business models, processes, systems, etc. All these will be imagined, designed and established from the ground up based on the capabilities, technologies, models, etc., that are at our disposal today. Therefore, in doing so, we will be leveraging, to the maximum extent possible, the technologies, business and operating models of the digital era. Now, I am not saying that we should go out and buy islands to create new countries.

Rather, I am suggesting that we embody the essence of thinking like a greenfield Digital Native Country and define a future state for our country that is unhindered by our constraints of today and one that is centred around its citizens and other stakeholders in order to enable true disruptive and breakthrough thinking. And only after this must the constraints of today be brought into consideration.

Taking this approach will enable countries to arrive at a visionary Future State Blueprint for the country that will take it the closest possible to becoming a Digital Native Country, and this blueprint will become the North Star that will guide and set the direction of future policies, initiatives, investments and roadmaps. In this Digital Native Country, data will be at the heart of everything ... we will be able to easily connect the dots between dispersed sets of data and create a unified view and approach .... Friction ... duplication, etc., will be eliminated. Artificial intelligence (AI), and especially generative AI will be leveraged to the maximum across all walks of life – personal, professional, organisations, etc., and the Internet of Things will play a central role.

Let's call such countries "Digital Nations"

A Digital Nation therefore could be considered as one in which all actors – citizens, residents, businesses, governments, legislators, judiciary, visitors etc. – are digitally doing all those things that are practically possible to do so. The economy is predominately made up of digital native businesses (ones that only or in the main operate in the online non-physical world), and non-digital native businesses are highly digitalized. Finally, emerging technologies, and digital era operating and business models are being leveraged to the maximum.

For simplicity lets define it as " a country where all societal actors operate seamlessly in a digital world, using digital-era technologies and business models for communication, work, commerce, education, and entertainment, predominantly through the internet".

In the digital nation, interactions are redefined... from fragmented, forced, siloed, reactive interactions... ... to seamless exchanges that connect digital nation actors when and where they need them.

For me this translates into the existence in the country of a Digital or highly Digitalized "Society", "Economy" and "Governance".

Digital Society is a social system where individuals engage, connect, and fulfil everyday needs through digital means. In this society, daily interactions are primarily conducted online, using digital products that enhance accessibility, inclusivity, and real-time connection, reshaping the ways individuals contribute to community life.

Digital Economy is an economic system where organisations and individuals create, deliver, and exchange value primarily through digital products and services. In this economy, value creation is rooted in digital-first models that enable seamless, online-driven transactions and interactions. And organisations are highly digital or digitalized.

Digital Governance is a governance system where all functions of public administration—legislative, executive, and judicial—operate digitally or are highly digitalized. This model enables as much as possible for government services, policymaking, and legal processes to be accessible, transparent, and responsive in a fully online environment.

At the core, Digital Nations requires the existence of robust and future-proof digital infrastructure akin to the physical infrastructure like roads, bridges, airports, railways, etc., which is necessary for our physical world to function. This includes devices like mobiles and laptops that can be used to access digital products and services, fast-speed digital highways to carry our data, digital IDs that can be used for authentication, digital payments to enable frictionless transactions, digital signatures to enable legal protection, secure and safe digital Communications, data exchange to enable easy access and transfer of information between people, organisations and devices, efficient data centres… and much more.

CHAPTER 2

Digital Governance Reimagined for the Digital Era and Adopting a Holistic Approach

Let me start by sharing my vision for the future of public sector interactions and services.

I believe the Digital Era technologies, business and operating models are leading us to a concept I call "Autonomous Governance" which will both significantly enhance the experience of users and employees and lead to tremendous efficiencies.

Let me elaborate on this by sharing three of my ideas:

1. 1-click-10-sec

Imagine a world in which a service provided by the public sector requires only one click and 10 seconds for it to be completely fulfilled, and that requires no forms to be filled out or documents to be provided. However, today, unfortunately, we as users are forced to provide the same information and documents each time we want to obtain a service, even with the same organisation.

Is this possible?

Yes, as all the information and documents that are normally required for the provisioning of a service are already sitting within the public sector ecosystem. It requires a change of mindset and approach.

2. Personal Profile Digital-Twin

Imagine a world in which all of our personal data, rights, eligibility, documents, records, etc., are contained in a single user-friendly personal digital profile – I have named this Personal Profile Digital-Twin.

I am not only able to access my information through this but also able to securely communicate through it with the public and private sector organisations in a seamless and frictionless way. Additionally, rather than having lots of digital documents in there – like a digital driving licence – it will just have a toggle button that will turn green if you have passed your driving test and are, therefore, eligible to drive a car.

Finally, it will be the secure and trusted way for you to receive official notifications from a public sector organisation and even cast your vote in country elections but of course, only if you are eligible to vote – which again will be indicated in your profile by a button for this specific thing showing as green because you have reached the voting age. There is no need to register separately to be a voter.

We can keep imaging more and more we can do through this mechanism – the key thing is that it will simplify all interactions and communications we have with organisations.

3. Personal Meta-Human Public Servant Assistant

Imagine a world in which AI-powered meta-human public servants will serve their users at any time of the day, and that will replicate human-like service. It will be like we are speaking and interacting with a real human. Moving from "Clicking" to "Asking" – we are social creatures and prefer to have a conversation with someone.

So in this new future world, which I believe is only around the corner, rather than clicking and searching through a portal, we will just go into our Personal Profile Digital-Twin and ask our meta-human personal public servant assistant for the information we need or the service we require and the assistant will not only go find and display it a bit like

ChatGPT does but also apply to the service on our behalf – if we have given it the consent to do so.

This same concept could also exist in a 3D VR experience created in a Metaverse that replicates and becomes the service centre for the public sector to not just

provide a human-like experience by having the meta-human public servant assistant but also provide a real-world-like experience through the metaverse.

Delving Deeper ....

I wanted to start this chapter with some futuristic thoughts, but now we can move to looking at governance in a broader way.

Let's kick this off by first reminding ourselves about what actually Governance is in the context of a country – it consists of the three pillars or branches - Legislature, Government (sometimes referred to as Executive) and Judiciary that all work in unison to ensure people live a secure, purposeful, fulfilling, healthy, and satisfying life, and the environment and our entire ecosystem is protected, sustainable and remains vibrant.

Countries around the world are investing millions of dollars in ambitious digital Initiatives to transform governance, and in my view, now is the prime time to guide these investments through a "purpose-driven" lens to avoid investing in quick-fix solutions at the cost of long-term sustainable solutions.

These digital transformation initiatives are major endeavours which present countries with the opportunity to reimagine governance rather than taking a digitalisation approach of layering technologies over current services and processes. A governance model that is truly citizen-centric and built ground up for the digital age BY DESIGN.

The approach of reimagining aims to change the thinking from merely - how can we more effectively and efficiently do the things that we have been doing to DISRUPTING the existing system with a completely different thinking.

This is similar to the private sector organisations that have not only used technology to enhance the way they do things but also adopted digital era business and operating models and modified the way they are designed to operate. For instance, streaming services and OTT platforms are digital by default and designed for today. They do not have any legacy systems and structures.

My vision of a governance model apt for this digital era is one where it is more of an "enabler" than a "doer", and one that is much more focused and aligned to its fundamental purpose of serving citizens.

At a high level, this means intelligently leveraging all the existing resources and technology capabilities to develop a citizen-centric system that is data-driven, proactive, predictive and connected. A governance system that can constantly identify/predict and understand the needs of its stakeholders even before they have figured these out. It can quickly derive insights from zettabytes of data and convert them into actions.

Let me demonstrate with two examples what I mean by reimagining for the digital era so that the difference and benefit of taking this vs the traditional digital transformation approach is clear.

1. Passports

Traditional Approach – we would look to make the end-to-end application process digital and online that has a simple and frictionless experience for the user; the processing of the application is also simple and frictionless for the officials that are responsible for undertaking this step or maybe is even made human-less with the help of technologies such as AI and the passport itself is made machine-readable, tamperproof etc. and once ready the delivery is automatically triggered and it reaches you. During all these steps, you have been kept fully informed and updated on the status of your passport application.

We may even introduce proactive and predictive aspects. Like the government organisation responsible for passports automatically reaches out to you through a push notification to inform you that your passport is experiencing in 3 months and asks you to swipe right if you want them to send you a new passport; once you do this, it takes you through some simple validation and security steps, and the job is done, and your passport arrives with you 7 days before the expiry of your passport.

We also may introduce a predictive model whereby despite the expiry date of your passport not approaching as you have been travelling a lot, there is a possibility that you have run out of pages. So once again, the responsible organisation for passports predicts that you may have run out of pages so automatically triggers of push-notification to say that whilst there is ample time before your passport to expires but as you have been doing so much travel, we are reaching out to see if you need a new passport due to the pages getting close to being fully used, and ask you to swipe right to trigger off the process.

Reimagined for the Digital Era Approach - In this Approach, we will start by asking ourselves some fundamental questions, starting with - why does a passport exist?

In other words, what is its core purpose?

And you, like me you, will most likely say its core purpose is to enable foreign travel – enter/exit your and foreign countries.

We will then ask ourselves the next question – how can we enable this foreign travel in this digital era we are living in?

Like me, you will say that technologies like facial recognition and biometrics can enable this.

We will reach the conclusion that the document called the passport has passed its sell-by-date as we have become the passport. And the "Problem" we really need to be solving is a policy, legal and operating model one, not how to transform the application and processing of passports.

2. Birth Certificates

Here, to save us time, I am just going to talk briefly about the reimaging of the digital approach.

So, again, we start by asking ourselves the question – why do birth certificates exist?

And we realise that on its own, it has no value - it is how it is used by many people or organisations to verify or validate when, where and to whom we were born for the purposes of determining if we are entitled to some benefits like inheritance, right to vote, eligible to drive and so on.

We come to the conclusion that, in essence, it is about "Verification".

So, rather than going down the route of transforming the physical form of a birth certificate, we should be looking to provide a secure and trusted digital verification service.

Don't get me wrong – the traditional digital transformation approach will absolutely and in a significant way improve the user experience, reduce the time spent doing things, and bring efficiencies. My view is that the reimaging for the digital era approach pushes us closer to solving the real problems and, drives breakthrough thinking, and enables us to make a step change and leapfrog.

In my view, public sector organisations in this digital era have an unprecedented advantage over such organisations of the past, as they have access to knowledge, business and operating models, technologies, computing power, communications infrastructure tools, innovations, etc., like no one has had before. Today, our average smartphone has more computing power than NASA's supercomputer that was used to put humans on the moon.

We, as countries, therefore, must go beyond the traditional digital transformation thinking and reimagine if we truly want to create a governance model that is fit for the digital era that we are living in today. We must ask questions such as:

1. Why do we do what we do today?
2. Are these things even needed, or have some of them become redundant or not created the impact that we thought they would?

3. If they are still needed, are we, as a public sector organisation, the right people to do them or should they be done by someone else?

And most important of all, we need to deeply investigate "what we are not doing today but should be doing and figure out ways to do these things efficiently & effectively" so that we can truly deliver what is expected of us.

Let's consider an example of public transportation. While there will always be a need for people to move from point A to point B, do we really need millions of people commuting within cities daily? The COVID-19 pandemic has shown that it is more of a mental block than an actual need in a hyperconnected world.

Several organisations have been able to successfully deliver on their projects without visiting physical offices. Therefore, the right solution may not be to build mega transport infrastructure and invest millions in complex traffic management systems but to focus on a more localised economy or leveraging technology and new business and operating models to reduce the need for people to move.

Similarly, if we take the example of education, we must look at the fundamental purpose, i.e. creating a skilled and productive workforce and, more importantly, sensible and responsible human beings. It then explores if the current way of delivering education is the right way to do it instead of just using new business and operating models and digital technology to disrupt the same education model.

When we take a traditional approach to the digital transformation of governance, we may miss the potential side effects that this may cause. For instance, when we only think about digital by default without considering inclusiveness, we are also creating a digital divide for the people who are either digitally challenged or come from marginalised groups with limited access or capability to access digital services.

In my view, we need to reimagine governance in order for it to be better connected to its core purpose of serving citizens. The future model of governance must be one that is minimalistic, more participative, and more responsive. And built around the following five principles:

Focus - citizen life experiences: for countries to be truly human-centric its primary focus must be to proactively design and activate life experiences for all stakeholders whether nationals, residents, visitors or others across the human life journey (cradle to grave) that enables them to live a secure, healthy, meaningful, content and fulfilled life. Countries must, therefore, elevate their thinking to a much higher level and look to enable all the elements that affect citizens, such as the living environment, the regulatory environment and the service environment.

Many governments, such as New Zealand, Singapore, Saudi Arabia, UAE, and Serbia, are trying to address this issue by changing their approach and adopting the concept of services based on life journeys – a departure from the conventional approach of arranging services around organisations. Although these efforts are still in their nascent phases, they can act as a guide for the country to get started with building an experience layer by design across the government.

To support the creation of this experience layer, countries can start by establishing an entity that cuts across different departments and agencies. This entity is expected to be continuously engaged in study and research to promote citizencentricity by applying behavioural science techniques, citizen journey mapping, design thinking, and collaboration.

Core - data & analytics: the new governance model should be built with a data-centric core with a central capability and capacity for data management and advanced analytics. This is critical if the principle of "focus on citizen life experience" is to be truly achieved.

Like the experience aspect in the public sector, advancements in analytics have been a relatively recent phenomenon for governance around the world. The public sector is building analytical systems on top of the existing processes and structures. Instead of analytics feeding insights to decision-makers to improve what exists today, it should be the driving factor behind what is developed and offered to the people in the first place and then act as an instrument for continuous improvement.

If countries carefully invest in creating a common technology stack, systems and tools, it will pave the way for harmonious integration and unlocking the flow of data that can be used for informed decision-making.

An analytics centre of excellence can help countries to have focused approach on building right capabilities and capacities to support whole-of-governance analytics needs. In addition to ensuring public entities have access to innovative analytical solutions, the centre can be a home to governance wide data standards, a repository of "how to" guidelines and advisory and provision for systems and processes to integrate data held with governance bodies.

Model - ecosystem based: the new model will leverage capabilities of academia, startups, technology companies and other organisations to design, develop and deliver citizen-centric services.

It is a more participative, lean and minimalistic governance model where the public sector is only doing what is a must to be undertaken by them.

This includes things that are not profitable for the private sector to do or things that require complete neutrality such as understanding citizen's needs, wants and expectations and translating them into policies, strategies, initiatives; protecting people from internal and external elements; ensuring their rights are protected and that public and private institutions treat them fairly.

Countries' public sector normally has a lot of burden on itself if seen through the lens of available resources. There are many avenues where private sector and other stakeholders can play a role in service delivery as well as solving social issues. Not only this has potential to lower resource burden on the countries, it also opens new opportunities for private sector, civil societies and other institutions. Moreover, this can create a competitive environment which will support open innovation and bodes well for user experience.

Public sector organisations in different countries are already opening up to private sector for them to deliver their services. For instance, Visa Facilitation Services Global (VFS Global), an outsourcing company currently processes millions of visa application on behalf of over 60 countries around the world1.

Examples can be also found from around the world where public sector organisations have found innovative ways like hackathons and crowdsourcing events to be more participative. In Luwero, Uganda, a mobile app is helping people share their feedback on roads and schedule their repairs.2 Because of this initiative, not only has community engagement gone up in Luwero, but more roads in rural areas are also being repaired at a quicker pace, directly influencing their experience with the government. Better road conditions improve road safety, reduce vehicle damages, and reduce instances of products being damaged in transit. Moreover, travel time and cost have halved for people.3

To engage with the people, the local Government of Luwero has collaborated with Mobilized Construction, a start-up that provides smartphone-based solutions to manage and monitor rural road repairs in developing countries. The phone is mounted on cars and is used to collect data on bad roads. The app uses the phone's accelerometer, GPS and video camera to identify if a road requires repair. Once the mapping of bad roads is complete, the app helps organise repair crews that are part of microenterprises involving locals.4

These approaches help governments leverage the power of many in a positive way, reducing strain on their limited resources.

Other countries have their own share of community engagement to tell. However, this remains more of an outlier than being a norm and the go-to approach of public sector organisations. Countries must travel the distance where this is no longer considered an "innovation", but a standard way of doing things.

To do that, countries will need to make significant changes to the governance framework, laws, and regulations, adjust organisational structures, and set new accountabilities and roles to bring this ecosystem alive. Additionally, a big shift will be required in the mindset of public sector organisations that allows the stakeholders the flexibility they need to solve an issue.

Emphasis - digital by default but not only: countries such as the UK have started to embrace this approach in their digital governance vision. This needs to be one of the salient features of the reimagined governance model in any country. However, while talking about 'digital by default', the focus is mostly on redesigning existing services and creating new ones through this approach. The concept of 'digital by default' must be extended beyond services to include:

- **Output of the services or "the product":** There is a lot of focus on redesigning services so that they become easily available through digital channels. However, the product of the service, in many cases, remains in its conventional or physical form. For example, a driver's licence. While you can apply for it online, the driving licence itself continues to remain in the physical form. While thinking 'digital by default', countries must investigate the possibilities of doing away with the need for physical documents and their delivery. So, in other words, taking the reimaging of the service or product for the digital ear approach rather than the digitalisation one.

One way to approach this is to ask a fundamental question, i.e. "What is this product trying to achieve, and is there an alternative to it?". For example, in the case of a driving licence, the idea is to establish a person's identity and prove that a person is authorised to drive a certain class of vehicle by competent authorities. Does this really require a person to carry a physical driving licence today?

In Estonia, the right to drive is established by the traffic register data. A driver is not obligated to carry the licence.[5] Is this approach not extendable to other countries – especially given the advancements in distributed ledger technology, which makes records immutable?

- **Day-to-day operations:** look at areas to automate and digitise in your core operations. Involve process re-engineering, adopt emerging technologies to minimise paper trail, and adopt policies to support a digital workforce such as remote working.

As an example, the UAE had set itself a target of conducting 50% of government transactions through blockchain platforms by 2021, saving around AED11b, 398 million printed documents annually and 77 million work hours every year.6 Although some years ago but it is still worth mentioning that in 2016, The HM Revenue & Customs (HMRC) in the UK inducted Robotic Process Automation into its operations, and within 18 months, 7.5 million transactions were managed by robots. This helped reduce the processing costs of these transactions by 80%, improved services by reducing call handling time by up to 40%, and achieved a 2X ROI within a year.7

Similarly, the COVID-19 pandemic pushed many public sector organisations around the world to adopt work-from-home or remote working solutions overnight. While this change was not planned, it was leveraged as an opportunity to introduce secure digital working tools and transform the culture.

- **Decision-making process:** advancements in technologies like predictive and prescriptive analytics, handling of big data, and artificial intelligence are allowing the collection and interpretation of data like never before.

Acting as core enablers, these technologies can be leveraged to build systems and tools to deploy, track, and monitor strategic goals, KPIs, and impact, helping countries make better, more informed, and data-driven decisions. In turn, this can help the government to reshape strategies, policies, institutional frameworks, programs and priorities, and optimise resource allocation to deliver on its promises to its people and the nation.

In the Netherlands, government has developed a National IT dashboard to keep track of IT projects in ministries and public entities[8]. The dashboard covers over a hundred IT projects worth at least EUR5m simultaneously, making it easy for decision-makers to track them all in one place. It provides information related to the progress of estimated costs, actual expenses and the lead time for all the projects.

Additionally, the dashboard records the benefits of different projects and their main suppliers, along with the recommendations of the ICT Review Office. Decision makers can also see the responses of ministries to understand if they are taking the right remedial steps where required.

The stress on the principle of making the government core based on data and analytics, therefore, becomes more evident.

- **Learning and development:** public sector organisations must explore ways to make learning and development programs and tools available through digital channels. As continuous skill development and lifelong learning concepts gather momentum, it will become challenging for any organisation to deliver required training through conventional means.

The COVID-19 pandemic has also created a case for facilitating learning and development programs through digital means. This trend is reflected in the increase in demand for MOOCs. For instance, Coursera recorded over 10 million course enrolment in April 2020 – an increase of 644% compared with the last year[9].

Integrating emerging technologies such as AR/VR and XR by design into learning programs can also contribute to enhancing skill development. For example, the US Air Force has adopted these technologies to improve its pilot training program as well as support crew[10].

A key thing to remember is that while making digital channels the primary way to interact and engage people, the design must consider how people with disabilities and special needs, those with limited access to required devices and the internet, and those with low levels of digital literacy can also complete a desired task conveniently.

Obsession - outcome-based results: strategies, policies, regulations, initiatives, projects, processes and investments of a reimagines governance model must be driven by outcomes. There should be an obsession towards return on investment whether it is in terms of quantitative impact, qualitative impact or, both.

A decision-maker should always scrutinise the actions of their organisation from the following lenses:

- Are end users or society better off than before?
- Are we more productive and efficient than before?
- How does this impact environmental and organisational sustainability?

In addition to these, public sector organisations must review the local societal contexts to check if any strategic priorities need attention, such as digital inclusion and equitable access to services for both genders.

It can be argued that even today, governance bodies have adopted KPIs and are investing in systems to track and manage performance. While this is true, the challenge lies with the use of an array of KPIs, lack of standardisation in measurement and individual capacity and capability of different public sector organisations. Moreover, often, the KPIs used are not helpful for decisionmakers in developing targeted strategies and initiatives to solve an issue.

For instance, The Digital Future Society and the United Nations University Operating Unit on Policy-Driven Electronic Governance have been working together on a study that aims to understand the challenges associated with the current approach and provide a framework to improve digital inclusion with the help of better data. Their study indicates that while over 300 indicators exist on the topic of digital inclusion, the majority of them are skewed towards access, usage and skills. Indicators related to user groups, such as gender-based information, are poorly covered. Similarly, KPIs related to issues like digital identities, security and trust are also missing to a large extent.

Again, the role of a core made of data and analytics is critical in this aspect. It can help governance bodies resolve challenges of appropriate capabilities and capacities. This will also allow organisations to focus and dedicate their resources to their core mandates and operations.

Finally, REIMAGINING governance for the digital era should be done holistically and not in some areas. And to achieve this we must, at a minimum, consider the following two dimensions:

1. Thinking digital in all interactions that the organisations of the three governance pillars will have. The aim of this approach is to ensure that all interactions are covered - whether it is with customers or organisations within the governance pillar or with organisations between the governance pillars are thought of and designed from the digital-first perspective while allowing room for digitally challenged individuals to opt for alternative ways. The following figure highlights typical interactions and transactions that a government must undertake.

2. Thinking digital across the entire organisation across all organisations that sit in the three governance pillars. The aim is to transition each and every layer within an organisation to be as digitally native as possible so that they all seamlessly and efficiently function together to deliver services for their customers with the best-in-class experience. The following figure provides my view of how an organisation can be deconstructed into four elements for this purpose.

Once a holistic perspective is developed, decision-makers need to look at each element to ask the following questions:

- What are the technologies that can be applied to these building blocks?

- Does the current structure and capabilities support a transformative change?

- How can we reimagine business and operating models, processes, procedures, and touchpoints across these elements that are fit for the digital era?

These questions will help anchor down the strategy and investments to a purpose. This is very important as, due to the rapid transformation of the digital landscape, investment decisions often lack the rigour of being truly purpose and benefit-led.

Countries need to ensure that the best value is achieved from digital transformation initiatives and investments associated with it. They should avoid falling into the common trap of pursuing an initiative just because it is today's trend. Every nation and society has unique needs which must be carefully considered while developing a digital transformation strategy.

To bring holistic digital transformation plans to life, countries will also need to develop some core enablers that can help people and entities responsible for bringing change to accelerate implementation. These enablers include creating tangible technical assets as well as standards, necessary skills and frameworks.

Let's look at digital leaders in government space like Denmark, the UK, Singapore, Saudi Arabia, UAE and other top-ranked countries in the UN e-Government Index 2024. The majority of them have established centralized digital transformation agencies, appointing government Chief information officers, Chief digital information officers, or Information Technology directors aiming to develop common systems and platforms and focus on other enablers to help government entities transform.

Countries like Singapore are further planning and investing in developing a nationwide sensor infrastructure and platform11 to facilitate data-driven changes in government and society that can improve lives of its people.

In addition to digital and technical assets, governments must have standards and governance systems in place that helps all government entities align in the same direction. For example, New Zealand's All-of-Government ICT Operations Assurance Framework which is to be used by all public service departments allows them to take a standardized approach towards ICT portfolio management.

Governments will also need to invest in creating a pool of workforce that can run government entities like digital enterprises.

Acknowledging these necessities, governments have started to establish digital academies for their employees and partner with private sector as well as academic institutions.

In Singapore, Public officers are being trained in digital capabilities such as data analytics and data science. The Civil Service College is collaborating with institutes of higher learning so that every public officer has access to tools and deepen their skills for digital age. Additionally, the Government Technology Agency (GovTech) had signed an agreement with the National University of Singapore (NUS) to collaborate in areas of technological innovation for manpower and capability development. The aim was for NUS to train around 10,000 public sector officials between 2017 and 2022 with focus on technological expertise and data science.

The idea behind creating these enablers is to solve one of the key issues of reinventing the wheel every time a public sector organisation wants to change itself.

CHAPTER 3

Exploring the State of Digital Governance in 198 Countries Across the World

AFRICA

Digital governance SUMMARY

This continent is often seen as lagging behind in digital development, but that's a perspective I find both outdated and unfair. While it's true that Africa faces significant challenges—like infrastructure gaps, political instability, and varying levels of internet access—there's also a story of incredible potential and growth. The UN's E-Government Development Index (EGDI)12 is a tool I find particularly insightful for measuring this progress. It considers factors like online services, telecommunications infrastructure, and human capital, giving a balanced view of where each country stands.

In Africa, the EGDI reveals a continent on the rise. Countries like South Africa and Mauritius are leading the charge, demonstrating that with the right strategies, even resource-constrained nations can excel in digital governance. However, the gap between these frontrunners and the rest of the continent is still very significant. This disparity highlights the importance of regional cooperation, investment in digital infrastructure, and (most importantly), education and training.

A snapshot into the African continent

That being said, I can't help but note the stark reality that many African countries, particularly the least developed ones, are still trailing behind the global average in terms of e-government development. The EGDI really drives this point home. It highlights just how significant the digital divide remains across the continent, especially when compared to other regions/continents of the world. Since 2010, African nations' efforts in digital governance have lagged behind those of other continents, and this is something that we can't ignore if we're serious about understanding the challenges and opportunities in this area.

While most African countries have laid down sectoral strategies or policies aimed at the digital transformation of their economies, these efforts often fall short when it comes to e-government specifically. Sure, there are policies that mention the digitalisation of public administration, but the lack of dedicated strategic frameworks for e-government is a major shortcoming. A good, comprehensive approach to digital governance needs more than just a section in a broader policy document. It requires a focused strategy, and especially one that can guide consistent development and adaptation over time.

Also, most of the e-government strategies I've come across in Africa are rooted in a critical assessment of the current situation within each country. They often include SWOT analyses, which are essential for understanding strengths, weaknesses, opportunities, and threats. But here's where I think the gap widens: while these strategies *do* take the local context and sector-specific peculiarities into account, they sometimes fall short in execution. Infrastructure and technical challenges are still major hurdles, and without addressing these, even the bestlaid plans can falter. One thing I've noticed, and something that I believe is a positive step forward, is the emphasis on digital literacy programs. Many African governments are rightly focusing on improving the population's digital skills, which is a foundational step toward successful e-governance. But this needs to be more than just an afterthought or a secondary objective. Without a digitally literate population, even the most advanced e-government systems will struggle to achieve their full potential.

What's holding the African continent back?

Out of the 54 countries in Africa, only six have EGDI values above the global average[13] of 0.6382. This tells us that while there are pockets of progress, the vast majority of African nations are lagging behind, and in some cases, the gap is alarmingly wide. I believe that part of the issue stems from the continent's ongoing struggle with telecommunications infrastructure.

High telecommunication cost

While there has been progress in improving telecommunications infrastructure across several African countries, this progress hasn't necessarily translated into a more digitally inclusive society. Sure, a stronger telecom infrastructure is a step in the right direction—it lays the groundwork for digital government services to thrive. But, the reality is that the cost of mobile broadband subscriptions (when measured as a percentage of per capita gross national income) remains staggeringly high in Africa compared to other parts of the world.[14]

Digital divide

This cost barrier is one of the critical reasons why the digital divide persists in Africa, and I would argue that it's a problem that needs urgent and targeted intervention. Without systematic measures aimed specifically at reducing these costs and making digital access more affordable, especially for low-income and lower-middle-income countries, the digital divides we see today are not just going to persist—they're likely to widen. According to a 2023 ITU report[15], roughly four in ten men and three in ten women use the internet across the continent.

Cyber attacks

Cybersecurity. A growing concern that's not getting enough attention in Africa. Unfortunately, the continent is increasingly becoming a haven for cybercriminals, largely because many countries on the continent are ill-equipped to deal with these threats. The statistics are alarming: between 2022 and 2023, 12% of all cybercrimes in Africa were directed at government agencies.[16] This isn't just about financial loss or data breaches—this is about the very credibility and functionality of government institutions being under attack. If people cannot trust that their information is secure when interacting with government services online, then the entire digital governance framework becomes undermined.

Digital governance in Africa: Regional leaders & laggards

To start with, I think it's crucial to recognise that Africa has the largest share of countries in the middle EGDI group—about 48 percent, or 28 countries. These are often nations in special situations, such as Least Developed Countries (LDCs), Landlocked Developing Countries (LLDCs), and Small Island Developing States (SIDS).

These categorisations are more than just bureaucratic labels; they represent real, on-the-ground challenges that these countries face in terms of infrastructure, economic stability, and technological advancement. The fact that Africa is home to so many countries in these special situations speaks volumes about the uphill battle many African nations are facing.

Southern and Northern Africa stand out as the most developed regions on the continent in terms of digital governance and that doesn't surprise me. These regions have made significant progress in many different areas like: infrastructure, education, and governance. Also, countries in these parts of Africa have been better positioned to leverage their resources and attract investments, which, in turn, has accelerated their development.

Middle Africa is the least developed region in terms of digital governance, and I think it's not hard to see why. Middle Africa struggles with some of the most severe infrastructure deficits on the continent, compounded by political instability and widespread poverty. I also believe that one of the biggest hurdles Middle Africa faces is its historical dependence on foreign aid and technologies. This reliance has, unfortunately, stunted its ability to foster homegrown technological innovations and take control of its destiny.

Top and bottom performers in Africa

The 10 most developed countries in terms of digital governance are:

1. South Africa

2. Mauritius
3. Tunisia
4. Marocco
5. Seychelles
6. Egypt
7. Ghana
8. Kenya
9. Cabo Verde
10. Botswana

These nations are clearly leading the way, and I believe their progress isn't just by chance. They've been making consistent efforts to enhance their digital infrastructure, improve online services, and invest in human capital.

The 5 least developed countries in Africa in terms of digital governance are:

11. Chad
12. Eritrea
13. Somalia
14. South Sudan
15. Central African Republic

Also, one of the most fascinating developments in Africa's digital governance story is the progress made by Rwanda, Côte d'Ivoire, and Zambia. Although their EGDI values still do remain below the global average, they moved from the middle to the high EGDI group for the first time in 2022. What's even more interesting is how Rwanda's high OSI (online service index) value contrasts with its other challenges.

Rwanda's focus on online services is allowing it to compete with the world's leading countries in this area, even if other aspects of its digital ecosystem are still catching up. I think this is a powerful example of how targeted investments can drive progress, even if a country doesn't necessarily have toptier infrastructure or human capital.

Opportunities moving forward

Since many African nations don't have to deal with decades-old policies that are often incompatible with today's technology, they are in a prime position to adopt cutting-edge digital solutions more swiftly. This is a great opportunity rather than trying to retrofit modern solutions onto outdated infrastructures. I would also add that this absence of legacy burdens means African governments can establish legal environments that are truly conducive to the growth of e-governance. They have the very rare chance to look at the successes and failures of other countries and then build regulatory frameworks that incorporate the best global practices. This, I think, is a significant advantage. If done right, they could even prove that starting late doesn't mean starting behind—it could mean starting smarter.

1. ALGERIA

Making (slow) progress but more can be done

Algeria is the largest country in Africa by area, with a population of more than 44 million people[17]. While the country has put an emphasis on digital government in Algeria (with heavy investment in the ICT sector) the progress has been slow. Algeria's ICT sector is continuously evolving but it has problems. From 2010 to 2019, the digital government in Algeria invested nearly $4 billion in its ICT infrastructure; from 2015 to 2019, total ICT equipment imports counted for $22 billion. The telecommunications and information technology segments dominate this sector.

Mobile adoption rates are high, with the number of mobile connections at the start of 2022 going up to 47 million, according to data from GSMA Intelligence[18]. Despite this significant progress in ICT infrastructure development over the last decade, the digital government in Algeria lags behind other African countries. Algeria's internet penetration rate stood at 70.9% of the total population at the start of 2023[19]. According to Kepios's[20] analysis, internet users in Algeria increased by +3.9 % between 2023 and 2024. However, there were 12.46 million people in Algeria who did not use the internet at the start of 2024.

On the other hand, while mobile broadband connectivity in Algeria is above the MENA average, the use of mobile money is very low[21]. According to a 2021 World Bank report, only 16% of Algerian adults and 11% of women used digital payments. For comparison purposes, the average in the MENA region is 23% of adults and 18%. However, according to the EGDI report, Algeria ranks 116th in the world and 13th in Africa[22], improving its position by 4 places in two years. It is among the countries with high EGDI with an E-Government Development Index of 0.5956.

Where to focus?

For a developing country like Algeria, productive participation in the digital economy represents a complex challenge. Without proper institutional support, policies, and strategies, pursuing digital economic integration can lead to job losses and increased inequality.

2. ANGOLA

Below Africa average in terms of digital governance

You know, when we talk about e-governance and e-participation, Angola's journey is quite an interesting one. In the big African picture, they're doing pretty well in terms of offering online services (according to the 2022 UN E-government survey[23]). Actually, in 2022, in a continent where the average was about 12 online services, Angola was offering more than 20. That's something worth noting, especially when you consider that even some European countries aren't hitting that mark. So, where does e-Angola stand? Angola finds itself in the middle ground in terms of its E-Government Development Index (EGDI) and Online Service Index (OSI) ratings. But there's a pressing need to ramp up e-participation efforts in e-Angola[24]...even though, in two years, Angola improved its position by 16 places in the e-participation rankings. This is a solid improvement, especially in a global landscape where digital engagement is becoming increasingly important.

Access to the internet in e-Angola has long been an area of concern, characterised by significant challenges. According to data from the National Institute of Telecommunications (INACOM), the number of mobile internet subscribers reached 9.35 million by December 2022, with nearly 740,000 fixed-line internet subscribers[25]. Internet penetration remains relatively low, standing at 39.3%, as reported in the Digital 2024 Angola report by DataReportal[26]. Issues such as lack of internet signal, network instability, and high prices continue to plague users, according to service providers.

What about the state of public services? The SEPE[27] website has become a hub for a variety of essential public e-services, offering convenience and accessibility to citizens. From enrolling in driving schools to accessing electronic student records and applying for various licences, the platform covers a wide spectrum of needs. Similarly, the General Tax Administration's[28] website serves as a central hub for taxpayers and it even provides access to a Tax Simulator[29] that helps calculate the taxes that need to be paid. Also, there have been significant advancements in identification methods, with the implementation of electronic signatures[30] since January 1, 2023. This serves as an additional means of secure identification alongside the universal electronic ID introduced in the mid-2010s.

Where to focus?

By addressing infrastructure gaps, promoting digital literacy, and prioritizing citizen-centric approaches, Angola can continue to advance its digital governance agenda and harness the full potential of technology for the benefit of its citizens.

3. BENIN

Here's how e-Benin has undertaken a"whole-of-government" approach

According to the latest available data from the UN[31], Benin has decent telecom infrastructure and development of its human capital, as well as pretty solid online services. Over the past years, Benin has shown notable improvement in its E-Government Development Index (EGDI) value, indicating a positive trend towards the adoption and utilisation of digital governance practices. Benin's approach to digital governance serves as an exemplary case of a "whole-ofgovernment" strategy, where various government agencies collaborate closely to achieve a common goal. This approach has been recognised as a model of success, with e-Benin being selected as one of the sixteen good-practice cases in GovTech focus areas by the GTMI in 2022.[32]

Also, recognising the need to modernise and streamline its digital governance framework, Benin's government reached out to none other than the Estonian government for partnership[33]. Drawing upon Estonia's expertise and innovative solutions, Benin sought to design and implement national e-government frameworks tailored to the needs of its citizens and businesses. The focus? Establishing government data interoperability. *(The backbone of modern digital governance.)* Benin's solution wasn't just a copy-paste job of Estonia's X-Road technology. They have developed their own proprietary software called UXP [34]. e-Benin, then developed an online government portal[35], which enabled access to over 200 public services. Additionally, innovative e-services such as the publication of national exam results, electronic driver's licence exams, and e-voting were introduced, enhancing efficiency and accessibility for citizens.

What's more, the focus on artificial intelligence (AI) in Benin, as showcased by events like the Digital Entrepreneurship and AI Trade Show (SENIA), reflects a commendable ambition to harness cutting-edge technologies for societal and economic development. The presentation of the GPT BJ chatbot exemplifies the potential of AI to streamline government services.

Unlike generalised AI models, such as Chat GPT, the GPT BJ is customised to address Beninese legal frameworks[36]. But the momentum doesn't stop there. e-Benin's recent launch of the National Artificial Intelligence and Big Data Strategy[37] signals a concerted effort to capitalise on AI's transformative potential. By prioritising sectors like education, health, agriculture, environment, and tourism, Benin aims to maximise the societal impact of AI applications... which I believe is a strategic move to address pressing socio-economic challenges and drive inclusive growth.

Also, in seeking partnerships to bolster its AI capabilities, Benin is turning to countries like Canada [38] renowned for their expertise in this domain. After all, partnering with established AI ecosystems can provide valuable expertise and resources to accelerate Benin's AI initiatives, promoting capacity building in the country.

Where to focus?

On nurturing more the local talent and their digital skills, on publicprivate partnerships, and embracing cutting-edge technologies for better telecommunication infrastructure.

4. BOTSWANA

A leading hub for frontier technologies in Africa

Looking at the latest available UN e-government survey[39], e-Botswana seems to be doing exceptionally well in terms of the Telecommunication Infrastructure Index (TII) and Human Capital Index (HCI). But then, again, it shows not that much development when it comes to the Online Service Index (OSI) and the low E-Participation Index (EPI).., even though for the latter I must add that it has improved its ranking by 27 places in 2 years. It's important to note that according to this year's report, Botswana also made it to the top 10 African e-governments, "taking" Algeria's place.

Now, according to the Africa Cyber Security Report of 2020/21, it seems like awareness of the data protection law in Botswana isn't too bad, with 55% of people surveyed knowing about it. *(The report's findings were released by Botswana Fibre Network (BOFINET) in June 2022.[40])*

Moving on to internet connectivity, it seems like there's a bit of a disconnect between public perception and official statements. While the regulator, BOCRA, insists that the perception of expensive and slow internet is off base, the reality paints a different picture. According to the 2024 Speedtest Global Index[41], Botswana ranks pretty low in terms of fixed broadband speed, sitting at 172nd out of 181 countries. That's not great. However, it's a different story when it comes to mobile internet, where Botswana fares a bit better, ranking 62nd.

On the other hand, one of the most transformative strategies, is "SmartBots." The initiative encompasses a range of goals, from enhancing digital connectivity within the country to digitising e-government services and cultivating an innovation ecosystem to support businesses. A cornerstone of this strategy is universal connectivity, epitomised by ambitious projects like the deployment of a 12,000 km fibre optic backbone and the village connectivity program (which aims to bring 500 villages online by 2025.) Now, according to the WIPO Global Innovation Index (2023)[42], Botswana is making waves as the third most innovative economy in Africa. That's an improvement from fourth place just a year prior. It shows that the efforts put into e-Botswana are paying off, and its potential for growth and development is looking brighter than ever.

Where to focus?

On providing more and better services to the citiznens and engaging them more in e-governance.

5. BURKINA FASO

Moving forward with the help of international partners

As revealed by the latest UN e-government survey[43], e-Burkina Faso falls within the Middle EGDI group, indicating a moderate level of e-government development. Similarly, it falls in the Middle OSI, TII, and HCI groups, suggesting a balanced yet unremarkable performance in online service delivery, telecommunication infrastructure, and human capital investment, respectively. However, what sets e-Burkina Faso apart (not in a good way) is its low EPI values, reflecting challenges in engaging citizens and promoting e-participation. This poses a critical obstacle in the nation's quest to harness the full potential of digital governance. It also falls below the averages of its region (Africa) and subregion (Western Africa).

To help with these challenges, the government of Burkina Faso is getting a financial boost from the World Bank's International Development Association[44] (IDA) to ramp up its digital public infrastructure (DPI) efforts. With this funding, the Burkinabé government aims to extend digital connectivity to reach more people, especially those in vulnerable situations like internally displaced persons (IDPs) and underserved communities. Plus, by training public administration staff and empowering young people with digital skills, they're investing in the future workforce.

Despite its geographical landlocked status, Burkina Faso has made significant progress in enhancing its connectivity through new regional network connections. This has resulted in a remarkable increase in available internet capacity and a notable uptick in broadband download speed *in the continent* from 2.68 Mbps in 2019 to 8.18 Mbps in 2022.[45] According to data from Ookla[46], Burkina Faso's fixed internet connection speeds have seen a considerable increase, with the median speed reaching a decent 42.46 Mbps. However, it's crucial to note the slight decrease in fixed internet speeds over the past year, signalling the need for continued investment and optimisation efforts. A total of 27.10 million cellular mobile connections were active[47] in Burkina Faso in early 2024, with this figure equivalent to **115.1%** of the total population. While this represents a significant leap forward (compared to the year before), there's still ample room for growth.... with internet penetration rates hovering around ONLY 19.9% of the total population.

Where to focus?

Looking ahead, it's essential to sustain the momentum gained by fundings through continued investment in infrastructure, digital literacy programs, and innovative solutions tailored to the needs of its own population.

6. BURUNDI

Well above region average in e-participation, but...

e-Burundi is a small country in East Africa, known for its beautiful landscapes and rich culture. For some years now, the government has been working to improve access to public services through digitalisation, but while progress can be seen in some areas, in others, not so much. As per the latest UN e-government survey[48], Burundi's digital governance profile reveals a mixed picture. It falls within the categories of Low EGDI, very low TII, where it has shown declining in OSI, HCI, TII and EPI. Also, it was among the few countries that actually fell behind from the Middle EGDI group in 2022 to the Low group in 2024. All this translates to this – while online services may be available, there is room for improvement in terms of accessibility, usability, and/or effectiveness. Burundi's telecommunication infrastructure — including internet connectivity and network coverage — is way below the regional average. Unsurprisingly, e-Burundi seems to be ranking lower than expected in terms of citizen engagement through digital channels. That's not a good sign, indicating that despite other challenges, there's not willingness among Burundians to engage with their government online.

On the other hand, according to the UN, Burundi had one of the winning initiatives in Africa. The UN Digital Government Awards 2023[49] showcased remarkable initiatives from across the globe, highlighting the progress made in using digital technology to advance public services in alignment with its Sustainable Development Goals[50] (SDGs). One notable winner of one of the awards was Burundi's *"Guichet* électronique *de création d'entreprise (Easy Business)"*. It won the award for "Best digital single window for creating or operating a business" which was a joint award it shared with Bhutan and El Salvador.

Another thing worth mentioning is that Burundi's journey with biometric ID cards has been both promising and fraught with delays. While successful trials have been conducted, the project has encountered significant setbacks, with registrations for biometric IDs commencing as far back as 2013[51]. Adding to the complexity, Burundi, like many African countries, has faced scrutiny over its handling of biometric data. A research report from 2022 raised concerns about data protection[52] and privacy practices among African governments, including Burundi. Nevertheless, the introduction of biometric IDs is seen as a critical step for Burundi's democratic process.

Where to focus?

e-Burundi's digital governance status shows concerning declines in many areas, which means there are clear opportunities for improvement, particularly in telecommunication infrastructure and human capital development.

7. CAMEROON

Relatively fair but inadequate performance in terms of e-governance

According to the latest (available) UN e-government survey[53], e-Cameroon falls within the Middle OSI group, reflecting its moderate performance in online service delivery. The country also boasts a medium level of telecommunication infrastructure (TII) and falls within the middle range in terms of e-participation (EPI). However, it's worth noting that e-Cameroon has a strong foundation in terms of skills and knowledge among its populace. A notable observation from a World Bank report[54] in 2020 sheds light on Cameroon's journey, describing its performance in digital infrastructure, financial services, and entrepreneurship as "relatively fair but inadequate" compared to regional counterparts. While this assessment might have been discouraging, it's important to note that progress has been made since then. In recent years, e-Cameroon has shown advancements in e-governance and e-participation[55].... surpassing the regional average.

In April 2022, the government launched *the Single Window for Foreign Trade Operations* (e-GUCE)[56], which makes it possible to pay customs duties, taxes, duties, and various fees online. Again, in 2022, the eVisa project was confirmed[57] by President Paul Biya. Also, the Master Plan[58] for the digitalisation of the civil registration system was adopted in 2018. As of 2022, Cameroon ranked 141th in the UN E-Government Development survey (out of 193 countries assessed), with an EGDI rating of 0.45. According to the 2022 World Bank's GovTech Maturity report[59], Cameroon moved up as well. Yet, reforms to their national ID are a must!

As of 2024, Cameroon ranked 155th in the UN E-Government Development survey (out of 193 countries assessed), with an EGDI rating of 0.4294...seeing a decline compared to 2022. Obtaining national ID cards has been a persistent issue in Cameroon over the past few years. Unfortunately, some individuals have even resorted to offering bribes to expedite the process or using fake IDs. The government's initiative to digitalise[60] the Civil Registration and Vital Statistics (CRVS) system could offer a solution to the issue of fake documents.

On the other hand, despite there being 12.73 million internet users, the internet penetration rate stands at only 43.9% according to Datareportal for digital Cameroon[61]. This uneven access to broadband internet, especially in rural areas lacking fibre optic networks, further exacerbates the digital divide.

Where to focus?

One significant challenge facing Cameroon's digital journey is the high cost of internet and mobile services. Limited competition and infrastructure contribute to these high costs, making them unaffordable for many citizens. Beyond infrastructure challenges, there's also a need to address inadequate digital literacy and skills among the population.

8. CABO VERDE

e-Cabo Verde is trying to become a major tech player in Western Africa

According to the UN e-government survey[62], e-Cabo Verde has secured the 111th spot out of 193 countries assessed. Now, what's interesting is that despite being a small island nation, it's doing more than others in similar conditions (in terms of e-governance), ranking way above the regional average for Africa. Actually, it is among the top 10 countries in Africa. That's quite an achievement.

Also, e-participation really improved these recent years. While it's commendable that e-Cabo Verde was the 9th country in Africa with the highest e-Government Development Index (EGDI) value in 2024, there's still more to be done to improve its e-governance. And I think it's worth noting that its *Online Service Index (OSI)* has seen so much improvement, with a score that surpasses the world's average.

Looking at NoSi's digital transition projects on their website[63], there's quite a bit of progress and potential here. One notable project, the Consular Portal[64] (launched in 2020) stands out for its impact on the diaspora population. One of the most ambitious projects underway is the Cabo Verde Technological Park[65]. Set to be completed by June 30, 2026 (the phase II), this initiative aims to transform the country into a digital and innovation hub, by providing modern infrastructure and workspaces tailored to the needs of both emerging startups and established tech companies.

The presence of the Ella Link cable[66], a vital undersea fibre-optic link, offers immense potential for economic growth and development. According to data from Datareportal[67], e-Cabo Verde had 433.7

thousand individuals accessing the internet at the start of 2024. However internet penetration stands at 72.1%, indicating that a sizable portion of the population remains unconnected. Also, according to a recent report from ITU[68] (International Telecommunication Union), which is the UN's ICT agency, Cabo Verde is the sixth country in Africa in terms of ICT development. In light of these challenges, the support extended by the European Union (EU) is of paramount importance. Aligned with e-Cabo Verde's long-term development goals outlined in 'Cabo Verde – Ambition 2030' and the EU's 'Global Gateway Strategy,'[69] this assistance aims to catalyse the country's transformation (among other things) towards digitalisation.[70]

Where to focus?

By enacting policies that promote innovation, safeguard data privacy and foster competition, the country can create a fertile ground for digital transformation to flourish. In light of this, there are some exciting opportunities on the horizon, particularly in e-government services and digital (private or public) services. With the right regulatory framework in place, e-Cabo Verde could really take off in these areas.

9. CENTRAL AFRICAN REPUBLIC

One of the 6 countries in Africa in the low EGDI group

The e-Central African Republic is one of the seven countries in Africa that are in the low EGDI group. According to the UN e-government survey in 2024[71], the e-Central African Republic's ranking was quite low with it "failing to move forward with e-government", ranking last in the world out of 193 countries assessed. To put this into perspective, the country's best ranking ever was back in 2008, when it held the 179th spot globally. So, there's been a noticeable decline in its digital governance performance over the years. Why? Due to widespread insecurity and a lack of state authority, particularly outside the capital city of Bangui. As a result, according to Freedom House[72], civil liberties and political rights are limited in the Central African Republic. This turbulent environment *significantly* impedes the government's ability to prioritise and implement digital governance initiatives. Even if the government were to offer online services, many people simply wouldn't have the means to access them.

For e.g. there were 616.6 thousand internet users at the start of 2023, when internet penetration stood at 10.6% according to Datareportal of Digital Central African Republic[73]. For comparison purposes, in Cameroon (the larger and more stable economy in the sub-region) the internet penetration is 29%[74]. Under these conditions, the government's approach toward digitalisation is driven by a strong desire to address the challenges resulting from the conflict. The Central African Republic adopted the cryptocurrency Bitcoin as a legal tender[75], making it the second country to do so after El Salvador. Going further, the National Assembly supported by the president's office seeks to develop a national crypto token called Sango Coin[76], built on the Bitcoin network.

Unfortunately, the Central African Republic does not have a national or sectorspecific cybersecurity strategy nor a national governance roadmap for cybersecurity. In the 2020 Global Cybersecurity Index[77], the country ranked 176th, only ahead of 8 other countries. What's even more alarming.... is the lack of cybersecurity education and training within the country. With ICT literacy rates being low and cybersecurity skills not taught in schools, the majority of the population is ill-equipped to protect themselves and their digital assets. The introduction of the national digital currency (Sango) further highlights the importance of digital skills development. BUT... the genesis paper of the project *fails to address* how consumers will acquire the necessary skills to use cryptocurrencies safely and effectively.

Where to focus?

With its digitalisation strategy still in development, it is important that the right policies and considerations are taken to support (and protect) the e-Central African Republic's digital economy. It still has a long way to go.

10. CHAD

In need of more international assistance

e-Chad, situated in the heart of Africa, faces many challenges. With a population of around 17.4 million, the majority of whom reside in rural areas, the country grapples with issues of marginalisation, particularly in the central and southern regions. The political landscape in Chad has been marked by instability[78], particularly since April 2021, when a military government took control following a coup d'état after the death of President Idriss Déby Itno. However, the challenges extend beyond domestic politics. Chad finds itself surrounded by neighbouring countries plagued by political volatility and internal conflicts, such as the Central African Republic, Niger, and Sudan. This regional instability has led to an influx of refugees seeking sanctuary in Chad, further straining its resources and complicating governance efforts.

In the midst of these complexities, Chad's aspirations for digital transformation face significant limitations. The ongoing political uncertainty and regional instability cast a shadow over efforts to develop a digital government and economy. So, where does e-Chad stand in the global scene? In 2024, e-Chad is classified among the seven African countries falling into the Low EGDI group according to the United Nations E-Government Development Index (EGDI).[79] But, if there's one thing you have to remember about e-Chad, it is that low levels of infrastructure and human capital development have not been an impediment to investment in online service delivery…at least in the sub regional level. Speaking of e-participation, it's noteworthy that e-Chad surpasses the regional average[80], indicating a growing engagement of its citizens in digital governance processes. This is a positive sign of democratisation and inclusivity. What's impressive is the significant improvement in e-participation it had in 2022..by 53 places. However, in 2024 I must add that it has fallen behind by 12 places, holding the 127th place globally.

Where to focus?

Prioritising initiatives to reduce internet costs, expanding infrastructure, enhancing digital literacy programs, and focusing on local innovation. Also, it's crucial to acknowledge that vulnerable groups often face barriers to accessing e-government services due to financial constraints or limited digital literacy. In some remote regions like northern Chad, a complete lack of digital access necessitates alternative measures to ensure inclusivity.

11. COMOROS

The small island with very low internet penetration rate

As a low-income island nation in Eastern Africa, Comoros grapples with the stark reality of very limited resources...which obviously hinder its ability to invest in important areas for e-government development. It falls into the low OSI group, reflecting its struggles in providing effective online services. The combination of middle TII (telecommunication infrastructure) and middle HCI (human capital) further exacerbates these challenges. Despite having some level of human capital development, the country ranks last globally in e-participation according to the UN's e-government survey, having a score of 0.000.[81] It landed at the 180th spot, with an EGDI of 0.2586. Comparatively, the average regional EGDI value is 0.4247... highlighting a significant gap in digital governance compared to neighbouring countries. Despite that, it's worth mentioning that over the span of two years, its ranking has improved slightly by 2 places.[82]

Now, let's talk about their online presence, which further reveals inconsistencies and deficiencies. Sure, they've got websites for public entities, but it seems like they're lacking consistency and quality control. The prevalence of bugs on certain websites, such as the Ministry of Tourism[83] or the Ministry of Finances's site, and the unavailability of others (like the General Administration of Taxes' site [84]) underscore the challenges in maintaining a functional and accessible digital infrastructure. Their first national digital strategy was adopted in 2019. Apart from a number of public entities managing the ICT sector in the country (such as the Ministry of Posts, Telecommunications and Digital Economy, ANRTIC[85]), in 2019, the National Digital Development Agency[86] (ANADEN, Agence Nationale de Développement du Numérique), overseeing digitalisation in the country, was established. Among other objectives, it is responsible for implementing the first national digital strategy adopted by the Council of Ministers in 2019 – Digital Comoros 2028 [87](Comores Numérique 2028). International organisations (such as the UN, the World Bank, and the ITU) provide tangible assistance in the development of e-government in the Union of Comoros. For e.g. In 2006, the International Telecommunications Union suggested the government *Intranet project*. Then, in 2021, the United Nations Framework for Cooperation for Sustainable Development[88] (UNSCDF) for Comoros (for the period 2022-2026) was adopted in Moroni covering digital development of the country. However, as of 2024, Comoros faces a significant challenge with internet penetration, standing at 27.3% of the population (according to recent research by Datareportal.[89]) This means that a substantial portion of the population still lacks access to the internet, hindering their ability to fully engage with digital government services and initiatives.

Where to focus?

So, I would say that for government efforts to succeed in e-Comoros, addressing the barriers to internet access and improving connectivity infrastructure are paramount. Initiatives to expand internet coverage, reduce costs, and enhance network reliability are essential to ensure equitable access to digital services for all citizens....Additionally, e-government platforms must be designed with accessibility in mind, catering to diverse user needs and accommodating individuals with limited digital literacy or access to technology.

12. DEMOCRATIC REPUBLIC OF CONGO

Digital D.R. Congo leapt forward in past years in e-governance

I believe the D.R. Congo holds immense potential for digital transformation, given its sizable, largely young[90] population of 5.7 million. Young demographics often embrace technological advancements, which bodes well for the future of digital D.R. Congo. However, the presence of armed conflicts in certain regions complicates the digital landscape further. Conflict zones often experience disruptions to essential services, making it difficult to deliver e-government solutions effectively. According to the UN's e-government survey[91], digital D.R. Congo has Low TII and falls in the middle HCI group. So, in simple words...on one hand, it has high human capital development (HCI), which is definitely a positive sign. However, its telecommunications infrastructure (TII) leaves much to be desired. Meaning that — while the population may possess the necessary skills and knowledge, inadequate infrastructure impedes the full realisation of these capabilities.

The improvements in EGDI values back in 2022[92] (e-Government Development Index) signified positive momentum in the country's e-governance efforts. Moving up nine places to rank 175th in e-governance and an impressive 44 places to rank 135th in e-participation within just two years was commendable progress. The same cannot be said for 2024, where D.R. Congo has clearly fallen behind by 4 and 11 places respectively. Moreover, the country's inclusion in Group C of the 2022 World Bank's GovTech Maturity report[93] indicated a growing focus on GovTech (Government Technology).

This presented an opportunity for digital D.R. Congo to leverage technology in governance and public service delivery more effectively. The adoption of the National Digital Plan Horizon-2025[94] in 2019 signalled the first solid step towards digital transformation. International organisations such as the UN and the World Bank have been pivotal in driving progress in this area. Take, for example, the World Bank's involvement in the development of the Public Procurement Platform (SIGMAP)[95]. Also, as of March 2024, we're seeing a growing trend of partnerships between the government and local fintech companies. The creation of the Congolese Fintech Network (CFN)[96] is another important signal of this trend.

But, despite recent initiatives like the launch of the Integrated Public Procurement Management System (the SIGMAP) in February 2022, many government websites remain underdeveloped and lack essential functionalities. Additionally, there's a lack of cohesion and organisation, with some sections being empty, like those of the General Labor Inspectorate[97], being found on other ministry websites. Perhaps... the most concerning aspect is the state of the E-GOV[98] website, which is supposed to provide citizens with access to electronic government services. However, as of now (the moment this section was written), it's *essentially* nonexistent, with only one page on the official government website displaying a 404 Error code.

Where to focus?

While there have been efforts to digitise public services, the current state of affairs in digital D.R. Congo highlights the urgent need for greater coordination, investment, and commitment from the government.

13. CONGO

Digital government of Congo is lagging behind

Despite sharing a similar name, these are two distinct countries with their own unique paths and challenges. The Republic of Congo, often just called Congo, is a mid-level income country and one of the most urbanized nations in Africa. According to the EGDI report, it falls in the middle OSI (Online Service Index) group[99], and it has fallen behind both in terms of e-governance and e-participation from 2022-2024. As with many mid-level income countries, there are hurdles related to infrastructure, funding, and policy implementation. Regarding internet usage, At the start of 2024, there were 2.24 million internet users in digital Congo[100], with an internet penetration rate standing at 36.2% of the total population. So, about 3.94 million people in the Congo were not using the internet at the beginning of the year. Today, 89% of the country has broadband coverage. Despite this, there's still a gap between coverage and actual usage, with just over 62% of the population using the internet. Also, the relatively low overall internet penetration rate suggests that there are still barriers to access, particularly in rural areas.

The launch of the Congo Digital Acceleration Project[101] in January 2023 was a very important moment in the history of this country. I believe it marked a significant step forward in bridging the digital divide... especially in rural areas. Moreover, the June 08, 2023, launch of the European component of the "Digital Transformation Acceleration Project"[102] added another layer of significance to these efforts. This project aims to accelerate digital transformation in Congo, not just as a source of job creation but also as a way to enhance governance. So, it supports the modernisationof public administration information systems and the development of the digital economy. What

I like most about these initiatives is that it doesn't just stop at providing internet connectivity...but they further ensure that technology's benefits are accessible to all, from urban centres to the most remote villages.

Where to focus?

The collaboration between the Congo government and international partners is promising, and I hope to see substantial progress in the coming years. What I'd like to add is that continuous monitoring, evaluation, and adaptation of these projects will be key to their success.

14. DJIBOUTI

A powerful engine with no steering wheel

Nestled at the crossroads of three continents, e-Djibouti may be small in size, but its strategic location has cemented its status as a vital transport and logistics hub for the Horn of Africa and the Middle East. According to the recent EGDI report, it ranks 174th in e-governance[103], having improved its ranking by 7 places (compared to 2022). Meanwhile regarding e-participation it hasn;t seen any changes whatsoever in terms of positioning. They also have some ambitious plans to become a digital hotspot for the region. The digitalisation efforts in the country started back in 2006 with an online customs system, but it wasn't exactly paperless at first (a factor that posed challenges and hindered efficiency.) Now, fast forward to today (2024), and we've got ASYCUDAWorld[104]. Crucially, the upgrade to ASYCUDAWorld was made possible through financing from the World Bank under the Djibouti Public Administration Modernisation Project[105] (P162904). And I think it's important to note that this project isn't *just* about customs... it's about modernising the whole government setup, making services more accessible online and tightening up revenue systems.

In the grand scheme of Djibouti's development trajectory, the "Vision 2035" strategy[106] stands as the beacon. Their national development plan, *"Djibouti Inclusion – Connectivity – Institutions,"* for 2020-2024, seems pretty ambitious too. What I'd like to add is the mention of the government's efforts to integrate all its services onto a single platform using the X-ROAD[107] system (from Estonia), which is a smart move for efficiency and accessibility. Also, e-Djibouti is benefitting from a World Bank-supported project[108] involving Ethiopia, which aims to extend digital services to the communities bordering the two neighbouring countries.

Where to focus?

e-Djibouti is slowly but surely moving forward in terms of governance and delivery of public services. However, it lacks a comprehensive strategic, legal, policy, and regulatory framework for digital service delivery. I think this is crucial because, without the right framework in place, they can't fully utilise the infrastructure they've already invested in (like the X-ROAD data exchange platform mentioned before).

15. EGYPT

Slowly but surely progressing forward

According to different reports, over half of the MENA countries surveyed have solid digital government initiatives in place, but there are still huge differences between them. Some, like Egypt, are rapidly moving forward with adoption; others are only taking baby steps towards modernisation if they're doing anything at all.

However, digital identity systems have provided Egyptians with greater access to key public services—such as education, health care, and financial services— and also help increase trust between citizens and government. By 2015, over 11 million citizens had received cards with embedded chips that are interoperable across state institutions. The Egyptian government has long prioritised ICT development. That's why, in mid-2020, the Ministry of Communications and Information Technology (MCIT) launched the project Digital Egypt, a comprehensive plan to shift towards a more digital society focusing on digital skills and jobs. One of the latest massive projects is the ICT 2030 Strategy[109], which includes provisions for the digital transformation of government services. Moreover, according to the UN E-Government Survey 2020[110], Egypt was one of the 16 countries in Africa that joined the high EGDI group in 2020. Meanwhile, the 2024 report, places Egypt among the top 10 African countries. The EDGI Index[111] shows that the country has improved its ranking by 8 places compared to 2020, and it's particularly worthy of note its impressive advancements in online services having high levels of infrastructure and human capital development. It is also one of the continent's six countries that has EGDI value above the world's average![112] Also, it only recently joined the top 100 countries for the first time (alongside Morocco.)

According to Boutheina Guermazi,[113] Director of Digital Development at the World Bank, the Egyptian government has done a great job in responding to the need for improved broadband networks internet services. This was especially noticed during the Covid-19 pandemic. It provided free Internet services to university professors and SIM cards for students to access e-learning platforms and improve online education.

Where to focus?

The government's digital initiatives will be further driven by the creation of smart cities, and disruptive technologies such as AI and IoT to improve the service delivery for all their citizens.

16. EQUATORIAL GUINEA

Huge potential wrecked by poor telecommunications infrastructure

Equatorial Guinea, located in Middle Africa, is categorised in the low OSI group, which indicates that the country is lagging in terms of online services and digital governance. While the country has a relatively well-developed human capital—think about education levels and the skills of its population—the telecommunications infrastructure is somewhat lacking. I think it's particularly interesting to note that despite these challenges, Equatorial Guinea managed to offer the highest number of online services (14) in 2022 within the low OSI group[114]. To put this into perspective, this placed it ahead of countries like Djibouti, Honduras, Sao Tome and Principe, and Tuvalu (all part of the same group), which offered between 8 to 10 services. *(Mind you, in 2020, the maximum number of services offered by any country in this group was nine.)*

According to the latest UN survey,[115] Equatorial Guinea ranked 176th in e-governance and 148th in e-participation. While these rankings may not seem impressive at first glance, it's important to note that the country has improved its standing over the past two years by 7 and 25 places respectively! This suggests that some great progress has been made...even though there's still a long way to go. Meanwhile, as of early 2024, Equatorial Guinea had 1.16 million internet users,[116] with internet penetration at 66.8%. This means that 575.6 thousand people remained offline at the beginning of the year. High connectivity costs remain a significant barrier to wider adoption and deeper digital engagement.

"Developing core infrastructure, systems, and competencies can also sustain new technologies and will help countries like Equatorial Guinea to skip the traditional model, and transition from a mainly extractive industries economy to a digital economy, leaping over intermediate steps "- World Bank states in its **Digital Economy Country Diagnostic for Equatorial Guinea.**[117]

Where to focus?

Regulatory barriers and a lack of healthy competition in the broadband sector are some main concerns for this African country. Also, the challenge is to create a digitally skilled population on a larger scale. This means more than just teaching basic computer skills; it requires a specific ICT policy in education that can lay the foundation for digital literacy across the country.

17. ERITREA

Digital Eitrea is among the least developed countries in the world

Since gaining independence from Ethiopia in 1993, Eritrea has been characterised by a highly militarised and authoritarian regime. I think it's important to highlight that the country hasn't held a national election since its independence. This, coupled with a Freedom House score of just 3/100[118], paints a stark picture of the lack of political freedom. This oppressive environment extends to digital governance as well. The authoritarian regime's tight grip on information and communication means that any digital governance initiatives are likely to be heavily controlled and limited in scope. In other words, the digital landscape in Eritrea is as restrictive as its political environment.

According to the UN's EGDI report[119], Eritrea ranks 190th in e-governance and in e-participation[120], holding the same position since 2022...highlighting significant challenges in these areas. As of early 2024, Eritrea had 1.01 million internet users[121], with an internet penetration rate of 26.6%. The 2022 UN report highlighted a critical issue: Eritrea was one of only three countries in the world without a national portal, the others being Belize and Mauritania. Moreover, access to electricity is heavily skewed towards urban areas.

Where to focus?

Given these circumstances, it is clear that Eritrea has substantial ground to cover. The low penetration rates coupled with the lack of a national portal, highlight severe infrastructural and systemic deficiencies. So, with the right political will and international support, Eritrea could begin to open up and leverage digital technologies to improve governance and public services. However, for now, the reality remains bleak, and the prospects for digital advancement are constrained by the broader political and social context.

18. ESWATINI

Has potential with its young and eager workforce

Digital Eswatini, this little country nestled between South Africa and Mozambique got a lot going for it, but there are some challenges too (especially when it comes to inequality and access to public services.) In two years, digital Eswatini vastly improved its e-governance[122] by 28 places and its e-participation by 61 places! I think it's safe to say that its among the best performers in Africa, ranking 11th in the continent. It is also one of the three countries (alongside Libya and Senegal) which moved up to the high EGDI group in 2024.[123] Its very well developed telecommunications infrastructure and sufficiently developed human capital can support future advancement in e-government. Also, one of the biggest issues in this country is that despite efforts to bridge the gap, inequality in both consumption per capita and access to public services remains glaringly high. Factors beyond the control of individuals...say - person education, parental education, place of birth, or of residence, explained 38.5% of consumption inequality back in 2017 (according to the World Bank.[124])

What's clear is that Eswatini is falling behind its neighbours when it comes to going digital. The numbers don't lie: with only 58% of the population using the internet as of 2022, they've got some catching up to do (according to ITU.[125]) And you know what? Even in 2024, not much seems to have changed. According to DataReportal[126], nearly 42% of the population was offline at the beginning of 2024. So, no real change has happened in 2 years.

In Eswatini, incomplete market liberalisation and limited competition are making internet access a luxury for many. With the Eswatini Post and Telecommunications Corporation holding a partial monopoly, it's tough for prices to come down. Plus, being landlocked means they don't have direct access to those vital submarine cables, which only adds to the problem. Secondly, in Eswatini, public sector platforms have limited availability and functionality, according to another recent World Bank report[127]. They're not securely sharing data between themselves, which is a missed opportunity for streamlining services and improving the user experience.

Where to focus?

In the end, I can say that the country needs to make massive investments to modernise its ICT infrastructure. For mobile broadband, there is room to increase access to high-speed, good-quality internet services. Also, currently, there is an incomplete feedback cycle in which user experience is sub-optimal and the benefits of using online governmental platforms remain unclear.... leading to reduced demand for such platforms and insufficient incentives to invest further in them.

19. ETHIOPIA

Moving on the right track, but at the wrong speed

I think it's important to look at a few key indicators here. We've got Middle OSI, Low TII, Middle HCI, and Low EPI. When we say *Middle OSI*, it suggests that there's some progress in service delivery, but it's not exactly leading the pack. *Low TII* means that Ethiopia's infrastructure isn't up to par. Regarding HCI, or *Human Capital Index*, it falls somewhere in the middle, which means some work to be done in terms of digital literacy and education. Lastly, we have EPI, or *E-Participation Index*. With a low ranking, it suggests that there's a lot of room for improvement in terms of involving Ethiopians in digital decision-making processes.

Despite some marginal gains in several areas Ethiopia still has a long way to go. Ranking 169th out of 193 countries[128]in the UN e-government survey[129]. is a stark reminder of just how far behind they are....improving its ranking by 10 places in 2 years. This is some great progress in the right direction. Also, according to recent data from Datareportal[130], there were 24.83 million internet users in Ethiopia at the start of 2024, when internet penetration stood at 19.4%. The International Telecommunication Union (ITU) cites [131] the same figure in its most recent data (from 2022.) However, one big challenge that stands out to is the impact of the civil war in the Tigray Region[132] on internet and electricity services since November 2020. This disruption has undoubtedly affected connectivity and access to vital services for the people in that region.

Launched back in July 2020, Ethiopia's Digital Transformation Strategy[133] has some big goals. One of the key pillars of this strategy is digital identification. It's seen as a game-changer for 'Digital Ethiopia 2025,' with the Prime Minister himself hailing it as a driver[134] of the country's digital vision. And it's not just talk. They've recently issued a procurement notice[135] for infrastructure hardware and IT components to support the digital ID project. In other recent developments, the country has also announced plans to issue at least 1.1 million refugee IDs[136] in the next year as part of a government strategy to facilitate the acquisition of services by forcibly displaced persons.

Where to focus?

First and foremost, Ethiopia must prioritise e-government services, and platforms designed for local products and digital tools that can empower citizens, businesses AND institutions. Of course, none of this can happen without internet access, so expanding internet connectivity is essential for ensuring inclusive participation in the digital economy.

20. GABON

Gabon has been falling behind

Gabon is a country nestled in Central Africa, boasting abundant natural resources. With its picturesque coastline along the Atlantic Ocean and borders shared with Cameroon, Equatorial Guinea, and the Republic of Congo, it is among the top 15 in digital transformation in Africa…despite losing some ground recently in the global scene. According to the UN's *E-Government Development Index* report[137] it falls in the high EGDI group and the middle OSI(online service index) group. This was the case in 2022 and it's still the case in 2024. This suggests a decent level of online service provision and a solid foundation for e-governance initiatives. Additionally, Gabon has shown very high levels of Telecommunication Infrastructure (TII) and high Human Capital Index (HCI) development, which are *crucial* pillars of digital advancement. All great signs and improvements compared to 2022.

Now, I think it's important to talk about the recent partnership between the Government of Gabon and the World Bank, which is poised to make a significant impact on the country's digital landscape. At the beginning of 2024, they sealed the deal on a $68.5 million loan[138] for the *Digital Gabon Project*, aimed at accelerating the adoption of digitalised public services and enhancing access to essential services for Gabonese citizens. Now...this is a substantial investment, and e-Gabon has the opportunity to modernise its legal identity systems (particularly through the digitalisation of the civil registration system.)

For over a decade, the country has not issued national ID cards[139] since 2013 - which has posed significant challenges for citizens. It's clear that this has been a pressing issue for some time. Despite previous attempts to kickstart the process, various government initiatives have faced setbacks along the way. However, there seems to be renewed hope with the recent progress highlighted by Immongault, as seen in the video recording[140] shared on LinkedIn by eGabon's presidency.

Where to focus?

The digital ID system of e-Gabon not only provides individuals with a form of identification but also opens doors to accessing essential services and participating more fully in society. It's a fundamental aspect of citizenship that has been missing for too long and that should be one of the main priorities of the government. Also, for the near future, more efforts should be focused on the *Online Service Index* so as to improve the number of services offered online as well as their delivery or accessibility.

21. GAMBIA

Where digital exclusion persists as a challenge

This high population density of Gambia presents both challenges and opportunities for digital development and connectivity. Gambia falls into the low OSI group[141], which suggests that there's so much room for improvement in terms of online service provision. It's even more discouraging the fact that there has not been any development or improvement in this area in the past 2 years (there's even been some regress.) In terms of key indicators like Telecommunication Infrastructure (TII) and Human Capital Index (HCI), Gambia sits in the middle range. Regrettably, even for these indicators, there has been some declining trend. So, it's important to acknowledge that there's still so much work to be done to fully harness the potential of digital technologies. In the latest UN e-government report[142], Gambia ranked 181st globally, falling behind by 7 places in just 2 years. Efforts have not been great regarding its E-Participation Index (EPI) either...with e-Gambia weakening its position by 21 places during the same time period. That being said...e-Gambia is way behind the region or sub-region average.

One initiative that's worth mentioning however, is the National Digital ID System (DIDS). It's great to see collaboration between the government, the United Nations Economic Commission for Africa (ECA), and the Ministry of Communication and Digital Economy (MOCDE) in shaping this strategy (Digital Transformation Strategy and the Digital ID Strategy[143].) Over the past 15 years, Gambia has issued various versions of national identity cards, each evolving to meet the changing needs of the digital age. The latest iteration, the biometric ID card, represents a significant leap forward in terms of security and reliability. According to the United Nations Economic

Commission for Africa (ECA) this national digital identity system has facilitated access to so many services while also cutting transaction costs.[144]

Regarding connectivity, at the beginning of 2024, there were about 1.52 million internet users in Gambia[145], which means roughly 54.2% of the population had internet access. That's a significant leap from the 18% internet penetration rate recorded back in 2019, according to an assessment by the ITU[146]. I think it's safe to say there's been quite an improvement in just five years. However, there's still work to be done.

Where to focus?

What I believe is important to highlight is e-Gambia has not made any progress, and there's still work to be done to ensure that digital development is inclusive and equitable. Addressing issues like access to technology, digital literacy, and ensuring that rural areas aren't left behind in the digital divide.

22. GHANA

Digital Ghana is one of Sub-Saharan Africa's leaders

Ghana has been making significant efforts and investments to position the country as a regional hub for digital services. It is one of those lower-middle-income countries that falls into the high OSI, TII and HCI groups.[147] Which is incredible! It ranks 108th in e-governance and 82nd in e-participation having improved its ranking by 4 places in two years for the latter. It recognises the opportunity that digital development has for stimulating jobs, enhancing productivity, and accelerating inclusive growth. That's why it has been undertaking a number of key projects. Also, why Ghana is one of the few countries in the continent with national digital IDs with electronic components and associated public-servicedelivery functions. In the 2018 survey of the UN's EGDI index[148], digital Ghana was the only African country that transitioned from the middle to high level. And today, according to the 2024 EGDI report[149], it has remained the sub-regional leader for the past few years.

There have been several recent initiatives by the Government to adopt new technologies, and some other developments in the private sector have also contributed to this demand as well. The launch of the Ghana.Gov[150] platform - a single digital payment and services portal - provides a single point of access to all ministries and public agencies' services. *GhanaPost GPS*-the National Digital Property Addressing System[151] launched in 2017 to facilitate the implementation of key government policies. The digital Ghana Community Network otherwise known as GCNet[152] - is an online system providing an end-to-end solution for handling all trade and customs operations at all ports in the country. Ghana's online passport application service[153] launched in 2016 to ease the application while ensuring maximum security for applicants.

In 2020, Ghana became the *first* African country to implement a universal quick response code payment system (GhQR)[154]. In 2019, the government organised the Ghana Digital Roadmap Conference[155] to review this policy document in line with digital opportunities to establish Ghana as the leader in ICT in Sub-Sahara Africa by 2023.

Where to focus?

Digital is one of Ghana's best-performing sectors, which grew by 19% on average between 2014 and 2020[156], according to the World Bank. But, most of the infrastructure in Ghana is concentrated in urban areas, with large sections of the country's rural population without effective coverage.

23. GUINEA

Digital Guinea is marred by inconsistencies and crucial service gaps

Guinea's unique position in West Africa often surprises many due to its notable progress despite facing significant challenges in telecommunications infrastructure. As a low-income country with limited resources allocated to technology development, Guinea has managed to defy expectations. According to the latest UN report[157], Guinea's e-governance ranking improved by 2 places from 2022-2024. But what's worth mentioning is its e-participation values which helped Guinea to move up from the 123rd to the 85th place during the same time period. An improvemend by 38 places in just 2 years! What stands out even more is Guinea's remarkable improvement in e-participation along the years, when between 2020-2022 it climed by 35 places. This leap is indicative of the country's commitment to enhancing digital engagement and inclusivity, despite its status as a Least Developed Country (LDC) back in 2022[158] and the economic constraints that obviously accompany it....something that the UN report doesn't fail to mention.

Despite this…Internet penetration rate needs *MAJOR* improvement. As of January 2024, Guinea had approximately 4.87 million internet users[159]. To put this into perspective, it means that about 66.1 percent of Guinea's population—roughly 9.49 million people—*remained offline* at the beginning of 2024. Guinea's low internet penetration rate highlights the disparities in digital access, particularly in rural and underserved areas where infrastructure remains inadequate... an issue that many African countries have.

As of April 2023, a few notable e-services have been successfully launched. For instance, the Guinean Agency for the Promotion of Employment and Entrepreneurship (AGUIPE-E)[160], supported by external funding, is operational, aiming to streamline employment services. However, there is a notable absence of essential digital services such as electronic signature capabilities, a registry for legal entities, and integrated platforms for surveys, feedback, and complaints.

Where to focus?

Digital Guinea has to focus more efforts on its ICT infrastructure and digital skills if it wants to keep the positive trajectory and be able to move from the middle to the high EGDI group in the years to come.

24. GUINEA-BISSAU

Digital Guinea-Bissau is trying to move forward…fast

Guinea-Bissau has the highest proportion of natural wealth per capita in West Africa.[161] Despite its enormous development potential, Guinea-Bissau remains one of the least developed countries in the world. This is partly due to the country's significant political and institutional fragmentation and instability which hamper the development of much-needed policy reforms. The government has not fully tapped into the potential of technology to lead transformative processes. This doesn't mean there haven't been initiatives. They have been initiatives but contrarily scattered, risking the increase of the digital divide…even though recently this doesn't seem to be the case (anymore.)

That's why on most digitalisation indicators, the country lacks behind its structural peers Burundi, Central African Republic, Gambia, and Sierra Leone on most digital economy indicators, as per the World Bank's latest Country Economic Memorandum [162]. For example, only 23% of Bissau-Guineans use the internet, compared to a global average of 63%, according to 2020 International Telecommunication Union (ITU) statistics.[163] Digital Guinea-Bissau ranks 170th out of 193 countries on the 2024 E-Government Development Index[164] (EGDI) - having improved its position by 16 places in 2 years. This is some huge progress considering that it had been "stuck" in the 180th-something position since 2012. Also, most importantly- this is the best ranking it has ever gotten.

According to a World Bank report[165], Guinea-Bissau's digital public platforms are at a nascent stage. Still, promising initiatives for automated tax filing, payments and business registration demonstrate the potential for developing digital services. Also, over the past few years, UNDP, World Bank and partners have stepped in to support activities to improve service delivery through digital technologies. For instance, the World Bank's Western Africa Regional Digital Integration Program[166] supports Guinea (among other countries) in developing a single digital market in the region.

Where to focus?

Guinea-Bissau must develop a countrywide digital transformation strategy with a whole-of-government and citizen-centric approach to harmonise existing and pipeline initiatives. Another priority for the government would be for it to undertake a digital skills needs assessment and develop the digital skills development section of the Education Sector Plan.

25. CÔTE D'IVOIRE

e-Côte d'Ivoire significantly improved its e-governance in only 2 years!

Situated in Western Africa, Côte d'Ivoire stands as a lower-middle income country, but its digital strides are....noteworthy. Back in 2022, it made significant progress by ascending to the high EGDI group[167], surpassing the continental average and positioning itself as one of the "top of the class" group in digital development within Africa. The 2024 UN e-government[168] survey paints a promising picture of progress, even though e-Côte d'Ivoire has seen some decline in both e-government and e-participation rankings. Over a span of just two years, the nation has lost 4 places in its e-government ranking and 7 places in e-participation.[169] However, while it falls into the high EGDI, OSI and TII groups there's still(always) room for improvement.

The government of e-d'Ivoire acknowledged the importance of strong digital infrastructure, and that's why it adopted back in 2021, the *National Digital Development Strategy (NDDS) 2021-2025* (S Stratégie Numérique de la Côte d'Ivoire à l'horizon 2025, SNCI 2025), the new *National Cybersecurity Strategy 2025* (Stratégie Nationale de Cybersécurité), and *the National Innovation Strategy* 2025 (Stratégie Nationale d'Innovation.) Also, the ambitious 2024 projects outlined in such strategies encompass several key areas of digital advancement.

Looking ahead... the projections from the World Bank[170] paint a promising picture for the future of Côte d'Ivoire's digital economy. With the right investments and policies in place, the digital economy is set to contribute significantly to the country's GDP, with estimates reaching over $5.5 billion by 2025 and a staggering $20 billion by 2050. Also, the fact that there were 11.23 million internet users in Côte d'Ivoire[171] at the start of 2024 highlights the growing importance of digital connectivity in the country. Internet penetration standing at 38.4% signifies a considerable portion of the population accessing online resources and services. As more people gain access to the internet[172], the potential reach and impact of e-government services expand, enabling the government to enhance service delivery, improve efficiency, and promote transparency. However, despite these advancements, the fact that 61.6% of the population remained offline at the beginning of 2024 shows the persistent digital divide in the country.

Where to focus?

Initiatives aimed at increasing internet penetration, enhancing digital literacy, and addressing affordability barriers are essential for promoting digital inclusion and democratising access to government services.

26. KENYA

One of the two countries in Africa with dedicated digital ID policy drafting

Despite being classified as lower middle income, e-Kenya is doing pretty well in terms of digital transformation. For example, it boasts high values in both the E-Government Development Index (EGDI) and it falls into the very high Online Service Index (OSI) as per the latest available UN e-government report[173]. Also, it's worth noting that its Telecommunication Infrastructure (TII) and Human Capital Index are rated at a high level as well. Also, while it's not the most developed country (e-gov wise) in the entire continent, it definitely is among the top 10 countries with the *highest* EGDI values… ranking 8th to be exact.. e-Kenya's global ranking of 109th out of 193 countries reflects its steady ascent on the world stage. Over a span of 2 years, the nation has made strides in improving its position, climbing 4 places— an achievement worthy of recognition. However.... its dropping in e-participation values[174] stands out (unfourtunately), with e-Kenya falling behind by 19 places during the same time period.

Its digital economy contributes a significant 7.7% to the country's GDP[175]—a feat that surpasses even more established economies like Morocco and South Africa. However, amidst these achievements lies a pressing challenge: the widening digital divide. Despite Kenya's leadership in digital innovation, *many* citizens still lack access to essential digital services and opportunities. Recognising this issue, the UNDP took a significant step by signing a Memorandum of Understanding (MOU) with the government of Kenya[176] in 2023. So...in line with this commitment, the government of Kenya has launched the 'Huduma Kenya Digitalization Plan,' [177] which aligns with the country's broader digitisation agenda. On the other hand,

Kenya, renowned for its pioneering role in mobile money and financial inclusion, has been on a quest to establish a comprehensive digital identification system. It is one of the two only countries in Africa [178] that have drafted a policy document specific to their digital ID systems. (Reminder: Ethiopia was the second country in case you were wondering.)

The transition from the Huduma Namba ID cards to the new Universal Personal Identifier (UPI) is a significant development in Kenya. Also, the Kenyan National Digital Master Plan 2022-2032 179 further solidifies the country's digital ambitions, with the creation of a Smart ID card emerging as a flagship program. This card aims to provide a unique identifier while facilitating access to government services through the e-citizen digital platform.

Where to focus?

Moving forward, Kenya needs to focus a little bit more on the development of its digital infrastructure and human capital as the UN's report suggests.

27. LESOTHO

One of the least developed countries (LDC) with the highest EGDI value

Situated in Southern Africa and affectionately known as the mountain kingdom, e-Lesotho grapples with being one of the least developed countries in Africa as well as globally. However, it falls in the middle E-Government Development Index (EGDI) group. Now, when we look at the numbers, it's in the middle EGDI, TII, EPI and OSI group. On the other hand I believe one of the driving forces behind e-Lesotho's progress is its high Human Capital Index (HCI) especially since it surpasses the region average. According to the latest available UN e-government survey, e-Lesotho ranked 157th out of 193 countries[180] assessed in 2024. Also, in terms of e-participation [181] (which measures citizen engagement in digital governance processes), the kingdom declined by 42 places in just two years ranking 159th globally. This is unfortunate considering it climbed an impressive 29 places back in 2022 (when it ranked 117th globally.

Not too long ago, the government took the decision to transfer functions, resources, and authority from the central government to local authorities is a strategic move aimed at addressing the country's governance challenges. However, the ministry *lacks the necessary* resources and expertise to monitor and advise local authorities. Also, local authorities struggle with limited revenue sources, hindering their ability to deliver essential digital or non-digital services to the community effectively. With 1.10 million internet users in January 2024(according to Kepios)[182], comprising 47.0% of the total population, it's evident that internet access is becoming increasingly prevalent. However, despite this progress, there's still a significant portion of the population—1.24 million people— who remain offline, representing 53.0% of the population at the beginning of the year. Comparing these figures to an ITU estimate from 2022 [183], which stated that only 47% of the population had internet access, I believe it's clear that there hasn't been significant progress in connectivity over the past two years.

Where to focus?

Factors such as infrastructure limitations, affordability issues, and digital literacy gaps need urgent attention in e-Lesotho. Efforts should focus not only on increasing connectivity but also on ensuring its affordability and accessibility to all segments of society. To address these issues, it's important to invest in capacity building at both the central and local government levels.

28. LIBERIA

Decent e-participation levels but needs to offer more services online

Situated in Western Africa, e-Liberia falls within the Middle EGDI group[184] indicating a moderate level of e-government development. While its Online Service Index (OSI) and Human Capital Index (HCI) also fall in the middle range, its Telecommunication Infrastructure Index (TII) is *notably* low, reflecting challenges in infrastructure development that have hindered its progress. Unfortunately this has been the case for the past few years now. One standout aspect of e-Liberia's digital advancement[185]....back in 2022. However, from 2022 to 2024, the country witnessed a significant decline in its e-participation index, falling behind by 45 places in the global ranking. Nearly undoing the progress it had two years prior. This demonstrates a shrinking engagement of Liberian citizens in digital governance processes, which is not a positive development for democracy AND civic participation.

Despite ongoing reform initiatives, the core public services still fail to reach all citizens and businesses efficiently, highlighting fundamental shortcomings in inclusivity. Even with seemingly basic services like birth and death registration, accessibility remains a challenge. Surprisingly, only 66% of the population[186] is registered at birth, according to WHO statistics, despite the availability of online registration options[187]. The key takeaway here is that sustainable reform requires not only policy initiatives but also *effective implementation* mechanisms (and especially accountability measures.)

Again...Looking at the establishment of regional "one-stop shops" in Liberia, I believe there's a notable gap between intention and execution. These County Service Centers (CSCs), envisioned to streamline access to public services, have faced significant hurdles despite being largely supported by the United Nations Development Program (UNDP)[188] under the Liberia Decentralisation Support Program (LDSP). Despite aiming to provide citizens with access to over fifty services, less than a third are actually accessible through these centres. And, the performance of e-Liberia on the GovTech Maturity Index[189] also raises concerns, particularly in the areas of service delivery and citizen engagement. Factors such as low population density and inadequate infrastructure exacerbate the situation, especially in rural areas. The lack of reliable electricity and road networks makes it difficult for the government to reach all citizens efficiently.

Where to focus?

It's important to address several remaining challenges, including interoperability issues, capacity building to effectively utilise system-generated data for efficiency analysis, and transitioning towards a more *whole-of-government approach* to digitalisation.

29. LIBYA

Amazingly overcame its infrastructure issues after the conflict

e-Libya, located in Western Africa, has made impressive progress on the E-Government Development Index (EGDI), reaching the high category for the first time. This big improvement is due largely to Libya's focus on building up its telecommunication infrastructure, which has seen major changes in just two years. Surprisingly, e-Libya is now performing above both the regional and global averages. Just two years ago, in 2022, it was in the low group for telecommunications infrastructure (TII). Now, it's jumped all the way to the Very High TII group. This amazing improvement shows just how much e-Libya has transformed in such a short time. This is a rare exception (seen in only a few countries), highlighting the potential for advancement in digital governance with the *right* investments in place.

What's also interesting is its exceptionally well-developed human capital[190], surpassing the region and sub-region average. On the flip side, e-Libya faces challenges in its online services, with a low OSI Index (which is an indicator of e-governance according to the DESA publication.)[191] Internationally, Libya's e-government ranked 125th out of 193 countries in the latest UN assessment. What's particularly worth mentioning it's that it improved its ranking by 44 places in just 2 years...indicating a promising trend. One area that stands out as a concern is Libya's e-participation score. From 2020 to 2022, the country held the 189th position, and in 2024, it dropped slightly to 190th place. This low ranking shows a clear gap in citizen engagement with the government's digital services. While progress has been made in other areas, this lag in e-participation suggests that many citizens may not be actively using or accessing these online platforms, or that more could be done to encourage their involvement.

It might be hard to believe, but just two years ago, Libya struggled with major internet connectivity issues. Understanding the factors behind these challenges shows just how impressive it is that they've managed to reach where they are today. High demand for internet services, coupled with damage to infrastructure from unauthorised construction, sabotage, and theft of ICT equipment, all played significant roles in the country's poor connectivity.[192] With approximately 25% of mobile towers damaged or stolen[193]physical infrastructure had been a target amidst the turmoil. This damage not only disrupted current connectivity but also posed obstacles to rebuilding efforts, which were essential for improving access and reliability.

Additionally, unauthorised construction and sabotage further exacerbated the situation, making it difficult to maintain and expand internet infrastructure. These activities not only undermined the stability of existing networks but also impeded efforts to introduce new technologies and services. According to an ITU report from 2022[194], the percentage of the population using the internet in e-Libya stood at 88%. According to another source[195] there were 6.13 million internet users in e-Libya at the beginning of 2024, with internet penetration reaching 88.4%. However, despite these figures, a significant portion of the population—approximately 801.6 thousand individuals—still do not have access to the internet.

Where to focus?

In light of these challenges, I believe addressing issues such as e-participation and instability caused by conflict will be crucial for further improving e-governance and ensuring widespread access to digital services for the Libyan population.

30. MADAGASCAR

e-Madagascar has has slightly fallen behind

Despite being a low-income nation and the world's fourth largest island, e-Madagascar has demonstrated significant improvements in its E-Government Development Index (EGDI)[196] values between 2020 and 2022.

However, in 2024, it seems to have fallen behind in e-governance and e-participation[197], according to the recent report. Also, the country's position in the medium Human Capital Index (HCI) category—a key part of the EGDI— isn't as strong as before. It dropped from the high HCI group it held back in 2022. Between 2022 and 2024, e-Madagascar dropped seven spots in the E-Participation Index (EPI) ranking[198]. This setback contrasts with the impressive progress made from 2020 to 2022, when Madagascar climbed 40 places in the UN e-government survey. This recent decline could indicate challenges in maintaining the same pace of digital development, especially in public engagement and accessibility. Despite this recent drop, Madagascar's previous leap shows the country's *potential* to improve its e-participation and digital services for citizens.

I think what's really crucial is the country's recognition of the limitations of relying solely on online platforms for citizen engagement, where internet access is still a luxury for many.[199] Looking at the Malagasy government's online platform, Torolalana[200], I believe it initially followed a trend seen in many countries worldwide, drawing inspiration from the GOV.UK model. However, this approach risked excluding a significant portion of the Malagasy population—approximately 80%—who lacked internet access.[201]

In these conditions, it's commendable that they've moved beyond just mirroring a model and taken proactive steps to ensure inclusivity by embracing multiple communication channels. Post offices emerged as a strategic partner in this effort, given their widespread presence and the trust they command among Malagasy citizens. Leveraging the existing infrastructure and credibility of post offices, the government introduced the Mahatoky service[202]—an in-person help desk located within post offices. (The name "Mahatoky," meaning "trust" in Malagasy)

Moving further, I think the situation in e-Madagascar regarding birth registration is quite concerning. While it's admirable that the coverage was at 80% in 2009, seeing it drop to 74% by 2021 was definitely a setback.[203] Fortunately, the Government of Madagascar has partnered with the World Bank on the Digital Governance and Identification Management System (PRODIGY) Project.[204]

This initiative aims to achieve universal birth registration and identity coverage while keeping costs low, particularly in light of challenges such as low digital literacy and mobile connectivity. Leveraging X-road[205] technology for secure data exchange between different government information systems[206] is a commendable approach.

Where to focus?

Sustaining and building upon those past gains will require ongoing commitment from the government as well as international support.

31. MALAWI

It has set its eye in bridging the digital divide

I think e-Malawi's positioning in the recent UN e-government survey[207] provides us with some interesting insights. Ranking 163rd out of 193 countries in e-governance might seem concerning at first glance, but I believe there's more to this story. Despite its low position, it's crucial to recognise the progress that e-Malawi has made, particularly in areas like telecommunication infrastructure (TII) and human capital (HCI). When we look at the specifics, e-Malawi's 99th position in e-participation[208] stands out. Especially seeing as it saw a slight improvement compared to the 101st ranking it held in 2022. However, there's undoubtedly room for more progress.

Malawi's digital infrastructure has seen advancements, but...there's stark disparity between network coverage and actual internet usage. There's an 86% 3G and 70% 4G coverage(according to ITU data)[209]. However, only 28% of the population is online.[210] That's a significant gap that signals underlying challenges. For perspective, these user figures reveal that 15.34 million people in Malawi *did not use* the internet at the start of 2024. This discrepancy suggests that while the infrastructure exists, there are accessibility gaps preventing the full utilisation of digital services and products. Also, access to electricity is low in e-Malawi[211], with only 18% of the population having access! However, I'm optimistic about Malawi's efforts towards inclusivity with the launch of the Inclusive Digital Transformation for Malawi (IDT4M) project[212] in collaboration with the UNDP in April 2024. This initiative holds promise in bridging the digital divide and ensuring that all citizens can benefit from the opportunities afforded by digital advancements.

Where to focus?

Updating key policies, strategies, and legislation is crucial to creating an enabling environment for the growth of the digital economy. For example - there is a need for *clear policy direction* and strategies to promote E-Government platforms and facilitate the digitisation of government payments, such as social payments.

32. MALI

It needs a new central policy to guide the digitisation of government services

Situated in Western Africa, Mali is a vast, landlocked nation that faces unique challenges and opportunities in its digital transformation journey. According to the latest UN e-government survey from 2024[213], Mali falls within the middle EGDI group, indicating moderate progress in its e-government development. However, one standout aspect is Mali's very *Low HCI* (Human Capital Index), highlighting a challenge in terms of human resources and (digital) skills development. Also, I have to mention that Mali has not seen any changes whatsoever regarding these groups in some time now. What's more… despite Mali showning some progress in its e-government and e-participation rankings[214] back in 2022, it seems it didn't manage to keep that same pace (or ranking for that matter). Falling behind by 5 places in e-government and 13 places in e-participation ranking is kind of a cause for concern. In 2022, Mali ranked 168th in e-government and 128th in e-participation, reflecting a negative trajectory towards digital engagement and inclusivity.

Regarding connectivity, issues persist. At the start of 2024, Mali had 7.82 million internet users[215], representing a 33.1% internet penetration rate. In this front, Mali has made commendable efforts to build its ICT infrastructure, including laying over 3,000 kilometres of fibre optic cable. The government's commitment to invest $117.3bn[216] in improving the fibre optic network is a great step forward (even though not enough in this case.) Political instability and conflict pose significant obstacles to further investment and infrastructure development.

Where to focus?

Moving forward, I think Mali would benefit greatly from developing and implementing a new digital transformation strategy that addresses current challenges and aligns with the country's long-term goals.

33. MAURITANIA

Has a long way to go in terms of digitalisation

Situated in Western Africa, e-Mauritania grapples with challenges typical of many developing nations. It falls into the high Telecommunication Infrastructure (TII) group and Human Capital (HC)[217], indicating a foundation for digital growth. However, despite these strengths, it falls into the Low Online Service Index (OSI) group, where it has been for the past few years now. However, I must add that e-Mauritania's has seen improvement in its EPI value[218], ranking 174th up from the 190th place it held in the 2022 UN e-government survey. Also it improved its e-governance ranking by 7 places in the same time period. This suggests that citizen engagement in digital governance processes is somewhat limited, even though on the right track . Keep in mind that low EPI values only exacerbate the gap between the government and its citizens.

I believe Mauritania's National Digital Transformation Agenda 2022-2025[219] signifies a significant step towards modernising the country's ICT infrastructure and government services. With a population coverage of at least 35% by a 4G mobile network in 2021 and an internet penetration rate of 98% in 2022[220], e-Mauritania has made significant strides in expanding its ICT infrastructure. However, while the internet penetration rate stands at an impressive 98%, recent data shows that 55.6% of the population remained offline at the beginning of 2024[221]. Looking at the numbers, it's clear that there's significant untapped potential for internet usage in Mauritania. With 2.19 million internet users at the start of 2024 [222], there's room for growth in expanding digital literacy and encouraging more widespread internet adoption.

However, there's a gap between people living in urban and rural areas who often find themselves disconnected from these digital advancements. In these conditions, one significant project supported by the EU is the establishment of a new submarine [223] to connect Mauritania, providing a backup solution to the current single submarine cable (African Coast to Europe - ACE). This initiative not only enhances Mauritania's connectivity but also benefits its landlocked neighbours by providing additional data capacity to accommodate the growing volume of digital traffic.

Where to focus?

While Mauritania's digital transformation agenda is ambitious and promising, it's essential to address the infrastructural challenges to ensure that the benefits of the digital revolution are accessible to all.

34. MAURITIUS

One of the few African countries above the global average

According to the latest UN e-government survey[224] from 2024, it's clear that e-Mauritius is making significant progress... especially considering the challenges faced by many nations on the continent. Mauritius boasts *very* high values in the E-Government Development Index (EGDI)[225], reflecting its advanced digital infrastructure and effective use of technology in public services. Actually, it was one of the two countries from the region that have ever reached the highest level. However, there's room for improvement in e-participation, indicating a need to enhance citizen engagement in governance processes. Countries with higher EGDI values usually have higher EPI values as well, but this is not the case for Mauritius. While it ranked 76th in e-governance in 2024, it ranks only 108th in e-participation (even losing 7 places compared to 2022.)

Ranked among the top 100 countries worldwide in overall EGDI (e-Government Development Index), Mauritius boasts values that surpass the global average. Interestingly, South Africa may take the lead regionally, but Mauritius is certainly not far behind, securing a close second spot in e-government development. But it's not just in Africa where e-Mauritius commands attention. Also, it is one of the only two SIDS (small island developing states) with very high EGDI values (alongside Singapore) in the world. Making these two and are the leaders in digital development within this group. This is one of the indicators of a thriving digital ecosystem, and I believe Mauritius is setting a stellar example for other island nations in the region to follow.

But it's not just in Africa where e-Mauritius commands attention. Globally, it stands tall as the fifth island-country in the world regarding e-governance, trailing only behind powerhouses like Singapore, Bahrain, Grenada, and Bahamas. This is a significant achievement for a small island nation.

Where to focus?

e-Mauritius has indeed made significant progress, but still... e-participation should be a main focus for the government in the years to come.

35. MOROCCO

Digital Morocco: Among the top 100 performers of the world (for the first time)

There are approximately 1 billion people in the world who have no means of identification, and African residents make up more than half of that number. This implies that African residents without identification cannot have access to basic social, digital and economic rights or cannot work official jobs. In digital Morocco, most citizens lack(ed) identification, prompting its government to introduce digital technologies, especially during the Covid-19 pandemic. These innovations include introducing vaccine passports, Covid-19 tracking technologies, and facial recognition systems.

According to the UN e-government survey, Morocco ranks 4th in Africa[226] - being among the top performers in the continent. This is a huge achievement, considering it is one of those countries that has lower-middle income but still managed to have high OSI (Online Service Index) values. Actually in Morocco surpasses the world average in terms of e-governance which is amazing. In the 2024 report it ranks 90th among 193 countries -having improved its position by 11 places[227] compared to 2 years ago. In terms of e-participation it also had great improvement, ranking 102nd, or a jump of 26 places since the 2022 report. This leap shows how much more accessible and interactive government services in Libya have become, allowing citizens to engage with their government online in new, more convenient ways.

Obviously, Morocco's strongest component is its telecommunication infrastructure where it even surpasses the global average...something that the UN report doesn't fail to mention. This is one of the main reasons it got into the top 100 performers of the world for the first time this year. The Moroccan government has chosen to work with third-party platforms to have an effective and productive digital ID system.[228] Although the user's personal information is shared with these third-party platforms, the DGSN ensures that all personal data is secured. The National Population Registry must provide unique registration for everyone, including minors and expatriates, so they can collect their biometric and demographic data. This registry also ensures a secured identity verification service both online and physically.

Where to focus?

Considering that not all Moroccans are digitally educated, the government needs to train more citizens[229] to cope with the challenges of the new digital environment. This way, citizens will benefit more from the digital transformation programs, and there will be fewer controversies.

36. MOZAMBIQUE

e-Mozambique is failing to keep a steady pace when it comes to digitalisation

e-Mozambique (nestled in Eastern Africa) finds itself in the Middle EGDI group[230], even on this year's report. This index essentially measures how well a country is doing in terms of its digital government services....denoting its moderate performance in e-government development. However, its progress seems to be overshadowed by its low Telecommunication Infrastructure Index (TII), which has been an issue for some time now. This means that compared to many other nations, it's lagging behind in leveraging technology for governance and public services.

In the UN e-government report of 2024, e-Mozambique was placed at a rather lowly 177th position in EGDI and 159th in e-participation.[231] What's concerning is not just the position itself but the fact that e-Mozambique has slipped even further behind in e-governance since 2018. This suggests a trend of stagnation or even regression. Even though I must add that it saw an improvement in its e-participation ranking as it went up by 4 places compared to the 2022 report. Looking at Mozambique's connectivity, I think there's a clear divide between urban and rural areas. Almost three-quarters of the population can't afford internet services or devices like smartphones and computers. Also, 76.8% of the population was offline [232] at the beginning of 2024. Imagine that! It's not just about affordability....a third of the population living in rural areas can't even access mobile broadband signals, no matter the cost.

One big initiative the country has undertaken is the integrated electronic tax filing system. By the end of December 2023, they aimed to have it in every tax office across the country [233], and it looks like they nailed that goal. That's a big deal because it means they're streamlining how they collect all taxes, which is crucial for keeping the country's finances in order and is one of the first. By March 2024, the goal was to have all taxpayers covered by this portal, although it's unclear if this objective was met or not.

Where to focus?

Despite everything, in general, I think it's clear that e-Mozambique has some catching up to do in terms of its digital governance initiatives. While some other countries in Africa are rapidly advancing in their digital transformations, it seems to be struggling to keep a steady pace. I believe this could have significant implications for the country's development and its ability to effectively serve its citizens in the digital age.

37. NAMIBIA

The first country in the world to implement UNDP's Framework

Situated in Southern Africa and surrounded by countries like South Africa, Botswana, Angola, Zambia, and Zimbabwe, e-Namibia occupies a strategic position in the region. However, its development in the digital sphere has been hindered by underdeveloped - or lets say - unevenly developed infrastructure, posing challenges to the advancement of e-government initiatives. One remarkable achievement of e-Namibia is its status as the first country in the world to implement the UNDP's Model Governance Framework for Digital Legal Identity (more on that below.) In terms of key indicators, e-Namibia is characterised by high Telecommunication Infrastructure (TII) and high Human Capital Index (HCI) [234]. Additionally, it falls into the high E-Government Development Index (EGDI) group [235], highlighting its progress in providing digital services to its citizens.

Looking at Namibia's pioneering efforts in digital ID, I believe it's truly a trailblazer in this field. Thanks to the groundwork laid by the UNDP Namibia's Accelerator Lab [236] and collaborative partnerships with government stakeholders, Namibia is poised to become the first African country (and indeed the world) to implement the UNDP's Model Governance Framework for Digital Legal Identity.[237] Also, looking at the government of Namibia's vision [238] to achieve full digital literacy by 2030, I believe it's a commendable vision. However, there are challenges to overcome... particularly in reaching rural communities and older populations. The collaboration with the e-Governance Academy, supported by the AU-EU D4D Hub project [239], is a promising initiative. Training 50 instructors in rural communities using a *Training of Trainers* model has the potential to exponentially increase digital literacy across the country. Workshops covering topics like online safety, information retrieval, and digital service usage are also important for empowering citizens with essential skills.

Where to focus?

Right now, it's important for e-Namibia to focus on improving its e-participation ranking, which would make it easier for citizens to engage with the government online. Another key area to work on is boosting its Online Service Index, which measures the quality and availability of government services provided online.

38. NIGER

Where less than 17% of the population is online

Niger is a large, landlocked country mostly covered by the Sahara Desert. It's one of the hottest countries in the world. The population is around 28 million [240], with many people living in rural areas and relying on agriculture. It's clear that the country faces significant challenges... particularly when it comes to GovTech. According to the recent World Bank's GTMI report[241], Niger has a "minimal focus on GovTech.". Niger also falls into the low EGDI group[242] which means that it is struggling with its digital governance capabilities. Being in this group typically means that a country faces significant challenges in digital development, and most countries in this category are either Least Developed Countries (LDCs) or Landlocked Developing Countries (LLDCs).. which Niger happens to be both. This dual classification highlights the compounded difficulties the country faces.... from economic constraints to geographical challenges.

In terms of e-governance, Niger was ranked 187th out of 193 countries assessed, which is quite low. When we look at e-participation, where Niger holds the 159th place. This ranking shows some huge dropping in engaging citizens online (compared to the 135th place it held in 2022) according to the UN E-government Knowledgebase [243].

However, at the start of 2024, the internet penetration rate in Niger [244] stood at a modest 16.9% of the total population. This means that, despite a growth of 172 thousand internet users between January 2023 and January 2024—a 3.8% increase—the vast majority of the population remains offline. Specifically, 23.02 million people, or 83.1% of the population, *did not* use the internet at the beginning of this year. Obviously, limited internet access is a major barrier. When only a small fraction of the population is online, the reach and impact of digital government services are inherently restricted.

Where to focus?

They show that progress is being made and that there is potential for further development. But, the focus now should be on leveraging these gains to enhance the overall digital governance.

39. NIGERIA

e-Nigeria and its untapped potential - The young and skilled talent

Looking at e-Nigeria's current state, it seems like there's a lot of potential waiting to be tapped into. With a Telecommunication Infrastructure Index (TII) and Human Capital Index (HCI) both classified as middle, alongside a high Online Service Index [245] (OSI), e-Nigeria finds itself in a unique position. According to the latest available UN data [246], e-Nigeria is ranked 144th in e-government and 115th in e-participation. This suggests a stable position but without *significant* progress or decline in recent years.

Addressing infrastructural gaps should be a priority for enhancing digital connectivity nationwide. According to some studies, any digital government is dependent on access to electricity.[247] One positive aspect is the increasing affordability of data services for mobile subscribers, which has contributed to greater internet access. Nigeria's ranking of 19th out of 72 low- and middleincome nations in the Alliance for Affordable Internet's 2021 Affordability Report [248] reflects commendable progress in implementing policies to make internet services more accessible to its citizens. Looking ahead, the government's new National Broadband Plan 2020–25 (NBP)[249] aims to expand broadband penetration to 70% by 2025 (replacing the previous plan from 2013–18.)

Ensuring a reliable digital identity is essential for any nation aspiring to build a robust digital economy. This begins with a single government database[250] to ensure that individuals are recognised consistently across all systems. But, repeated biometric enrollment[251] for various purposes such as the National Identification Number (NIN), Bank Verification

Number (BVN), SIM registration, voter's cards, and passports has led to widespread frustration among Nigerians. Truth be told...this redundancy not only increases program costs but also fails to deliver the intended benefits efficiently. It's worth noting that Nigeria has shown interest in integrating the Modula Open Source Identity (MOSIP)[252] with its digital ID system. This integration could further streamline identity management processes and improve the overall efficiency of digital service delivery.

Where to focus?

One thing that stands out to me is the abundance of young talent in the country. With such a large population of young people eager to learn and innovate, Nigeria has a valuable resource that it can leverage to drive its digital evolution forward. What this suggests is that e-Nigeria could greatly benefit from investments in both telecommunication infrastructure and human capital development.

40. RWANDA

One of the beacons of digital governments in Africa

While many parts of the continent still rely on paper-based systems that are expensive, slow, and difficult to access, e-Rwanda stands out as one of the beacons of digital government in Africa today. Thanks to an ambitious plan launched by President Paul Kagame back in 2012, this small East African country soon became one of the world's fastest adopters of technology—a pioneer in digital transformation, e-governance, and e-democracy.

According to the 2024 UN E-Government Survey[253], e-Rwanda was particularly noted as a country that despite having poorly developed infrastructure, its online services are well developed compared to most other countries in Africa. Actually, Rwanda is one of those Least Developed Countries (LDC) that has been hailed for its efforts for many, many years now. The Rwandan government set up a single, secure platform in 2014 where citizens could access government services with relative ease. The platform is named Irembo[254], and at first, the idea was to help citizens submit applications and make payments for various services. Moreover, the government has announced its *Vision 2050 strategy* and the *Smart Rwanda Master Plan*, which emphasises creating a prosperous and knowledgeable society through smart information and communications technology strategies.

What's noteworthy is that despite having limited resources, the country has made great strides in offering public services online. That's how Rwanda has set the bar regionally in terms of mobile network coverage since 97% of its population has access to mobile phone services [255]. The country also boasts a high internet penetration rate for an African nation. The investments and enabling regulatory reforms have helped e-Rwanda achieve some of the highest 3G and 4G network coverage rates on the continent [256], bringing virtually all Rwandans within the range of mobile broadband. That's why in e-participation it ranks 42nd out of 193 countries[257], even improving its ranking by 11 places compared to 2022. It is the second country after South Africa in the whole continent in this regard.

Where to focus?

The apparent problem is that Rwanda needs to invest more in human capital— people with skills to take advantage of ICTs—to build its digital skills base. A better-educated workforce will help accelerate change and ensure that Rwanda's strategic investments create more jobs and opportunities for all.

41. SÃO TOMÉ AND PRÍCIPE

São Tomé and Príncipe faces challenges as a low income country

São Tomé and Príncipe (STP), a small island developing state nestled close to the equator off Africa's western coast, has been facing some challenges in its digital transformation path. It is among the world's least developed countries[258], and it actually presents a stark example of the challenges faced by low-income states seeking to enhance their digital infrastructure and governance capabilities. The country struggles with a predominantly agricultural economy and nascent tourism industry, relying heavily on external aid for economic sustenance.

When it comes to e-government, São Tomé and Príncipe's position is low, ranking 154th globally in e-government[259] (unchanged ranking since 2018) and a promising improvement in e-participation at the 166th place (from 187th) according to the UN's metrics[260]. This reflects a deficiency in online service provision *but* also progress in harnessing digital tools for governance and citizen engagement. Such rankings show a glaring gap between infrastructure development and the capacity to effectively utilise it for public benefit. The World Bank's GTMI report for East and Southern Africa[261] paints an equally bleak picture, categorising STP among nations with *"Minimal focus on GovTech,"* alongside countries like Eritrea, Sudan and South Sudan. Being both a Small Island Developing State (SIDS) and a Least Developed Country (LDC), São Tomé and Príncipe confront persistent challenges that hinder progress in telecommunications infrastructure, online service provision, and human capital development. These challenges stem largely from limited resources, which constrain investments crucial for advancing e-government initiatives. At the start of 2024, São Tomé and Príncipe had 133.4 thousand internet users[262], representing a 57.0% internet penetration rate. Additionally, there were 167.7 thousand active cellular mobile connections, equivalent to 71.6% of the total population. Recognising the critical role of connectivity, particularly in education, the Ministry of Education and Higher Education has partnered with UNICEF[263] to implement a complete digital learning strategy.

Where to focus?

According to a recent World Bank report [264], "The reduced availability of external financing, continued disruption of global supply chains, and climate-related events could weaken STP's prospects for growth and further impede poverty reduction." So, with targeted investments, innovative policy frameworks, and external funding, the country can aspire to a thriving future...digitally and economically.

42. SENEGAL

A low-income country with great potential and progress

I think e-Senegal is an intriguing case study in digital development, especially considering its position as one of the least developed countries with one of the highest EGDI values, according to the UN's e-government survey [265]. This is pretty significant because it sheds light on how a nation's digital advancement doesn't *always* correlate directly with its overall development status. In the 2024 UN e-Government Knowledgebase [266], Senegal climbed to the 135th position worldwide, a notable improvement from its 143rd position in 2022 and the 150th place in 2020. Additionally, the World Bank's GovTech Maturity Index Update[267] placed Senegal in Group C, indicating that the country has some focus on GovTech initiatives. What's impressive about e-Senegal is its highly developed telecommunication infrastructure, which always serves as a strong foundation for digitalisation efforts. *(Being one of the most advanced in West Africa.)*

According to DataReportal[268], there were approximately 10.79 million internet users in the country at the start of the year, representing 60.0% of the population. This figure hasn't shifted much since 2022 (ITU data)[269]. Similarly, the total number of cellular mobile connections remained at 21.92 million, which interestingly amounts to 121.8% of the total population. Meanwhile Senegal's recent collaborations with international organisations like the World Bank, the African Development Bank (AfDB), and the Smart Africa Alliance are a significant step towards boosting its digitalisation efforts.

Take, for example, the agreement signed in April 2023 with the World Bank[270], totalling 150 million USD for the Digital Economy Acceleration Project (PAEN). Similarly, the additional funding of 5.01 million EUR from the AfDB in December 2022 for the construction of the Diamniadio Digital Technology Park[271] is another great example. Also, I believe that collaboration is key when it comes to complex projects like national data strategies. That's why it's encouraging to see initiatives like the two-day workshop in [272]. March 2023, led by MCTEN in partnership with Smart Africa and GIZ(German agency for international cooperation and development). Bringing together expertise from different sectors and countries can lead to more effective strategies.

Where to focus?

It should focus more on improving the connectivity and the access to the internet for more people.

43.SEYCHELLES

This African island-nation in top 100 countries globally

This high-income island nation stands out for its notable performance in digital government, ranking among the top six countries in Africa according to the United Nations e-Government Development Index (EGDI)[273]. It has a very we-developed technological infrastructure and a well-educated populace, which are crucial factors in driving its digital advancement. Also, it's noteworthy that Seychelles is among the elite five African nations (alongside South Africa, Mauritius, Tunisia, Marocco) to rank within the top 100 countries globally in terms of overall EGDI ranking. However, despite its overall strong performance, it has seen a decline in e-governance[274], dropping from the 85th place in 2022 to the 92nd in 2024. Meanwhile, it's e-participation score has seen an improvement, placing it in the 130th position this year, or 18 places higher compared to 2022. When examining internet usage statistics, I find it encouraging that Seychelles has achieved a commendable internet penetration rate. With 93.6 thousand internet users at the start of 2024 (according to Datareportal)[275], representing 86.7% of the population, it's evident that a significant portion of the populace is connected online.

The recent introduction of the SeyID digital identity platform by WISeKey[276] in April 2024 marks a significant milestone in Seychelles' digital journey. Launched in 2022[277], the SeyID platform aims to enhance the country's digital government, tourism, and health initiatives, streamlining processes and improving efficiency. And truth be told, a great majority of government services do use at least one digital system to enable their delivery...reducing reliance on paper-based processes. These systems (often database-driven applications) empower public servants to efficiently handle various applications, from building permits to customs documentation.

Where to focus?

Considering the insights from a recent World Bank report [278], it's evident that e-Seychelles face challenges in fully embracing digitalisation due to limited end-to-end processes and a lack of focus on user-centricity. This has resulted in a relatively low uptake of digital services. However, despite these challenges, Seychelles possesses a high-quality national identity register, providing a strong foundation for developing a digital identity system.

44. SIERRA LEONE

e-Sierra Leone is struggling with connectivity issues

Sierra Leone (situated in West Africa) might be small in size, but its digital aspirations are big. The National Innovation and Digital Strategy (NIDS) 2019-2029[279], spearheaded by the Directorate of Science, Technology, and Innovation (DSTI), laid out a comprehensive vision for the country's digital transformation. Also, they were among the early adopters of a "Mobile First" digital strategy back in 2019. As highlighted by the UN's data[280] it has a ranking of 172nd in e-government and 120th in e-participation among 193 countries assessed, having seen improvement in both indicators (by 13 and 37 places respectively) in just 2 years.

Also, Sierra Leone has taken significant steps to improve connectivity, being among the first countries in West Africa to prioritise access to high-speed internet through initiatives like the Africa Coast to Europe (ACE)[281] submarine fibre optic cable. But, looking at the data from Datareportal[282], we can see that there were 2.70 million internet users in e-Sierra Leone at the start of 2024, with internet penetration standing at 30.4%. Despite 60% of the country having at least 3G network coverage, only 21% have active mobile broadband subscriptions (ITU data from 2021)[283]. This reveals a gap between coverage and actual usage, highlighting issues with affordability and accessibility. In terms of network quality, Sierra Leone ranks 137 out of 181 countries for quality and speed according to Speedtest Global Index[284] of April 2024. Another huge challenge hindering the progress of digitalisation in Sierra Leone is its unreliable electricity supply. In April 2024, Sierra Leone's Energy Minister Kanja Sesay resigned amidst a prolonged electricity crisis. According to Reuters[285], this crisis has left major cities like Freetown, Bo, Kenema, and Koidu experiencing multi-day stretches without power.

I believe that for e-Sierra Leone to truly harness the benefits of digitalisation, there needs to be a concerted effort towards investing in human capital development. According to an IMF report, the country falls behind the regional average in both literacy rate and internet penetration. With an average literacy rate of around 65%, e-Sierra Leone faces challenges in providing its citizens with the necessary foundational skills to thrive in the digital age.

Where to focus?

There are clear opportunities for improvement through targeted investments in human capital development and the broader digital infrastructure.

45. SOMALIA

Among the 3 least digitally developed in the world

When we look at e-Somalia's situation, it's clear that it's facing some significant challenges in terms of its digital development. However, it's crucial to consider the context in which e-Somalia operates. The country has endured prolonged civil conflict, frequent droughts, and floods, which have severely impacted its human and physical resources, hindering its overall economic development.

Also, when we take a closer look at e-Somalia, it becomes evident that several challenges hinder the effective use of digital technologies in the country. These challenges range from inadequate infrastructure to low-quality and slow internet connections, frequent power outages and high internet costs relative to the income of the majority of the population. According to UN data[286], Somalia ranks 191st globally in e-government adoption and 137th in e-participation. These rankings underscore the immense gap that needs to be bridged in terms of digital governance and citizen engagement. With Somalia positioned just above South Sudan and Central African Republic (there are 193 countries assessed in total) it's clear that there's a long, long way to go to improve access to inclusive e-government applications and services.

Only 27% of the population is online based on data from the start of 2024 (according to Datareportal)[287], where there were around 5.08 million internet users in the country. One of the biggest challenges here is infrastructure. Deploying and maintaining networks in rural areas can be tough and expensive. There's the issue of electricity, or rather, the lack of it. Most rural areas in Somalia don't have access to electricity, making it hard to power up those cell towers. And even if they do have power, the cost is among the highest in the world, which doesn't help matters.

Where to focus?

With the ongoing challenges this country faces, it's understandable that efforts towards digitalisations might take a backseat to more immediate concerns like rebuilding infrastructure and ensuring basic needs are met.

46. SOUTH AFRICA

The leader of the entire African continent

e-South Africa stands as a great example of e-government development on the African continent... positioning itself as the regional leader. With an EGDI (E-Government Development Index) value of 0.8616 [288], South Africa stands proudly in the highest rating class (VH) for the (alongside Mauritius). This marks the first time ever, African countries have reached this rating class. This achievement is not only significant on a regional level but also puts South Africa among the top 100 countries globally in terms of overall EGDI ranking.

However, while it leads the region in overall e-governance, it's interesting to note that it (finally) holds the top spot in e-participation, outranking Rwanda for the first time. Obviously, it is one of the six countries in the region to now have EGDI values above the world average[289]. It ranks 40th in e-governance and 29th (!) in e-participation.

Internet penetration has expanded rapidly in e-South Africa. According to DataReportal's *Digital 2024* [290] *report*, the internet penetration rate in e-South Africa reached an impressive 74.7% by January 2024. To put this into perspective, out of the total population, 15.35 million people were *not* using the internet at the start of 2024, or about 25.3% of the population remained offline. Since the SA Connect program was introduced back in 2013 [291], there has been a clear focus on improving internet connectivity across the country. In the 2023–24 budget [292], the government allocated approximately $176.2 million for the second phase of this program.

This funding is set aside for capital equipment and new fibre infrastructure [293], as well as leasing existing fibre, all aimed at expanding communication networks to underserviced areas.

Moreover... the improvements in internet speed are noteworthy. Data published by Ookla[294] in April 2024 show that the median mobile internet connection speed via cellular networks was 50.70 Mbps (which is a 38% increase compared to 2023.)

South Africa's approach to digital development is quite impressive....especially considering their long-term vision. The National Development Plan: Vision 2030[295], which was developed in 2012 really sets a strong foundation for making e-South Africa an inclusive digital society.

What I like most about this initiative is the National e-Government Strategy and Roadmap[296], which was outlined in 2017. This strategy brings a fresh approach to electronic government development, laying out a comprehensive programme of action. The e-Government Portal[297] is a standout feature in this strategy. It's a single point of entry to more than 100 services...covering a wide range of needs such as birth registration, parenting resources, health services, education, agriculture, employment, and social services. I'd say an important G2B service is the BizPortal[298], which was developed to streamline business operations in e-South Africa.

Where to focus?

Doing what works. South Africa clearly sets a benchmark for other African countries to follow.

47. SOUTH SUDAN

The battle to connect a country

In 2011, e-South Sudan became the world's newest nation after a referendum was held on its independence from Sudan. Although the vote was largely peaceful, South Sudan still struggles with many of the same problems that plague other new countries, including poor infrastructure and political instability. However, the country's distance from the world's foremost IT hubs, combined with limited resources and security concerns, has made it difficult to develop its digital sector in tandem with its traditional economy.

South Sudan has been unable to provide consistent electricity or Internet connectivity for its citizens. More than 37% of the population don't have access to electricity[299], which in rural areas is significantly lower (35%) than in urban areas (55%). A low phone penetration level (45%) is also a significant structural barrier, specifically in rural areas and among women. Without consistent electricity, phone usage, or Internet connectivity, those who own mobile phones cannot access any governmental services online, which many other African countries have already achieved. According to the EGDI report, for South Sudan "significant investment is needed in all areas"[300] In the 2022 report, it was the least developed country in the entire world (regarding e-governance). In this year's report, South Sudan ranks second last[301] compared to all 193 other countries analysed…thus surpassing the Central African Republic. Regarding e-participation things are not this bleak where it has once again moved up from the last place. Now it ranks 177th (or up by 16 places compared to 2022.)

Where to focus?

To conclude, the government needs to address the ongoing instability and conflict; structural barriers (poor network coverage and limited access to electricity); socioeconomic barriers (chronic underdevelopment and low literacy rates); and, to a lesser extent, behavioural barriers (lack of knowledge of available services.) Considering South Sudan's sheer size and the vast number of citizens, digital government is far from being an easy task. A cohesive e-governance plan that takes into account all layers of political bureaucracy will need strong leadership and support.

48. SUDAN

Digital Sudan and its role in economic transformation

The Digital Sudan Prime Minister, Dr Abdalla Hamdok, was given a Sudaneseissued Visa card on March 14, 2021. The visa card signifies the crucial moment in the country's rejoining the global economy and the increasing progress of financial inclusion in one of Africa's biggest markets. For years, Sudan had been left out, but recently, they're retaining a spot in the global economy, with international sanctions progressively lifted from 2017 and a new government installed in 2019.

For the past ten years, Sudan's economy has suffered rising inflation, oil price fluctuation, sanctions, and institutional crises. In Africa, cross-border e-commerce is expected to improve by 25% annually or twice the growth rate of domestic e-commerce. Regional and global trade through e-commerce will help to boost gains for both micro, small and medium-sized enterprises (MSMEs) in Sudan.

Digital Sudan has a high chance of being successful with the introduction of e-commerce into its government. Due to its phone penetration of 70.4%, its citizens have more internet access, which will make up for the lack of e-payment systems, high cost of access to bandwidth, and limited financial inclusion. Also, adopting the cash-on-arrival method will compensate for the deficiency in financial inclusion.

According to the DESA publication[302], Sudan remains in the middle category of the E-Government Development Index (EGDI) and also in the Human Capital Index (HCI) and Telecommunication Infrastructure Index (TII) groups. This means that there hasn't been much improvement since the 2022 report. For example, Sudan now ranks 178th in e-governance, a small drop from 176th in 2022. However, there's been a bit of progress in e-participation, where Sudan moved up to 184th place from 187th in 2022.

Where to focus?

As a country, digital Sudan has a lot of catching up to do. Even among surrounding countries, Sudan is lagging in digital and technological advancements. To advance and introduce digital government into their system, the Sudan government has to invest significantly in digital transformation.

49. TANZANIA

e-Tanzania suffers from a wide digital divide

e-Tanzania, a country located in Eastern Africa, falls within the Middle EGDI group[303]. Also, in the latest UN survey, Tanzania is ranked 153rd out of 193 countries in e-government[304]. I have to note that it has been holding the same position since 2020. It has a middle Human Capital Index (HCI), showing that the population has a somewhat good level of education and skills needed for e-government. Tanzania's ranking in e-participation, which measures the involvement of citizens in the government's decision-making processes through online tools, is 137th. This is a drop of 9 places in just two years.

However, its connectivity infrastructure has made impressive progress over the last two decades. This growth has been driven by access to international submarine fibre cables[305], the construction and expansion of the national fibre backbone, and a competitive market among mobile network operators (MNOs). According to DataReportal's 2024 Digital Report on e-Tanzania[306], there were 21.82 million internet users in Tanzania at the start of 2024, with internet penetration at 31.9%. However, these numbers reveal that 46.60 million people in Tanzania did not use the internet at the beginning of 2024.

A huge challenge for the country remains the digital divide - an issue that has been seen across Africa. According to ITU, in 2022[307], 64% of urban dwellers in Africa used the internet, compared to only 23% of people in rural areas. I'd say there are two main challenges to improving connectivity in rural Tanzania: the tough terrain and the sparse population. Also...comparing Tanzania to its neighbours like Kenya, Mozambique, and Uganda, the absolute levels of internet usage are pretty low. Unfortunately, the gender gap is considerably much wider in Tanzania[308] due to several factors, including sociocultural norms that might discourage women from using technology.

Where to focus?

Ultimately, the connectivity issue is a major roadblock to Tanzania's overall digital and development goals.

50. TOGO

Togo has been using AI to solve some social & economic issues

According to UN data[309], e-Togo's e-government and e-participation standings are like this: 161st in e-government and 99th in e-participation among 193 countries, as of 2024. And...despite falling into the Middle EGDI [310] group, e-Togo stands slightly below the regional average in e-governance. However, its e-participation score places it way above the regional and sub-regional averages, indicating a promising trajectory in its e-government initiatives...such as the NOVISSI Program. The use of AI-enabled mobile data and satellite imagery[311] facilitated the efficient distribution of financial aid to vulnerable residents during the pandemic, totalling $22 million. Originally designed to assist low-income urban populations, the program quickly expanded its reach to include rural communities in Togo's 200 poorest cantons.

By providing monthly financial aid, NOVISSI has helped alleviate poverty[312] and hardship for thousands of Togolese citizens whose livelihoods were disrupted by the crisis. The success of the NOVISSI Program[313] was thanks to government, philanthropic organisations, and academia coming together. What's even more promising is that e-Togo is collaborating with organisations like the World Economic Forum's *EDISON Alliance*[314] *Lighthouse Countries Network* to amplify the impact of digital inclusion initiatives. However, one thing that needs more attention is the internet penetration which remains low despite the growing number of cellular mobile connections. According to DataReportal's *Digital 2024 report on Togo*[315], *at* the beginning of 2024, there were 3.44 million internet users in Togo, accounting for 37.6% of the population. The decrease in fixed internet connection speeds in April 2024, as indicated by Ookla's data[316], further exacerbates this issue. Slow internet speeds can hinder access to online services, limit participation in digital governance initiatives, and impede the overall development of the digital economy.

Where to focus?

While e-Togo's rankings are promising, continued efforts are needed to further strengthen its digital infrastructure and promote digital literacy. Of special importance is increasing the (now) low internet penetration rate and decreasing fixed internet speeds to bridge the digital divide.

51. TUNISIA

The leader of Northern Africa when it comes to digital governance

According to the latest UN survey[317], Tunisia ranked 87th (up from the 88th place in 2022) in e-government and 99th (down from the 67th place in 2022) in e-participation among 193 countries assessed. Despite all this, Tunisia ranks third in Africa regarding EGDI (right after South Africa and Mauritius)[318]. They are among the top 100 performers globally. Its EGDI value is above the global average of 0.6382….making it the leader of Nothern Africa.

I believe another noteworthy point is from the 2023 World Bank's GovTech Maturity report on the Middle East and North Africa[319]. According to this report, e-Tunisia is categorised in Group B. This group includes countries that invest significantly in GovTech development but still have areas where they can improve. However, connectivity could be better. According to DataReportal's Digital 2024 report[320], at the start of 2024, there were 9.96 million internet users in e-Tunisia (79.6%). When we look at internet speeds, the picture becomes even clearer. According to Ookla's Speedtest Global Index[321], as of April 2024, the median mobile upload speed was relatively low at 13.96 megabits per second (Mbps). The median fixed broadband upload speed was significantly lower at just 2.97 Mbps. These slow speeds, particularly for fixed broadband, can hinder the efficiency of digital communications.

Regarding digital services, citizens tend to interact more with the government during significant moments like the birth of a child, getting married, enrolling in a social protection program, entering retirement, or starting a company. These are times when people need the government's support the most, and simplifying these processes can make a huge difference. In these conditions, the TERI Umbrella MDTF[322] is particularly committed to this cause.

Where to focus?

The country's focus on improving e-participation is particularly noteworthy, as it shows an effort to involve citizens more directly in governance processes. However, continued investment and attention to areas needing improvement will be crucial for maintaining and building on this progress.

52. UGANDA

E-Uganda has seen more improvement in citizen participation than e-gov

Despite being considered one of the least developed countries, Uganda has achieved a notable position in the United Nations e-government development index [323]. It falls into the high *Online Service Index (OSI)* group... which indicates that it offers a good range of online services compared to many other nations. It's also worth noting that it is among the *least* developed countries with the *highest* EGDI value. This highlights the country's efforts and progress in e-governance despite its overall economic challenges.

What's more....according to the UN Knowledgebase data[324], e-Uganda is currently ranked 150th in the world for e-government, and 102nd in e-participation. Unfortunately, the country has seen a decline in its rankings. Compared to earlier reports, Uganda has lost ground in e-governance. This year, it dropped 6 places in e-governance and 9 places in e-participation. This shows that Uganda is facing challenges in keeping up with progress in digital government and citizen engagement.

One thing I have to add is that the UN lauded several countries for consistently using effective strategies to ensure affordable public access in 2022. Uganda was one of those countries. One standout move is their *National Backbone Infrastructure Project*, which helps spread affordable internet access to regional government offices. This is what the 2024 report says about Uganda *"..has leveraged its human capital to achieve notable progress in online services delivery despite having an underdeveloped telecommunications infrastructure. "*

What I like most about this is how it addresses a critical issue: low internet penetration. With only 27% of individuals using the internet, according to DataReportal's 2024 Digital report on Uganda[325], there's a clear need for improvement. To put it in perspective... that means over 35.95 million people in Uganda didn't have internet access at the beginning of 2024. Government initiatives are crucial steps in addressing these challenges. For instance, the funding Uganda received from the World Bank in June 2021[326] aimed at expanding access to high-speed and affordable internet, improving digital public service delivery efficiency, and strengthening digital inclusion across the country.

Regarding its initiatives, back in 2023, e-Uganda launched a digital transformation plan[327] supported by the UN Development Program. It's a comprehensive strategy with a long-term vision to connect 90% of Ugandan households to the internet by 2040. But Digital ID remains a sticking point, and it's a serious one because the Ndaga Muntu program faced legal action[328].

Where to focus?

Uganda stands to benefit greatly from investment in both telecommunication infrastructure (TII) and human capital development (HCI). TII lays down the groundwork, but without investing in people, in their skills and education, the impact might not be as profound.

53. ZAMBIA

Has had huge progress even though it's not a high income country

In 2022, Zambia was one of the three African countries (along with Côte d'Ivoire and Rwanda) to join the high EGDI group for the first time[329]. This was a huge achievement considering that it's classified as a lower-middle-income country. Actually, one of the main challenges of Zambia has been its underdeveloped or unevenly developed infrastructure. Yet in 2024, it seems to have overcome this issue as it falls within the high TII group[330]. I have to add that it's one of the Landlocked Developing Countries (LLDCs) that has seen the most dramatic improvement in its EGDI values and ranking in a short time period. And now, according to the 2024 report, its *"telecommunications infrastructure and human capital are sufficiently well developed to support accelerated advancement in e-government if investments are targeted towards improving services delivery."* According to the UN Knowledgebase [331], e-Zambia ranked 130th in e-government, improving its position by 1 place. Even though it dropped down by 7 places in e-participation.

What most people don't know is that Zambia was actually one of the pioneers in sub-Saharan Africa when it came to adopting the internet. But DataReportal's report[332] for 2024 on e-Zambia shows a significant drop in the number of internet users to 6.51 million compared to 2022, with a penetration rate of 31.2%. Looking ahead, the government has set an ambitious target of issuing digital IDs to at least 10 million citizens[333] over the next decade. However, the year 2024 has brought some challenges. The Zambian government had to reallocate funds initially budgeted for the digital ID project to address a drought emergency[334] causing widespread hunger. This shift in priorities is understandable, given the immediate need to respond to the crisis, but it does slow down the digital ID initiative. On a positive note, I'd say that Zambia has made impressive progress in digitising records. According to a LinkedIn post[335] by a senior technical advisor for the World Bank, Zambia managed to digitise 81% of its legacy paper ID cards in just three months. It's a great example of how quickly and effectively digital transformation can happen with the right focus and resources.

Where to focus?

They need to keep building up their digital infrastructure and finding more ways to use the national ID across different sectors for more and more citizens before they focus on offering more public services online.

54. ZIMBABWE

Struggling with low participation of citizens in 2024

Zimbabwe—a low-income country in Eastern Africa. With about 17 million people[336], it was once known as "the jewel of Africa" for its great prosperity. However, over the past two decades, Zimbabwe has been experiencing prolonged economic distress, exacerbated by external shocks and internal instability. These conditions have created a challenging environment for any form of progress, including digital transformation. Looking at the specifics, the UN e-government Knowledgebase[337] ranked Zimbabwe 149th in e-governance and 148th in e-participation out of 193 countries assessed in 2024. It saw improvements in e-participation but not in e-governance scores. Now, according to the World Bank's GovTech Maturity Index (GTMI) report on East and Southern African countries[338], digital Zimbabwe has *"some focus on GovTech"* along with 13 other countries in the region. This means that while there are initiatives and policies aimed at leveraging technology for government operations and services, these efforts might not be as advanced as those in countries with a stronger emphasis on GovTech.

Internet access is severely limited, and this problem is made worse by an ongoing economic crisis and inadequate electrical infrastructure, which often cause power cuts[339]. At the start of 2024, there were 5.48 million internet users in Zimbabwe[340], Which means that internet penetration stood at just 32.6%. To put this into perspective, that leaves 11.36 million people without internet access. Zimbabwe's international connectivity infrastructure is relatively well-developed and fibre optic cables connect major cities and urban areas[341], which sounds promising. But, large gaps remain in rural areas.

Meanwhile, Zimbabwe's journey with mobile money has had its ups and downs. It was among the leaders on the continent in the use of mobile money[342]. However, in 2020 the government decided to shut down mobile money services, blaming them for the collapse of the Zimbabwean dollar and the subsequent economic turmoil. Fast forward to 2024, Zimbabwe is now considering[343] allowing mobile money agents to resume their operations. The timing is crucial, given the introduction of the new gold-backed currency, the ZiG (Zimbabwe Gold), launched in April 2024. This new currency was designed to replace the beleaguered Zimbabwean dollar and help stabilize and boost the economy.

Where to focus?

For the country to truly move forward, there needs to be a concerted effort to improve both the reach and quality of internet services, especially in rural areas.

ASIA

Digital governance
SUMMARY

Asia is the second-best continent in terms of digital governance, which shows how committed many countries here are to using technology to improve government services and engage with citizens. For example, Asia has 25 countries in the very high EGDI (E-Government Development Index) group out of 76... which is a huge progress considering there were only 15 countries in this group back in 2022. According to the recent UN report *"Asia has achieved the most rapid advancement in digital development"*. In addition, Asia is also the second-best continent in terms of the number of countries in the high EGDI group, with 14 (out of 62 nations in the whole world. This further confirms that many Asian countries are investing in the right areas, like online services, digital infrastructure, and education, which are all key to good digital governance.

One country that's worth mentioning is Singapore. It's not only a leader in Asia but is also considered one of the best in the world...the third in the world, to be exact. For the first time, Singapore is the top EGDI performer in Asia. It managed to surpass the previous leader which was South Korea. Its success shows what's possible when a country fully uses digital tools, with advanced online services and efficient e-procurement systems that set a high standard for others. It's also worth noting that in Asia, just like in Europe, most countries that have e-procurement systems also use digital invoices. Specifically, about 90 percent of these countries in Asia have adopted digital invoicing, which is a big contrast to other regions where it's less common. Nearly 80% of Asian countries offer more[344] than the global average of 18 online services, which I believe shows how dedicated the region is to making government services more accessible online.

What's holding Asia back?

However, it's important to recognise that Asia also faces some challenges. The continent has a large number of countries in special situations, such as Least Developed Countries (LDCs), Landlocked Developing Countries (LLDCs), and Small Island Developing States (SIDS). These countries often face unique difficulties that make it harder to develop strong digital governance. For example, LLDCs often struggle with issues like not having access to the sea, being far from major markets, and high costs of trade, which can slow down their progress... especially when it comes to their telecommunication infrastructure. There are currently 12 LLDCs in Asia, which highlights the challenges they face...even though they have successfully managed to reach the high or very high EGDI groups. However, there's more to this and I will explain in a bit.

Also, countries in Southern Asia often struggle with issues like low internet penetration, inadequate infrastructure, and limited government capacity to implement digital initiatives effectively. These factors combine to create a significant digital divide within the continent. While there are pockets of progress, like in India, the overall landscape remains uneven *and* underdeveloped.

Digital governance in Asia: Regional leaders & laggards

There's a noticeable divide between the subregions, with Eastern and Western Asia leading the way, while Southern Asia lags behind. I think this isn't surprising, given the economic powerhouses that dominate these areas. Countries like South Korea and Singapore have long been trailblazers in the digital world, and their leadership in digital governance reflects that. South Korea, for instance, consistently has ranked among the top globally, not just in Asia. I believe this is largely due to its forward-thinking policies and a strong emphasis on integrating technology into every aspect of governance. The same goes for Singapore, where the government has been relentless in pushing for a smart national vision, ensuring that digital services are seamless, efficient, and accessible to all citizens. That's why they became the top performers in just 2 years.

The 10 most developed countries in terms of digital governance are:

1. Singapore
2. South Korea
3. Saudi Arabia (huge improvement)
4. UAE
5. Japan
6. Bahrain
7. Israel
8. Kazakhstan
9. Turkey/Türkiye
10. China

There are 47 countries that have been analysed.

Singapore, and South Korea as I mentioned, are in a league of their own, but I would also highlight Saudi Arabia and Bahrain for their consistent innovation and high standards in digital services that managed to push them up to the V2, V1 rating class. On the other hand, Kazakhstan, has been steadily improving its digital infrastructure and services, aiming to become a regional leader in Central Asia. Turkey is leveraging its strategic position between East and West to develop a digital governance framework that serves both its domestic needs and its ambitions on the global stage.

Meanwhile I want to take some time to focus on the best countries that are in special or restricting conditions (in some way.) Take Bangladesh and Bhutan, for instance. These two countries, both located in Southern

Asia, are classified as Least Developed Countries (LDCs). Yet, they've managed to achieve some of the highest EGDI values among all other LDCs in the world. Moving on to Landlocked Developing Countries (LLDCs), I find it equally impressive that Kazakhstan, Mongolia, Armenia, and Uzbekistan top the list with *the highest* EGDI values. Being landlocked often poses additional challenges, and yet these countries have prioritised digital governance and, in doing so, have outperformed many others in similar circumstances. And then we have Singapore, Maldives, two Small Island Developing States (SIDS) that have also achieved high EGDI values. In my view, their success is particularly noteworthy because, as islands, they face unique challenges such as vulnerability to climate change and limited natural resources. Yet, they've managed to excel in digital governance, setting an example for other small island nations.

As you can see, Asia is home to the top countries of the world that have turned their restrictions into opportunities.

The 10 least developed countries in Africa in terms of digital governance are:

In my analysis of digital governance across continents, I've typically highlighted the 5 least developed countries in each region. However, when it comes to Asia, I believe it's important to expand this list to include ten countries. The reason for this is that the last five countries on the list may not come as a surprise, given their challenging circumstances.

1. Pakistan
2. Myanmar
3. Turkmenistan
4. Iraq
5. Lao People's Democratic Republic
6. Timor-Leste

7. Syrian Arab Republic

8. Democratic People's Republic of Korea

9. Yemen

10. Afghanistan

Opportunities moving forward

In the coming decades, Asia is poised to experience urbanisation at an unprecedented rate. This growth is going to reshape cities across the continent, bringing more

people into urban centres where they'll increasingly rely on local public services. With this surge in urban expansion, it's clear that strong e-government structures must be a priority at the local level. I see this as not just a matter of convenience but a necessity to meet both present and future demands. If governments don't act now to strengthen these structures, I think they'll struggle to keep up with the expectations of a digitally connected urban population.

Countries around the world, especially in Asia, are recognizing the power of digital identity as a foundational platform. It's impressive that it's the secondhighest continent, just after Europe, in terms of the proportion of countries with laws or regulations on digital identity. This is a solid foundation, and I believe it's something that can be leveraged further. Civil registration and the establishment of legal identity will become even more important in empowering vulnerable groups (but not only limited to them.) Without these, I see a significant risk of leaving the most vulnerable behind, unable to access the digital services that could improve their lives.

However, I would also add that having these laws is only the beginning. What really matters is how these frameworks are implemented and how inclusive they are in practice. There's a huge opportunity here, and I think the region could lead the way globally if it focuses on expanding access to these digital identities and ensuring that they are used to connect people to a wide range of services.

1. AFGHANISTAN

Digital Afghanistan has underdeveloped telecommunication infrastructure.

The Taliban's resurgence in 2021 has severely limited the access of Afghan women to vital services like education and healthcare information, highlighting the importance of digital infrastructure for humanitarian purposes. Since the Taliban takeover, Afghans have encountered numerous digital security and trust issues. Many individuals have reported incidents of hacked accounts or inaccessible accounts, while certain government websites were also compromised.

According to the 2024 UN's EGDI report[345], Afghanistan is positioned quite low, holding the 188th spot out of 193 countries assessed. This low ranking reflects the country's middling performance across various digital indicators. It's worth noting that Afghanistan, along with Yemen and North Korea, are among the countries with the lowest EGDI rankings in Asia[346]. According to the latest ITU data[347], only 58% of the Afghan population has access to at least a 3G mobile network, and just 18% use the internet. Despite some indications of a slight increase in internet users between 2022 and 2023 [348], various challenges persist. Technical issues, such as potential damage to fibre optic cables and financial constraints, including restrictions on moving money in and out of the country, pose significant obstacles to internet development [349]. One such challenge is the decrease in cache servers and the suspension of the World Bank's project to fund internet infrastructure, which has led to a substantial decrease in internet traffic at Afghanistan's only Internet Exchange, NIXA[350]. However, I think it's important to note that even before the Taliban regained control, internet access was limited to a small segment of the population due to infrastructure deficiencies and widespread poverty. But, since then, access has become even more restricted, with frequent suspensions of connectivity in Kabul and other areas.

Where to focus?

With the right support, digital initiatives aimed at expanding internet access, enhancing digital literacy, and promoting online safety and security for Afghan citizens *can* be implemented, but I don't see it being a priority any time soon.

2. ARMENIA

Digital Armenia: The Silicon Valley of the Caucasus

Armenia is a country in the South Caucasus region of Eurasia. It's a small country, and one interesting fact about Armenia is that it's one of the oldest countries in the world. The country has been working on developing its economy, particularly in the technology and public sectors, often referred to as the "Silicon Valley of the Caucasus."

Looking at Armenia's digital development, it's clear that they're doing pretty well. According to the UN's 2024 EGDI report[351], digital Armenia ranked 48th out of 193 countries, which is quite high and quite an imporvement compared to the 64th place it held in 2022. They're making good progress in providing digital services to their citizens. The most impressive achievement is that it holds the 27th place in the world in e-participation, moving up by 37 places[352]. In 2 years Armenia moved up from the high to the Very High EGDI group...which is amazing considering it's a Landlocked Developing Country. It is the second country after Mongolia to have such a huge upward shift. Their telecommunication infrastructure is also strong, which means people have good access to communication networks. The country's Digitalization Strategy for 2021-2025 aligns well with the UN's broader Public Administration Reform strategy and the Sustainable Development Goals (SDGs)[353]. Also, thanks to support from the World Bank[354], several e-government innovation projects have kicked off this year, with some digital transformation initiatives already underway to meet the objectives of the 2030 Agenda[355]. One noteworthy project is the E-Health in digital Armenia initiative[356], currently in the implementation phase. There's also the development of the e-justice system— a two-year project (finished in 2023) that sought to establish a unified e-justice platform[357] for all interconnected information systems.

Armenia is making significant progress in modernising its public services delivery through the launch of the *'Strengthening Transparency, Accountability, and Access to Public Services through GovTech'* project[358], initiated at the end of 2023. This initiative, funded by the UK Good Governance fund and implemented by the Armenian Government, is a very important step forward in aligning Armenia's public services with modern digital standards.

Where to focus?

There is still room for growth, especially in areas like digital infrastructure development and cybersecurity. With continued investment and international support, Armenia can further advance its digital capabilities and better serve its citizens.

3. AZERBAIJAN

2024 has marked a year of impressive progress for Azerbaijan

Over the years, the digital government in Azerbaijan has embarked on significant projects such as the Baku–Tbilisi–Ceyhan oil pipeline, Southern Gas Corridor, and Trans-Caspian International Transportation Route. However, recently, the country has made significant progress in becoming a digital hub. A lot of countries and companies have also expressed their support for Azerbaijan's initiative. Numerous advances have been made to bring the Azerbaijan digital initiative to fruition.

To make Azerbaijan a regional digital hub[359], several necessary reforms have been made in the public administration.Information/Communications Technology also plays a significant role in the growth of the Azerbaijan economy apart from the oil and gas industry. Hence, the Azerbaijan government is encouraging digitisation reforms to improve the regional digital ecosystem[360] and economic welfare of the nation. It also launched several technological parks across the country to facilitate tax breaks and exemptions for companies. Although these initiatives and projects are meant to liberalise the telecommunications sectors, they need improvements to make Azerbaijan a better regional hub.

In 2024, Azerbaijan made significant strides in digital development, becoming one of the few landlocked developing countries (LLDCs) in Asia to join the very High EGDI group.[361] It achieved high scores in both telecommunications infrastructure (TII) and overall EGDI values, but there is still room to grow. Specifically, Azerbaijan could further accelerate its digital progress by enhancing online services and investing in human capital to build digital skills. To support this growth, Azerbaijan is working on a national strategy for artificial intelligence (AI), which aims to develop smart cities and strengthen the country's technological infrastructure. Also, Azerbaijan's improvements in digital governance are clear.. it now ranks 74th in e-governance and 88th in e-participation. This represents a jump of 9 and 10 places, respectively, which means Azerbaijan has now surpassed the world average in both categories. Altogether, 2024 has marked a year of impressive progress for Azerbaijan.

Where to focus?

A priority should be the improvement of e-participation of its citizens as it's below the world and region average. [362]

4. BAHRAIN

The sixth top performer in Asia

Despite its small size and unique challenges as a small island developing state, digital Bahrain has achieved remarkable success. They have very high scores in various areas like the E-Government Development Index (EGDI)[363] remaining one of the few countries with a very high EGDI. Also, in this year's UN report, Bahrain finally graduated from it's SIDS (Small Island Developing States) status. According to data from the International Telecommunication Union (ITU)[364], 100% of the population in Bahrain had access to the internet in 2022, with at least a 4G mobile network available.

Looking at Bahrain's e-government services, it's clear they've made significant progress. So, for example, the national portal in digital Bahrain[365] serves as a central hub for accessing various e-services, ranging from passport and visa issuance to utility bill payments and licence renewals. In 2022, these channels served over 18 million visits[366], indicating a growing reliance on digital platforms. Also, Bahrain's digital initiatives extend beyond basic services. For example, the open data portal and the MoIC's Sijilat portal[367] facilitate business registration and renewal processes online, streamlining operations for entrepreneurs. Other noteworthy programs include the Sehati National Health Insurance Scheme[368] and platforms for hosting and integrating digital government services.

In digital Bahrain, the widespread broadband access supported the 2017 Cloud First Policy[369]. Also, the ability to work remotely and monitor COVID-19 cases through the BeAware Bahrain app[370] highlights the importance of cloud-based solutions in crisis management and response efforts. Something worth mentioning Bahrain was the first in the region to implement multi-cloud and hybrid cloud systems in e-government, as stated by the government back in 2023[371]. And in 2024 it's the 6th country in Asia regarding advancements in digital governance.

Where to focus?

Further investment in e-participation would likely yield substantial benefits for Bahrain's digital governance efforts as it's slightly below the world average.

5. BANGLADESH

Digital Bangladesh managed to surpass the global average in 2024

Digital Bangladesh has been a buzzword in Bangladesh ever since Prime Minister Sheikh Hasina first coined the phrase. While government officials have been promising a digital government of Bangladesh since 2010, the country's infrastructure has hardly improved during this time frame. An important programme from the collaboration of the ICT Division of the Bangladesh government and UNDP Bangladesh is the Access to Information (a2i) Programme[372], which started in 2007. It has been one of the key drivers of the government's public service innovation agenda because it improves the service delivery model to enable the citizens in a simplified, low cost and timely manner. The country has also built on digital health platforms developed to tackle the COVID-19 pandemic and facilitate real-time monitoring of health threats, anticipate new threats, and increase transparency. And the A2i platform[373] has been a great example of this.

Moreover, the EDGE Project (Enhancing Digital Government & Economy)[374] - is another important project with the World Bank that has major implications for the country. This project was approved in 2020 and aims to support part of the 'Digital Bangladesh' program, focusing on investments that will strengthen digital government and service delivery foundations. Nonetheless, according to the recent United Nations 2020 report[375], Bangladesh is among the least developed countries in Asia (along with Bhutan and Cambodia) that have been celebrated as "leaders" in digital government development since 2022, reaching the H3 rating class within their EGDI group. What's more, according to the EGDI index, Bangladesh has moved up by 11 places[376] down to the 100th place compared to 2022(in e-governance). And in e-participation it ranks 70th (again moving up by 5 places)..meaning that now it has surpassed the global average for both these indexes.

Where to focus?

If the country wants to make its visions a reality, other extensive and fundamental reforms are needed to strengthen the legal environment to support the next wave of digital development.

6. BHUTAN

A "leader" among other underdeveloped countries

Only a few years ago, digital Bhutan has evolved from the medium E-Government Development Index (EGDI) to an advanced-level EGDI group. According to the study[377], Bhutan was ranked 103rd in 2024 among the 193 UN member states. With this current standing, Bhutan is now considered the second top performer in digital government development among other least Developed Countries (LDCs). In this year's report, Bhutan was actually passed by Bangladesh, which has now moved ahead. Just 2 year ago, back in 2022, Bhutan was leading in this area.

The government launched its master plan in 2014, and the master plan includes ICT initiatives and projects...and since then a lot has changed. However, the Kingdom of Bhutan has not always been a developed one. The country was isolated from the world and only started experiencing modernisation about 20 years ago. Bhutan's first television broadcast was in 1999, which shows how late they were exposed to technology. Then in 2005, the government launched the Government to Citizen (G2C) program, a one-stop-shop for over 100 services, including acquiring a passport.

With all these achievements, Bhutan has the potential to attain greater heights in technology[378] and innovation. Bhutan ranked 117th among 175 countries in the 2016 ICT Development Index. Bhutan still has a long way to go; there's still so much to be done regarding digital literacy and increasing Internet accessibility. Also, there's a need for more professional training (regarding this, the country established its first ICT college in 2017, which is a good start).

Where to focus?

The best move the digital Bhutan government can take in building a strong digital government is investing in the next generation to become ICT professionals. This means reducing the cost of accessing ICT training. The IT companies in Bhutan face the challenge of high prices and a lack of support from international broadband connectivity. Addressing these issues will help Bhutan build a better digital government.

7. BRUNEI

Brunei Darussalam: The second-highest level of digital connectivity in the region

Looking at digital Brunei Darussalam, it's clear they're doing quite well overall. Their E-Government Development Index (EGDI) ranks them at 75th out of 193 countries assessed in the 2024 UN report[379], moving up from the high to the *very high* EGDI group for the first time. They have very high scores in areas like *Telecommunication Infrastructure Index (TII),* but "only" high scores in *Human Capital Index (HCI)*, and *Online Service Index (OSI)*. But what's interesting is that despite these high scores, their E-Participation Index (EPI)[380] is only in the middle range. This means that while Brunei Darussalam excels in providing digital infrastructure and services, there's room for improvement when it comes to engaging citizens in decision-making processes through digital platforms.

One of the key things the Digital Economy Council has done is launch the Digital Economy Masterplan 2025[381]. There's also the Brunei Open Data portal (data. gov.bn)[382], which allows government agencies to share non-sensitive information with the public. This helps facilitate access to data and promotes transparency in governance. Additionally, the GOV.BN portal[383]provides access to hundreds of e-services from various government systems, making it easier for citizens to access government services online.

Brunei is considered to have the second-highest level of digital connectivity in the region. This information comes from a 2023 report by Information and Communication Technology (ICT)[384], which looked at 169 economies worldwide to measure how well they provide universal and meaningful internet access. According to the

International Telecommunication Union (ITU), Brunei scored 94.8 in their assessment, which is quite high. This score is based on how many people can connect to the internet and use fast mobile networks like 4G or LTE. These results show that Brunei is doing well in providing universal and meaningful connectivity to its citizens.

Where to focus?

One area that Brunei Darussalam could focus on improving is the Local Online Service Index (LOSI), which is rated as low. LOSI measures how well local services are provided online, and having a low score in this area is not a good sign for citizens.

8. CAMBODIA

One of the leaders in e-government among lower income countries

Despite being classified as a lower-middle-income nation, digital Cambodia demonstrates strong performance in key digital governance indicators. The country has high scores in both the EGDI[385] and the Telecommunication Infrastructure Index (TII), indicating a robust digital infrastructure and a significant level of technological readiness. Also, Cambodia exhibits high levels of human capital development, as reflected in its high Human Capital Index (HCI), which further supports its digital advancement efforts. However, while Cambodia excels in providing some digital services, there may be room for enhancing the transparency and accessibility of these services to ensure they meet the needs of all citizens.

The Cambodian government has reaffirmed its commitment to digital development through the Cambodian Digital Government Policy 2022-2035[386]. This policy aligns with the UN's Sustainable Development Goals (SDGs) and the Digital Economy and Society Policy Framework 2021-2035. To make all this happen, Cambodia has set up the National Council for Digital Economy and Society[387]. This council is really important because it's in charge of making sure the digital government plans are put into action. To support this, the government has set up the Digital Government Committee (DGC) to oversee comprehensive digital transformation across all government sectors. Also, collaboration between UNDP Cambodia[388] and the Cambodia Academy of Digital Technology (CADT) in providing training to senior-level government officials plays a significant role in laying all the groundwork for digital Cambodia.

With one of the world's fastest digital adoption rates, it's clear that more and more people in Cambodia are getting connected online. According to recent data[389], there were 9.66 million internet users in Cambodia at the beginning of 2024, which is quite a significant number (considering the economic status of the country.) This means that about 56.7% of the population had access to the internet, allowing them to connect with others and access information and services online..

Where to focus?

It's crucial to address issues like quality education for all, ensuring that everyone has equal access to digital learning opportunities. Additionally, they need to think about social inclusion and justice (so making sure that digital advancements benefit everyone), especially marginalised communities.

9. CHINA

Digital China is among the world's leaders when it comes to e-participation

I believe digital China is incredibly impressive, especially considering its very high rankings across various indicators of the E-Government Development Index (EGDI)[390]. Actually, for the pas 4 years China has been among the top 10 countries in Asia with the highest EGDI values[391], according to the UN's E-Government report. Additionally, Shanghai (one of China's leading cities) was among the top cities globally with the highest LOSI values, reflecting its exceptional performance in local online service provision.

China's issuance of the 'Overall Layout Plan for the Construction of Digital China[392]' in 2023 marked a significant milestone in the country's digital governance journey. This plan outlines China's ambition to become a global leader in digital innovation and technology by 2035. In addition, China's Ministry of Foreign Affairs recently (in 2023) released a document called *China's Positions on Global Digital Governance*[393]. This document builds on China's *Global Initiative on Data Security*[394] – earlier efforts on data security and talks about the importance of getting data from other countries through the right channels.

China places a very, very strong emphasis on the importance of achieving fair and universal access to the Internet, and enhancing digital connectivity. They believe it's important for people to be able to get online easily and use digital technology. According to recent data[395], there were 1.76 billion mobile connections in China in early 2024, which is more than the total population! What's even more impressive is that China has managed to cover 100% of its population with at least a 4G mobile network[396]. This means that no matter where you are in China, you should be able to get a good mobile internet connection. Connectivity is an important part that then leads to improved e-participation. And in 2024, China ranked 12th out of 193 countries assessed (!) regarding e-participation[397] (moving up compared to 2022). Also, I find it really interesting how China is working to bridge the gap between different regions[398].

Where to focus?

They're really focusing on new and cutting-edge technologies that are just starting to emerge. They're setting the pace for what's possible in the digital world, and it's exciting to see where they'll go next.

10. INDIA

India has the world's largest biometric identity program

Despite being a low-income country with a poorly developed telecommunications infrastructure, digital India has made huge progress in terms of human capital development and online service provision. This is quite impressive, given the challenges posed by its not highly-developed telecommunications infrastructure. On one hand, there's a solid foundation in terms of human capital, indicating a skilled workforce capable of engaging with digital technologies effectively. On the other hand, the infrastructure remains a bottleneck, (potentially) hindering the *full* realisation of digital potential.

But, India has made remarkable progress by leveraging its pool of skilled technical labour to develop digital services for its citizens. A standout example is Aadhaar, which means "foundation" in several Indian languages. It's (still) the world's largest biometric identity program, covering nearly the entire population of 1.4 billion[399]. Aadhaar is a great example of how an effective digital identity system can increased the efficiency and effectiveness of public services provision. Originally aimed at curbing fraud[400] in social benefit programs, Aadhaar has evolved to become integral to various aspects of daily life in India, including banking and mobile phone activation. I believe the success of India's digital public services is also evident in initiatives like Transactions on its United Payments Interface (UPI)[401], which has witnessed exponential growth in transactions, making financial dealings more accessible.

Additionally, DigiLocker has simplified bureaucracy by providing a convenient online repository for official documents (like licences and tax records.) The UPI witnessed significant growth, with over 10 billion payments and transfers in August 2023. MyGov.in[402] is another important platform for improving participatory governance. With millions of registered users, it offers various tools for participation, such as discussions, polls, and surveys. This not only encourages citizen involvement but also strengthens democratic processes.

But, the increased prominence of India's technology on the global stage has inevitably attracted scrutiny, particularly concerning data security and privacy concerns. Instances of data leaks from India's digital systems[403] (such as the vaccination database and identity system) only highlight the vulnerabilities that exist within these complex technological infrastructures.

Where to focus?

By addressing concerns surrounding data security and privacy while continuing to use its skilled workforce and expertise, digital India can continue to play a very important role in e-governance, both domestically and internationally.

11. INDONESIA

Amazing progress since 2018

Infrastructure is considered a significant factor in digital transformation, and the government has invested in ICT infrastructure development, including installing 4G infrastructure in more than 10,000 subregions since 2022. Also, the country's government has included ICT infrastructure development[404] in the national medium-term plan.

Actually, the Indonesian government released Presidential Regulation 95/2018 since before the pandemic, in 2018. The regulation includes providing strategies for the eGovernment system that centres on different sectors such as budget planning, data and information, business processes, eGovernment applications, eGovernment infrastructure, and other eGovernment services. The goal is to make quality accessible data that can be distributed across the country. What's more, according to a survey, the Indonesian digital economy is estimated to be above USD 124 Billion by the end of 2025.

The government is working on bringing more than 64 million micro, small and medium enterprises(MSMEs) aboard all over the country and helping them go digital. The government is planning on helping 30 million MSMEs go digital by the end of 2024. Also, the GoTo Group formed by the merger of Gojek and Tokopedia is working on a super app capable of merging eGovernment, transport, education, logistics, financial services, and communications. The Indonesian government keeps introducing different programs[405] to help achieve a digital society. Some of these initiatives include the National Movement on Digital Literacy and the Digital Talent Scholarship. The government is working with prestigious technology companies to make this happen. According to the UN data, Indonesia has advanced from high to very high EGDI groups as it improved its ICT infrastructure and focused more on digital literacy programs to increase access to e-services. It ranks 66th globally in e-governance[406] and 35th in e-participating as it constantly keeps improving its position...far surpassing the regional and world averages.

Where to focus?

The digital government in Indonesia has done a great job when it comes to running a digital government in the sense that it made sure all the sectors and areas in the country experience digital transformation. Regardless of their achievement, there's still room for improvement especially in increasing e-participation of the populace.

12. IRAN

A balance between technological advancement and governmental control

Digital Iran is a lower-middle-income country, that falls in the middle EGDI group (part of the UN's E-Government survey[407]). Unfortunately, while it has a strong telecommunication infrastructure and human capital..the Online Service Index is below average. Research suggests that the development of e-government is tied to that country's economic status. And indeed, while its per capita GDP ranks among the upper-middle-income countries, the development of e-government is lagging behind. One possible explanation for this disparity could be the prioritisation and allocation of resources within Iran's development agenda.

Having digital skills has never been a problem. Unfortunately, Iranian hackers have made headlines for their activities targeting other nations (like Albania[408], US states/cities[409], UAE TV streaming services[410], etc.), showcasing a significant presence and capability. Yet, despite this prowess, Iran struggles with low levels of e-participation, with a score of 0.1781 (on a scale of 0 to 1.) Comparing this to South Asian countries' average EPI of 0.4064 and the world average of 0.4893, it's clear that Iran's government initiatives to engage citizens in collaborative governance are *severely lacking.* In the global ranking of e-participation, Iran sits at 164th out of 193 countries assessed in 2024[411] .

Connectivity is an issue, even though there has been improvement, with internet penetration reaching 81.7%[412] by January 2024. But fixed-line broadband connections are slower compared to mobile options. In January 2024, the median download speeds for mobile and fixed-line broadband[413] were 32.77 megabits per second (Mbps) and 13.58 Mbps, respectively, in digital Iran.

Where to focus?

Overall, if digital Iran wants to develop in the international sphere, it needs to pay more attention to increasing the e-participation. Despite nominal improvements in reducing the urban-rural digital divide, inequalities persist, particularly in regions inhabited by ethnic minorities. However... the regime's reluctance to address these disparities suggests a prioritisation of maintaining control over fostering inclusive digital development.

13. IRAQ

Digital Iraq has a long way to go!

While digital Iraq possesses the necessary technological and human resources to support digital initiatives, the actual delivery of online services lags behind expectations. The low values of the E-Participation Index (EPI)[414] indicate a significant gap between the availability of digital platforms AND citizens' engagement with them. This suggests that while there may be digital platforms and services in place, they are not effectively utilised by the population for active participation in decision-making processes. Or they don't engage with government initiatives. According to the UN's E-government report[415], Iraq's ranking of 148th among 193 countries assessed reflects this disparity. Moreover, its even lower ranking of 179th in e-participation highlights the urgent need for improvement in participatory governance practices within the country.

The absence of a comprehensive e-government policy in Iraq presents a significant obstacle to modernisation efforts. Right now, getting funding for digital projects is a struggle, and many institutions lack the basic infrastructure needed for digital operations. That's why UNDP suggests[416] creating a transparent and predictable funding mechanism to allocate resources effectively. Iraq is also facing a big challenge when it comes to information security for the public sector. Without a clear policy in place, it's tough to provide electronic services securely. Another problems is the lack of a unified national identity register. Without this register, the government doesn't have a clear picture of the country's population, making it difficult to identify individuals using public services. However, before before getting to that, it's important to first increase the uptake of the National (non digital) ID.

Where to focus?

Prioritising the development of a coherent information security policy, extending cybersecurity requirements (to ALL critical infrastructure providers) and addressing infrastructure gaps within government institutions are the main steps for Iraq. The government must develop and adopt a long-term digital transformation strategy. This means creating a clear plan for how digital technologies will be used across all government organisations. This plan should come from the top, with political leaders leading the charge.

14. ISRAEL

One of the Asian countries with the highest EGDI values

The war conflict aside, the progress that Israel has made in recent years, especially in terms of its E-Government Development Index ranking is impressive[417]. According to the latest UN survey from 2024, Israel ranked 23rd out of 193 countries, down from the 16th place in 2022. It has still managed to maintain its top Asia performers position even on this year's report..ranking 7th among the other countries. Another key highlight was Israel's participation in the Digital 7 (D7)[418], a coalition of the world's leading e-governments. Being part of the D7 allows Israel to collaborate with other top-performing nations like the UK, South Korea, Estonia, and New Zealand (among other countries.) This collaboration facilitates the sharing of best practices, joint projects, and support for growing digital economies.

The "Digital Israel" initiative is a cornerstone of Israel's digital transformation. The initiative is a collaborative effort involving key organisations such as the Bank of Israel and the Israel Consumer Council[419]. The National Digital Program, reflecting the government's digital policy for 2017-2020, served as a digital compass for all ministries and government bodies. One thing that I think is important to mention is that Israel's national AI program is set to revolutionise government services[420]. The initiatives under this program address challenges within the government's operations, promoting efficiency and focusing on citizen services.

Israel's focus on digital transformation is evident in its investment in high-speed digital infrastructure, including the deployment of broadband and 5G networks across the country which is one of the most essential things to do in 2024 and onward. Why? Because it's important for an inclusive digitalisation process[421]. The official launch of the 5G network in September 2020 marked a significant step towards enhancing Israel's telecommunication market, characterised by high mobile penetration[422] (92% in 2022 according to ITU) and a sophisticated network. Unique digital IDs have been introduced to facilitate easier access to a range of services through multiple digital channels. These IDs streamline[423] the process of interacting with government services, making it more efficient for citizens to obtain the assistance they need.

Where to focus?

Regarding digital governance Israel has been in the top 5 Asian countries, so it should just focus on improving the capabilities, scope and service of public institutions.

15. JAPAN

Having trouble implementing digital ID initiatives

With a population of nearly 127 million and one of the world's largest economies by GDP, Japan has only recently been looking to technology to improve lives and government services. According to the recent UN report[424], Japan ranks as the top 5 performer in Asia and 13th in the world[425] (regarding e-governance.) Still, a significant portion of administrative tasks still requires in-person visits – whether it's banking, filing taxes, or handling paperwork for moving homes. The My Number ID card, designed to facilitate digital verification, aimed to shift some of this burden online. However, since its introduction in 2015, no political leader has been able to make it widely accepted – in 2019, a mere 15% of the population[426] made use of it, partially due to concerns about data privacy. In 2022, Kono Taro, Japan's Minister for Digital Transformation, decided to give the digital ID program another shot. In October 2022, Kono took a bold step to push this digital ID into the mainstream. He issued an ultimatum: Starting in 2024, Japanese residents were required to possess a My Number card if they wished to access their hard-earned health insurance benefits at the doctor's office. This move was aimed at driving greater adoption of the digital ID. (Despite this, the journey has been far from smooth.)

Even Japan's Digital Minister Kono Taro was quick to point them out when he appeared[427] at the Tallinn Digital Summit. By the government's own figures[428], less than half of the population thinks the digitalisation of society is a good thing, and only 28% feel they are adapting to it. What's more, only 29% of those who have used the country's digital government services are satisfied with them. Also, I have to mention that Japan's Digital Agency is a relatively new entity, having been established in September 2021. It's just 3 years in the making. In September (2023), the agency published its Annual Report[429], aimed at providing insights into the path that Japan's digital path might take in the future.

Where to focus?

The main priorities should be breaking down barriers to technology adoption, standardising the government's digital approach, and addressing internal issues within the organisation.

16. JORDAN

Jordan has finally reached very high OSI levels

While numerous initiatives have been introduced over the last decade to develop and enhance e-government in Jordan, results indicate that there's still room for improvement in effectiveness and efficiency. His Majesty King Abdullah II was the first to give attention to the importance of the e-Government program in 2001 when he announced the initiative and assigned the Ministry of Communications and Information Technology implementation. On the Official Site of the Jordanian e-Government[430], people can access the governmental portal, which aims to give citizens and businesses better service delivery and transparency. However, there is still much room for reforms, such as increasing the usefulness of government websites and ensuring security from cyberattacks.

But, according to the UN's EDGI Index, Jordan's [431]e-government ranking had been falling from 2014 to 2022. However, in 2024, it went up by 11 places now ranking 89th out of 193 countries. The concept of e-government has become more appealing among citizens...with Jordan falling into the *Very High* Online Service Index Group. Even though I must add that this hasn't been easy due to long years of low service quality and poor online experiences at various government departments. As a developing country with a small economy (considering its population and GDP), Jordan is not struggling anymore to keep up with technological advancements that help significantly enhance its e-government program.

Where to focus?

Jordan needs to start thinking differently and raise its level of ambition so as to keep up with the top performers in the Western Asia region. This requires an urgent need to review the strategies that are currently being employed for digital government transformation.

17. KAZAKHSTAN

The leader of Central Asia in e-gov and e-participation

Despite being classified as an upper-middle-income country, Kazakhstan has achieved remarkable success in e-governance by leveraging its *very high* levels of human capital development and infrastructure development. The country has been actively pursuing digital transformation through its Digital Kazakhstan program, leading to significant improvements in ICT infrastructure over recent years. Making it also the LLDC with the highest EGDI value in 2022[432] and again in 2024 according to the UN[433]. *It's important to note that LLDCs (landlocked developing countries) typically face more challenges in terms of connectivity and e-governance compared to other countries.* Despite these obstacles, Kazakhstan has made remarkable progress, particularly in expanding internet access and mobile connectivity. To illustrate this progress, let's look at internet access: In 2018, only about 100,000 people in 55 rural settlements had internet access via fibre optic cable. By 2023, there were 17.73 million internet users in Kazakhstan[434], with internet penetration reaching 90.9%. In terms of e-participation, Kazakhstan ranked 15th globally out of 193 countries[435] assessed in 2022. This indicates a high level of citizen engagement in governance through digital platforms, which is quite impressive.

The Digital Family Card[436] (DFC) represents a significant step forward in using digital technologies to enhance the well-being of people in Kazakhstan. It's designed to analyse vulnerabilities, pinpoint target populations, and offer comprehensive public services to vulnerable groups proactively throughout the country. Operated by the domestic company "National Information Technologies" in collaboration with UNDP Kazakhstan and relevant government ministries, the DFC is a joint effort to make social services more accessible and effective. One notable aspect of the DFC is its ability to streamline the assessment of family vulnerabilities *without* requiring direct involvement from citizens. This means that support measures can be implemented automatically - even for families who may not have access to online platforms for public services. With the government's Digital Kazakhstan program, Kazakhstan successfully achieved its goal of increasing the internet penetration rate to 82.3% by 2022. Also, in 2022, the International Telecommunications Unit (ITU)[437] reported that 92.3% of the population had internet access, with 15.4% using fixed broadband and 94.5% using mobile broadband.

Where to focus?

Continued investment in expanding this broadband infrastructure and mobile networks, as well as closing the digital divide, will be very important to sustain these positive trends.

18. NORTH KOREA

Digital North Korea has made 'progress'

When it comes to North Korea, often referred to as amongst the world's worst country in terms of e-government, the challenges are glaringly obvious. The nation's isolation, restricted access to the global internet, and limited information infrastructure are significant barriers to digital transformation as per the latest UN e-government survey[438]. Between 2022 and 2024, North Korea has been falling behind in e-governance and e-participation as well. Also, it still remains one of the countries with the lowest EGDI scores in Asia, alongside Yemen and Afghanistan. According to the UN's E-Government Knowledgebase[439], North Korea ranked 184th in e-governance and 192th in e-participation out of 193 countries assessed.

However, internet access remains extremely limited, with only about 2,000 of North Korea's elite military officers and diplomats reportedly granted access to external communications[440]. Also, as of now, it's the only country where internet access remains below 10%[441]. Actually, analysis suggests that fewer than 10,000 people in North Korea can access international websites. This tiny group likely includes foreign expatriates and the country's political elite. So, more than 99.9% of the population remained offline at the start of 2024 (over 26 million people.) Interestingly data from GSMA Intelligence shows that there were 7.51 million cellular mobile connections in North Korea at the start of 2024. This figure indicates that mobile connections were equivalent to 28.7% of the total population in January 2024. This number increased by 206 thousand (+2.8%) between the start of 2023 and the start of 2024. This increase, although small, suggests a gradual shift. Mobile technology is becoming more prevalent, even though under *strict* state control.

Where to focus?

While internet access in North Korea remains virtually nonexistent for the vast majority of its citizens, there's a slow rise in mobile connectivity and digitalisation efforts. It's a complex situation, deeply intertwined with the country's political dynamics and isolationist policies. I find it fascinating, yet troubling, how digital access—or the lack thereof—can shape the lives and opportunities of an entire nation.

19. SOUTH KOREA

Has topped the OECD Digital Government Index for the second time

South Korea has once again claimed the top spot in the OECD 2023 Digital Government Index[442] for the second time, showcasing its strong commitment to digital governance. Joining South Korea in the top ranks are countries like Denmark, the United Kingdom, Norway, Australia, Estonia, Colombia, Ireland, France, and Canada. South Korea is leading the OECD countries with an impressive score of 0.935 out of 1. That's no small feat, especially when you consider that the average score across these countries is 0.605. It's important to note that this version of the Index is the first to be published since its pilot in 2019. *(While the methodology remained consistent between the 2019 and 2023 Indexes, changes to the survey used to collect data mean that direct comparisons between the results cannot be made.)*

According to the rankings, Korea is leading the group in this dimension, followed closely by Denmark, Norway, and a handful of other countries like Austria, Australia, and Estonia. Now, it's interesting to note that the gap between the top and bottom performers isn't as pronounced as in some other dimensions. In other words, there's a more even spread of development across countries, as the report suggests.

Meanwhile, regarding the EGDI score, it ranks 4th in the world and (unfortunately this year) 2nd in Asia (after Singapore.) In e-participation, South Korea has still managed to gain traction and improve its ranking by 5 places. So that means that it's the 4th country in the world with the most engaged citizens with governmental e-services and platforms.

Where to focus?

When we look at the rankings and assessments, it's evident that South Korea is often at the forefront, whether it's in terms of e-government services, digital infrastructure, or government as a platform. They're setting the bar high and showing the world what's possible when it comes to leveraging technology for the benefit of citizens. And I believe their continued leadership in this field will only inspire further innovation and progress on a global scale.

20. KUWAIT

Insights and problems of its digital transformation

Within eight years (2012-2020), digital Kuwait rose in rank[443] in the United Nations e-Government Development Index (EDGI). Even though between 20222024, it keeps losing its position 15 places in its ranking, nearly reaching the low ranking it had in 2005(!). Even though it managed to move up from the *High* to the *Very High* EGDI group in 2024, its e-participation score leaves much to be desired. Actually it declined from the 67th to the 130th position this year. That being said, the new national eID card is one of Kuwait's main steps toward digital transformation. The eID card served as a means of providing seamless administrative procedures and supporting Kuwait's vision of a digital government. And it's a way for the citizens to gain easy access to daily services. What's more, the government launched home delivery programs for these cards[444] which they later suspended in 2023[445].

Google Cloud is moving to expand its territory in the Middle East and, as a result, entered into a strategic agreement with the Kuwait government[446] back in 2023. The digital Kuwait government and Google Cloud company will join forces to create a comprehensive digital transformation roadmap that will affect both the government and privately owned sectors. The strategic alliance between both entities will enable the Kuwait government to use Google Cloud's technology and expertise in artificial intelligence, cybersecurity, and data analytics to fulfil its vision of making Kuwait a top digital nation in the next few years. With the assistance of the digital Kuwait Direct Investment Promotion Authority(KDIPA), the Central Agency for Information Technology (CAIT), and the Communication and Information Technology Regulatory Authority (CITRA), Google

Cloud opened a base office in Kuwait[447] and then reach out to other regions from there.

Where to focus?

The digital Kuwait government is making severe plans and efforts to ensure that their country becomes a top digital state in the coming years. At this pace, they will be able to achieve their vision of running a digital government by 2035.

21. KYRGYZSTAN

Has had some solid progress these past few years

Digital Kyrgyzstan is one of those lower-middle-income nations with remarkable progress when it comes to e-governance. Its focus is reflected in its very high TII value meaning that the telecommunications infrastructure and the high HCI are among its strongest components. However, the once high EPI[448] couldn't even reach the world's average according to this year's report, even though it still reflects a well-educated and engaged population when it comes to digital matters. This indicates that Kyrgyzstan should be investing more in strengthening its human capital and online services provision. That being said, in the UN's E-Government survey of 2024[449], digital Kyrgyzstan ranked 78th out of 193 countries assessed in e-governance...an improvement compared to the 81st place in 2022.

Analysing internet access in Kyrgyzstan, I think it's evident that there's been significant growth in recent years. With 6.5 million active subscribers out of a population of 7 million back in 2022, it's clear that internet usage is becoming increasingly widespread. In 2021, there were 5.8 million subscribers[450]. And according to data from DataReportal in February 2024[451], Kyrgyzstan's internet penetration rate was reported to be 79.8%. Also, according to data from Ookla's Speedtest in May 2023[452], the median download speed on mobile internet was just 26.65 Mbps, whereas fixed-line connections boasted a median download speed of 55.25 Mbps.

Kyrgyzstan has been receiving significant international support and funding to boost its digital transformation efforts. For instance, under the EU-funded twinning project "*Support to Digitalisation Agenda in Kyrgyzstan,*" experts from Estonia, Finland, and Italy provided over 900 days of consultations and engaged hundreds of government officials through seminars, meetings, and workshops between 2021 and 2023. Moreover, at the beginning of 2024, the World Bank approved an additional $7 million in financing[453] for the ongoing Digital Central Asia South Asia (Digital CASA) project in the Kyrgyz Republic. This funding supplements the original $50 million Digital CASA – Kyrgyz Republic Project[454], which was initiated in March 2018.

Where to focus?

Alongside infrastructure development, I think it's important to focus on raising awareness and educating citizens about the benefits of digital services. While internet access is becoming more accessible in digital Kyrgyzstan, there are still challenges to overcome, particularly in ensuring consistent and high-quality connections, especially on mobile networks.

22. LAO P.D.R

Lao P.D.R. is struggling to keep up with its neighbours

As a landlocked country in Southeast Asia, digital Lao PDR is surrounded by rapidly growing economies like Thailand and Vietnam, presenting both inspiration and challenges for its digital aspirations. Lao P.D.R. is classified as a lower-middle-income country with a population of 7.42 million, most of whom reside in rural areas.

Analysing the global ranking of Digital Lao PDR in e-governance, I think it's essential to consider its performance in various indices. According to the UN's e-government survey of 2024[455], Digital Lao shows a mixed picture. Its overall E-Government Development Index (EGDI) value places it at 152nd out of 193 countries assessed[456] an improvement from the 159th position in 2022. However, in e-participation Lao declined by 5 places in 2 years.

Analysing the main challenges faced by Laos in its digital economy journey, I think it's evident that the country lags behind in several key areas. One significant challenge is the low adoption of mobile broadband subscriptions, with less than half of the population having access. With only around 60% of the population having access to the internet[457], connectivity remains a significant barrier in digital Lao, particularly in isolated rural areas where over 60% of the population resides. And then there's the lack of a comprehensive government strategy for digital Lao P.D.R. This has led to fragmented systems and processes across different departments, making it harder to coordinate efforts. Lastly... I believe the legal and regulatory framework for the digital economy requires further strengthening,...particularly in areas of data protection.

Where to focus?

Despite many challenges, I'm optimistic about the potential for improvements through targeted projects and initiatives for digital Lao. They need to implement projects aimed at enhancing digital infrastructure and promoting digital literacy, which can play a significant role in bridging the digital divide.

23. LEBANON

Struggles and strategies for government modernisation

Lebanon faces significant challenges stemming from the country's deep-rooted financial crisis[458], which has persisted since 2019. This crisis has severely impacted the livelihoods of Lebanese citizens and the functioning of public institutions. As a result of this prolonged crisis, Lebanese municipalities are grappling with numerous difficulties.

On the positive side, it achieved a significant milestone by entering the high EGDI group for the first time in 2022, as noted in the UN's E-government survey[459]. This suggests that efforts to enhance digital government services have yielded some success. One major challenge has been the underdeveloped or unevenly developed infrastructure, even though in 2 years major progress has been made in this direction. Moreover, despite achieving high EGDI values, the country's E-participation Index (EPI) remains below the world's or the regional's average[460]. So, while digital government services *may* be accessible, there is room for enhancing citizen engagement and participation in governance processes.

Municipality decentralisation in digital Lebanon presents a complex issue with significant implications for local governance and service delivery. Despite there being over 1,000 municipalities across the country[461], their authority as outlined in the *Municipal Act of 1977* is largely constrained by centralised oversight, leading to what is often termed as 'faux decentralisation.'[462] While municipalities theoretically possess extensive powers to manage their budgets, collect taxes, and oversee local infrastructure and services, the reality is quite different. The heavy reliance on the Independent Municipal Fund as a primary revenue source has limited municipalities' incentive to seek alternative funding avenues[463] or tailor services to their communities' specific needs. From a digital governance perspective, this centralised control can impede the implementation of technology-driven solutions at the local level.

Despite increased demand for both fixed and mobile services, access to the internet remains constrained. Investment has been hindered[464] by the economic and monetary crises and by the lack of maintenance to the infrastructure. According to data from Lebanon Digital 2024[465]: Global Overview Report, a significant portion of Lebanon's population (4.7 million)were internet users at the start of 2023, when internet penetration stood at more than 86%.

Where to focus?

By investing in infrastructure upgrades, developing innovative solutions, and expanding internet access, government entities can help bridge the digital divide and improve connectivity across the country.

24. MALAYSIA

Among the first to develop a digital strategy

According to the OECD, digital Malaysia is among the first and only in the region[466] (along with Indonesia, Myanmar and Vietnam) to develop a national digital government strategy at all levels, including its municipalities. However, it's quite interesting to see that the Asia-Pacific region (which Malaysia is part of), despite having some of the fastest-growing economies and over half of the world's internet users[467], remains one of the most diverse and digitally divided areas. Anyway, getting back to Malaysia, MyDIGITAL[468] is probably one of the most outstanding achievements the government has made. This is the first Digital Economy Blueprint where the government carefully considers the vision and growth of its digitalisation. It complements national development policies such as Wawasan Kemakmuran Bersama 2030 (WKB 2030)[469] and the Twelfth Malaysia Plan (RMKe-12)[470] . Also, in Malaysia, as in many Southeast Asian countries, the government has been working on strategies to provide online services to its citizens and businesses, such as permits, licences, and certificates. They've not only focused on the central level[471] but also extended their digital government strategies to the subnational and local levels.

Now, on the global stage, Malaysia is making a mark with the Centre for the Fourth Industrial Revolution (C4IR)[472], a partnership between MyDigital and the World Economic Forum. The C4IR is the 19th of its kind worldwide and the first in Southeast Asia. According to their strategic blueprint, digital Malaysia set a target of attracting RM70 billion in digitalisation investments by the year 2025. However, recent announcements from The Malaysian Digital Economy Corporation (MDEC) suggest that Malaysia has already exceeded this ambitious goal[473], surpassing RM70 billion in digital investments ahead of schedule. Also, according to the UN report, in 2024 the country was characterised by very welldeveloped telecommunication infrastructure and and very high EGDI values.

Where to focus?

The government should prioritise citizen engagement and involvement as well as their skill development, especially when developing digital government services. Building trust with citizens can be challenging, especially when there's a history of low trust in the government[474], and people may not fully understand why they should engage with authorities.

25. MALDIVES

Has been amazingly progressing since 2020

Analysing the digital Maldives, I believe it's clear that the country has made notable progress in technology adoption. It is an upper-middle-income nation that relies heavily on a few industries, highlighting potential vulnerabilities in its economy. In terms of e-governance, I think the Maldives shows promise with its high EGDI (E-Government Development Index) value[475] ranking 94th in e-governance (with a value that's above the global average) and 92nd in e-participation. One of its strongest components is the telecommunication infrastructure.

One great initiative and great first step was when authorities in the Republic of Maldives introduced in 2023 a mobile app for their national digital ID system[476] called eFaas. One of the key features of eFaas is its use of facial recognition and biometrics for self-verification, which enhances security and privacy. Seeing as e-participation needs some encouragement in the Maldives, this is a great first step toward that road. The introduction of One-Gov is another game-changer in terms of digital governance. Initially, the portal provided services from five government bodies. Now, with 4 *more* government entities[477] the scope of services available to citizens has expanded even further.

Analysing the issue of connectivity in the digital Maldives, I believe it's clear that while internet penetration is relatively high at 83.9%[478], there hasn't been a significant improvement from 2022, according to data from the ITU[479]. This suggests a stagnant growth rate, which may hinder the country's digital development efforts. Which may be attributed to factors such as infrastructure limitations, geographical challenges, or affordability issues, which could be inhibiting wider access to the Internet.

Where to focus?

Overall, I think addressing e-governance issues in the digital Maldives requires a multifaceted approach, including investment in infrastructure, improving connectivity and/or its affordability and enhancing the quality of internet services.

26. MONGOLIA

e-Mongolia has made some impressive progress in the past 4 years

Analyzing e-Mongolia's digital progress, I think it's remarkable how, despite being a lower-middle-income country, it boasts above-average EGDI values. Ranking 46th in e-government in 2024, according to the UN's report[480], e-Mongolia has shown substantial improvement... particularly among landlocked nations. In 2024, Mongolia experienced one of the most significant leaps in EGDI values and ranking, rising by more than 28 positions. This remarkable progress also extended to e-participation[481], with a notable jump of 20 positions. During this time it also moved up to the very high EGDI group. So, it's safe to say it has had impressive progress in just 4 years. With it also being the second largest landlocked country globally (which means it doesn't have direct access to the sea and submarine cables) it still manages to maintain a decent telecommunication infrastructure. Data from the International Telecommunication Union[482] shows a significant rise in mobile broadband subscriptions. From 2017 to 2022, subscriptions shot up from 80 to 118 per 100 people. That's quite the leap! Plus, over 99% of the population now has access to 4G/LTE networks, which is pretty impressive in terms of internet accessibility.

But, while Mongolia has made progress in its digital development, there are still hurdles to overcome, particularly when it comes to bridging the gap between urban and rural areas - both physically and digitally. In rural parts of the country, access to reliable ICT infrastructure and the internet remains a challenge. This means people living in these areas might not have the same opportunities to connect and engage in the digital world as their urban counterparts. Additionally, access to affordable financial services isn't readily available for everyone, which can further widen the gap between different segments of the population. Then there's the issue of logistics. Mongolia's vast and thinly populated landscape poses quite a challenge.

Where to focus?

Overall, I'm optimistic about Mongolia's digital future. So, finding solutions to these urban-rural divides and logistical hurdles will be crucial for Mongolia to fully leverage the potential of digital technologies for its economic and social advancement.

27. MYANMAR

Some digital successes but many obstacles to still overcome

Years ago, on February 1, 2021, Myanmar experienced a significant shift in power as the military junta seized control in a violent coup. So, keep this fact in mind when analysing the digital governance in e-Myanmar.

But, despite being categorised as one of the Least Developed Countries, Myanmar has shown commendable progress in improving its rankings on the E-Government Development Index (EGDI)[483]. By 2022, it had moved up to the Middle EGDI group for the first time. And in 2024, it joined the top performers among the Least Developed Countries (LDC). However, it's worth noting that Myanmar's ranking in the UN's 2024 e-government survey wasn't as high as one might expect, given its progress. Placed at 138th out of 193 countries assessed[484], it fell behind by 4 places compared to 2 years ago.

Internet penetration in Myanmar has ....reversed. In recent years, internet penetration hasn't seen much expansion. In fact, it's faced setbacks due to various factors such as damaged infrastructure, frequent internet shutdowns, and high costs imposed by the military regime. According to a *2023* report[485], by January 2024, only 44% of the population had access to the internet. This indicates a stagnation rather than growth in internet accessibility. Also, the International Telecommunication Union (ITU)[486] reported a slightly higher internet penetration rate of 48% in 2020.

However, daily power outages (throughout the coverage period)[487], lasting from 5 to 16 hours, have impacted connectivity[488]. Furthermore, there exists a gender digital divide, with fewer women having internet access compared to men. According to an ITU estimate[489] from 2017, only 19% of women in Myanmar have internet access, compared to 29% of men. Barriers for women include perceived lack of relevance, high costs, and insufficient literacy skills, particularly in utilising mobile phones for internet access.

Reflecting on the situation in Myanmar, it's concerning to see how the military is leveraging e-government projects to strengthen its surveillance capabilities rather than focusing on enhancing public services for the benefit of the people. The military's initiatives, such as the national census[490], e-ID system[491], and the establishment of a "National Database,"[492] appear to be geared towards collecting vast amounts of data, including sensitive personal information and biometric data, under the guise of improving governance.

Also, despite the military's efforts to seek support from international organisations (UNFPA[493] included) and other countries for its e-government master plan, the absence of such support really just shows the scepticism surrounding the military's intentions and the potential misuse of collected data. Currently, the military's e-ID system[494] houses the personal data of more than 50 million individuals, along with geographic data from over 13 million households.

Where to focus?

Balancing all factors will be crucial for Myanmar's path forward, particularly in ensuring that digital development aligns with principles of democracy, human rights, and accountability.

28. NEPAL

One of the leaders in digitalisation among the least developed countries

As a lower-middle-income country, Nepal transitioned to the high EGDI group in 2022[495], indicating progress in digital governance. However its ranking in 2024 of 152nd in e-participation among 193 countries shows limitations in engaging citizens in collaborative governance. Looking at connectivity in Nepal, it's clear that there are challenges that need to be addressed. While there are around 15.85 million internet users in the country, internet penetration is 49.6% which is lower than the 2023 data (51.6%)[496], indicating that a significant portion of the population lacks access to digital services. One major issue has been the lack of digital infrastructure, but in 2024 things have improved dramatically in this dimension.

The education system also plays a role in perpetuating this challenge. With only 20% of university graduates choosing to stay in Nepal to work[497], the outdated curricula fail to adequately prepare students for the digital demands of the job market. Moreover, Nepal's economic situation exacerbates the issue, with a significant portion of the population living below the poverty line[498]. For these individuals, access to digital tools and technologies remains a distant dream, further widening the digital divide. However, according to the new UN report, Nepal now has the sufficient human capital to progress its digital governance efforts. But only if it focuses its efforts in improving the OSI values (Online Service Index.)

Where to focus?

One major obstacle they need to overcome is the lack of digital literacy among both urban and rural populations, which hampers their ability to effectively engage with digital services. Moving forward, I believe addressing infrastructure gaps and enhancing e-participation initiatives will be essential for maximising the benefits of digitalisation and inclusive development in e-Nepal.

29. OMAN

Ranks among the top 50 countries in the Government AI Readiness Index

e-Oman is a small but strategically located country in the Middle East, known for its diverse landscapes and rich history. Despite its size, it's made significant progress in technology and online services. These factors contribute to its high ranking in the United Nations e-Government Development Index (EGDI)[499], placing it among the top performers in the Asian continent (in the 12th place to be exact). Also, as a member of the Cooperation Council for the Arab States of the Gulf (GCC), Oman shares similarities with other Gulf countries in its approach to e-government. In the UN's survey, Oman was classified in the very high EGDI group. Yet, despite its high EGDI ranking, Oman has not shown significant improvement in recent years (2022-2024) in e-participation[500] - falling behind by 11 places. This suggests that while the country has made progress in e-government, it may be facing challenges in further advancing its digital initiatives, particularly in engaging its citizens.

Looking at Oman's plans for the future, particularly outlined in Vision 2040[501], it's clear that the country is placing a strong emphasis on developing its ICT sector. The launch of a significant digital transformation program in 2022 (backed by a substantial investment of $442 million) was one of the many initiatives to advance e-services and digital infrastructure. Regarding Oman's initiatives in developing smart cities, there are some promising steps being taken. Sultan Qaboos University's establishment of an IoT laboratory[502] and a communication and information research centre is a positive move. Also, the announcement of an artificial intelligence zone in Duqm[503] for research and experiments is another signal of the focus of e-Oman on emerging technologies. Furthermore, the establishment of Oman's first cyber-security centre as part of the *Oman National Computer Emergency Readiness Team (OCERT)*[504] is crucial for safeguarding government institutions from cyber threats.

Where to focus?

There remain opportunities for further improvement, particularly in enhancing online service provision and promoting greater citizen engagement in digital initiatives. The stagnant ranking in the (latest available) UN's e-government survey, coupled with the decline in e-participation, suggests that there may be gaps in citizen engagement and the delivery of online services.

30. PAKISTAN

Trying to close the connectivity gap

Like in most other countries around the world, E-government in Pakistan has its roots deeply embedded in the public sector reforms of the 1990s. While there has been significant progress since then, it's clear that e-government in Pakistan still has a long way to go to truly deliver on its potential. Why? The underlying infrastructure doesn't exist, and most of the digital services offered by the government are needlessly complex and difficult to use. More than half of its population lives in rural areas without access to broadband connections. In other words, despite having some of the world's fastest-growing mobile users, fixed broadband penetration rates remain low at below 1%[505]. However, there's tremendous potential for growth from fixed-to-mobile substitution here—and e-government could be a big part of enabling that growth.

Since 2007, Information Technology (IT) services have been governed by several different laws and acts, each of which aims to create or update some aspect of IT infrastructure within the country. The incremental update of these laws affected government IT infrastructure development and caused considerable confusion for both consumers and service providers. According to the EDGI Index, Pakistan is ranked 136th out of 193[506], improving its ranking by 14 places compared to 2022. The 2024 UN report[507] mentions its fragmented and siloed approach, lack of enabling telecommunication infrastructure and low affordability, digital skills gap, cyber security, data privacy and lack of trust, service design maturity, and limited citizen participation as factors responsible for Pakistan's ineffective digital government development. However, recently Pakistan has invested heavily in online services which has resulted in a higher level overall of e-government compared to other countries within the Middle TII and HCI groups.

Decades of mismanagement and lack of focus on information technology (IT) has severely hampered Pakistani governments' ability to make IT strides. While efforts have been made to develop e-governance initiatives and policies, such as taxation and public health systems, there is still a long way to go. Also, e-governance is not about developing policies (for which Pakistan is making efforts) but ensuring that they are properly implemented and monitored. The majority of e-governance applications are written in English, even though the country's English literacy rate is very low.

Where to focus?

Even with the growing number and popularity of e-governance applications, there is a significant lack of understanding regarding their potential and how they can benefit the masses. It needs more concerted efforts and correct implementation.

31. PHILIPPINES

Top priorities for digital gov in the Philippines: Developing digital skills

The Philippines is a country made up of thousands of islands, each with its own unique communities and challenges. Now...imagine trying to create a national identification system that covers over 110 million people spread across all these islands. Sounds like quite the feat, right? Well, the Philippines has done just that and, that's how it was in the spotlight at the UNDP's Future of Government 2023 awards[508]. Their national ID system, PhilSys[509], earned them recognition in the Open Source Adaptation category. And let me tell you, it's no small achievement. With over 85 million people already registered, PhilSys is making waves when it comes to digital governance. A great achievement...and a great reminder.

But here's the thing: as impressive as this accomplishment is, it's also a reminder of the work that still needs to be done. You see, while we celebrate milestones like this, we can't lose sight of the bigger picture. And in this case, that means recognising that there's still a gaping urban-rural gap that needs to be addressed. Of course, proficiency in navigating digital platforms, understanding online safety measures, and utilising digital tools for various purposes are indispensable skills. However, marginalised communities often lack access to resources and opportunities to develop these skills, placing them at a disadvantage in the digital world. By emphasising the significance of digital literacy, the initiative aims to bridge this gap and empower individuals from all walks of life to actively participate in the digital economy and society. Also, recognising the widespread impact of digital literacy initiatives, the program also prioritises the dissemination of these initiatives across the province. I've always said that collaboration with local government units is crucial in ensuring the effective reach and benefit of these capacity development sessions.

Through some amazing initiatives and investments, the Philippines managed to move to the very high EGDI group in 2024.[510] Its ranking improved by 16 places in two years, holding the 73rd position[511] among 193 countries in e-governance. Its e-participation score that was below the region and sub-region averages back in 2022 has seen major progress...moving up by 31 places as well.

Where to focus?

The Philippines needs to focus a bit more on investments in the human capital development.

32. QATAR

Has the infrastructure but needs more focus on digital skills

Despite being small in both population and geographical size, digital Qatar is highly urbanised and boasts a high-income status. These factors provide a solid foundation for its digital initiatives as the UN E-Government Survey (2024) suggests[512]. It ranks 53rd in e-governance and 92nd in e-participation having improved its position by 25th and 9th places respectively in 2 years. Additionally, Qatar has a highly developed telecommunications infrastructure. This infrastructure enables widespread access to digital services and facilitates communication and connectivity across the country. It has set an ambitious goal of digitising 90% of citizen services by 2030. This initiative, outlined in the Third National Development Strategy (NDS3)[513], sets a clear vision for enhancing citizen satisfaction and improving service delivery through digital channels. To support these efforts, Qatar plans to establish a Digital Centre of Excellence[514] for data and emerging technologies, with a focus on artificial intelligence (AI). This centre will drive initiatives to develop a comprehensive national data governance and management framework (which will enhance data availability and quality.)

Looking at the announcement of the Unified E-Payment Gateway Project[515] in digital Qatar, I believe it's a significant step towards modernising government services and promoting electronic payments. The introduction of multiple payment options, including credit cards, debit cards, prepaid cards, and bank transfers, through various channels such as the internet, cell phones, and points of sale (POS), will make it easier for people to pay for government services. This convenience will encourage more individuals AND companies to transition to electronic payments, reducing reliance on cash transactions and improving overall efficiency. Something I think is particularly important about this initiative is its potential to streamline operations and reduce costs for government entities. By centralising e-payment processing through the Unified E-Payment Gateway, government agencies can minimise the resources required to manage payment systems independently. This will ultimately lead to cost savings and increased efficiency in delivering services to the public.

Where to focus?

Looking ahead, I think Qatar should continue to focus on enhancing digital literacy and inclusion, particularly among underserved populations. This will help ensure that all citizens have access to and can benefit from the opportunities afforded by digital technologies.

33. SAUDI ARABIA

e-Saudi Arabia: 3rd in Asia and 6th in the world!

According to the latest United Nations Economic and Social Commission for Western Asia (ESCWA) index[516], Saudi Arabia reclaimed its spot as the top performer in e-government services across the Middle East and North Africa (MENA) region back in 2023. And it has been consistently leading the region for the past couple of years, maintaining its position at the forefront of digital transformation.

In the Govt Electronic and Mobile Services Maturity Index (GEMS) of 2022, it's the top country in the Middle East and Africa[517], showing a big improvement of 27.4% since 2020 (out of 18 countries.) Additionally, in the GovTech Maturity Index (GTMI)[518] of 2022, Saudi Arabia is among the highly developed countries that provide government services and engage with citizens. It has climbed up by 37 ranks since 2020, which is impressive. Also, Saudi Arabia was one of the leaders in the Arab region, Asia and the world according to the UN 2024 E-Government Development Index[519]. According to these reports, I can say that Saudi achieved the best historical result of the kingdom, improving by 25 ranks its e-governance position and by 36 places its e-participation position. This means that it holds the 6th and 7th position respectively among 193 countries assessed.

Obviously, it has done a great job in expanding *virtual* public services. The Seha Virtual Hospital[520] in Saudi Arabia is breaking new ground in the region's healthcare landscape. It's a prime example of how advanced digital platforms can significantly expand healthcare services. Since its launch in 2022, doctors have successfully performed 13 remote heart surgeries[521], reducing hospital stays for heart failure patients by up to 40%. Similarly, the Najiz portal[522] offers a wide array of 150 electronic government services, ranging from virtual court sessions to handling business paperwork, serving around 180,000 visitors daily[523]. Every week, around 90,000 interactions take place on this platform. Also, if you haven't heard, Saudi Arabia plans to invest $40 billion into Artificial Intelligence, as some news outlets have suggested[524]. This huge investment would make them the biggest AI investor globally. Historically, the country has relied heavily on oil, but with the rise of renewable energy and concerns about climate change, they're looking for new ways to grow their economy. AI offers a promising opportunity for economic growth by fostering innovation and creating new industries.

Where to focus?

With AI being a top priority for Saudi Arabia, data privacy, algorithmic bias, and ethical concerns need to be very *carefully* navigated to make sure that it is used responsibly and ethically.

34. SINGAPORE

For the first time ever leads Asia, surpassing South Korea

In the 1990s, Singapore was among the first countries to have broadband links nationwide, while in the 2000s, they developed a fibre broadband network and wireless hotspots throughout the island. Right now, four million[525] Singapore residents (around 70%) can access 500 digital government services online using facial verification. Also, about 97%[526] of Singapore's population now has access to superfast internet connectivity. There are many policies and initiatives that are responsible for this success, but I want to highlight one of the most important: *the Smart Nation Initiative*. Singapore's Smart Nation initiative was launched by Prime Minister Lee Hsien Loong on 24 November 2014. Through the Smart Nation initiative, Singapore's government aims to make Singapore[527] *"an outstanding city in the world...for people to live, work and play in, where the human spirit flourishes."*

The ambition and clarity of Singapore's digital vision are a driving force in the country's digital transformation process. In particular, Singapore's implementation of ICT infrastructure strategies, like fibre network rollout and 5G development plans, underpinned its top billing. Fast, reliable, and affordable connectivity is not the only way to create a brilliant platform for digital transformation, but it is considered the most important one, and digital Singapore is the global leader. Also, according to the 2024 EGDI report, Singapore is in the top three *in the world (!)* regarding e-governance[528]. Obviously, it managed to surpass South Korea in this year's report as the top leader in Asia in both e-governance and e-participation.

What's more, annually, the government spends roughly 1%[529] of the country's gross domestic product (GDP) on research and development

(R&D). Most of this spending is directed by Singapore's National Research Foundation, an organisation that funnels billions of dollars into research with potential government and business applications. Another huge focus is the tremendous investments in talent. One of the most significant challenges to the success of digital transformation in Asia is not, but it is that of talent[530]. Singapore[531] is in the most vital position across Asia to address talent and skills challenges.

Where to focus?

Singapore needs to just keep leveraging its momentum for more and better services.

35. SRI LANKA

No concerted effort at building a digital government

I think it's clear that digital Sri Lanka (this lower-middle-income country) faces challenges in building a digital government, especially when compared to other countries. Sri Lanka lags behind in terms of e-government development, as shown by its ranking of 98th out of 193 countries in the UN's E-Government Survey 2024 (down by 3 places). Sri Lanka's e-participation ranking also went down by 1 position to the 108th place in 2024. This suggests a significant need to focus investments and efforts in both these areas.

While there has been an increase in internet access and broadband subscriptions in recent years, the quality and consistency of service remain inconsistent. The data from the Telecommunications Regulatory Commission of Sri Lanka (TRCSL) indicates significant growth in mobile broadband subscriptions, reaching over 20.3 million, and fixed-line broadband subscriptions, totalling 2.5 million as of December 2023[532]. But, the *Digital 2024* report *by* DataReportal[533] shows a notable decrease in internet users and penetration rate, reaching 12.34 million users and 56.3% penetration rate by January 2024 (down from the 66.7% in 2023). I think that the government's decision to impose additional taxes on telecommunications services, along with the approved tariff hike of 20%[534] for mobile, fixed, and broadband services, could potentially hinder further progress in connectivity and affordability.

As mentioned in the title, the lack of a systematic effort toward e-governance in Sri Lanka is concerning and represents a missed opportunity for the country's economic development. The President's 2024 Budget speech[535] emphasised the importance of digitalisation for building a new growth model; but it's unclear how these plans will be implemented and whether they will effectively contribute to the development of a digital economy. Despite mentions of activities like improving the Revenue Administration Management Information System (RAMIS) and establishing a Data Protection Authority, there is little clarity on the progress or effectiveness of these efforts.

Where to focus?

Sri Lanka needs to focus more on strengthening human capital and the online services it provides.

36. SYRIA

Digital Syrian Arab Republic is plagued by conflict...

Digital Syrian Arab Republic (a lower-middle-income country in Western Asia) has faced significant challenges in many years. These challenges stem from a combination of external factors, including the 2019 financial crisis in Lebanon, COVID-19, the ongoing war in Ukraine and obviously the civil wars. Each of these events has played a role in further eroding the welfare of Syrian households. When we look at the e-governance indicators (according to the UN report)[536], the digital Syrian Arab Republic is characterised by a mix of strengths and weaknesses.

The UN e-government Knowledgebase's[537] latest rankings for Syria paint a bleak picture: 162nd in e-governance and a staggering 184th in e-participation out of 193 assessed countries as of 2024. This represents a decline of 6 places in e-governance even though its e-participation improved by 1 place this year. According to the World Bank report[538] on the Middle East and North Africa, the digital Syrian Arab Republic has "some focus on GovTech" along with three other countries in the region.

Truth be told, the ongoing civil war, compounded by a highly repressive regime and the involvement of multiple belligerent forces, *severely* limits the government's ability to prioritise digital governance. Obviously, the focus understandably shifts towards managing political instability and humanitarian crises rather than advancing digital infrastructure and services.

The economic fallout from over a decade of conflict has only exacerbated Syria's already dire situation, plunging households into greater hardship since 2023[539]. This socio-economic crisis not only deepens the digital divide but also highlights the government's struggle to offer or focus on offering basic services... let alone invest in comprehensive e-governance frameworks.

As of early 2024, Syria had 8.51 million internet users[540], representing 35.8% of the population, and 17.21 million active mobile connections, covering 72.3% of the population. Despite these challenges, there are promising initiatives that focus on skills and education, like UNICEF's digital learning program (particularly in conflict-affected areas like) Al-Hasakeh governorate[541]. Also, the Ministry of Education of Syria[542] is integrating 3D virtual reality technology, which are particularly noteworthy. Through an ambitious project, 750 teachers have been trained to develop VR and AR-based curricula, enhancing educational content delivery. Moreover, 5,000 student licences have been distributed, enabling virtual learning experiences and tutorials.

Where to focus?

The truth of the matter is that without meaningful political reforms and societal stability, any digital governance efforts in Syria are likely to remain superficial, unable to bridge the vast gaps in participation and service delivery that are critical for national recovery and development.

37. TAJIKISTAN

Digital Tajikistan? International help is on the way

While digital Tajikistan has made some progress in its digital development, there are still significant challenges to overcome. According to the UN's E-Government survey[543], Tajikistan ranked 123rd out of 193 countries assessed, which indicates that there's room for improvement in its e-government initiatives. On a positive note, Tajikistan reached the high EGDI group for the first time in 2022. This suggests some advancements in digital governance within Tajikistan (by 6 places to be exact). The Conference on Elevating Global Access through E-Commerce (E-GATE) in Tajikistan[544], which was held on March 1, 2024, is a significant event. It was supported by big organisations like the World Bank and its private sector arm, the IFC, along with the UK Foreign, Commonwealth and Development Office (FCDO), and other international groups. This conference is important because it marks the beginning of strong connections between Tajikistan and global resources.

Also, I believe that the support from the ADB (including financing for project preparation and digital transformation initiatives) will play a crucial role in strengthening Tajikistan's infrastructure, promoting food security, and enhancing social services. ADB stands for the Asian Development Bank, which has launched a new country partnership strategy (CPS) for digital Tajikistan[545], focusing on improving the quality of the country's economic growth by supporting government efforts to increase productivity. The ADB has been a major supporter of Tajikistan's development since 1998, providing over $2.2 billion in assistance, with a large portion in grants.

If we look at Tajikistan's unevenly developed ICT infrastructure, it really poses significant challenges to the country's digital transformation efforts. It's concerning that only 36% of individuals in Tajikistan have access to the internet, according to data from the ITU in 2022[546]. This limited internet access hinders opportunities for economic growth, social inclusion, and, most importantly, access to information and services. Also, the widespread reliance on outdated 2G mobile[547] connections, covering 95% of the country's territory, highlights the urgent need for infrastructure upgrades. Modern online needs, such as accessing information, conducting business transactions, and participating in e-government services, require faster and more reliable internet connections.

Where to focus?

By investing in infrastructure upgrades and promoting a free and open internet environment, digital Tajikistan can create (more) opportunities for digital growth and social development for all its citizens.

38. TAIWAN

Digital Taiwan: Initiatives and challenges

I believe that Taiwan's Information and Communication Technology (ICT) sector plays a crucial role in its economy. It's actually one of the most important sectors in the world when it comes to contributing to the country's GDP[548]. However, despite this, there's still a big gap when it comes to digital access in Taiwan. This means that not everyone has the same opportunities to use the internet, and factors like gender, age, income, education, and job status all play a role in this divide. Another important point to consider is that even though the ICT sector is a big part of Taiwan's economy, not everyone benefits equally from it. There are disparities in employment opportunities and income within the sector, which leads to wider income gaps in society.

Taiwan's DIGI+ initiative[549] (or Development, Innovation, Governance, and Inclusion) is a great initiative that seeks to promote a "smart government." Taiwan's DIGI+ initiative is a great effort aimed at driving digital transformation and fostering a "smart government" approach. One key aspect of the DIGI+ initiative is its focus on infrastructure development, talent cultivation, and crossindustry transformation. The country has successfully integrated information technologies into government operations, making it easier for citizens to interact with various agencies. This integration is exemplified by platforms like join.gov. tw[550], which allows citizens to file petitions and participate in policymaking. The digital democracy in Taiwan is also supported by initiatives such as vTaiwan[551], a platform that combines online and offline interactions for national deliberation.

However, despite these advancements, there are areas that require attention. The public sector websites face challenges such as accessibility issues, inconsistent navigation, and a lack of uniform design[552]. Also, Taiwan's digital footprint and strained relations with mainland China have also led to significant cybersecurity challenges, with government agencies facing millions of cyberattacks monthly. In terms of public services, initiatives like the T-Road, which connects agencies and facilitates data reconciliation, and platforms like the 111 SMS service aim to reinforce trusted government information sources.

Where to focus?

To further improve Taiwan's digital government, there is a need for a clear commitment to procedural and structural justice.The government must also continue to empower the workforce with digital skills and cross-boundary governance abilities.

39. THAILAND

Amazing e-participation levels but issues with data leaking

With very high levels of human capital development and moderate to very high levels of infrastructure development, digital Thailand has capitalised on its resources to achieve significant progress in governance. One significant aspect of Thailand's digital advancement is seen in its E-Government Development Index (EGDI[553], which measures how well governments use technology to provide services to citizens. Since 2014, Thailand has been consistently improving its EGDI ranking, moving up from 102nd globally (then) to 52nd in 2024.

Another noteworthy achievement is Thailand's performance in the World Digital Competitiveness Ranking[554]. In 2023, Thailand jumped to the 35th position out of 64 countries, a significant improvement from the previous year when it was ranked 40th. Thailand's rise in this report and its high rankings in the Global Cybersecurity Index (GCI)[555] in 2020 reflect the country's growing competitiveness in the digital arena. The Thai government plans to launch a digital identification program in 2024[556] which is a significant step towards modernising their systems and making transactions more efficient.

But, data leakage has been a great issue for digital Thailand, especially recently. Such issues only highlight significant challenges in the country's cybersecurity practices (particularly within the public sector.) For instance, in 2021[557], the personal data of millions of visitors to Thailand became accessible online, exposing a major breach in data security. Then, in April 2023[558], personal information from 55 million Thai citizens was hacked from the national public health portal and put up for sale on the dark web. And recently, in 2024, a cybersecurity firm found once again that the personal information of 20 million Thais had been leaked from government agencies[559] and is on sale. What's concerning is the apparent lack of response or statements from the Thai government regarding these breaches. While identifying the perpetrators *IS* challenging, the government's negligence in *addressing* cybersecurity issues and safeguarding citizens' personal data could undermine trust in its (current or future) digital governance efforts.

Where to focus?

However, as mentioned, digital Thailand needs to focus a little bit more on building trust and confidence in digital governance as well as in providing more and better online services.

40. TIMOR-LESTE

Timor-Leste's strongest component is its human capital

Countries like Timor-Leste *(seeking to uplift their economies)* often face barriers in building telecommunications networks and expanding online services. This not only impacts their ability to connect globally but also limits opportunities for economic growth and human capital development. The UN survey[560] suggests that Timor-Leste has a somewhat moderate availability and quality of online services for its citizens as well as infrastructure with strong investment in education and (digital) skills development, which are very important for advancing digital initiatives.

According to the UN e-government Knowledgebase[561], Timor-Leste ranked 159th in e-governance and 120th in e-participation out of 193 countries assessed in 2024. Unfortunately, Timor-Leste has seen a notable decline in both these scores. Also, in the World Bank's report on East Asia and Pacific countries[562], TimorLeste is noted to have *"some focus on GovTech,"* alongside three other nations. This suggests that the country is *trying* to explore and invest in government technology solutions to improve service delivery and administrative efficiency.

With 742.4 thousand internet users and a penetration rate of 54.2%, it's clear that a significant portion of the population remains offline in digital Timor-Leste[563]. This suggests that despite increasing access, barriers like affordability, infrastructure limitations, and digital literacy still impact connectivity. Factors like network coverage, data costs, and the relevance of digital services play crucial roles in determining who can effectively use the internet. Also, Timorese adults have achieved moderate levels, scoring an average of 20.47 out of a possible 52 points on the Digital and Financial Literacy (DFL) Index[564]. This index - developed by UNCDF and UNDP in collaboration with Tebbutt Research - provides a snapshot of how well individuals understand and navigate digital and financial concepts.

Where to focus?

To further accelerate progress, *continuous* investment in telecommunications infrastructure and digital literacy programs will be essential. Strengthening these areas can ensure that all citizens, including those in remote areas, can fully access and benefit from digital services.

41.TURKEY/ TÜRKIYE

Among the top digital governments in Asia for 2024

In evaluating Turkey's digital governance standing, it's notable that the country has emerged as one of the top performers for 2024 in Asia..again. This achievement is underpinned by Turkey's commendable Online Service Index (OSI) levels, which have been driven by strong human capital development and infrastructure investments as well as a huge focus on AI and blockchain technology.

As per the 2023 E-Government Benchmark report[565], Turkey secured an impressive 10th position out of 35 EU countries. This marks a noteworthy ascent, improving its ranking by 6 places compared to the previous year, culminating in a total score of 81. Moreover, on a global scale, Turkey maintains a solid position, ranking 27th out of 193 countries in the EGDI report[566] (up from the 48th place in 2022). I believe these rankings at both EU and global levels reflect Turkey's focus on enhancing its digital governance.

In 2019, the Grand National Assembly of Türkiye greenlit the Eleventh Development Plan (2019–2023)[567]. I find it pertinent to discuss this plan now because it holds significance as the initial development roadmap crafted under the newly adopted Presidential Government System.

Here are some noteworthy aspects:

1. 98% of government services are available online in Turkey, surpassing the EU average of 84%.

2. Transparency remains an area of concern, as only 11% of governmental platforms disclose the use of personal data for services. This is notably lower than the EU average of 56%.

3. Turkey excels in accepting eID logins, with 94% of online services accommodating this feature (compared to the EU average of 70%.)

4. Challenges persist in cross-border accessibility, with only 38% of services catering to users beyond national borders. Although slightly below the EU average of 49%, this presents an area for improvement.

5. In user-centric services, the country stands out, earning 99 points(out of a total of 100), along with Malta and Finland.

What's more, in the EU's assessment, Istanbul, the capital city of Turkey, stands out as one of the top cities globally when measured against 146 other cities using the Local Online Service Index (LOSI)[568]...once again. This index evaluates various criteria such as institutional framework, content provision, service provision, participation and engagement, and technology.

Where to focus?

Turkish authorities could enhance their use of information systems and technical architectures to better accommodate multilingualism...especially when aiming to establish services that align with European standards.

42. TURKMENISTAN

Digital Turkmenistan has the right human capital and technology but still…

Despite improving its ranking as reflected in the UN's 2022 E-government report[569] the same thing cannot be said for this year's report. It still has values below the regional and global averages, dropping in its ranking by 8 places, reaching the 145th position out of 193 countries assessed[570] in e-governance. This is unfortunate, considering that back in 2022, it was recognised as one of the four Landlocked Developing Countries (LLDCs) that experienced significant improvement in EGDI values.

However, I must add that Turkmenistan's efforts to enhance digital services and telecommunications infrastructure are commendable and indicate a commitment to advancing its digital transformation agenda. The presence of over 500 public service portals on the www.e.gov.tm[571] website, along with the availability of online payment and information services, demonstrates a solid effort to improve access to services for citizens…even though more needs to be done in this direction. UN agencies have played a vital role in supporting Turkmenistan's journey towards digitalisation. They've provided crucial assistance across various areas, aiding in the simplification and harmonisation of processes and fostering better collaboration among different public institutions. Something I think is particularly important about this partnership is the focus on digital transformation in the public sector.

What's more, Turkmenistan is also trying to innovate by itself. In 2023, the government signed a new project, *"Assistance in the implementation of a pilot system of interdepartmental electronic information exchange in Turkmenistan"*. The project, funded entirely by the Government of Turkmenistan, aims to develop and deploy an electronic data interchange system using the X-road platform[572]. The success of X-road in other countries, including Estonia, Finland, and Japan, highlights its potential as a reliable solution for electronic information exchange. Once again, even with this project, UNDP is a partner of choice[573] in promoting the digital transformation of Turkmenistan.

Where to focus?

By focusing on improving e-participation and addressing other areas of digital governance, Turkmenistan *CAN* build a more inclusive and responsive digital government ecosystem. Also, by sharing experiences and best practices from successful e-leaders, Turkmenistan can accelerate its progress even more.

43. UNITED ARAB EMIRATES

Digital UAE advances via emerging tech and service rating systems

The global recognition in the UN's 2024 EGDI report[574] solidifies the UAE's leadership in digital governance, securing a top spot in Asia and trailing only Singapore, South Korea and Saudi Arabia. Moreover, Dubai's recent achievement of being among the top 10 in the Global Power City Index 2023, issued by Japan's Mori Memorial Foundation's Institute for Urban Strategies[575], demonstrates the UAE's ascending global significance.

UAE is a leader in adopting new, emerging technologies. They've made a plan called the AE National Strategy for Artificial Intelligence 2031[576]. They're serious about AI and want to be the best at it. They're so serious that they even have a whole Ministry for Artificial Intelligence[577] (perhaps the only government in the world with one)! Also, the recent collaboration signed in March 2023, forming "The UAE Centre for Government Digital Excellence" supported by Microsoft and PwC Middle East[578], is a strategic move. It demonstrates a willingness to leverage industry expertise and cutting-edge technologies to enhance government operations and government services.

Have you heard about the UAE pass and its benefits? It's a digital ID system[579] that allows its users to access all of their government documents, services or different payments. While other countries grappled with the challenges brought by the pandemic in a bid to digitalise their governments and public agencies, the UAE was several steps closer to its citizens[580]. Actually, the UAE pass follows in the footsteps of similar systems already in place in countries like Estonia and Singapore[581], where digital IDs are accepted as valid forms of identification in most day-to-day situations.

Each year, the government makes a comprehensive evaluation is conducted on approximately 124 government services. This year's evaluation[582] resulted in six service centres achieving top ratings. Among the services that performed below expectations was Kalba Hospital. In response, Sheikh Mohammed announced, via communication on the X platform[583] the decision to replace its director. For those who don't know, the implementation of the Global Star Rating System for Services[584] since 2011 was later expanded in 2019 to cover various service channels (websites, applications, etc.) This system's evaluation process considers customer satisfaction surveys and mystery shoppers, ensuring that only the highest quality services are delivered to the citizens.

Where to focus?

Maybe they could focus more on the human capital index to improve it more since that's the only place where it's lacking…and not a leader of the subregion. More education and more digital skills should be in the focus.

44. UZBEKISTAN

Digital UAE advances via emerging tech and service rating systems

The global recognition in the UN's 2024 EGDI report[585] solidifies the UAE's leadership in digital governance, securing a top spot in Asia and trailing only Singapore, South Korea and Saudi Arabia. Moreover, Dubai's recent achievement of being among the top 10 in the Global Power City Index 2023, issued by Japan's Mori Memorial Foundation's Institute for Urban Strategies[586], demonstrates the UAE's ascending global significance. UAE is a leader in adopting new, emerging technologies. They've made a plan called the AE National Strategy for Artificial Intelligence 2031[587]. They're serious about AI and want to be the best at it. They're so serious that they even have a whole Ministry for Artificial Intelligence[588] (perhaps the only government in the world with one)! Also, the recent collaboration signed in March 2023, forming "The UAE Centre for Government Digital Excellence" supported by Microsoft and PwC Middle East[589], is a strategic move. It demonstrates a willingness to leverage industry expertise and cutting-edge technologies to enhance government operations and government services.

Have you heard about the UAE pass and its benefits? It's a digital ID system[590] that allows its users to access all of their government documents, services or different payments. While other countries grappled with the challenges brought by the pandemic in a bid to digitalise their governments and public agencies, the UAE was several steps closer to its citizens[591]. Actually, the UAE pass follows in the footsteps of similar systems already in place in countries like Estonia and Singapore[592], where digital IDs are accepted as valid forms of identification in most day-to-day situations. Each year, the government makes a comprehensive evaluation is conducted on approximately 124 government services. This year's evaluation[593] resulted in six service centres achieving top ratings. Among the services that performed below expectations was Kalba Hospital. In response, Sheikh Mohammed announced, via communication on the X platform[594] the decision to replace its director. For those who don't know, the implementation of the Global Star Rating System for Services[595] since 2011 was later expanded in 2019 to cover various service channels (websites, applications, etc.) This system's evaluation process considers customer satisfaction surveys and mystery shoppers, ensuring that only the highest quality services are delivered to the citizens.

Where to focus?

Maybe they could focus more on the human capital index to improve it more since that's the only place where it's lacking…and not a leader of the sub region.

More education and more digital skills should be in focus.

45. VIETNAM

Digital Vietnam has taken many initiatives in 2024 despite stalling

Digital Vietnam has taken several initiatives in 2024 to advance its digitalisationn efforts. And that's a good sign, seeing that for many years now, it hasn't had any real progress compared to other countries. Despite its ranking of 71st out of 193 countries in the UN's E-government survey of 2024[596], I have to say that Vietnam's position has seen substantial change. Actually, from 2022-2024, the country has moved up by 15 places in the global ranking[597], indicating a newfound focus of *substantial* improvement in its digital governance initiatives. This is the best ranking it has had since the first report in 2003. On February 23, 2024, Vietnam's Ministry of Information and Communications shared a detailed plan for building up the country's digital infrastructure – *Information and Communication Infrastructure Master Plan for the Period 2021-2030, with a Vision to 2050*[598]. This plan lays out how digital Vietnam will use new technologies like artificial intelligence, big data, and the Internet of Things to boost its IT industry and to integrate digital applications into all aspects of life, from the government to business to everyday activities.

What's more, Vietnam's government has launched a comprehensive national digital transformation project known as Project 06[599], aimed at developing an application for population database, digital ID, and authentication from 2022 to 2025. I believe that one of the notable aspects of this project is the inclusion of DNA biometrics alongside other forms of biometric data such as face, fingerprint, iris, and voice. By integrating digital ID cards with chip-based technology, citizens can access a wide range of services, from cashless payments to medical diagnoses, with increased convenience and security. Also, it's important to recognise that not everyone has equal access to digital technologies. Vulnerable groups (such as persons with disabilities) may face barriers to accessing digital services. So, support should be provided to ensure that these groups are not left behind in the digital age. Something I think is particularly important about this issue is the need for inclusive policies and initiatives to facilitate digital inclusion for all members of society. Something that Vietnam has been trying to do. In digital Vietnam, incentives such as tax savings and concessional loans are offered to support the research, manufacture, and production of products and services that enable persons with disabilities to access digital services.

Where to focus?

While it's on the right track, continued efforts are needed to ensure that all citizens can benefit from the opportunities offered by technology as well as to include them more in e-governance.

46. YEMEN

Digital Yemen is not yet a reality

Once a land marked by smaller internal conflicts, Yemen has been thrown into turmoil by a devastating civil war involving regional powers since 2015. This conflict has taken an enormous toll on the civilian population, who have suffered not only from direct violence but also from hunger and disease due to the disruption of trade and aid. "Digital Yemen" is not a reality yet. In these conditions, it's no surprise that Yemen ranks so poorly in terms of digital governance. According to the latest UN e-government survey[600], Yemen is placed 185th out of 193 countries assessed. This low ranking is shared by other conflict-ridden or isolated nations like Afghanistan (188th) and the Democratic People's Republic of Korea (184th).

According to the UN e-Government Knowledgebase[601], Yemen ranked 170th in e-participation out of 193 countries assessed in 2024. This places Yemen well below both the region and subregion averages, highlighting just how far it has to go in terms of digital development. Also, a World Bank report focusing on the Middle East and North Africa[602] identified Yemen, along with Libya and Iraq, as the only countries with minimal focus on GovTech. It's not surprising when you consider that all three countries are suffering from conflict.

On the human capital front, Yemen's middle ranking suggests that while there are some 'pockets' of skilled individuals, the overall level of education and digital literacy is not sufficient to drive widespread adoption and innovation in digital services. At the start of 2024, there were 6.16 million internet users in Yemen[603], with internet penetration at just 17.7%. This low penetration rate means that the vast majority of Yemen's population is still offline. The low telecommunication infrastructure index in Yemen is a major roadblock. Many areas lack basic internet connectivity, which is essential for any e-government services.

Where to focus?

I find it particularly concerning that Yemen has such a minimal focus on GovTech, especially given the potential benefits it could bring in terms of transparency, efficiency, and citizen engagement. GovTech solutions can help streamline administrative processes, reduce corruption, and improve service delivery—all of which are crucial for a country in crisis. However...the ongoing conflict makes it difficult to prioritise these and similiar digital initiatives.

EUROPE

Digital governance SUMMARY

Europe is home to 36 of the 76 countries of the world classified in the "very high" category of the UN's E-Government Development Index (EGDI). That's more than half of the world's top performers in digital governance, and it speaks volumes about the continent's focus. In fact, Europe hosts the two top-ranking countries in e-government development, which I'll talk about later. But what's more striking to me is how consistently high Europe's performance is across the board. It's not just about a few standout countries; there's a general trend across the continent towards excellence in digital governance. This consistency shows that Europe isn't just leading the way—it's doing so as a unified region with shared goals and standards.

On average, they provide more services online than any other region in the world. This means that European citizens have easier, quicker access to government services right from their computers or smartphones. Whether it's paying taxes, accessing healthcare, or even engaging in public consultations, the digital tools are there to make these interactions smoother and more efficient.

A snapshot into Europe

An area where Europe really stands out is in the use of geospatial technologies for service provision. A significant number of European countries have integrated these technologies into their public services. Geospatial tech allows governments to offer more precise and personalized services, whether it's mapping out public health resources or optimizing urban planning. This kind of technology is becoming a necessity for efficient and effective governance in the modern world.

What's also worth noting is that Europe has the lowest variance in EGDI scores among its countries. To me, this is an indicator that the continent is moving towards a more uniform level of digital governance. In other words, the gap between the top performers and those further down the list is narrowing.

This region has set the standard in many ways when it comes to digital governance, especially in providing online services for vulnerable populations. I think it's impressive how Europe consistently leads in this area. For quite some time now, the continent has had the highest proportion of countries offering online services tailored specifically for people in vulnerable situations...Whether it's services for the elderly, disabled, or other marginalized groups.

Some areas that need a little bit more attention

However, I can't help but notice that while Europe is doing well overall, there are still gaps that need to be addressed. In particular, I think it's important to focus on immigrants and people living in poverty, who, despite being some of the most vulnerable, seem to be underserved in terms of e-government services. These groups are slipping through the cracks, even in a region that's otherwise excelling in digital governance. And I believe this is a significant oversight that needs more attention.The challenge here is twofold. First, there's the issue of language and cultural barriers for immigrants, which can make it difficult for them to navigate online services even when they are available. Second, people living in poverty often lack access to the technology needed to benefit from these services in the first place. If you don't have reliable internet or a computer, how can you take advantage of online government services? These are the kinds of questions I believe European policymakers need to grapple with more seriously.

When talking about transparency (whether it's transparency in service delivery, the design of these services, or how personal data is handled) there are still gaps. I've seen that some countries lag in being open about how their digital services are designed and delivered. This lack of transparency can erode trust, which is crucial when it comes to government services, especially those aimed at vulnerable populations.

Top and bottom performers in Europe

When we break down Europe by region, it becomes clear that Northern and Western Europe are the frontrunners in digital governance. In contrast, Southern Europe lags behind, and I think that's not just a coincidence. There's a significant historical, economic, and political context behind this divide. It has a lot to do with their long-standing investments in education, innovation, and a strong welfare state that prioritises accessibility and transparency in government services. There are 43 countries in the continent.

The 10 most developed countries in terms of digital governance are:

1. Denmark
2. Estonia
3. Iceland
4. UK
5. Finland
6. Netherlands
7. Germany
8. Sweden
9. Norway
10. Spain

For example, when we look at the top performers in digital governance, the list is dominated by Northern countries like Denmark, Estonia, Iceland, and the UK. These countries are not just leading in Europe; they're leading globally. Unfortunately, Finland, which held second place in 2022, has fallen far behind this year. On the other hand, Spain still made the list (again) and is the only country from Southern Europe to do so this year. I think this disparity can be attributed to several factors, including economic challenges, differences in infrastructure development, and varying levels of digital literacy.

The 5 least developed countries in Europe in terms of digital governance are:

1. Monaco
2. Andorra
3. North Macedonia
4. San Marino
5. Bosnia and Herzegovina

Fun fact: this list has not changed one bit from the 2022 report. Monaco and Andorra, despite being wealthier, haven't translated their financial resources into advanced digital governance. This is where I think the complacency factor comes in—there might not be a strong push for change. Contrast this with Bosnia and Herzegovina, or North Macedonia (a landlocked country) where limited financial resources are likely a significant barrier to developing digital governance systems. For some of these countries, the economy is centred around specific industries—Monaco on luxury, Andorra on tourism, and San Marino on heritage and banking. This economic focus might lead to a conservative approach to governance, where maintaining the status quo is prioritised over innovation.

While these countries are diverse in many ways, their common (low) ranking in digital governance highlights how both wealth and size can be doubleedged swords. Wealth can lead to complacency, and small size can reduce the *perceived* need for digital services. Even though in most cases, the small size has been an advantage in the countries with a clear focus. Meanwhile, those countries facing economic and political challenges might simply not have the resources to invest in digital governance, even if the will is there.

Opportunities moving forward

I believe there's a significant opportunity to advance digital governance in some European countries by placing more emphasis on cross-border services and transparency. We often talk about the European Union as a single market, but when it comes to digital services, there's still a lot of fragmentation. I think there's a real need to focus on making digital services work seamlessly across borders. This would not only simplify processes for citizens who live, work, or do business in multiple countries but also strengthen the sense of unity within the EU. Cross-border services are particularly important for businesses and individuals who work/live/travel/operate in more than one country.

Also, transparency is another area that some European countries can or should focus on. When it comes to transparency, I believe this is an area where Europe could set a global standard. Digital services are becoming more complex, and the amount of data governments collect is growing. But with that comes a responsibility to be open and clear about how this data is used. Many people are increasingly concerned about privacy and data security. By being more transparent about digital service design and data usage, governments can build trust with their citizens. I would also add that this transparency shouldn't just be about ticking boxes or fulfilling legal requirements. It needs to be meaningful and easy to understand so that ordinary people can feel confident that their data is being handled responsibly.

Transparency also ties back into the idea of improving cross-border services. If European countries can work together to develop shared standards for data usage and service design, it could lead to a more unified and transparent digital governance system across the continent. For instance, if a citizen from one country moves to another, they should be able to easily understand how their data is being used in both places, without worrying about inconsistencies or gaps in information.

1. ALBANIA

Moved to the Very High EGDI group this year (for the first time)

Albania, a small country in Southeastern Europe, is making decent progress in public administration reform. According to the EGDI report, Albania falls into the upper-middle-income category, and has moved up for the first time to the very high EGDI group[604]. Albania stands out as a country with well-developed infrastructure and a skilled workforce, positioning it to potentially reach a very high EGDI level in the near future. The nation is on a positive trajectory.

According to the eGovernment Benchmark 2023 report[605], a notable 61% of services in Albania are accessible online, and an encouraging 71% of these services accept eID logins. However, there's a noteworthy gap when it comes to cross-border accessibility, with only 14% of services available for users outside the country, which is considerably lower than the EU average of 46%. Refering to the EGDI report, there has been a significant decline in e-participation[606] over the past two years, moving down from the 22nd to the 49th position in 2024.

But, while the e-Albania platform has seen significant improvements in digitising service delivery, the closure of contact centres back in 2022 raised concerns, particularly for citizens who may struggle with digital skills or lack access to IT equipment. Ongoing efforts to improve the online portal's user experience are also in the works (especially the smart chatbot). Also, the Albanian School of Public Administration (ASPA)[607] has been working on adapting its training programs, focusing more on EU integration. Although progress has been made, there's still a need for further efforts to improve both ASPA's physical and digital infrastructure. Digital security and safeguarding personal data are vital aspects that require increased attention, too. Cybersecurity is of utmost importance, especially after a temporary suspension of digital services due to cyberattacks in 2022[608].

Where to focus?

It's imperative for Albania to continue these efforts and consider upgrading its regulatory framework for data protection to align seamlessly with EU standards. This would not only enhance cybersecurity but also establish trust in the digital ecosystem (which is fundamental for a society.)

2. ANDORRA

Strong infrastructure, weak digital skills, limited services

Andorra, being one of the small mountainous microstates in Europe, has some interesting lessons for both its peers and more marginalised areas. According to the EGDI report[609], Andorra has made progress in e-participation (up by 23 places) but not in e-governance (down by 12 places) in 2024. Also, according to the DESA publications[610], Andorra scores very high on the Telecommunications Infrastructure Index (TII), emphasising the importance of quality broadband for digital advancements. Remarkably, 92% of the people in Andorra are connected to the internet, showcasing the broad accessibility of digital resources. But, going digital requires people with the right skills, and Andorra, being a small country stuck between France and Spain, finds it hard to attract and keep talented individuals.

The recent Law 42/2022[611], passed on December 1, is a significant move for entrepreneurs, especially in the digital era. It specifically addresses start-ups and tech-driven companies, offering them a regulated framework for growth. In addition, the government took another step in 2023 by introducing the Digital Nomad Visa regulation[612]. This document sets criteria for Andorran companies looking to boost the digital economy, entrepreneurship, or innovation. These companies may hire non-resident foreign workers with salaries below the minimum wage under certain conditions. I think this legislative push not only encourages entrepreneurs to set up shop in Andorra but also creates opportunities for those driving the digital economy. It seems the government is keen on leveraging the country's stable legal framework and established ecosystem to enhance its economy.

Where to focus?

I believe Andorra has a good digital setup, but there's room for improvement in the services it provides to its citizens and the development of its people. While the digital infrastructure is solid, I think putting more emphasis on enhancing public services and investing in the skills and knowledge of its residents is crucial.

3. AUSTRIA

What is holding digital Austria back from being a top performer in the EU?

Since 2003, the government behind digital Austria has frequently presented digital action plans, each containing a strategic framework for digitising services. By establishing a Federal Ministry for Digital and Economic Affairs[613] to promote e-government among the population, Austria was the 10th in the European Commission's Digital Economy and Society Index (DESI) 2022 (the latest report available)[614]. No change whatsoever from the 2020 report.

However, there is a looming deadline. Digital Austria needs to automate its public services ahead of a significant demographic shift. The median age of the population in the country is 44 years old [615]. By 2040 probably half the population will be aged 65 or over[616].

Actually, in 2003, the Austrian Federal Government launched an eGovernment initiative that aimed to coordinate all activities by setting up two cross-departmental coordination bodies. This made it one of the first EU Member States to adopt *comprehensive* legislation on eGovernment.

The eGovernment Act[617] entered into force in 2004, and it was a milestone achievement. Today, the Digital Austria 2050 Strategic Action Plan[618] puts forward initiatives focused on improving digital skills for the labour force, general citizens, and the education sector. These and several other governmental efforts have helped the Alpine Republic rank among the EU's top five for the indicators "transparency" and "key enablers".

The initial point of contact for all issues relating to eGovernment services is the oesterreich.gv.at[619] portal, which offers online services according to the "onestop principle". The business community can take care of any formalities online using the corporate service portal USP [620] particularly tailored to their needs. Digital Austria[621] is a unique platform model that has served as the coordination and strategy committee for eGovernment since the year 2005. Parallel to Digital Austria, the eGovernment Innovation Center[622] (EGIZ) was also set up in 2005. This initiative supports public authorities in developing the Austrian ICT strategy and conducts research in an eGovernment environment. However, it has fallen behind in e-governance by 2 places[623] and in e-participation by 16 places according to the UN report (2024.)

Despite these, the country needs to focus on some key areas if it wants to catch up to the frontrunners. So, for example, according to the DESI index, in 2022, Austria was one of the poorest performers regarding broadband coverage (ranked 14th out of 27 member countries)[624]. Meanwhile, some countries like Malta, Luxembourg, Denmark, Latvia, Spain etc., have achieved 100% (or nearly complete) coverage. Indeed, Austria has successfully launched several services developed jointly with the private sector, like Smart City Vienna[625] and GovLabAustria[626]. However, more effort is required.

Where to focus?

The government needs to focus on equipping citizens with digital and technical skills to enable them to use "digital media competently" and qualify them for participation in modern society.

4. BELARUS

Tech-forward Belarus falls short on digital public services

Belarus has made significant strides in digital governance, especially with its high EGDI (e-Government Development Index) level. While Belarus scores impressively in the EGDI report[627] as its e-participation index shows, the same cannot be said for its e-governance scores where it lost 19 places in the global ranking in 2 years. It even declined from the highest EGDI group it held in 2022.

When the Soviet Union dissolved, Belarus took advantage of new opportunities. In 1993, two Belarusian programmers founded EPAM Systems[628], which later became the biggest custom software developer in Central Europe and the first IT company from the region listed on the New York Stock Exchange. In the early 2000s, the Lukashenka government initiated a Hi-Tech Park to boost digital businesses. Unlike typical technology parks, Belarus' Hi-Tech Park is unique[629] – it's virtual, covering the entire country. However, despite this focus on digital technology and the economy, a setback occurred when databases of the Belarus Ministry of Internal Affairs suddenly went offline[630], prompting many IT specialists to leave. Neighbouring countries, especially Poland, took advantage of this situation. For example, in September 2020, Poland launched the Poland Business Harbour (PBH) scheme, making it easier for Belarusian professionals to relocate.

Despite that, one of the strongest points of Belarus is connectivity. An impressive 85.09% of Belarusian individuals are connected to the internet, showcasing widespread digital access. The telecommunication infrastructure is top-notch, earning a Very High TII index value of 0.9156 in the EGDI report.

Where to focus?

I think when considering the future of Belarus's digital development, two crucial areas that deserve attention are service provision and the human capital. As of now, Belarus holds a rank of 88 out of 193 countries[631] globally in e-participation. Looking ahead, I've learned that Belarus plans to establish a centre dedicated to implementing cybersecurity measures and responding to cyber incidents. I think this is a crucial step in ensuring the safety and security of the digital environment.

5. BELGIUM

Digital Belgium efforts stall even though it has everything to move forward

Digital Belgium lacks digital skills which is cited as the main reason why it is failing to meet EU targets on digitisation, according to a new report published by the European Commission[632] as well as the EGDI report. The European Commissions' findings were based on an assessment of how far the 27 member states have advanced toward achieving key goals set out in the Digital Agenda for Europe. Belgium ranks 6th in the EU regarding the integration of digital technology, with the country showing a high uptake of digital technology within their operations. Meanwhile, on the global scale, it ranks 56th in e-governance (down by 17 places compared to 2022) and 85th in e-participation (up by 1 place.)

Its federal portal *www.belgium.be* was first launched in 2002. It provided a single and multilingual entry point to information and services for citizens, businesses and civil servants. However, it has also made specific portals to meet the needs of every user and ethnic group. For example, the government portal of the Flemish Regional Government – vlaanderen.be[633] - was launched in 2003. The wallonie.be[634] portal is the source of information about Wallonia for French citizens and businesses. The ostbelgienlive.be[635] is another portal dedicated to the Germanspeaking Community. By 2021, all levels of government set up a new federal digital strategy - #SmartNation[636].

But, according to the European Commission's report, Belgium ranks last in terms of connectivity, showing that it has not made a lot of progress toward reaching the Digital Decade targets[637]. The country has largely completed coverage of NGA(Next Generation Access) networks and performs better than the EU average. However, the rollout of Very High Capacity Networks (VHCN)[638] has progressed slowly, with coverage reaching only 69% of households. This is below the EU average. On the other hand, according to the European Commission, the country ranks 13th of the 27 EU countries on human capital. The chronic lack of ICT graduates in Belgium hasn't improved since 2016. According to one study by Agoria[639], digital Belgium will need 600,000 more IT profiles by 2030 to make up for this shortage. The different Belgian governments have their own measures to improve the population's basic digital skills and foster digital inclusion. For example, at the federal level, the Digital Belgium Skills Fund (DBSF)[640] focuses on developing the digital skills of socially vulnerable children, teens and young adults.

Where to focus?

While people in Belgium have taken up digital administration, more intense coordination between different levels of government is required to improve online services and digital skills through educational programs.

6. BOSNIA AND HERZEGOVINA

Digital Bosnia and Herzegovina remains the least developed in Europe

The journey of digital transformation in Bosnia and Herzegovina has bit been picking up momentum, with its full potential remains largely untapped. To build a public sector ready for the future, governments must undergo a process of reinvention. As of the EGDI Report 2024, Bosnia holds the 107th position out of 193 countries[641] or down by 11 places compared to 2022. It stands just ahead of Ghana or Kenya in the global ranking (!). The same thing can be said about its e-participation score, ranking it 78th or down by 6 places this year.

I believe the inaugural Digital Innovation Hubs Forum (DIH Forum)[642] held in Sarajevo in 2023 marked a significant step forward for digital governance in Bosnia and Herzegovina. It provided a unique platform for all digital innovation centres to showcase their activities in Sarajevo. Also, the European Union's Digital Agenda for the Western Balkans[643] is accelerating efforts in Bosnia and Herzegovina as well as the entire region.

Yet, the level of digitalisation in the public sectors in Bosnia and Herzegovina can be higher. Despite some progress in recent years, particularly in the development of regulations for digital transformation (such as laws on administrative procedures, e-signatures, e-documents, and e-commerce), the existing legislation remains fragmented and incomplete. The limited, scattered, unharmonised, and (sometimes) incompatible nature of e-services in Bosnia and Herzegovina is another area of concern. While there are various "stand-alone" e-services, such as those for issuing residence permits, passports, driving licences, identity cards, and handling tax contributions, the siloed approach to digitisation poses obstacles to their consolidation and interconnectedness. I believe this fragmented service delivery process also hampers the future development of a fully integrated e-service system.

Where to focus?

A relevant and logical approach would be the establishment of a centralised virtual or physical management space. This would support the comprehensive design and delivery of e-services, particularly considering the complex governance structure in Bosnia and Herzegovina.

7. BULGARIA

Digital Bulgaria's growth rate is not sufficient to catch up with other EU states.

Bulgaria initiated its e-government journey two decades ago, concentrating on building and enhancing infrastructure and key systems. However, early on, it became evident that there was a need for better coordination between the overall policy for providing administrative services and those delivered electronically. Despite having a regulatory framework that could accommodate e-government, it wasn't encouraging its growth.

In the recent European Commission Digital Economy and Society Index (DESI) for 2022, Bulgaria finds itself in the 26th position[644] among the 27 EU Member States, which is somewhat.... Middling. Even though Bulgaria's DESI score has been growing by an average of 9% annually over the past five years, this rate of progress isn't quite enough for the country to catch up with the other EU Member States (given its current ranking.) However, on a more global scale, the EGDI report paints a slightly different picture[645], placing Bulgaria at the 55th position out of the 193 countries covered..just ahead of Belgium and Malaysia. The 'Digital Bulgaria 2025'[646] National Programme and the roadmap[647] for its implementation are very important for steering Bulgaria towards a digitally empowered future. This program has a clear objective: to modernise the integration of intelligent IT solutions across all aspects of the economy and social life.

The country falls significantly below the EU average, scoring 32.6 compared to the EU average of 45.7 (according to the Digital Decade 2023 report.)[648] The proportion of individuals with basic and above-basic digital skills is notably *lower* than the EU average, especially in the latter category (8% in Bulgaria versus the EU average of 26%). There's also a shortage of ICT specialists in Bulgaria, which is 3.8% of total employment and below the EU average of 4.6%. However, looking ahead to the EU's ambitious target of having 80% of adults with basic digital skills[649] by 2030, Bulgaria needs to step up its efforts. Shifting the focus to connectivity, Bulgaria performs very well in fibre-to-premises coverage, reaching 85% of households compared to the EU's 50%. However, both fixed and mobile broadband take-up is low.

Where to focus?

To overcome the shortcomings, there needs to be a continued, sustained effort at the political and administrative levels. However, I think that political instability may significantly affect attempts in this area (as it has done before).

8. CROATIA

Digital Croatia has seen some major progress these past years

Croatia first adopted the Law on the State Information Infrastructure[650] in 2014. It introduced the communication of public institutions with citizens via a Stateissued mailbox — a national identification and authentication, creating the preconditions for the "paperless government" project. In 2017, the new Decree on Organisational and Technical Standards for Connecting to the National Information Infrastructure[651] was adopted.

Then, in June 2019, the Decree on The Provision and Use of Trust Services[652] was published, laying down the measures and the forms of protection of electronic trust services. The size of the ICT market in terms of percentage contribution to GDP is around 4%, according to the World Bank report[653], which is comparable to the overwhelming majority of EU countries fall. What's more, Croatia's 20212030 Development Strategy[654] recognises the digital transition of society and the economy as a strategic objective. It has taken several steps to provide more digital access to the public administration, especially through the eID notification platform. Now, Croatian citizens can log into public e-services in the other EU Member States using their Croatian Electronic Identity Card (eOI)[655]. The National Healthcare Information System (CEZIH)[656] offers eBooking, ePrescription, eRefferal, Electronic Health Record, eSickLeave, and many other similar services for employers. Currently, less than 2% of all prescriptions are issued on paper[657]. Croatia was among the first EU countries to start the implementation of crossborder services and access to patient data by physicians in other EU countries.

But, although the Croatian regulatory framework is fully aligned with the EU frameworks, it fails to harmonise different and specific laws[658]. Moreover, according to the five categories compiled by DESI (Digital Economy and Society Index), digital Croatia underperforms compared to both EU and peer group averages[659] in terms of connectivity and digital public services. It ranked 21st of 27 EU Member States in the 2022 edition of the DESI Index. What's more, according to the EDGI (E-Government Development Index) index, digital Croatia improved its global ranking in 2024 by 12 places in e-governance and by 14 places in e-participation compared to 2022[660]. Meanwhile it moved up among the European countries, holding the 17th position compared to the 28th it held in 2022.

Where to focus?

It needs to focus more on improving its technology and infrastructure so as to catch up with the regional average.

9. CZECHIA

Lack of digital technology hindering digitalisation efforts

In the past few years, digital Czech Republic has been trying to digitalise its economy, with some solid progress in some areas. However, the lack of integration in digital technology has been hampering its growth, according to the European Commission experts[661]. Obviously, it has made relatively solid progress in the overall DESI score since 2017, which improved at a marginally higher pace than the score of the Union as a whole. It ranked 19th among the 27 EU Member States in the 2022 edition of the Digital Economy and Society Index (DESI)[662]. *(For comparison, the country ranked 18th one year before.)*

In the Human capital dimension, Czechia ranks 15th of the 27 EU. 60% of Czechs have at least basic digital skills, which is well above the 54% of the EU average. Its connectivity reforms were translated into some improvements in the country's performance in connectivity. Some of these reforms include the 'Strategy on the Implementation and Development of 5G Networks in the digital Czech Republic'[663] and the 'National Plan for the Very High Capacity Networks Development'[664]. But, while the share of e-government users has grown significantly to 76% and is now well above the EU average (65%), the lack of ICT specialists is one of Czechia's biggest obstacles to digitalisation. According to Eurostat,[665] 76% of Czech enterprises have reported difficulties in hiring ICT specialists. To put it into perspective, the EU average is only 55%. A survey shows that the economy can absorb an additional 14,000 ICT specialists. To overcome this problem, the central Digital Czech Republic strategy[666] and the Education strategy 2030+[667] are the most critical documents the government has issued to coordinate actions and policies on human capital. Moreover, The Czech

National Coalition for digital skills and jobs (DigiKoalice)[668] is an active partnership focusing on education.

According to the DESI index, Czechia ranks 19th out of 27 EU countries in the Integration of digital technology dimension — four positions below its 2021 ranking. The proportion of SMEs with at least a basic level of digital intensity is 2% lower than the EU average (55%). That being said, Czechia is still far from the Digital Decade target[669] of at least 75% of enterprises using cloud computing, AI or big data. Also, in the global scene, it has fallen behind both in e-governance and e-participation rankings.

Where to focus?

In order to move closer to its targets, it needs to increase the proportion of companies that use advanced digital technologies, train more ICT specialists and ensure cross-border interoperability of digital public services.

10. CYPRUS

Government initiatives are a work in progress

The Digital Strategy for Cyprus[670] was approved by the Council of Ministers on 8 February 2012. It was a comprehensive plan for 2012-2020 with a holistic approach to developing the information society in Cyprus. Based on the Digital Agenda for Europe[671], the stated overall vision of this strategy was to provide *"information and communication technologies to support the development of the economy and citizen participation in the social and political domains."* A great focus of the government was improving its citizens' e-skills. That's why the digital Cyprus Productivity Centre[672], in association with the Department of Electronic Communications[673], launched a strategic initiative to improve digital literacy and further promote eGovernment services. Moreover, the government has paid special attention to AI and blockchain development in the country. For instance, the "Research and Innovation Strategy Framework (2019-2023)"[674], "the Artificial Intelligence Strategy Report," and the "National Strategy for Distributed Ledger Technology (DLT).[675]"

According to the DESI index, in 2021, digital Cyprus showed significant improvement in most categories. Overall, Cyprus ranks 20th out of 27 EU Member States in the 2022 edition of the Digital Economy and Society Index[676], with the most progress made in connectivity. So, Cyprus ranks *above* the EU average on mobile broadband take-up, improving its coverage of Very High Capacity Networks (VHCN) and 5G readiness. However, disappointingly, Cyprus ranked 23rd in the EU on Human Capital, which is below the EU average. This means that, compared to the other EU Member States, there aren't enough ICT specialists in the country. That's why, during 2023-2025[677], the country plans to make over 460 training programs for everyone covering several areas of use of smart devices, e-government services, digital marketing, etc.). Also, the level of online interaction between public authorities and the general public is below the EU average[678]. Only 59% of Cypriot internet users *actively* engage in using e-government services.

Where to focus

The government should integrate digital skills into the educational curricula to fit the industry's needs. Also, it still has room for improvement regarding interaction with the general population.

11. DENMARK

NemID is the key to a successful digital Denmark.

Denmark is the absolute global leader in digital public services, with high levels of interaction between citizens and all levels of government. According to the UN's 2024 EGDI report[679], digital Denmark has held the top position since 2018, showcasing its sustained leadership in this area. It holds first place according to the Economist Impact's Digital Cities Index[680] in 2022, too. Denmark has a remarkable track record in government digital transformation, setting clear goals for over 20 years. They continuously update their digital strategy through the Agency for Digital Government[681], releasing new reports every 4 years. Also, this year it is the second best country in the world when it comes to e-participation ..up from the 12 place it held in 2022 (according to the EGDI report.)

One remarkable aspect worth mentioning is Denmark's e-identification solution, NemID (or easyID). Initially introduced after a pilot project for digital signatures in 1999, NemID started with a less convenient two-factor authentication system, requiring a physical key card for identity verification. With just one identity number and log-in code, Danish people can access nearly all digital services, making it a widely used and effective system.

With approximately 95% of the Danish population[682] using NemID, it's evident that this digital ID solution plays a significant role in the country's digital landscape. Moreover, the '*borger. dk*' portal stands as a great example of seamlessly integrating services from central, regional, and local authorities into a single platform. The portal is linked to the Danish eID solution, providing a secure digital mailbox for citizens to communicate with central and local government bodies.

Remarkably, over three-quarters of government organisations[683] allow users to receive correspondence via email.

Something that's worth mentioning about Denmark that not many other countries have is this: different governmental levels have similar levels of digitalisation. Interestingly, digital Denmark even tends to offer slightly more online services at regional or local levels compared to central government services.

Where to focus?

The only goal Denmark can have at this moment is to become the world's leader in e-participation too.

12. ESTONIA

In digital Estonia, the phrase 'small but mighty' resonates with their transformation.

In the 2023 eGovernment Benchmark[684], there were two names mentioned as leaders. One of them was digital Estonia. Of course, this is no surprise to those who have followed Estonia's digital government journey. In 2024, Estonia became the second-best country in the *world* in e-governance, up by 6 places compared to 2022. I've been a long-time admirer of Estonia's digital government[685] initiatives, and it's a nation that consistently impresses me.

Digital Estonia, also known as E-stonia, has been making headlines again with its cutting-edge tech advancements. Back in 1996, the Tiger Leap Foundation[686] (supported by the government) kickstarted Estonia's tech journey. With a population just shy of 1.4 million, Estonia can be compared to some cities in larger countries. Yet, in terms of its transition to a digital economy, it stands as a true giant.

It's small...but mighty. Estonia is like a digital powerhouse despite its small size.

They have more new tech companies per person than any other European country, and they're also the top in Europe when it comes to investing money in tech projects per person. No wonder Estonians have founded several "unicorns"[687] – startups that have grown to over 7 billion dollars in value[688]. Also, recently, Estonia's public sector has taken a strong interest in making its tech more eco-friendly across different (think agriculture, manufacturing, and services.) This focus actually began last year (2022) when the Ministry of Economic Affairs and Communications commissioned an analysis by Ernst & Young[689] to assess the environmental impact of various ICT aspects in the public sector.

Here are some statistics about Estonia's digital government. I got all the facts and figures mentioned here on their website[690].

- One of the strongest digital ID since 2002
- 100,000 e-residents (services given to every world citizen by the Estonian government)
- First state ever to use blockchain technology.
- The first and (still) the only country in the world to introduce i-voting since 2005 (voting online, which is optional, of course)
- 98% of income taxes are declared online (with pre-filled forms, I might add)

Estonia has long been hailed as a pioneer in digital governance, and their forwardthinking vision, as encapsulated in the *Digital Agenda 2030*[691] released in 2021, truly underscores this reputation. Currently, Estonia boasts over 100 AI initiatives[692] within its public sector.

One of the most impressive initiatives, in my opinion, is *Bürokratt* often dubbed Estonia's 'Siri' [693].As their website at e-estonia.com[694] proudly states, "We have built a digital society, and we can show you how." For that, Estonia provides various resources to help other countries achieve what they have.

Where to focus?

Estonia's internet penetration rate stood at only 93.7 % of the total population at the start of 2024 so I believe that that should be a key focus of the government - further improving its connectivity.

13. FINLAND

Has slightly been falling behind

Digital Finland has a proactive approach to digital advancement is evident in several ways. They were one of the first EU countries to make a national AI strategy about artificial intelligence back in 2017. They wanted Finland to be the best in digital governance. And guess what? They're aiming to rule the metaverse world by 2035![695] For that, they outlined a detailed strategy called 'Metaverse Initiative by the Finnish Ecosystem: Virtual Potential into Real-World Impact.'[696] And they've done a wonderful job, as seen by different international reports. The Finnish government's dedication to digital leadership is evident, reflected in the country's top ranking in the 2022 Digital Economy and Society Index (DESI)[697] among EU Member States. Finland particularly excels in indicators measuring human capital related to digital skills. They've come up with what they've called 'A Digital Compass.'[698] To make this happen, they're aiming for innovative businesses (of course) but with a huge focus on top-notch education and digital skills.

What sets digital Finland apart is its high percentage of employed individuals working in ICT (Information and Communications Technology) roles, surpassing the EU average (7.4% against 4.5%.) Around 79% of the people there have a good grasp of basic digital skills, way more than the average in the EU[699], which is only about 54%. All former and current Prime Ministers have had digitalisation high on their government programs. One of the key moments was presenting the report' Productive and innovative digital Finland — digital agenda for 2011– 2020"[700] to the parliament. It defined future objectives for the development of the information society to promote growth and productivity.

The EU's plan (outlined in the Path to the Digital Decade)[701] sets an ambitious goal for 2030: ensuring at least 80% of citizens possess basic digital skills. Only Sweden and Finland have the highest percentage of people working in these tech jobs – Sweden with 8% and Finland with 7.4%. Also, a remarkable 82% of Finnish SMEs[702] showcase a basic level of digital intensity, indicating a strong embrace of digital tools and technologies. But despite that, Finland fell behind from second place in 2022 to 9th place in 2024 in e-governance. It also didn't manage to hold its position in e-participation...dropping from the 6th to the 19th position this year.

Where to focus?

The goal is clear: Finland wants to be at the forefront of the digital game, and they're doing and should continue to do some serious planning to make it a reality.

14. FRANCE

From being a leader to lagger?

French President Emmanuel Macron did not waste any time tackling the French government's digital transformation after his election on May 7th 2017. From the release of the digital roadmap to the large investment made in digital government innovation, the government was clearly serious about using technology to improve its efficiency and provide better services to French citizens. According to a report from the UN, France currently ranked only 12th out of the 28 countries[703] of the European Union (EU) in terms of integration of digital technology, which is a good ranking back in 2022. It also ranks 34th among 193 countries[704] of the world, a huge decline from the 19th place in 2022 or the 9th place it held back in 2018. All this has raised several questions about this digital transformation of France's government! A similar trend can be seen in the smaller EU scene, where France has dropped from 11th place to 20th place in the rankings this year.

The Public Action 2022[705] was the first to be presented, which set out actions in a concrete way. In September 2018 the National Strategy for an Inclusive Digital Society and the initiative Digital in Common[706] was launched, which aimed to train 1.5 million people in digital literacy to provide equal opportunities for everyone throughout the country. The actions under this French National Plan for Digital Inclusion were launched within the framework of the 2030 targets set by the European Commission's Digital Decade[707]. According to the EU report[708], France's position has worsened in the human capital dimension, mainly due to the low share of people with "above basic digital skills" and the connectivity dimension, remaining below the EU average.

Where to focus?

Generally speaking, digital tools used by most public institutions are not very user-friendly, and interactive online consultations do not work for many people. Overall, the digitalisation of administrative documents and procedures remains vastly unequal among different ministries, and some are falling behind.

15. GEORGIA

Digital Georgia "suffers" from underutilisation of public services

Digital Georgia shows promising signs of advancement in its digital infrastructure and capabilities. With *very high* levels of the Telecommunication Infrastructure Index (TII) and Human Capital Index (HCI), Georgia has achieved a commendable level of digital readiness. These factors contribute significantly to Georgia's very high level in the E-Government Development Index (EGDI)[709], indicating a strong foundation for digital governance and service delivery. In fact, in 2022, for the first time, Georgia moved to the higher EGDI levels[710]. Looking ahead, Georgia's ambition to become an ICT hub and digital corridor from Europe to Asia is a promising strategic direction outlined in the National Broadband Development Strategy of Georgia 2020–2025 (NBDS)[711] and Government Program for 2021– 2024 *Towards Building a European State*[712].

As I mentioned before, while infrastructure in digital Georgia is well-developed, gaps still exist in urban-rural connectivity. So, despite reaching 100% 4G coverage in 2022 (ITU data of Georgia)[713], there are areas, especially in rural regions, where access to high-speed internet remains limited. Initiatives like the *Universal Internetization program and, Log-in Georgia Project*[714], and *Login Georgia Project* are really important for addressing last-mile connectivity challenges AND bridging the geographic digital divide.

Yet, various studies and reports, show that there's an underutilisation of public services in digital Georgia. Many citizens may not even be aware of the existence of these services, let alone how to access and utilise them. This lack of awareness can be attributed to insufficient promotion and outreach efforts on the part of the government. Additionally, the design of digital government services often falls short in terms of user-friendliness. A user-centric approach is crucial for ensuring that services are intuitive and accessible to all citizens, regardless of their level of digital literacy. Without prioritising user experience, adoption rates are likely to remain low. In the UN's EGDI report[715], Georgia ranked 77th in 2024 in e-participation of citizens in designing and using public services.

Where to focus?

More continued efforts are needed to ensure that all citizens can fully benefit from the digital transformation.

16. GERMANY

Huge progress in a short time: 4th in the world for e-participation

The German government has lately focused on innovation & digital transformation of the public sector as the two most critical areas and top priorities. For this reason, it has created an e-government strategy for 2025[716] and has consolidated all IT/ Software systems at the federal level. Even though digital Germany is one of the largest economies in the world with the most prominent ICT Industry in Europe, this country has consistently been ranked in the low- to mid-field of digital government rankings…up until the 2024 UN report where it showed some huge progress.

According to DESI (the Digital Economy and Society Index)[717], back in 2022, digital Germany performed below many other European member states. As a result, it is 13th out of 28 countries. But, as the EU's largest economy, it could do better, and Germany's progress with digital transformation since then has been crucial. Not only for the country itself but also to enable the EU as a whole to reach its 2030 Digital Decade targets[718]. That's why in 2024, it finally managed to make the list of top performers in the EU, ranking 7th, up from the 14th place in 2022. The biggest improvement, though, is in its e-participation score. Germany jumped all the way from 32nd place to 4th place in the world! This is a huge leap, showing how much progress they've made.

What's more, is that a previous Eurostat statistic[719] revealed that German citizens were very hesitant to manage administrative acts with public authorities digitally. So, it's not only about the mere lack of innovative capacities or policies but also about the cultural barrier...which the country managed to overcome. Indeed, citizens were reluctant to use information technologies. The pandemic, however, forced many people's hands and in 2020, 54% of Internet users used digital administrative services for the first time. However, in recent years, many digital issues have gained political traction with the adoption of several key strategies, such as the Digital Strategy or the Gigabit Strategy. Which I believe was also the reason for such huge progress.

Where to focus?

It needs to continue doing what's working because it finally managed to resign its "EU's sleeping beauty" status.

17. GREECE

Digital Greece remains behind the EU average despite its initiatives

Digital Greece was one of the first countries in Europe to initiate large-scale digital transformation efforts and has been doing so for several years. However, according to recent data by the European Commission[720], Greece remains ranked behind other EU countries regarding connectivity infrastructures as well as digital skills. According to the EGDI Index[721], digital Greece has declined in its ranking among 193 countries from its 33rd place in 2022 to its 36th place in 2024. Also, it ranked 25th of 27 EU[722] states back in the 2022 edition of the Digital Economy and Society Index (DESI). This doesn't mean that there have not been any achievements. On the digitalisation of public services, in 2020, Greece scored above the EU average in the number of e-government users, while it far exceeds the EU average in open data readiness. And it also scores 99% in the 5G readiness indicator[723].

Yet, Greece consistently has ranked low on the DESI index (Economic and Society Index). The country has been significantly slower than the rest of EU in making fast broadband available to its citizens and digital government services. In 2020, digital Greece acted swiftly amid the COVID-19 crisis to make public services available online in time for its citizens. A unified government portal (gov.gr)[724] is currently providing more than 6000 different government services, which is widely used by the general public. Then in June 2021, Greece adopted the 2020-2025 'Digital Transformation Bible'[725], a new holistic digital strategy. Greece has also accelerated legislative reforms to create the right supporting framework conditions for implementing the new digital strategy. An example is the adoption of the Code of Digital

Governance[726] on 22 September 2020. As for digital skills, digital Greece has made slight progress in 2023, but it still remains below the EU average. However, only 51% of the citizens have basic digital skills, and according to the European Commission[727], the progress has been slow. The share of employed ICT specialists remains low in 2020 (2%) compared to the EU average (4.3%).

Where to focus?

Looking forward, digital tools will be leveraged to expand access to public information and make it easier for citizens to engage with public agencies online.

18. HUNGARY

Hungary is struggling in the online service provisions front

Digital Hungary has grown increasingly popular over the last decade or so, with more and more citizens choosing to interact with their government through the Internet instead of in person. However, as demand for services increases, so does the pressure on Hungary's digital government to deliver its services effectively and efficiently – not an easy feat when faced with limited resources. According to the DESI report[728], it remains a leader in broadband connectivity, as 22% of households subscribed to such a service in 2021 (compared with 7.6% in the EU.) Also, according to the Digital Decade Report 2023[729], its broadband connectivity

(70%) is above the EU average (55%.) Kepio's[730] analysis indicates that internet penetration rate in Hungary in 2024 was 91.8%.

Additionally, the country scores above the EU average on *Overall fixed broadband take-up*, *5G*, and *Fixed very high capacity network coverage*. This is also important in light of the Digital Decade target[731] to achieve 100% coverage of all households of gigabit networks by 2030. Regarding digital policies, the National Digitalisation Strategy 2021-2030[732] provides the strategic policy framework for this period. However, Hungary is giving mixed signals regarding public services. It ranked 22nd out of the 27 EU States[733] in the DESI 2022 report. The progress is not bad, as it has moved in line with the rest of the EU, but there is still room for development.

Meanwhile, in the 2024 EGDI report, it is evident that it has fallen behind both in e-governance and e-participation.

Where to focus?

Hungary needs to pay close attention to increasing the number of ICT specialists and the digital skills of its citizens. With a solid foundation in place, it should focus on further developing its online services and increasing citizen participation.

19. ICELAND

Fifth top performer in the world (2024 report)

Many countries have succeeded in digital governance, but replicating their success isn't straightforward because each country is different. After all, if it were easy, every country would be at the same level. Digital Iceland (it seems) has mastered the art of harnessing the best of technological expertise while fostering collaboration with a diverse array of private sector innovators from several companies and/or countries. According to the UN's annual digital government assessment, the eGovernment Development Index[734], Digital Iceland is ranked fifth globally (out of 193 countries). This is up from the country's 12th-place ranking in 2020.

Iceland's digital infrastructure has two elements. One is the creation of an 'e-ID' that citizens use as a digital signature to access different public services, with more than 90% of adults having one. The second is digitising documents and services used to prove who someone is, such as driving licences - used by more than 50% of the population. According to European Commission's Benchmark report[735], Iceland is one of Europe's eID frontrunner. Also, for those who don't know, the country was recognised as 4th place in Europe for digital innovation in the European Commission's eGovernment Benchmark 2022[736].

A cornerstone of Iceland's digital governance triumph lies in its astute approach to building upon existing solutions. They've not only borrowed concepts that have worked in other countries but have also tailored these concepts to fit seamlessly into their unique national context...helping it become the 5th country in the world and third in Europe in e-governance. Another important step in building momentum in Digital Iceland is shining a light on all the agencies (including private companies) that have done excellent work. Iceland holds a yearly conference for the local community where they share success stories, products, and their strategy. This conference is crucial for growing their movement, and it is an approach I don't see many countries practice. Iceland manages to use digital technologies to stimulate citizen engagement and policy participation[737]. That's how it managed to improve its global e-participaton ranking by 10 places in 2 years (ranking 7th in the world).

Where to focus?

Iceland is doing amazing, improving its strategies each year, so it should keep focusing on using that same momentum to move forward.

20. IRELAND

The promising digital economy of e-Ireland in Europe

Ireland currently holds a strong position overall when it comes to the digital economy in the European region. That's how Ireland has managed to rank 5th among the other 27 EU Member States in the 2022 edition of the Digital Economy and Society Index (DESI)[738]. The average yearly relative growth of its DESI score in the last five years is approximately 8.5%, one of the highest in the EU.

The country has one of the highest ICT specialists (including females), well above the EU average. It ranks 6th in digital public services. In 2022, the share of e-government users increased remarkably from 67% to 92%, according to the report. The country continued to review and improve the user-friendliness and quality of the public services provided by the government services portal 'Gov. ie.[739]' In the 2023 Digital Decade report[740], e-Ireland has shown a high level of digital skills, proving the potential to improve further its performance in digital infrastructure and the digitalisation of businesses

What's more, Ireland has set a highly ambitious target of 100% online provision of critical public services. It also aims to ensure that by 2030, 90% of these services are actually used online, and more than 80% of its eligible citizens[741] are using its MyGovID solution[742]. Having 80% digital ID coverage is a target set by the European Union[743]. The onset of subsections of the Data Sharing and Governance Act 2019[744] in 2021 enabled the creation of The Data Governance Board[745]. Following the announcement of the development of a new National Digital Strategy two years ago, the government launched the new national digital strategy, Harnessing Digital – The Digital Ireland Framework[746], in

February 2022. Then, one month later, the country published the Connecting Government 2030[747] in March 2022, setting out an approach to deliver digital government for all. This is how Ireland was able to improve its e-participation ranking by 32 spots in just two years, and also boost its e-governance ranking by 10 spots during the same period. It's a huge leap, showing real progress in both areas.

Where to focus?

It needs to ensure complete interoperability across all levels of government and across all public services. Moving forward, it's important that when digitalising public services, it implements and follows a user-first and business-first approach.

21. ITALY

Is digital Italy moving.. backwards?

While the country has been embracing digital government and technology on multiple levels, it has fallen behind considerably in just 2 years. It has tried various options for digitally transforming the public sector. Different governments introduced several types of governance throughout the years, but, unfortunately, the situation has not improved as much as it was expected.

In September 2016, Diego Piacetini, the Italian Government's High Commissioner for the Digital Agenda, was appointed by the President of the Council of Ministers to lead and relaunch the "Digital Agenda" implementation. During this time, the Digital Transformation Team, supervised by the same commissioner, was also launched. Later on, important strategies were introduced, such as the *20142020 Strategy for Digital Growth*[748], the *Ultra-Wideband Plan and the National Broadband Strategy.* The Italia Login project[749], which stems from the abovementioned projects, seeked to build the so-called *Citizens House*. Then in 2019, there was a heightened focus at the political level on boosting the digitisation of the Italian economy and society. The latest project is the 2025 National Innovation Plan[750], which includes 20 main digitalisation actions to be put in place by 2025, trying at the same time to promote more democracy, ethics and inclusion.

However, despite these strategies, there are still disparities in the growth and geographical distribution of digital transformation. According to the 2022 DESI Index, Italy ranks 25th out of 28 EU[751] Members, despite data (before the pandemic) showing that the country had a good ranking in terms of 5G preparedness. Meanwhile, according to the EGDI index, Italy ranks 51st out of 193 countries[752] in e-governance and has fallen behind by 14 places compared to 2022.

What's even worse is that its e-participation score places it 29 spots lower than 2 years ago (in the 61st place.) Although the country ranks relatively high in its offer of e-government services, public take-up remains low. There are significant human capital gaps because digital Italy records very low basic and advanced digital skills levels compared to the EU average.

Where to focus?

If Italy wants to deliver citizen-driven services, it needs to transform its technological systems to overcome its analogue structures. Like many other countries, it is faced with an outdated legacy that doesn't allow for interoperability, and that has, until today, limited itself to translating processes created for an analogue bureaucracy.

22. KOSOVO

From high connectivity to a push for enhanced services

Kosovo has made significant progress in digital reforms, particularly in achieving one of the highest levels of connectivity in Europe. However, the challenge lies in translating these advances into *tangible* improvements in service delivery for both citizens and businesses. After gaining independence from Serbia, the Kosovo government (alongside some serious donor organisations) aimed to replicate Western experiences. Unfortunately, this approach led to the emergence of various platforms that faced challenges. These hurdles included a lack of sustainability, difficulties in adapting to the local context, and a lack of design thinking and user-centricity.

Then again, Kosovo has made great progress in achieving connectivity for everyone through its five-year Kosovo Digital Economy Project (KODE)[753], which kicked off in 2018 with support from the World Bank. The results were impressive, with nearly everyone in Kosovo using the internet by 2023 and the country boasting one of the highest subscriber rates for fixed broadband services in Europe. What's interesting is that this access wasn't concentrated in just a few areas – it was spread out evenly across the whole country, making Kosovo a leader in internet penetration in the Western Balkans[754].

They've also made progress in digitising its public sector. For instance, e-Participimi[755] fosters direct communication between citizens and parliament members, enhancing public-private dialogue. Meanwhile, E-Kosova[756], a statewide portal, facilitates electronic access to public services like health, taxes, and police. But, according to UNDP findings[757], a large number of Kosovars lack digital skills beyond basic social communication and internet surfing. While the Digital Skills Programme Bootcamps[758], launched in 2022 with the support of UNDP and GIZ, are a step in the right direction, there's a need for more concrete action. It's essential to integrate comprehensive ICT education programs into earlier stages of education, ensuring that people are equipped with the necessary digital skills from the beginning. On the other hand, I think UNDP's involvement in consultations for the Digital Agenda 2030[759] and input in the E-Government Strategy 2023–2027 are crucial.

Where to focus?

As Kosovo navigates its digital landscape, continued collaboration, investment in education, and a user-centric approach will be key to ensuring that the benefits of digitalisation reach every corner of society.

23. LATVIA

Not much has improved in 2 years

I've been observing Latvia's digital performance, and it's been quite impressive, particularly in fixed connectivity and digital public services. According to the EGDI report[760], Latvia hasn't made any leap forward in e-governance, still holding the 29th place in the global ranking. Also, Latvia moved from the 29th place to the 37th in e-participation, indicating a decline in engagement with digital initiatives. However, Latvia surpasses the EU average in the use of prefilled forms, streamlining processes for citizens and businesses.

Also, the country's Digital Transformation guidelines[761] for 2021-2027 serve as an important strategy for Latvia's digital evolution. Which has helped it stand out as a leading Member State in the digitalisation of public services. The country not only performs above the EU average in this area but *excels* at acquiring and providing innovative digital services. It has high level of digitalisation in public services for both individuals and businesses in Latvia. An impressive 77% of internet users in the country[762] utilise e-government services (for comparison, the EU average is 74%.)

The E-Government Benchmark 2023[763] paints a consistently positive picture for Latvia. The country exceeds the EU average in all dimensions. 91% of all services are online (compared to the EU average of 84%.) Something that's worth noting is that all government platforms disclose if personal data was used (a level of transparency that far exceeds the EU average of below 50%.) And 67% of e-services are available cross-border, ranking Latvia 6th out of 27 EU countries in this aspect. It is actively fostering citizen and business interaction with public administrations by participating in the GovTech consortia called 'The incubator for knowledge sharing and collaborative delivery for all GovTech initiatives in the EU (GovTech4all)'[764].

Where to focus?

In my assessment, while a significant portion of Latvians already utilise e-Government services, there's untapped potential to enhance the appeal of public services, especially for those who don't use them regularly. I believe Latvia should expedite its efforts in the digitalisation of public services. Also, ongoing improvements in accessibility and functionality will contribute to a more inclusive and user-centric approach to e-government services in Latvia.

24. LIECHTENSTEIN

Liechtenstein is losing ground despite having a solid foundation in place

Liechtenstein, this tiny country with around 40,000 people, situated between Switzerland and Austria, ranks 44th in the world according to the e-government survey[765]. Additionally, the country performs amazingly well in terms of public services inclusion and accessibility, surpassing the EU average.

Liechtenstein's eGovernment Strategy 2019-2023[766] was built upon insights gained from a decade-old strategy. The government's vision involves enhancing access to administrative services for citizens and streamlining business transactions. Also, the Digital-Liechtenstein[767] initiative brought together over 50 companies and organisations to position Liechtenstein as a leading digital business location. The subsequent Digital Roadmap, created in 2019, outlines the comprehensive plan for digitising society.

Looking at the EGDI report[768], it's pretty clear that Liechtenstein has been falling behind. In 2024, they are in the 44th spot out of 193 countries, a noticeable decline from their 25th place in just two years. However, not all hope is lost as it has seen some kind of achievement in e-participation. In 2022, they were holding down the 67th spot, and in 2022, they've moved up to the 61th place. This shows that even though Liechtenstein is lagging behind in improving its e-governance, it's doing really well in getting its people involved in the process. The country is putting a lot of effort into making sure citizens can actively participate, which is paying off.

Where to focus?

While Liechtenstein boasts excellent digital infrastructure and a strong emphasis on human capital, there's a crucial area that requires focused attention— improving online service provision. Investing in optimising online service provision aligns with the country's commitment to efficiency and accessibility in digital governance. It should place a greater emphasis on evaluating the effectiveness and efficiency of interoperability solutions and technology options. This involves considering user needs, maintaining proportionality, and finding a balance between costs and benefits.

25. LITHUANIA

GovTech Lab Lithuania: Encouraging innovative solutions for the government

The Baltic nation has made great progress as well in using digital technologies to enhance the efficiency and accessibility of public services. That's how it has been positioned at the forefront of e-governance, earning it recognition on the global stage....As reflected in its impressive overall maturity score of 85 points (out of 100 points in total) in the E-government Benchmark 2023 report[769]. This places Lithuania in the 7th position out of the 35 countries surveyed.

In 2023, they included a project to modernise the state information platform (Electronic Government Gateway)[770] by enabling users to do an advanced search for information on public and administrative services. *(This reform is expected to be completed by 2026.)* GovTech Lab Lithuania[771] is an inspiring example of how the public sector can drive innovation. It has won multiple public-sector innovation awards and in 2022, it was named one of the top three GovTech initiatives in the world. GovTech Lab is its flagship program, the GovTech Challenge Series[772]. Arune Matelyte, who is the manager and Co-founder of GovTech Lab Lithuania, has said that a trip to Edinburgh's CivTech office[773] in 2020 set her team on its current trajectory. And that it was that collaboration and cooperation that could help a country move forward at a faster pace. Regarding its progress, the E-Government Development Index[774], published by the United Nations, really shows this change…especially in e-participation where it moved up by 38 places. What's even more impressive is Lithuania's performance in the GovTech Maturity Index[775] published by the World Bank. In 2020, they were ranked 39th, but by 2022, they had moved up to 8th place. Their rating of 0.981 out of 1.0 is quite remarkable, especially when you consider that the world average is 0.522 and the European average is 0.698. I'd say this shows how quickly and effectively Lithuania has enhanced its public services digitalisation maturity. The European Commission E-Government Benchmark[776] also highlights Lithuania's achievements. They are ranked 8th out of 35 countries in Europe. They are praised for their use of eID and pre-filled forms, which make accessing services much easier for citizens. These improvements not only streamline processes but also demonstrate how the country values efficiency and user-friendliness in public services.

Where to focus?

By investing in such initiatives such as the GovTech Lab Lithuania and creating conducive environments for innovation, governments can not only solve current issues but also future-proof their operations.

26. LUXEMBOURG

Luxembourg: Needs to put more efforts in engaging citizens

The country's digital transformation has had some pretty positive ripple effects, especially in innovation with data centres and digital administration. Not to mention, they've increased their workforce skills. Over the past few years, the digital scene has become quite a hot topic in Luxembourg's political circles. One noteworthy aspect is the high satisfaction with public services, surpassing the OECD average[777] across various service categories.

This satisfaction not only reflects effective governance but also correlates with increased compliance with policies, heightened participation in public life, and enhanced social cohesion. Luxembourg also secured a great position in international rankings, notably ranking 8th out of 27 EU Member States in the 2022 Digital Economy and Society Index (DESI)[778]. While the country boasts a higher-than-average share of ICT specialists and graduates, a shortage in this skilled workforce poses a potential challenge to the full digitalisation of Luxembourg's economy.

Also, according to the eGovernment Benchmark 2023 Insight Report[779] (which assesses 34 EU countries), Luxembourg emerges as one of the top three leaders, securing an impressive 89 out of 100 points, following in the footsteps of Malta and Estonia.

2023 key figures of Luxembourg's digital governance (the latest available report comparing only the EU countries)

- 95% of services in Luxembourg are available online, surpassing the EU average of 84%.
- About 64% of the population in Luxembourg possesses basic digital skills (which is notably above the EU average of 54%.)
- An impressive 100% of all government platforms in Luxembourg transparently communicate whether personal data is used when accessing a service. This is in stark contrast to the EU average of 56%.
- An impressive 91% of internet users in Luxembourg engage with e-government services, surpassing the EU average of 74%.
- Luxembourg takes the lead by making 91% of its services available for cross-border usage, ranking *first* among the 34 EU states assessed.
- Luxembourg secures the 3rd position among the 34 EU states in transparency concerning service delivery, design, and personal data.
- Luxembourg earns its place as one of the EU's best performers in digital infrastructure.

But in the 2024 EGDI report, things don't seem this bright. Luxembourg has fallen behind by 19 and 43(!) places in e-governance and e-participation respectively. *(Fun fact: since the 2020 EGDI report, it has always been behind Liechtenstein for some reason.)*

Where to focus?

Once a leader in the EU, it seems to have fallen quite behind, so it needs to put more strategic efforts into its human capital and the provision of online services.

27. MALTA

Is not in the top 10 performers list of Europe anymore

Malta earned its title as the digital leader of Europe, as indicated by its remarkable performance in the eGovernment Benchmark 2023[780]. This report evaluated the digitalisation of public services across 35 European countries) where Malta emerged as the standout performer in 2023, securing an impressive total score of 96 out of 100 points. But, in the recent (2024) EGDI report, Malta ranked 28th globally out of 193 countries[781], falling behind by 13 places in just 2 years. Meanwhile, the improvement in the e-participation index that Malta managed to achieve in 2022, was undone this year as the small nation fell from the 22nd place to the 44th.

While it improved its telecommunication infrastructure, it has been lacking in the human capital and the online service provision. Which is a shame since in 2023, in Europe, where 84% of government services can be completed fully online, Malta took the lead alongside Denmark by providing a remarkable 100% of its services online to national users. One notable aspect contributing to Malta's digital success has bee user convenience, having 90% of its services accepting eID login. Malta's groundbreaking transparency initiatives deserve recognition. Being the first country to offer users[782] insights into how their personal data is a huge commitment to transparency and citizen engagement. Also, with an impressive 96% of services available for cross-border users, Malta has always exemplified a commitment to inclusivity and accessibility in digital governance. Also this not only has helped enhance the user experience for non-nationals but also has positioned Malta as a model for effective cross-border digital service delivery...despite all the setback it has seen recently.

Where to focus?

I believe Malta is not heading in the right direction with their digital transformation. Even though the launch of the Malta Diġitali Strategy 2022-2027[783] was supposed to help. They should be working on coordinating digital policies more efficiently. A key aspect of Malta's strategy should involve enhancing cooperation with industry and civil society to continually assess and adjust education and training programs according to evolving labour market needs.

28. MOLDOVA

Digital government of Moldova finally moved up to the very high EGDI group

Moldova, this landlocked country located in Eastern Europe, bordered by Ukraine and Romania to the west, gained independence from the Soviet Union in 1991. Since then, it has faced economic challenges and political complexities, especially when dealing with digitalisation. I think Moldova is doing well in terms of e-government, falling into the *very* high EGDI group[784] according to the 2024 e-government survey…ranking 70th out of 193 countries. In the past four years, it has improved its ranking by 9 places. Even though Moldova has had a less developed infrastructure compared to the rest of Europe, it has finally stood out with a strong performance in the human capital index.

However, challenges persist, with reported gaps in ICT skills and low levels of digital literacy. The accessibility of digital public services[785] varies among socioeconomic groups, highlighting disparities in quality and affordability, especially between richer and poorer households. According to an OECD report[786], less than 17% of these SMEs have successfully integrated digital tools into their operations. I believe this might be due to ongoing skill shortages and mismatches. In response to these challenges, Moldova has taken proactive steps since 2021, introducing key digital solutions to catalyse the transformation of public services. These include the MobiSign digital signature/identity application and the MWallet digital wallet, both developed with the support of UNDP[787].

Also, while the legal framework *is* there it needs to be solidified. A crucial development for Moldova is the approval of the 2023-2030 Strategy for Digital Transformation[788]. This strategic plan, given the green light in September of last year (2023), outlines Moldova's vision for the next 7 years. Experts from U4Digital, along with various stakeholders, international donors, associations, and both public and private institutions, collaborated in extensive consultations to shape this strategy[789]. I believe this collective effort reflects the Moldovan government's commitment to creating a digital future for the country.

Where to focus?

Moldova needs to keep pushing legislative reforms to fully support the digitalisation of public services. There should be a stronger focus on enhancing digital public services.

29. MONACO

Must improve online services to match digital infrastructure success

Monaco is a small sovereign city and state located on the French Riviera, known for its luxury, casinos, and as a tax haven. However it is also quite advanced in government technology and human capital, according to the E-government 2024 report[790]. The Principality is leveraging cutting-edge technologies[791] (like big data analytics) to shape its smart city strategy. An urban hyper-vision system plays a crucial role in efficiently monitoring and managing various municipal functions, ensuring optimal urban governance. Even though it must be said that Monaco has left its best days behind..in 2018 to be exact). Since then it has continuously failed to make progress or at least keep up with other neighbouring peers.

Extended Monaco Programme[792] (initiated in April 2019 by HSH Prince Albert II) reflects a solid approach to leveraging digital technology for societal *and* economic transformation. It simplifies many processes, like obtaining a residence card or applying for government housing, by allowing them to be completed online using a digital identity or signature. Monaco has a great, top-notch digital infrastructure. A staggering 97% of the population were internet users in 2022, reflecting widespread digital connectivity.

An early adopter of 5G in 2019 (the first in Europe[793], to be precise), Monaco is not anymore the lead in digital innovation. However, the introduction of Monaco Cloud[794], developed in collaboration with Amazon and Dell but operated by a local Monégasque company, is a great achievement. In 2023, Monaco took a huge step forward by adopting a VMware Sovereign Cloud facilitated by Monaco Cloud[795].

This strategic move not only enhances data security and confidentiality but also accelerates the realisation of Monaco's digital service goals. Moreover, since 2018 (as part of the Extended Monaco program) the government has been using a 3D digital model[796] (twin city) of the Principality for urban development studies.

Where to focus?

I believe that even with all the technological progress, Monaco needs to put more emphasis on improving its public services. There's so much room for growth, and the focus should be on designing and delivering more effective and enhanced services to the public. Unfortunately, based on the 2024 EGDI survey[797] Monaco is trailing behind both the regional and global averages in these aspects.

30. MONTENEGRO

Lagging in governance compared to Balkans and EU

In 2022, Montenegro made noteworthy progress in e-government, achieving a commendable improvement in its global ranking. According to an E-government survey798, Montenegro fell behind by 10 more places, ranking 81st out of 193 countries, with an EGDI value of 0.7211. The same thing happened for its e-participation score, where the country fell by 2 places in 2 years. In Europe, there's a noticeable gender gap when it comes to top positions in e-government leadership. Out of 111 countries with chief information officers (CIOs) or similar roles, only 11% were women in 2022. To break it down regionally, there were just four female CIOs in the whole of Europe[799]. Remarkably, Montenegro had one of them, marking a noteworthy achievement in promoting gender diversity in this field. While Montenegro has seen amazing improvement in its infrastructure and digital skills, it still needs to focus on offering its citizens more and better online services. So, according to the 2024 EGDI report, and the E-Government Benchmark 2023[800], Montenegro is behind many other Balkan countries, such as Slovenia, Croatia, Bulgaria, Greece, Romania, Serbia, and Albania. (The latter report assesses 35 countries in the EU with a score from 1-100 on different key dimensions.) As per this report, it ranks 34th (out of 35 countries in total), surpassing only North Macedonia in the Balkans *and* the EU.

Here are some key figures to remember:

- Only 53% of Montenegro's services are online compared to 84%, which is the EU average.

- Only 33% of the governmental platforms show if personal data was used to offer a service. –>Also, only 20% of the services accept eID login, compared to 70%, which is the EU average.

The Government of Montenegro took a proactive step by adopting the Digital Transformation Strategy[801] in 2021. This strategy serves as a roadmap, outlining the conditions and initiatives necessary for digital governance. To support this digital evolution, Montenegro enacted the Law on Electronic Administration[802] in January 2020. However, based on UNDP[803] observations, it's clear that the pace of progress has been somewhat slow. The country hasn't fully harnessed the potential of digital transformation to ensure an efficient and transparent state administration.

Where to focus?

So, moving forward, strategic interventions should prioritise expanding online service offerings, enhancing transparency measures, and fostering the widespread adoption of key enablers.

31. NETHERLANDS

Netherland UN's position at 10th globally reflects emphasis on public services!

In a recent UN report/survey[804], it secured the 10th position out of 193 countries, falling behind (even if only by one place) since 2022. Also, the country's ascent to the 3rd spot in the Digital Economy and Society Index 2022 (DESI)[805] speaks volumes about its relentless pursuit of technological advancement. What's intriguing is how the Netherlands has managed to consistently elevate its status on these global scales. Notably, it has cemented its place as a digital frontrunner, showcasing continuous progress...despite the recent "front lagging."

The first movement that initiated the beginning of digital public service in the Netherlands was in 1994. In the mid-90s other phases were introduced, continuing with the phase of the transaction, which created an online environment that would be safe to use. During the final phase the attention was put on creating a 'new government' that stimulates citizens to participate in the decision-making process and provides faster service. All things considered, today, the Netherlands has made improvements in the development and execution of it's e-Government strategies, which are noticeable at all the rankings, but to stay in the top ten it needs to continue innovating and make it easy for start-ups to be involved and play a greater role.

When the new cabinet was formed in January 2022, the National Digitalisation Strategy (then) was replaced by a fresh blueprint known as the Priority Framework for Digitalisation[806]. These broad government-wide priorities weren't just ideals but were methodically dissected and expanded upon through separate agendas. One such comprehensive agenda, the Value Driven Digitalisation Work

Agenda[807] established on November 4, 2022, took an important stance by placing public values at the forefront of the entire digital metamorphosis. It addressed important topics like online identity, digital inclusion, privacy, and democracy, aiming to make government services more accessible for everyone.

Cybersecurity is a big deal in the digital Netherland. They want people to feel safe when using online services, and that should indeed be a huge focus for every government out there.

That's why they've made some important plans and laws to protect everyone's information online. First, in August 2022, they published a new policy for the use of cloud solutions[808]. These rules help keep information safe and make sure the government doesn't rely too much on just one company for technology.

The government is also changing some laws to better match our digital world.

Then, they created The Netherlands Cybersecurity Strategy 2022-2028[809] in October 2022. Apart from describing the government's vision of the security of the digital society, this strategy is accompanied by an action plan with clear steps to ensure the country is safer online. These changes show that digital Netherland is serious about making the Internet a safer place for everyone. They want people to feel secure when using online services and are taking important steps to make that happen.

32. NORTH MACEDONIA

North Macedonia is the third least developed country in Europe (gov-wise)

The progress in e-governance across Montenegro is not consistent. While some institutions are leading the way in utilising new technologies to enhance their operations, there's a notable variance in progress due to differences in available resources, extending to municipal levels. The United Nations Development Programme (UNDP) has been actively supporting North Macedonia's digital initiatives. Through its projects, UNDP played a key role in implementing LOGES[810], the country's first e-services software, at the local level.

This system is already up and running in 18 municipalities, showcasing successful local-level digitalisation. Switzerland has emerged as a major supporter of democratisation and decentralisation in North Macedonia. They recognise the crucial role of digital transformation in these processes. Digitalisation is a central focus of the Swiss development program in North Macedonia, notably within the Swiss-supported project Empowering Municipal Council[811]. However, North Macedonia ranks last among 35 EU countries. This poor ranking is attributed to subpar performance in various e-government dimensions[812], such as transparency, key enablers, user-centricity, and cross-border services.

Let's delve into the figures to understand why this is the case:

- Only 44% of services are available online (a significant contrast to the EU average of 84%).

- Shockingly, none of the governmental platforms disclose whether personal data was utilised to provide a service, showcasing a substantial lack of transparency.

- A mere 6% of online services accept eID login, hindering users from authenticating with their IDs to access needed services. This is strikingly below the EU average of 70%

- (For context, other Balkan countries outperform North Macedonia in these metrics. Albania boasts 71% of services accessible with eID, Bulgaria stands at 73%, and Greece at 67%.)

- In the global scene it has fallen behind by 4 spots in e-gov and 33 spots in e-participation (2024 EGDI report), merely surpassing the Dominican Republic and Trinidad and Tobago.

- On a positive note, North Macedonia excels in pre-filled information, with 73% of services having prefilled details, surpassing the EU average of 68%. However, this may be explained by the relatively low percentage of available online services.

Where to focus?

Collaborative efforts and learning from regional counterparts with better results could offer valuable insights into North Macedonia's digital advancement. It has the sufficient telecommunication infrastructure but it needs more international support to keep up with its neighbours.

33. NORWAY

E-government in Norway is great but behind many other Nordic countries

In the 2024 EGDI report[813], Norway secured the 15th global rank out of 193 countries. A noteworthy strength lies in Norway's commitment to the security and privacy of public service delivery, surpassing the EU average in this critical dimension. The judiciary and education systems enjoy an impressive 87% satisfaction rate among Norwegians, far surpassing OECD averages[814] of 56% and 67%, respectively. The health care system satisfaction, at 80%, outstrips the OECD average by 12 percentage points. However, a contrasting narrative unfolds in the Digital Economy and Society Index[815], where Norway finds itself among the last in the Nordic region. This index suggests room for improvement in certain digital aspects compared to neighbouring countries.

However, let's focus a bit on the achievements

1. Almost all government services in Norway (95%), can be accessed online, way more than the EU average of 84%.

2. An impressive 95% of online services in Norway allow you to log in with eID, which is much higher than the EU average of 70%.

3. Unlike the EU's 49% average, Norway stands out with 56% of services available for people across borders, making things easier for users from other countries to access their services.

4. When it comes to convenience, 75% of Norwegian online services come with prefilled details, surpassing the EU average of 68%.

5. Its e-participation ranking impressively improved by 27 spots in 2024.

Norway is one of Europe's eID frontrunners. MinID[816], a key player in this domain, empowers citizens to access public services that demand a medium to high level of security. With a substantial user base of 2.6 million Norwegians, MinID operates through the ID-Gateway, a shared platform for eID in the Norwegian public sector. Surprisingly, Norway, alongside Denmark and the Netherlands, achieves a perfect score of 100% on the online availability indicator for regional government services[817], showcasing a rare uniformity in eID access across different government tiers.

In 2023, The Ministry of Local Government and Regional Development published a new Strategy for Electronic Identification (eID)[818]. The premise of this strategy is "one person, one identity." The main goals for the eID are laid out in the One Digital Public Sector[819] strategy. Also, what's worth mentioning is that all groups (including foreign nationals *without* a Norwegian national identity number) and even children should be able to obtain an eID at the level they need.

Where to focus?

In essence, Norway's digital landscape is a tale of two narratives — a global frontrunner in e-governance and citizen satisfaction, juxtaposed with a comparative position that provokes a closer examination within the Nordic digital context. Balancing these elements will likely be a focus area for Norway's ongoing digitalisation journey.

34. POLAND

Challenges and prospects of digital Poland: The government perspective

Before 2006, in Poland, only a few government services were available online. However, within a few years, almost all major functions have migrated to digital platforms. The Ministry of Digital Affairs[820] has been responsible for digital policies, public administration reform, public sector digitalisation and the development of electronic government since 2015. The Polish public administration is actively involved in open data initiatives. A good example is Open Data Portal[821]. This portal allows everybody to get information about different areas: from education, economy or transport to environmental issues and water resources. The ePUAP Portal[822] (Electronic Platform of Public Administration Services) allows government institutions to provide services to the public via electronic communications channels. The obywatel.gov.pl[823] portal has dozens of the most popular services provided by the public administration available for easy access and convenience.

Digital Poland ranked 37th out of 193 countries[824] according to the E-Government Development 2024 Index (EDGI). Meanwhile, it ranked 42nd out of 193 countries in e-participation, according to the same report...an improvement by 9 spots in 2 years. Meanwhile the 2022 DESI index[825] (which takes into account only countries within the EU) congratulated Poland's efforts in public digitalisation even though it ranked 24th out of 27 (an unchanged position). According to this study, the government made progress in many indicators. Still, given the equally positive developments in other countries, this was not translated into a change in its overall position.

Where to focus?

Finally, Poland's performance is offset by a below EU average scores in digital public services. Currently, the government needs to improve its performance regarding public services. It can remedy this by encouraging citizens and businesses to procure and complete certain transactions online.

35. PORTUGAL

Why is it failing to keep up?

In digital Portugal, the technological evolution (and not only that) has not been that impressive since 2018 when it held the 29th position globally in terms of e-gov. Even though, considering that it was a mainly paper-based administration just a few years ago, it has changed mindsets and the traditional culture of the Portuguese administration, putting citizens at the centre.

Some important digital initiatives include:

Citizen Card[826] – the national identity card as physical and digital documents.

Digital Mobile Key[827] - an authentication mechanism that allows users to access public and private services, sign digital documents and more.

Zero Licensing[828] – a simple and time-saving service that simplifies the process of issuing specific business licences.

e-Portugal[829] – a platform that provides a single digital point for accessing all public services to citizens and businesses.

SIMPLEX Program[830] - an administrative simplification and modernization program launched in 2006 that follows a citizen-driven approach.

LabX[831] – a governmental laboratory used for experimenting with innovation in the public sector.

AMA Academy[832] – a program that focuses on encouraging new forms of participation of civil servants, promoting their achievements, and developing digital skills.

The Action Plan for Digital Transition[833] was published on the 21st of April 2020, and it outlined the strategy set for the country's future digital transformation. The Portugal Digital Mission Structure[834] oversees every component of this digital plan toward making the country more competitive in the digital arena. While there are still quite a few people in digital Portugal who have never used the internet (16% in 2021)[835], that number keeps decreasing yearly. According to the UN EGDI Index, Portugal ranked 66th (out of 193 countries) in e-participation in 2024[836]. Meaning that it fell behind by 34 spots in just 2 years. To overcome this issue, the government should be engaging and providing users and professionals with the support and training needed to get started with digitisation – helping them build their capacity to gain confidence in using e-services.

Where to focus?

They should keep looking for new ways to help citizens facing specific challenges related to technology or needs specific to certain groups, such as minors or people with disabilities. Also, they need to invest more in digital hubs that help SMEs and startups test new digital technologies, get access to digital skills, access funding for their growth etc.

36. ROMANIA

Digital Romania is EU's laggard

Romania's digital development is still trying to keep up with Western countries. The government is also having a tough time keeping pace with the rest of Europe, especially the EU, when it comes to online governance. There hasn't been any progress, and catching up seems almost impossible. Among the Very High EGDI group it is in the last place. It ranks 49th in the world in e-gov and 66th in e-participation (in 2024) among 193 countries.

According to the European Commission's Digital Economy and Society Index report from 2022[837], the country ranked last out of all EU members, highlighting challenges around regulation and the lack of digital public services in Romania. According to the report, although the country has one of the highest numbers of ICT graduates, it's the shortage of ICT specialists that limits the country's capacity to innovate and reap the benefits of digital transformation. In 2023, the country was lagging behind even in the human capital dimension, with a very low level of basic digital skills (compared to the EU average) but maintaining its high rankings in the proportion of female ICT specialists in employment and ICT graduates.

However, technology and connectivity aren't an issue for the country. It ranks 10th on connectivity. It improved in terms of coverage, with the fast broadband coverage increasing to 87%, reaching the EU average.

Until the outbreak of COVID-19, the digitalisation of public services had been progressing - but only slowly. In 2007, the Public Procurement Electronic System (SEAP)[838] was launched. Meanwhile, in 2010, the Single Electronic Point of Contact (PCUe)[839] was developed. However, a crucial element of e-government is an electronic payment system.

That's why in 2011, the Ministry of Communications and Information Society launched the SNEP (National Electronic Payment System.)[840] This system enabled individuals to pay their obligations to public administration entities (at the local and central levels) using payment cards. However, it had limited efficiency and did not appeal to a significant part of the population.

That's why in 2020, the new government established the Ministry of Research, Innovation and Digitization[841]. This ministry would be responsible for and oversee the Authority for the Digitalization of Romania (ADR).[842]

The key document concerning the country's digitisation is the *National Strategy on Digital Agenda for Digital Romania for 2014-2020*.[843] But despite the key objectives outlined in the document being achieved, this success came mainly from its modest assumptions.

Where to focus?

Romania needs to address the shortage of ICT specialists, boost business digitalisation, close the urban-rural digital gap, improve connectivity, and modernise the public administration to offer more (and better) digital services.

37. RUSSIA

Digital Russia: How the government is trying to compete

In recent years, before the beginning of the war, digital Russia was working hard to become a world leader in digital government. Digital government has become an increasingly popular term in Russia, as the country has aimed to reduce paperwork and provide more government services electronically. While these goals are largely positive, it's essential to realise that this type of digital government can also help close the digital divide between those who have internet access and those who don't, particularly in rural areas of the country. Russia's government realises that the country needs to start taking advantage of the internet and technology's massive benefits.

In digital Russia, almost 60% of the population[844] has internet access. However, for any country's digital transformation to be successful, everyone should have equal access to communication technologies and services without discrimination on any grounds such as gender, age, or disabilities. Electronic Russia was a reform created in 2002 under the Federal Target Program. However, it was wrought with multiple setbacks, including critical underfunding, lack of coordination, inefficient use of budget funds, and a comparatively low priority from the government. Then, in 2011, with Putin's endorsement, the e-Government reform was harmonised with another overarching Federal Program *Information Society 2011-2020.* It was launched as an effort to upgrade Russian public services and make them available online. In practice, this approach has not resulted in a costeffective IT infrastructure. Then, in 2016 the government focused on creating a more user-friendly platform focusing on higher internet penetration rates and inclusivity.

Where to focus?

However, to fully accelerate its digital leap, Russia needs to address certain infrastructural weaknesses[845]. According to the EDGI Index 2024[846], digital Russia has fallen down compared to 2022, ranking 43 out of 193. Even though it has one of the most tech-savvy populations[847] globally, its ranking was lower than the majority of the European Union (EU) countries. The Russian digital government is being affected by the low digitalisation of services. Many remedial measures are being taken for smart cities and digital regions, but not enough is being done.

38. SAN MARINO

Digital San Marino is struggling with very low e-participation rates

San Marino, Europe's third smallest microstate, stands out not only for its rich history as the world's oldest republic but also for its high-income status. This tiny country, nestled within Italy, adopts a somewhat digital positive approach to governance, aiming to enhance the well-being of its citizens through information and communications technology (ICT). But, while the available data doesn't provide a comprehensive evaluation of the country's performance across all e-government key performance indicators, I will specifically refer to the 2024 E-Government Survey (EGDI)[848].

San Marino, with its high EGDI (E-Government Development Index) ranking and very well-developed telecommunication infrastructure, doesn't showcase commendable achievements in e-government. It has very high TII and High HCI values, reflecting strong and developed telecommunications infrastructure and a well-educated population in digital skills. However, I think there's a notable concern when it comes to the Online Service Index (OSI)...a concern that's been evident for many years now. Despite having advanced infrastructure and connectivity, San Marino falls into the Middle OSI values category. This indicates that although the country has the necessary foundations for digital services, there's a gap in providing these services online to its citizens. The discrepancy between high EGDI values and a middle score on the OSI highlights an opportunity for San Marino to leverage its existing strengths in infrastructure and human capital to improve its citizens' online service experiences.

Examining the e-participation levels in San Marino, the findings suggest limited government efforts in actively involving citizens in collaborative governance. In the global context, the country ranks 174th out of 193 nations, signalling a comparatively low level of engagement. Examining the figures more closely, it becomes evident that San Marino's e-participation index falls considerably *below* both the world average of 0.4893 and the regional average for Southern Europe, standing at 0.6526. This points to a substantial gap in involving citizens in decision-making processes through digital platforms.

Where to focus?

The 2024 EGDI report reveals a need for increased attention to providing online services to citizens and actively engaging them in collaborative governance. Additionally, concerted efforts to elevate e-participation levels should be prioritised, employing strategies that focus more on citizen involvement and promote transparency in decision-making processes.

39. SERBIA

Digital Serbia - The digital transformation giant

Governments around the world have made great strides in using digital technologies/innovations to transform themselves. And digital Serbia is one of them. In general, the UN's 2024 E-Government Survey has beautifully highlighted these achievements. It now ranks 39 globally in e-gov and 19 in e-participation (among 193 other countries.)

To dissociate itself from a technology-first mindset, digital Serbia has started thinking of becoming a "Smart Government" instead of a "Digital Government". The key difference is that a smart government goes beyond technology to consider a holistic picture, including technology, people, processes, and other missing pieces, such as policies and regulations. Prime Minister of digital Serbia - Ana Brnabić, has continually stressed that digitalisation and education are the most important catalysts of Serbia's innovation, growth and competitiveness. She aims to future-proof the administration's capabilities for rapid deployment of costeffective and citizen-focused e-services while coordinating the implementation of ICT policies.

Speaking about the development of digitalisation, Serbia's Prime Minister Brnabić has pointed out that[849] the country has a stable digital society and that she is committed to supporting the development of the Serbian people. When it comes to the development of telecommunication, according to Brnabić, Serbia's market is highly competitive, resulting in a high rate of coverage with 4G technology, which now stands at 99.5% of households with at least one mobile provider[850]. According to A global study of "digital progress in 2020"[851], which assessed over 90 economies across 160 indicators, Serbia is a "break out" economy. What does this mean? This means that despite having limited digital infrastructure, it is a rapidly digitalised country.

Where to focus?

Despite all the achievements, Serbia needs to focus a bit more on improving its e-governance ranking as it's a bit low compared to the e-participation one.

40. SLOVAKIA

Digital Slovakia can't seem to keep pace with the EU average

Slovakia (nestled in the heart of Europe) is a country rich in history, culture, and of course beauty. With a population of around 5.4 million people[852], Slovakia emerged as an independent nation in 1993 following the peaceful dissolution of Czechoslovakia. Also, as part of the European Union, Slovakia has aligned its digital strategies with EU directives for better collaboration and interoperability on a continental scale. The country boasts a very high EGDI level[853], primarily driven by the impressive digital skills of its citizens and great telecommunication infrastructure. According to the 2024 UN report, Slovakia is ranked 60th in e-government and 53rd in e-participation. The big news, though, is that Slovakia has improved its e-participation ranking by 30 places in just two years. However, there's a need for a more focused approach to improving the provision of online services...which has ben the case for some years now.

Slovakia has shown notable progress in the digitalisation of public services. The country has achieved scores of 67 for citizens and 77 for businesses (as indicated by the E-Government 2023 Benchmark report)[854], reflecting advancements in online services. However, there is still work to be done to meet the EU's ambitious target score of 100. Slovakia is actively engaged, through collaborations between public and private entities, in a large-scale pilot project testing the European Digital Identity Wallet[855] in various everyday situations and is funded under the Digital Europe program.

Transparency emerges as a concern, with only 11% of governmental platforms disclosing the use of personal data for services (the EU average is 56%.) On a positive note, 70% of online services in Slovakia accept eID login, aligning with the EU average of 70%. Regarding digital skills, Slovakia faces a digital literacy gap[856], with nearly half of the population lacking basic digital skills. Furthermore, the proportion of ICT specialists in Slovakia's total employment stands at 4.3%, just below the EU average of 4.6%. Despite this, there has been a steady increase of ICT specialists since 2017[857]. The 2030 Strategy for the Digital Transformation of Slovakia[858] holds significant importance in the nation's journey toward great digital maturity. This strategic framework aligns with *and* builds upon the priorities of the EU Digital Single Market.

Where to focus?

As I reflect on the findings, it becomes apparent that challenges persist, particularly in the usability and transparency of digital public services. Improving online service provision should be a focal point, addressing reported difficulties and ensuring a (more) transparent experience for users.

41. SLOVENIA

One of the most connected countries failing to keep up

Digital Slovenia became a leader in digital technologies, with some of the fastest internet speeds in Europe back in the day. But, according to the 2024 EGDI report, Slovenia ranks 33th in the world in e-governance[859]. It now holds the 33rd spot in e-governance, dropping 12 places over the past two years. As one of the most connected countries globally, Slovenia is working hard to support its economy through digitalisation. Citizens can access several government services online, including filing taxes and making social security payments, through the eUprava[860] government portal. It is managed by the Ministry of Public Administration and is offering and developing eServices for citizens. For years, digital Slovenia has been among the top countries in Europe in terms of internet connectivity and internet penetration. That helps public authorities to grow faster and allows citizens to take full advantage of online services to boost their productivity and quality of life. In 2020, 67% of Slovenians[861] aged 16-74 used the internet to interact with public authorities, obtain information from government websites, or completed and sent interactive forms. One of the most critical tools for promoting and implementing better regulation principles is the Stop the Bureaucracy website[862]. It helps make the decision-making open and transparent.

By 2030, Slovenia hopes to become a digital society[863] with 100% coverage of fibre optics and internet access available to all citizens. That means that all schools, public institutions, and businesses will have access to high-speed internet. It also aims to improve its ranking according to the Digital Economy and Society Index[864]. According to the 2023 report[865], Slovenia ranks 13th among the EU Member States and 9th in connectivity. The Ministry of Public Administration[866] deals with the different policies and strategies on e-government and administrative processes. It has a clear vision of the country's future in which all citizens and businesses will be connected. Digital Slovenia has already achieved so much due to their investment in digitalisation. But there's still more work to be done! According to the OECD[867], "*the Slovenian government should build on this social and economical digital eagerness and create a sense of urgency, leveraging the current digital disruptiveness to strengthen the country's economic development and social wellbeing.*"

Where to focus?

If it wants to increase the trust of its citizens, the government should try to address security concerns and that of low interoperability. Also, it is crucial to ensure that the digital economy and digital government agendas are working in concert with one another.

42. SPAIN

Finally joined the very high EGDI group

Digital Spain, one of the Eurozone's most vulnerable economies, is one of the most digitally advanced countries in Europe and may soon see one of its cities become the continent's most connected urban centre. The rise of Spain's Digital Economy can be traced back to the Spanish government's decision to put digital technology at the centre of its economy and society in 2013. Then, back in 2021, the President of Spain, Pedro Sánchez, presented three new plans for the development of the Spain 2025 Digital Agenda[868], with an investment of more than 11,000 million euros for the next three years. These new plans are the *Digitalization Plan for SMEs 2021-2025*[869], the *National Plan for Digital Competences* and the *Digitalization Plan for Public Administrations*. They were added to the other three plans presented last December: the Connectivity Plan[870], the Strategy to Promote 5G[871] and the National Strategy for Artificial Intelligence[872].

Spain's digital government efforts are paying off. The country ranks at or near the top of rankings for internet access, e-government services and use of social media to interact with citizens. According to the 2022 DESI index[873], the country ranks 7th of 28 EU Member States. Moreover, digital Spain ranks 5th in the EU on digital public services thanks to its well-timed implementation of a digital-by-default strategy throughout its central public administration. The EDGI index shows that the country has not had any major changes in its position for 8 consecutive years, ranking 17th out of the 193 countries in 2024[874]. This makes Spain the leader of e-government in southern Europe and one of the top ten leaders of Europe as a whole. Meanwhile in e-participation it saw a major dropping by 8 spots, landing it in the 33rd position. This means that while Spain has made progress overall, it still faces some huge challenges in getting citizens more involved online.

Where to focus?

Spain faces two hurdles on its path to digital success: first, many Spaniards aren't online yet; second, traditional industries, which include large numbers of small businesses that find running an online business expensive and complex, are proving challenging to digitise. Regarding human capital, digital Spain is a relatively good performer on basic digital skills but below the EU average as regards the proportion of ICT specialists and graduates. The government should focus on laying the necessary foundations and building up the required digital skills within society, companies, and universities.

43. SWEDEN

Is the digital government in Sweden "lagging" ahead?

The contribution of the ICT industry to Sweden's economy, as a share of GDP, is among the highest in the world. According to the EDGI index, in 2022, Sweden ranked 5th out of 193[875] countries when it comes to e-government. In 2024, things seem more bleak as it ranks 14th in e-gov and 35th in e-participation (down by 3 places.) Even though I must say that the digital government in Sweden has begun at an early stage, and the country has a long history of high connectivity and making use of digital tools. So, as a digitally mature country, it continues to perform well across all dimensions of the EU's 2030 Digital Decade[876]. The government entrusted DIGG (Agency for Digital Government)[877] with the strategic task of expanding the public sector's competence to increase access to public information through open government data. In January 2020, DIGG released its report on Promoting public administration's[878] ability to use AI within the public sector.

One of the pillars of Nordic cooperation is freedom of movement, and the political objectives are high. These ambitions were outlined in the NordicBaltic ministerial declaration on Digital North. The Nordic-Baltic eID Project (NOBID)[879] is a collaborative arena between Sweden and Denmark, Estonia, Finland, Iceland, Latvia, Lithuania, and Norway, enabling access to national digital services to users from other countries. The government presented the first National Cyber Security Strategy in June 2017. Then, at the beginning of March 2019, several government agencies in the field of cyber security presented a Comprehensive cyber security action plan for 2019- 2020[880] to implement the strategy at the agency level. While accelerating public service digitisation, the government must understand citizens' relationship with technology. According to a recent study[881] made in the Nordic countries, 62% of citizens believed that technology makes life better, and 69% agreed that it's needed to solve future problems. According to OECD[882], Sweden needs strong institutional leadership, backed by the government's political support and mechanisms that foster collaboration among public sector ministries, agencies and other stakeholders.

Political willingness and announcements alone do not lead to results.

Where to focus?

Countries like Sweden are often seen as models, but it is far from being considered perfect regarding digital solutions in the public sector and how it affects its citizens. This is especially true since the nation has failed to keep a consistent progress in e-participation (having many ups and downs). More needs to be done to address the reasons for this year's decline.

44. SWITZERLAND

Switzerland can do more to increase the participation of its citizens

Switzerland is a landlocked country renowned for its stunning landscapes, precision engineering, and commitment to... neutrality. This neutrality has made it an international hub for diplomacy and home to numerous international organisations, often being referred to as the "heart of Europe." When it comes to e-services, Switzerland's standing is equally noteworthy. The country has secured a prominent position on the global stage, securing the 26th spot out of 193 nations in the UN's E-Government Survey 2024[883] – an impressive feat.

This high ranking is substantiated by Switzerland's notable values in essential indexes like Human Capital and Telecommunication Infrastructure. However, a closer examination reveals a nuanced aspect: the country appears to face challenges in gov technology and e-participation in recent years. In 2022, it landed in the 41st spot, marking a notable decline from the 18th place it held in 2020. And while in 2024 it moved up by 9 places…it still isn't good enough considering this country. On the other hand, analysing Zurich's performance in the Local Online Service Index (LOSI)[884], the city emerges as a global leader in providing online services to its residents. According to the E-Government survey report, Zurich secured an impressive 26th place out of 193 cities assessed.

According to the OECD, the Swiss express exceptionally high satisfaction[885] with traditional public services, with 92% reporting contentment with the health care system and 84% with education and the judiciary. These figures notably surpass the OECD averages. However, insights from the 'Swiss Digital Government Survey

2023'[886] by Deloitte reveal a more nuanced perspective on e-government services. The survey (encompassing 1,000 participants aged 18 and over) indicates that only 48% are satisfied with the current range of e-government services, believing them to be available to the required extent.

Where to focus?

There's room for improvement, particularly in boosting e-participation levels. While Switzerland excels in various aspects, initiatives targeted at strengthening public interaction are very important moving forward.

45. UKRAINE

In times of war, Ukraine's e-governance triumphs inspire USA and Estonia

Reflecting on Ukraine's recent events, it's evident that even in the face of immense challenges like pandemics and wars, life can persist, and digitalisation becomes a crucial lifeline. However, it's disheartening that it often takes global crises (such as the Covid-19 pandemic and recent conflicts) to accelerate the adoption of digital solutions. The urgency of the war prompted not only Ukraine but also neighbouring countries (like Poland, for example) to swiftly develop digital services to aid the Ukrainian population. It really shows how crises can act as powerful motivators for adopting and expanding digital solutions to meet the urgent needs of the people. Ukraine's e-government performance is a testament to this resilience. In the 2024 EGDI report[887], Ukraine made an amazing leap, improving e-governance ranking by 16 places. But what's more noteworthy is that it improved its e-participation ranking from the 57th spot to the number 1 leader in all of Europe! The government even moved all public data and services to public cloud platforms abroad for safety purposes and so that they're easily accessible. The commitment to prioritising user and data safety became even more apparent on the eve of Russia's full-scale invasion. Critical decisions were made to bolster security measures, including a strategic move to transition the entire *Diia* infrastructure to a cloud format.

Analysing Ukraine's Diia app[888], I believe it stands out as a crucial component of the country's digital infrastructure. Since its launch in September 2019, the Diia app has gained immense popularity, with over 19.2 million Ukrainians currently using it—installed on around 70% of the smartphones in the country. In regions of Ukraine affected by Russian occupation, the Diia app often serves as the sole means for Ukrainians to access government services or receive assistance. Beyond its wartime utility, Diia has been a transformative force in Ukraine's digital governance over the past five years. It also has served to jumpstart the adoption of such systems in other countries. For example, in 2023, USAID Administrator Samantha Power reiterated[889] that they would be working to make Diia an opensource digital public good to give to other partner countries as well. Even Estonia (a global leader in the field of digital government for so long) will be implementing a similar app based on Diia[890].

Final words

The Diia app (a key player in Ukraine's digital landscape) has not only proven its worth during wartime but has also become an essential part of everyday life for millions of Ukrainians. The fact that even Estonia, a long-standing global leader in digital governance, is looking to implement a similar app based on Diia speaks volumes about the app's effectiveness.

46. UNITED KINGDOM

UK's new digital strategy (2024-2030): What I think

So, the Foreign, Commonwealth & Development Office[891] has rolled out a plan to boost digital technologies in low- and middle-income countries. Digital technologies have the power to transform lives, whether it's by opening up new economic opportunities or improving healthcare research. But here's the thing – not everyone has access to these benefits. In fact, 2.6 billion people worldwide still lack internet access[892], with women and girls in poorer countries being particularly disadvantaged. By 2030, the UK aims to halve the gap between those who have internet connectivity and those who don't in at least 20 partner countries[893]. That's a bold goal....but it's one that's crucial for bridging the digital divide and ensuring that everyone has a fair shot at benefiting from the digital revolution.

The United Kingdom is in a strong position to address global digital development challenges, thanks to its extensive history of pioneering digital innovation. In 2018, the UK became the first bilateral donor to formulate a comprehensive strategy for 'Doing development in a digital world'[894]. Moreover, the UK has earned impressive rankings in global assessments of digital governance. According to the latest available UN e-government survey[895], the UK ranked 7th out of 193 countries assessed and 6th in e-participation (up by 4 places compared to 2022). It holds the 4th place in the world for e-participation and the 4th place in Europe for its overall digitalisation efforts. But it's not just about rankings. For example, the Digital Access Programme's UK Tech Hubs[896] is making a real impact on the ground. With Tech Hubs in places like South Africa, Nigeria, and Kenya, they're supporting local entrepreneurs, SMEs, and tech start-ups to thrive in their digital ecosystems. In 2023 alone, these Tech Hubs trained over 55,000 local tech entrepreneurs, with 80% of them being women. They've also provided support and mentorship to around 10,000 digital SMEs. Talk about driving growth and creating opportunities! Also, the UK is actively participating in shaping international norms/standards related to digital government as applauded by the 2024 UN report. Among other things it even hosted the first global summit of its kind the"AI Safety Summit" in November 2023.

Where to focus?

The UK has certainly learned how to lead the charge in addressing its challenges and has to keep using this momentum forward.

47. VATICAN CITY

Online services and innovations

The Vatican, known for its rich history and religious significance, has embraced digital transformation to offer a variety of online services. This report explores the digital services provided by the Vatican, focusing on the Vatican Library, communication platforms, and other essential services. The Digital Vatican Library (DVL)[897] is a significant initiative that provides free access to the Vatican Library's extensive digitised collections. These collections include manuscripts, incunabula, archival materials, graphic materials, coins, medals, and printed materials from special projects. The Vatican Apostolic Library has undertaken extensive digitisation projects to preserve and make accessible its vast collections. As of recent updates, over 19,000 manuscripts have been digitised[898] and are available online. The library aims to digitise approximately 40 million pages of documents, ensuring long-term preservation and accessibility. The Vatican offers several online services[899] to facilitate visits to its renowned sites. Visitors can purchase tickets for the Vatican Museums, including guided tours, educational activities, and special events, through the Online Ticket Office. Under the leadership of Monsignor Lucio Adrian Ruiz, the Vatican has significantly updated its communication technologies[900]. The Vatican Internet Service, the telecommunications department behind the Vatican's web services, has been instrumental in this transformation. Pope Francis established the *Dicastery for Communication*[901], consolidating nine separate communication entities under one unified direction to streamline and enhance the Vatican's digital outreach. As we all know, the digital world is a significant part of young people's identity and way of life. The Vatican's efforts to engage with the digital generation[902] include vocational training programs like "Faith Communication in the Digital World," which harness the native understanding of digital platforms among young professionals to enable meaningful dialogue and connection within faith communities. These initiatives ensure that the Church remains relevant and accessible to younger generations. The Vatican has launched a new portal and app for the Jubilee Year 2025[903], available in nine languages. This platform provides essential information about the Jubilee event, including details on the Holy Door of St. Peter's and other Roman Basilicas.

Where to focus?

Despite these advancements, the Vatican faces challenges inherent in integrating digital technologies with its longstanding traditions and practices. These challenges include ensuring data privacy and security, maintaining authenticity and authority in digital communications, and addressing the digital divide that may limit access to online resources for several communities.

NORTH AMERICA

Digital governance
SUMMARY

When we look at the progress of e-government development across the North American continent, we see a region that's holding its ground with steady advancements. It's interesting to observe that most countries in this part of the world have managed to stay within the same EGDI groups for several years now. This consistency suggests that while progress is being made, it's happening at a somewhat predictable and stable pace. However, this could also indicate that there might be a certain level of stagnation in some areas, where more could be done to push the boundaries further.

If I had to mention two main things from the continent it would be Belize and Haiti as two different examples of what's possible. On the one hand, Belize made an impressive leap[904] from the middle to the high EGDI group back in 2022, which highlights the potential for growth even in smaller nations. This kind of movement is what I find encouraging because it shows that with the right focus and resources, countries *can* improve their digital governance frameworks significantly.

On the other hand, there's Haiti's situation. It's the only country in the region (not only in the Northern America) that experienced a downturn, moving from the middle to the low EGDI group in 2022 and not showing any progress in the 2024 report. I believe this shift is a stark reminder that progress in e-government isn't guaranteed and that challenges like political instability, economic difficulties, and infrastructure issues can severely impact a country's ability to develop its digital governance.

When we look at the bigger picture, the EGDI report groups both North and South America together, placing the Americas as a whole in second place after Europe in terms of digital governance initiatives and successes. However, I think it's important to recognise that this high ranking is largely driven by the USA and Uruguay, both of which are well above the world average in e-government development.

These two countries are the powerhouses in the continent(s), setting the pace and standards that many other countries in the continent are yet to meet. In contrast, many other nations in the (both) Americas are still catching up, and this disparity within the region is something that shouldn't be overlooked.

I would argue that North America's advantage lies in its consistency. The proportion of countries in the high or very high EGDI groups is increasing steadily, which signals that even those countries not at the top are making gradual improvements. I believe this trend is a positive indicator.

What's holding some of these countries back?

First off, many of the underdeveloped countries in Northern America are Small Island Developing States (SIDS).

This status brings with it a unique set of difficulties that are hard to ignore. SIDS often face limited resources, both financially and in terms of human capital, which makes it tough to build the robust digital infrastructure necessary for effective governance. So, they need better digital infrastructure to grow economically, *but* they also need economic growth to invest in that very infrastructure.

The same can be said about low- and low-middle-income countries. This financial constraint inherently limits their ability to invest in the necessary technologies and infrastructure to support robust digital governance. Once again - without adequate funding and investment, these nations are at a disadvantage from the very start. Also, the gap between countries within the same region can be staggering. Take the United States, for example—it offered 22 public services online in 2022, which is impressive. But then you look at Haiti, which only offered 2, and you start to see just how wide the disparity is. Cuba is somewhere in between with 7 services, but even that pales in comparison to what's available in the U.S.

Something that's particularly concerning is that regional strategic instruments for digital government are often part of broader digital agendas that span multiple countries. In theory, this sounds great—collaboration and shared goals *should* be beneficial. But in practice, these agendas often lack a comprehensive focus[905] on digital government priorities. I would also add that there's usually an absence of effective monitoring mechanisms. Without proper oversight, these agendas risk becoming little more of a formality than an effective tool for change. Another thing is the lack of innovation in public procurement processes in most Caribbean and Central American countries. Despite recent initiatives, these countries have not been able to *fully* make good use of modern procurement methods to enhance their digital capabilities. This is a missed opportunity, as innovative procurement could be a game-changer in equipping public services with the necessary digital tools. Without it, the progress remains slow, and the potential for digital transformation is severely limited. There's also the digital divide. As you can guess, the urban-rural gap is the smallest in regions with high penetration. The ratio stands at 1.2 in both Americas[906].

Digital governance in Northern America: Leaders & laggards

If we divide the region into three subregions—North, Central, and the Caribbean—it becomes evident that the northern part is by far the most developed in terms of digital governance. The United States in particular, is not just a leader in its own region, but it's also far above the global average when it comes to integrating technology into governance and among the world's top leaders. It has invested heavily in digital infrastructure, online services, and human capital, making it the benchmark for what effective digital governance can look like. This isn't surprising, considering the resources and focus these countries have dedicated to digital transformation. On the other hand, I think it's important to acknowledge that the Caribbean countries are doing fairly well, especially given their size and resources. Countries like the Bahamas, Grenada, and Barbados are outperforming many larger nations on the continent.

Top performers out of 23 countries in Northern America:

1. USA
2. Canada
3. Costa Rica
4. Mexico
5. Panama

Top laggers out of 23 countries in Northern America:

6. Saint Lucia
7. Cuba
8. Belize
9. Honduras
10. Haiti

Opportunities moving forward

Many governments have already started integrating digital functions into their operations, which is a positive move. However, there's a chance to give digital government authorities more influence, especially when it comes to setting standards and making key investment decisions. Strengthening their role could help drive even more progress.

Another key opportunity I see is in the evolution of digital government strategies. These strategies are already mainstream (which is a great starting point) but there's room to make them even more ambitious and/or comprehensive. I believe that by aiming higher, these strategies can catalyze a system-wide digital transformation that could redefine public sector operations. So- from simply adopting digital tools to fully embracing a digital-first mindset. A mindset that permeates every aspect of governance. The development of digital talent within the public sector is another area brimming with potential. I see this as a foundational opportunity—one that can have a ripple effect across all aspects of digital governance. There's also a chance to create more inclusive government services by designing and delivering them in a way that considers all levels of government and all citizens. This could involve strengthening collaboration between federal, state, and local governments (where needed) and creating a more integrated digital service delivery system.

Lastly, dedicating specific resources and capacities to investing in digital government can lead to long-lasting results in Northern America. This isn't just about securing funding—it's about creating sustainable investment strategies that align with long-term (this is the keyword here) digital transformation goals. Unfortunately, without focused investment, many digital initiatives might fall short of their potential.

1. ANTIGUA AND BARBUDA

Among the most developed Small Island Developing States (SIDS)

This small island nation gained independence from the United Kingdom in 1981 and has since developed a diverse economy, with tourism, offshore banking, and the digital government of Antigua and Barbuda. The Prime Minister of Antigua and Barbuda's focus to achieving complete digitalisation of public services by 2030[907] is a forward-thinking and commendable initiative. This decision stems from the recently conducted Digital Readiness Assessment (DRA)[908] by the UNDP, which, I must say, is a crucial step in aligning the country's digital strategy with the acceleration of Sustainable Development Goals (SDGs).

In November 2023, the UNDP organised a workshop to discuss the findings[909] of the Digital Readiness Assessment (DRA). The aim was to collaboratively shape the country's digital transformation vision. The Barbados and Eastern Caribbean UN country team played host to around 50 participants (including representatives from the government, private sector, civil society, and the UN.) Examining Antigua and Barbuda's role as the host for the 4th International Conference on Small Island Developing States (SIDS)[910] in May 2024, I believe they have a significant opportunity to shape the digital development agenda for small islands, not just in the Caribbean but on a global scale.

Small islands face unique challenges, and a collective effort in steering the digital development agenda can lead to solutions that suit the specific contexts of these nations. Looking at the data provided from the UN E-government survery[911], I think this island-nation is in an interesting digital position. With a very high Telecommunication Infrastructure Index (TII) and a high Human Capital Index (HCI), it seems to be well-equipped both in terms of technology and the skills of its people. The fact that it falls into the category of 12 out of 37 Small Island Developing States (SIDS) with an EGDI (0.6428) value[912] above the *global* average is quite commendable. This indicates that, compared to many similar nations, it's making significant progress in using digital technologies for governance *and* development. However, I still must add that in 2 years it dropped in ranking both in e-governance (by 6 places) and in e-participation (by 27 places.)

Where to focus?

This country appears to have a solid foundation in terms of telecommunication infrastructure and human capital, positioning it well in the global digital landscape. The key now would be to capitalise on these strengths, address any gaps in e-participation, and focus a bit more on offering more and better online services.

2. BAHAMAS

Has an EGDI value above world's average

Over the years, the digital government in the Bahamas has been working on different programs to maximise the benefits of ICT. However, not all of their efforts have been able to achieve great results except in the case of the digital transformation program. Residents of the Bahamas may soon begin to use digital assets to pay for taxes, including the CBDC (central bank digital currency).

The digital government in the Bahamas officially launched the Department of Transformation and Digitization (DTD) back in November 2019. This program is designed to make all government services available on online platforms, resulting in a smooth and effective business process both locally and internationally. The project aims to improve competitiveness in the Bahamas and reduce the costs of doing business with the Government. When this project is completed, it will reduce the cost of red tape and delays, increase the country's Gross Domestic Product through the financial service sector, attract businesses locally and internationally and improve transparency in government activities. Additionally, government activities will be less susceptible to vulnerability and other issues with a paper trail, such as the misplacement of documents and disasters (hurricanes, fires).

The digital government in the Bahamas also plans to bring this tech initiative to the cabinet Office and make it into an e-cabinet management system. When there's an e-cabinet system, all the operations run by the cabinet office become digitised. Also, there will be updated security measures to enable the ministers and permanent secretaries to deliver the best government services. How is the Bahamas doing on the global stage? According to the 2024 EGDI report, the Bahamas dropped 17 places in its e-governance ranking and fell even further in e-participation, slipping by 32 spots over the past two years. Now it stands in the 83 and the 127 position.

Where to focus?

While it has a good infrastructure in place, the Bahamas government needs to pay more attention to service delivery and people's skills.

3. BARBADOS

Great infrastructure, data governance but low e-participation

With a rich history influenced by British colonialism, Barbados gained independence in 1966. Geographically, digital Barbados is compact and one of the most densely populated countries in the Eastern Caribbean. Despite its size, the country exhibits high human development, strong governance systems, and noteworthy levels of technological connectivity.

When it comes to analysing Barbados from a digital perspective, the country boasts high EGDI values, indicating a strong performance in digital public services and/ or governance in general. In the UN's e-government report of 2024[913], digital Barbados secured the 91st position out of 193 countries.

This is a decent ranking, considering the global context, however, for context purposes you must know that it dropped in ranking by 12 spots. This achievement also puts Barbados among the top Small Island Developing States (SIDS) that have gone beyond the global average in EGDI scores. Barbados now holds 6th place, showing real progress for a small island nation.

This transformation gained momentum with the Barbados Economic Reform Transformation Plan (part of the IMF's Extended Fund Facility) initiated in October 2018. As highlighted in a 2023 OECD report[914], Barbados is actively enhancing its digital public services. This progress aligns with the objectives of the Modernisation of the Public Sector Programme supported by[915] the InterAmerican Development Bank (IDB). The primary goal of this program is to address gaps in digital public infrastructure and accessibility, aiming to promote greater digitalisation of government services and encourage the use of digital channels. The island stands out for having a central service delivery platform offering both informational and transactional services. It's worth noting that, apart from Jamaica, Barbados was (up until recently) the only other country providing informational services through digital channels.

Examining the progress towards a digital ID in Barbados, I think it's a significant step forward for the country's technological advancement. The assurance from Minister Davidson Ishmael that Barbadians could have a digital ID this year (2024) indicates a tangible outcome of the government's persistent efforts over the years. However, it's worth noting that the introduction of a digital ID has faced resistance from some segments of the population[916].

This is a common challenge when implementing such transformative changes, and addressing concerns from the public is crucial for successful adoption.

Where to focus?

The average EPI value suggests there may be areas for improvement in terms of e-participation (citizen engagement in digital platforms and services.) While the infrastructure and governmental aspects seem strong, enhancing e-participation and providing more and better online services could further strengthen the digital ecosystem.

4. BELIZE

Digital government of Belize is far behind many countries in Central America

Belize, this country located in Central America has only recently shown interest in advancing digital governance to enhance administrative efficiency and public services. Despite that, the digital government of Belize has made progress in adopting technologies to streamline government processes, even though it's still behind many other countries of the same income level.

In 2022, Belize made a notable leap, entering the high EGDI group[917] for the first time and securing a ranking of 133 out of 193 countries. In 2024, Belize dropped 8 spots in e-governance, landing at 141st place. This drop caused Belize to lose its spot in the high EGDI group. However, there was some good news—Belize moved up 9 places in e-participation this year.

This achievement is significant, even though more could be achieved especially considering Belize's status as an upper-middle-income country. Looking at the broader Americas region, the majority of countries have maintained their EGDI groups since 2020. Unfortunately, Belize, was one of the only six countries in the world to move to a lower EGDI group. This doesn't match what Belize is capable of, as the country already has a solid base in terms of technology and the skills of its people. Belize has the right infrastructure and a capable workforce to do more, so it's surprising it hasn't reached its full potential yet.

The ongoing redesign of Belize's national/governmental portal adds a layer of complexity to the assessment, making it challenging to provide a comprehensive analysis. The portal underwent redesigning during the 2021 EGDI assessment, as reported by the EGDI report, and as of now (2024) is "under maintenance" [918], the last time I checked. The E-Governance and Digitalisation Unit have successfully integrated key entities[919] such as the Belize Police Department, Customs and Excise Department, and Magistrates Court[920] into the same system as the Department of Transport. This integration fosters seamless data sharing and enhances coordination in handling accidents and violations.

A significant development is the official partnership forged in 2023 with Giga, a global initiative by the United Nations Children's Fund (UNICEF)[921] and the International Telecommunication Union (ITU). The collaboration aims to connect every school to the Internet and provide young people with access to information, opportunities, and choices.

This initiative aligns seamlessly with the Ministry of Education, Culture, Science, and Technology's MoECST's BESPlan 2021-2025[922] and the ongoing national curriculum reform focusing on competency-based learning and STEAM initiatives. The government's focus on using technology for education is further underscored by the alignment of this initiative with the National Digital Agenda of the Ministry of E-Governance[923]. This agenda prioritises the use of technological applications and advancements to bring about transformative changes in people's lives.

Where to focus?

It's evident that when it comes to the digital government of Belize, there are challenges related to unevenly developed infrastructure, which poses constraints on the development of e-government initiatives. I think more efforts are needed to establish fully functional governmental platforms that facilitate citizens' seamless access to various services…something that was noted even in the new EGDI report.

5. CANADA

Digital Canada needs to (urgently) increase efforts to attract the skills they need

I believe that Canada is facing a crucial need to boost its efforts in attracting digital skills - especially after seeing its current EGDI ranking in the Americas. According to the Information and Communications Technology Council (ICTC), there's a projection that digital Canada will need around 250,000 more jobs in the digital economy by 2025[924] (making a total of 2.3 million digital workers.) Now, if this prediction holds true, it would mean that about 11% of all jobs in Canada would be in the digital sector.

I think the efforts made to bridge the digital talent gap in Canada are notable, particularly with initiatives like the proposal for visas allowing skilled tech workers to enter the country *without* a job offer.[925] These steps are aimed at strengthening the competitiveness of the tech sector and expanding the available talent pool. In July 2023, IRCC launched a one-time, specialty-occupation, open work permit initiative, which reached its goal of 10,000 applications within 24 hours[926]. However, these measures might only bring in a relatively small number of the digital experts needed to fill the gap. While digital Canada has shown progress in attracting tech talent, notably with the implementation of its tech talent strategy[927], I don't believe it's sufficient to meet the overall demand.

In my articles[928], I've consistently highlighted that citizens nowadays possess an increasing level of technological literacy. They expect government services to offer a seamless digital experience that mirrors their interactions with private sector products and services.

This concern is not merely my personal opinion. Ottawa is already grappling with an estimated 30% shortage in its IT positions[929], facing limitations in attracting new talent to government roles.

Also, although Canada's public service agencies made strides during the pandemic in leveraging digital technologies for better service delivery, the country still trails global leaders. The United Nations' 2024 e-government survey[930] has revealed a continuous drop in Canada's ranking from 28th (2020) to 32nd (2022) to 47th (2024). So, in 2022, Canada was doing really well in digital government, ranking second in *both* North and South America for its efforts. However, by 2024, things have changed.

Canada has slipped to 5th place, now ranking behind the United States, Uruguay, Chile, and Argentina. Moreover, there's a substantial gap between government and industry investments in technology. For instance, research conducted by Accenture[931] revealed that 49% of global public sector respondents intended to make significant investments in data solutions over the next three years, whereas the figure stood at 71% across all industries.

Where to focus?

Three key aspects take centre stage for digital Canada: competitiveness, attracting global investment, and devising and implementing smart public policies.

6. COSTA RICA

Huge progress: Costa Rica ranks 3rd in Northern America for the first time

The digital government of Costa Rica has actively worked towards providing digital access to its citizens, promoting e-government services, and creating a tech-friendly environment. The country boasts a very high E-Government Development Index (EGDI)[932], primarily driven by impressive levels of the Human Capital Index (HCI) and Telecommunication Infrastructure Index (TII).

However, there's a notable area that warrants attention – the provision of online services. This was a major issue pointed out in the 2022 report, and it's still the same concern being raised now. It shows that while some progress has been made, there's still work to be done in this area.

The digital government of Costa Rica secured the 61st position in the 2024 EGDI ranking among 193 assessed countries. Diving into the specifics, the *Online Service Index* for Costa Rica[933] was measured at 0.8009 in 2024 surpassing even the Central America's leader back in 2022 - Mexico.

In examining the digital government of Costa Rica and its approach to data interoperability, there's a noteworthy reliance on the European Interoperability Framework (EIF)[934] as reported in the OECD's "Digital Government Review of Latin America and the Caribbean."[935]

The report indicates that Costa Rica stands out as the only country in the region actively employing EIF to advance its public sector interoperability efforts. However, my observation raises a concern regarding the *absence* of specific regulations on open data in Costa

Rica. The roles of Access to Information Officers, outlined in the 2017 Decree 40200 on Transparency and Access to Public Information[936], become necessary.

On the other hand - in terms of existing regulatory instruments related to data in Costa Rica, several key documents are in place. Such as:

- 2018 Executive Decree 41190 on the Reform of Executive Decrees No. 38994, "Promotion of Open Government in Public Administration and Creation of the National Commission for Open Government"937, No. 40199, and Decree No. 39372
- Decree 40200 on Transparency and Access to Public Information of
- 2017938
- Decree 40199 on Open Data Publication of 2017939
- The Regulations of the Law on Personal Data Protection in 2012940 • The Law 8968 on Personal Data Protection in 2011941.

I have to say that Costa Rica has made great progress in digital service delivery through its central platform (http://gob.go.cr/)[942]. This platform serves as a hub for *both* informational and transactional services (yes, there are countries that still don't offer transactional services in their central platforms). It even has a service catalogue covering between 10% to 50% of services. While this range is modest, having a service catalogue is a positive step. These catalogues play a very important role in mapping government services and streamlining interactions, contributing to a more cohesive and user-friendly experience.

Where to focus?

I believe the digital government of Costa Rica could benefit from strategic efforts to refine and expand its online service offerings. This might involve streamlining existing services, introducing new ones, and ensuring a userfriendly interface.

7. CUBA

Digital Government of Cuba has one of the lowest e-participation levels in the world

Cuba has a unique political and economic history characterised by socialist governance. And if we have to look at it through another lense, the digital government of Cuba has faced challenges in terms of internet access and digital infrastructure, with limited connectivity and strict government control over online content.

In 2022, the digital government of Cuba provided only seven services online[943], a stark contrast to the majority of countries in the Americas and the Caribbean, where 63% offer more than 16 services. The *Online Service Index* for Cuba is quite low, standing at 0.2298, well below both sub-regional (0.4256) and global (0.5754) averages. *E-participation* in Cuba is exceptionally low too, with a value of 0.0548, highlighting a minimal and low level of citizen engagement in digital governance. Additionally, the country's telecommunication infrastructure (TII)[944], with a value of 0.5318, falls considerably below the global average of 0.6890. Despite efforts like price cuts and promotions, internet services in Cuba remain expensive for most citizens. While some can connect through state institutions, the quality is often low[945], shared among users, and subject to censorship.

On a positive note, Cuba has higher values in Human Capital Index (HCI) compared to the global average. This suggests a well-educated population in digitalisation, and it also suggests a population with untapped potential for contributing to the digital economy and governance. In the overall assessment, the digital government of Cuba is ranked 139th out of 193 countries in the 2022 report. According to the 2024 E-government report[946], the country has a sufficient human capital base and infrastructure to progress its digital governance efforts.

Where to focus?

Cuba's absence from many international reports on digital governance is primarily due to a lack of transparency in responding to survey questions. This gap in information makes it challenging to assess and compare the performance of the digital government of Cuba on a global scale.

But focusing on improving internet accessibility, enhancing online services, and addressing gender diversity in leadership are key steps that I believe would significantly elevate the digital government of Cuba.

8. DOMINICA

Great infrastructure but very low e-participation

The Commonwealth of Dominica (not to be confused with the Dominican Republic) is a small island nation in the Caribbean. It is a 750-square-kilometre. Eastern Caribbean island with a population of more than 72,000[947] . One of the first things noticeable about digital Dominica in the UN's 2024 E-government survey[948] is the decline in EGDI values.

But, despite having a middle Online Service Index (OSI), Dominica boasts high values in both the Telecommunication Infrastructure Index (TII) and Human Capital Index (HCI). In fact, Dominica has such a huge focus on developing the infastructure, that in 2023, the partnership with decentralised autonomous organisation (DAO) Tron[949] marked a significant step in that direction. This collaboration aims to develop the country's digital ID infrastructure, with Tron being designated as the national blockchain.

The project includes the creation of the Dominica Digital Identity (DDID), a "Dominica Metaverse," and a digital currency named "Dominica Coin" (DMC). This initiative would allow Dominican citizens to use DMC and other Tron-based tokens for payments.

Despite these advancements, the 2024 EGDI values of Dominica (0.5445)[950] remain lower than in previous years and there's a concerning trend of decline, ranking 127th out of 193 countries assessed...compared to the 109th spot in 2022. This signifies a drop of 18 places in just 2 years, indicating potential challenges in sustaining or improving its digital governance capabilities.

However, one thing where Dominica saw some huge progress during the same time period is the e-participation index. Back in 2022, it was ranked very low, sitting at 183rd place. But by 2024, it climbed an impressive 53 spots to reach 130th place. This improvement is a huge step forward, especially since it helps make up for the big drop of 41 places that Dominica experienced in 2022. While there's still room to grow, this leap shows the country is moving in the right direction

Digital Dominica has had huge support from international organisations, specifically the United Nations Development Programme (UNDP) and the World Bank. One notable initiative, the "Work Online Dominica"[951] program, started by the Government of Dominica's Ministry of Public Works and the Digital Economy in collaboration with UNDP Barbados and the Eastern Caribbean, was particularly successful (even though the website has some issues not allowing people to apply.) There's also, the Caribbean Digital Transformation Project[952] which is a digital economy development initiative financed by the World Bank. As part of this initiative, the UNDP Chief Digital Office took a proactive step by conducting a digital readiness assessment in Dominica[953]. This assessment played an important role in framing digital governance, identifying opportunities, and understanding challenges.

Where to focus?

Actively involving citizens in the decision-making process and seeking their feedback can contribute significantly to the success of digital initiatives. Refining digital service delivery is another critical consideration.

9. DOMINICAN REPUBLIC

Digital Dominican Republic has had some good progress in 2 years

In examining the digital governance of the Dominican Republic, it's clear that while it has maintained high E-Government Development Index (EGDI) values in the range of 0.50-0.7, its progress has been somewhat stagnant. Being a small island developing state, the EGDI value of the Digital Dominican Republic surpasses the world average[954], indicating praiseworthy progress in digital governance.

The Dominican Republic's EGDI value[955] in 2024 is 0.7013 positioning it at 85th among the 193 countries assessed. This ranking shows how much progress the country has made in developing its digital government services. When it comes to the e-participation index (EPI), the Dominican Republic scored 0.6575, placing it at 61st in the world.

Because of these improvements, the Dominican Republic climbed 7 spots and an impressive 25 spots in the respective rankings. These jumps show just how much effort the country has put into growing its digital systems and involving people in the process.

The Dominican Republic's Agenda Digital 2030 is an important framework[956] aimed at enhancing the efficiency and transparency of public administration. What's more, the rise in mobile device coverage and connectivity has notably influenced the adoption of mobile apps across governments in the region, including the digital Dominican Republic. The *Servicios Públicos RD*[957] mobile app is a practical manifestation of this trend, offering citizens convenient access to digital services. Interestingly, the Dominican Republic stands out as a country regularly using public-private partnerships (PPPs) to address digital transformation needs, according to a recent OECD report[958].

Measuring user experience in digital government services is a crucial aspect, and it's interesting to see how the digital Dominican Republic is actively engaging in this area. The Ministry of Public Administration (MAP) has taken on the responsibility for maintaining service quality. The issuance of resolution 03/2019[959] is a proactive approach to citizen satisfaction assessment across various layers of the public administration, encompassing central government, local governments, and autonomous institutions.

Moreover, the fact that each institution is entrusted with conducting the survey and (subsequently) reporting the results to the MAP demonstrates a decentralised yet coordinated effort. Another important fact is that the government is "taking lessons" from global (digital) leaders, particularly by looking into implementing Estonia's X-Road platform[960] along with its open-source code. I think this move indicates a strategic effort to enhance data interoperability and streamline data flows within the public sector.

Where to focus?

Continuous monitoring, adaptation, and addressing areas identified through surveys should be a priority for the years to come.

10. EL SALVADOR

What's holding digital El Salvador back?

While most of the Latin American and Caribbean countries are leading the way in terms of digitising government services, digital El Salvador lags behind others in the region. With only about half of the country's population using the internet and the lack of trust in digital ecosystems, there's still a long way to go before it can be considered on par with its neighbours. El Salvador's first steps toward a more digital public sector started in 2016 when the government formed a dedicated unit – the **Electronic Government Directorate** (Dirección de Gobierno Electrónico[961].) Today, to guide policymakers, the government has developed the Digital Agenda (DA) 2020-2030[962] - the main reference document for promoting and encouraging the digital government of El Salvador. The Digital Agenda is aligned with the United Nations Sustainable Development Goals[963] and other national strategic projects.

According to recent data, El Salvador's total population was 6.53 million at the beginning of 2023[964]. Mobile penetration is remarkably high in the country, considering its economic indicators. Data from GSMA Intelligence[965] indicates that there were 9.77 million cellular mobile connections at the start of 2022 - even exceeding figures for the total population. And there were only 3.30 million internet users in January 2022. Yet, in 2024, the internet penetration rate was 71.7%. Kepios's[966] analysis shows that internet users in El Salvador increased by 0.6% between 2023 and 2024. And that's a good step in the right direction.

Regarding access to digital technologies, the government has made significant advances providing high-quality computers[967] for students and teachers across the country. However, Despite these efforts, El Salvador still lacks a national framework for digital skills[968] development. This framework is essential to guide how students acquire digital skills to the highly-specialised level in higher education and close the country's digital divide. Also, high school students can decide if they want to follow the technical path and connect with MEGATEC[969]. This program offers over 30 technical programs to help students strengthen their technical and digital skills and continue an extra year at the TVET institution, where they obtain a higher technical degree.

Where to focus?

Increasing investment in telecommunications infrastructure, repeaters, and encouraging an innovative digital economy while avoiding unnecessarily costly policies are some of the main future priorities for El Salvador.

11. GRENADA

Digital Grenada is hoping to become a Small Smart State

With a population of over 126,000 people[970], digital Grenada is a sovereign state located in the Caribbean Sea. It comprises Grenada, Carriacou, Petite Martinique, and several smaller, uninhabited islands. These islands together form the nation of Grenada. In analysing its international EGDI ranking, it's evident that the country has shown some progress in recent years even though its high EGDI values show a decline in 2024 with a score of 0.6458[971] (values range from 0-1.) Also, the low EPI values of 0.2466 indicate that there's room for improvement in actively engaging people in collaborative governance.

Between 2020 and 2022, Granada made great progress, jumping from 102nd place to 66th in the rankings. However, things have taken a step back since then. By 2024, it has dropped back to its earlier position (worse actually), ranking 104th out of 193 countries assessed.

One other aspect of Grenada's "regress" is shown in its O*nline Services Provision* and *Telecommunications Infrastructure Indexes*. This is reflected in the decrease in OSI value[972] from 0.5507 to 0.5056 and TII value from 0.7770 to 0.6767, respectively. Grenada may still be in the same EGDI group, but in 2024 it stood out for having one of the strongest human capital bases. This strong foundation in skilled people could really help push Grenada's digital government efforts forward…if used right.

What I think is worth noting is that digital Grenada ranked as one of the Small Island Developing State (SIDS) with the EGDI values above the world's average. It has also been working towards becoming a Small Smart State (SSS)[973], with support from the United Nations Development Programme (UNDP) since 2020.

Given Grenada's vulnerability to climate change impacts (like extreme weather events and changing rainfall patterns,) adopting climate-smart agriculture practices is necessary for safeguarding the country's food security and rural livelihoods. One such project is the Blue Bot initiative[974], which utilises artificial intelligence to analyse images captured by underwater reef robots. On land, the *Climate Smart Agriculture and Rural Enterprise Programme* collects data to monitor real-time changes in climate, soil conditions, and market prices.

This information is then used to make informed decisions throughout the food supply chain and to promote more climate-resilient and sustainable agriculture[975]. Additionally, the Climate Resilient Infrastructure for Integrated Landscape[976] initiative has launched a mobile app to provide citizens with real-time information and alerts during natural disasters. Lastly, Grenada's involvement in the CariSECURE[977] initiative highlights its focus on enhancing public safety through digitising data collection and analysis by the police.

Where to focus?

The next step for digital Grenada should be digitalising public administration, providing more high-quality online services, and creating an innovation hub platform to meaningfully engage citizens.

12. GUATEMALA

Guatemala still lacks a central strategy for the digitalisation of government services

Digital Guatemala, this Central American country rich in cultural heritage and natural beauty, has been gradually (and slowly) advancing its digital governance. In the latest UN E-Government Survey[978], Guatemala ranked 122nd out of 193 countries assessed, still part of the high EGDI group. While this indicates some level of advancement. Guatemala is still behind when it comes to important things like human capital and infrastructure. This means it doesn't yet meet the average standards of its region or the world in these areas. However, there's one place where Guatemala is doing really well: online services. In this area, it has gone far beyond both the regional and global averages, showing real progress in how it provides services online. It's a bright spot for the country, even as there's still work to be done in other areas. Over the past two years, Guatemala has moved up two spots in the EGDI rankings, keeping pace with its regional neighbours. The country has a strong EGDI value of 0.5738, showing good progress in e-government development. However, its EPI score of 0.4658 is average, suggesting there's room to improve how citizens engage with online government services.

One significant positive aspect is the government's commitment outlined in the Digital Government Plan for 2021-2026[979]. In terms of connectivity, digital Guatemala has achieved somewhat of an impressive coverage[980]. However, while Guatemala has the necessary elements for innovation (such as human capital and public institutions), these components seem less coordinated. Over the past decade, the Government of Guatemala has implemented long-term policies to support the development of the digital economy. While progress in this area may not be entirely clear, data suggests[981] that there has been some impact on financial inclusion, indicating that efforts to promote digital inclusion are beginning to yield results. The launch of the Open Data Portal by the Ministry of Finance was a step forward, but issues like outdated data and insufficient governance persist.

Where to focus?

I think one key area that requires immediate attention is the lack of a central strategy or policy for the digitalisation of government services or systems (yes, they lack a central policy.) Another important thing to note is that while the country has relatively high network coverage, there are still segments of the population that lack access to the internet, especially in rural and underserved areas. This digital divide persists[982] across various factors such as gender, geography, income, education, literacy, and ethnicity.

13. HAITI

Natural disasters and lack of resources keep leaving it behind

The digital government of Haiti is falling behind compared to other countries. Only 57% of the population is covered by at least a 3G mobile[983] network, and only 47% own a mobile phone. According to the latest UN survey on e-government[984], Haiti ranks among the lowest in the world for digital governance, ranking 186th out of 193 countries assessed. Haiti's digital performance has not improved over the past two years, even though it moved up by just one spot in the global scene. It's clear that much more work is needed. Significant investment is required in every part of digital governance, and more effort is needed across the board to make real progress. This reflects the country's ongoing struggle with limited resources and damage to its telecommunications infrastructure caused by natural disasters. With a low EGDI value of 0.2116, coupled with very low Online Service Index (OSI)[985] and low Telecommunication Infrastructure Index (TII) values, the digital government of Haiti faces an uphill battle.

The fact of the matter is that the lack of access to national ID cards is a major obstacle, as most Haitians do not possess one. In February 2023, the Haitian government registered 5.3 million Haitian adults, but only 4.4 million received the new ID card. This leaves a substantial gap, with an estimated 2 and 2.6 million[986] people still needing new ID cards. The process of obtaining identity cards and passports in Haiti is plagued by long wait times and bureaucratic hurdles, leading to frustration among Haitian citizens. In this place where food insecurity is a pressing issue affecting nearly half of the population, such initiatives can lay the groundwork for greater financial resilience and (especially) women's economic empowerment. Take, for example,

Klere Chimen, Haiti's largest safety net program[987], funded by the World Bank(WB). This US$75 million initiative not only provides cash transfers but also offers voluntary training related to health, nutrition, and financial inclusion. One notable achievement of the program is the significant increase in digital cash transfers. In March 2023, approximately 60% of recipients received their cash transfers digitally[988], a substantial jump from just 3% in May 2022.

Where to focus?

From fixing the infrastructure to offering more services online to funding digital education initiatives and training programs for the whole population - there's a whole lot to be done.

14. HONDURAS

Still faces substantial digital gaps despite major progress

While Honduras demonstrates moderate levels of telecommunications infrastructure and human capital, its online services provision has always lagged behind. However, for the first time, in 2024, it saw some progress in this dimension. So, in terms of online services, Honduras falls within the middle OSI group, even though it still indicates huge room for improvement. In the UN's recent E-government report, Honduras ranks 142nd out of 193[989] countries, having moved up 13 places in ranking in just 2 years. When it comes to e-participation, it rsaw some amazing progress moving up by 50 places in 2 years, holding the 130th spot in 2024.

It's the Honduran Digital Republic[990] that leads the digital initiatives for the government. One of its most important steps has been the creation of the **DIGER** (Results-Based Management Directorate)[991]. With a direct line to the presidency of the Republic, *DIGER* functions independently in the administrative, financial, and budgetary aspects of the government's digital agenda. Another noteworthy aspect is that Smart Cities are at the forefront of the government's long-term ICT goals. The city of San Pedro Sula[992] and the Port of Cortes are leading the charge[993] with different ambitious programs aimed at the modernisation of infrastructure, digital connectivity, and e-participation. It's a solid effort but still not enough. Connectivity and digital skills present significant challenges for Honduras, with low affordability, availability, and utilisation of digital infrastructure. Inequities in internet access are pronounced[994], with a substantial 58% gap in internet use between affluent and underprivileged households in Honduras. Its initiative to improve its identity verification services is a significant step towards enhancing access to essential services for its citizens. With funding from the World Bank totalling $40 million[995], the country aims to digitise its civil registration and vital statistics system, ensuring that every Honduran has access to a legal identity. This project is crucial as it not only guarantees the right to identity but also facilitates access to social programs, education, healthcare, financial services, and more.

Where to focus?

Despite progress Honduras still faces substantial gaps in infrastructure, online services, and human capital. Without adequate investment Honduras may struggle to enhance its digital government capabilities and meet the evolving needs of its population.

15. JAMAICA

Digital Jamaica has been steadily improving its e-government ranking since 2018

Digital Jamaica shows promising signs of progress in its digital governance landscape. With a high Telecommunication Infrastructure Index (TII) and Human Capital Index (HCI), the country is well-positioned to leverage digital technologies for societal advancement. It has high EGDI values[996] even surpassing the world average (for the first time). The country has been steadily improving its EGDI ranking since 2018, and has shown huge progress in the past 2 years, indicating a positive trajectory in its digital transformation journey. In the latest UN E-government survey of 2024[997], digital Jamaica ranked 96th out of 193 countries assessed (up from 102nd in 2022).

This improvement in ranking reflects the country's efforts. Jamaica has also made progress in getting more citizens involved in digital governance. In 2022, it was ranked 123rd for e-participation, but by 2024, it improved to 102nd. This shows that more Jamaicans are using digital platforms to engage with their government, making it easier for people to get involved and have a voice in important decisions.

In 2023, Jamaica took significant steps towards its digital transformation journey, with the European Union (EU) partnering with the government to launch the *Digital Jamaica* program, worth 9.5 million EUR[998]. This marks a milestone as the first major grant-funded initiative aimed at supporting Jamaica's digital agenda (across various sectors.) Its *National Identification System* (NIDS) is another significant step forward. The pilot for the digital ID[999] was launched in

December 2022, marking a crucial milestone in Jamaica's construction of a digital society.

One notable aspect of the NIDS rollout is the expansion of enrollment centres, including the transformation of Post Offices into NIDS centres. Furthermore, the government's plan to upgrade border management systems, including implementing a biometric passenger screening system at Sangster International Airport[1000], shows another focus on digital border management. As Jamaica Information Service reports[1001] the government plans to upgrade its border management systems in order to enhance security even more in the near future.

2023 was also the year where the government proposed a unified application named 'One Jamaica.'[1002] This app is designed to bring together the different virtual services offered by various government agencies into a single, easy-to-use digital platform. More and more people are using mobile apps for various tasks, and there's also a growing focus on protecting people's data, as shown by the recent Data Protection Act[1003].

Where to focus?

Although digital Jamaica has an ICT Council[1004] in place, it's not working as it should be[1005]. This means there's a gap in the oversight and coordination of digital initiatives. Also, Jamaica doesn't have a recent comprehensive plan specifically for digital government.

16. MEXICO

Evolving from e-government to digital government

e-Mexico has made progress in the digitalisation of its government through the years, especially in 2024 when it finally moved up to the very high EGDI group. It is one of the most digitally advanced countries in the Northern America continent..ranking 4th out of 23 countries. Mexico has made some progress in the last few years, partially because of its booming economy. It's also due to how they've embraced the digital world.

The Mexican government started to use information and communication technologies (ICT) in the 1990s, though there was no central government e-Government strategy. The Institute for Statistics, Geography, and Informatics (INEGI) was in charge of the Mexican government's IT policy. In 2001, the president officially introduced e-government as an initiative to digitalise and modernise the government. Since then, Mexico has sought to make the most of its digital opportunities to improve government performance. The government's official portal, *gob.mx* has been a powerful force in the country's transformation[1006]. Mexico's 65th ranking in the 2024 UN E-Government Survey[1007] is a good progress in the right direction. Also, I believe it is critical to mention the fact that it's a leader compared with countries with similar per capita GDPs - a laudable standing.

Since 2012, Mexico has delivered outstanding results in line with the objectives of its National Digital Strategy. It has set up essential initiatives, such as MéxicoX[1008], an online learning platform for specialised and academic training for teachers, benefiting millions of users. Similarly, prende.mx[1009] is a knowledgesharing platform for teachers using technology as part of the learning process. InteroperaMX[1010] (inspired by the Estonian X-Road) is a platform that allows government agencies to securely share reliable and trustworthy data. This effort, which has been operational since 2018, is driven by the vision of having the user only provide the same information once to the public sector.

Where to focus?

Because technology is rapidly evolving, e-Mexico might benefit from a plan to quickly upgrade its government systems to attract the best tech talent to the public sector.

17. NICARAGUA

In digital Nicaragua infrastructure impedes progress

Digital Nicaragua, a lower-middle-income country in Central America, has not shown much progress in e-governance. The main culprit? The online service provision. According to the World Bank's GovTech Maturity Index (GTMI)[1011], Nicaragua is categorised in group C, which means there is *"Some focus on GovTech."* This classification indicates that while there is an awareness of the potential of digital government technologies, the efforts and implementations might not be fully comprehensive.... Yet. I'd say another critical point to consider is Nicaragua's standing, according to the United Nations report on e-governance[1012]. The country is characterised by a High Technology Infrastructure Index (TII) and Human Capital Index (HCI). This means that its telecommunications infrastructure and human capital base are sufficiently well developed to drive forward digital transformation of the government.

Interestingly, despite its high human capital index, Nicaragua has seen a decline in its overall digital governance performance. From 2022 to 2024, digital Nicaragua's EGDI (E-Government Development Index) values[1013] declined, leading to a ranking of 132nd in e-governance. In terms of e-participation, Nicaragua has dropped even further, now ranking 148th out of 193 countries that were assessed. This is a big fall, as the country has lost 2 spots in e-governance and 13 places in e-participation. This decline is worrying and shows that there may be bigger, deeper issues in the country's digital systems that need to be fixed. At the start of 2024, there were 4.36 million internet users in the country, putting internet penetration at 61.5%[1014]. On the surface, this sounds pretty solid, but when you dive deeper, you realise that it means

2.73 million people are still offline. That's 38.5% of the population without internet access, which is a significant gap. Frequent power outages[1015] remain a major issue, caused by both poor infrastructure and natural disasters. For instance, a failure in the Central American electrical system in July 2021 led to a total blackout in Nicaragua that lasted five hours. Similar blackouts reported in June[1016] and many other months of that year. These outages severely disrupt internet connectivity, making it unreliable for many users.

Where to focus?

Ensuring reliable power, making internet access more affordable, and bridging the geographical divide are critical steps towards achieving more comprehensive and inclusive connectivity. The goal should be not just to increase the number of e-services but to ensure that access is equitable and reliable for all Nicaraguans.

18. PANAMA

Digital Panama: On its way to becoming a Digital Hub

Panama has shown a huge commitment to leadership in terms of the accountability and transparency of government. With that in mind, in 2013 it was created the National Authority of Transparency and Access to Information (*Autoridad Nacional de Transparencia y Acceso a la Información*) or ANTAI[1017]. According to the World Bank and the World Economic Forum, Panama ranks second place in terms of ease of doing business in Latin America and 86th worldwide[1018], thanks to its forward-looking government and its successful efforts towards digital transformation. What's more, according to the EGDI report, Panama improved its ranking compared to 2020[1019]. The National Authority for Government Innovation (*Autoridad Nacional para la Innovación Gubernamental)*[1020], otherwise known as AIG, has had a massive role in digitalisation. It was established in October 2009 as the e-government agency in charge of designing, implementing and managing the digital agenda. Thanks to their efforts, in the 2024 EGDI report, Panama made a solid improvement by moving up three spots in the rankings. Now, it stands at 79th place out of 193 countries.

The Internet for All (Internet Para Todos, IPT)[1021] project is one of the most prominent initiatives geared towards increasing internet penetration rates by providing free broadband internet across the nation. This project is administered by AIG and is part of the strategies for modernising the infrastructure. To that end, more than 11,000 Wi-Fi hotspots were installed by early 2010, covering 86% of the population. The Panamanian government's other initiatives include modernising public procurement, aimed at more transparent and efficient resource management through Panamá Compra[1022], an e-procurement platform. As part of Digital Agenda 2020, it recently launched the Panama Digital Hub[1023] with hopes of turning the country into an international centre for digital innovation. It is a public policy intended to make digital Panama the most competitive country in Latin America in terms of knowledge and technology. Also, it is part of the "*Strategy for the Development of the ICT Sector 2025*" and has four human talent pillars, physical and social infrastructure, financial resources, and legal, regulatory framework. Moreover, to combat the Covid-19, the government introduced the "Solidary Panama" (Panamá Solidario) Plan[1024]. It was a temporary emergency and social assistance plan which consisted of cash allowances and bags of food for people in need where they used identity cards as debit cards.

Where to focus?

Panama needs to build institutional capacities by developing a procurement policy for information and communication technologies. It should focus on implementing an e-government infrastructure that helps strengthen the country's ongoing efforts towards a coherent and sustainable digital government.

19. SAINT KITTS AND NEVIS

Infrastructure is not enough, more focus on services needed

Digital Saint Kitts and Nevis (also known as the Federation of St. Christopher and Nevis) shows very high levels of technological infrastructure and human capital, positioning it well for digital development. However, despite these advantages, the country also faces challenges in effectively engaging its citizens in collaborative governance, as reflected by its low EPI levels[1025]. In the UN's E-Government Survey[1026], Saint Kitts and Nevis dropped in ranking from 87th in 2022 to 110th out of 193 countries.

The Ministry of Social Development and Gender Affairs has taken a bold step towards modernisation by committing to digitising all its application and payment processes by the end of 2024. By transitioning to digital processes, the ministry wants to make it easier for people to access the support they need. The recent makeover of the ministry's website[1027] is a promising start to this digital transformation journey. The updated website now features simplified online application forms for various services[1028], ranging from community centre reservations to benefit enrollment. Still, it's far from perfect and far from online. Also, ICT infrastructure, particularly broadband (but not only), plays an important role in the modernisation of Saint Kitts and Nevis. Currently, the country boasts an impressive mobile penetration rate of 137%, indicating widespread access to mobile services among its population.

Moreover, all connections are 3G/4G broadband enabled[1029], ensuring fast and reliable internet access for users across the Federation. But, the Human Capital Index (HCI) stands at 59%, indicating that a child born today will be 59% as productive when they grow up if they have access to complete education and full health. I have to admit that this figure is higher than the average for Latin America and the Caribbean region. However, it falls below the average for high-income countries. To address these challenges and enhance human capital development, Digital Saint Kitts and Nevis partnered with the United Nations (UN) and three other Eastern Caribbean countries (Anguilla, British Virgin Islands, and Grenada) to pilot the Resilient Caribbean: Engaging and Training Youth, Strengthening Integrated Social Protection Sector Delivery Joint Programme[1030].

Where to focus?

Thanks to its infrastructure and human capital, it *could* improve its international ranking (in the EGDI report), but to do that it needs to pay more focus in offering more and better services online. E-participation is another important focus area if it really wants to succeed as Digital Saint Kitts and Nevis.

20. SAINT LUCIA

Empowering the blind and low vision with digital skills

Digital Saint Lucia, as a founding member of the Organisation of Eastern Caribbean States (OECS), holds significant regional importance, hosting the headquarters of the OECS and the Eastern Caribbean Supreme Court. This positioning proves its role in regional cooperation and governance. But what about *digital* governance? With high scores in both the Telecommunications Infrastructure Index (TII) and the Human Capital Index (HCI)[1031], Saint Lucia has a solid foundation for digital advancement. This means the country has good infrastructure and a well-educated workforce in digital skills, which are essential for using digital technologies effectively. In the UN's E-Government Survey[1032], Saint Lucia ranks 133rd out of 193 countries (which is below the global average.)

Additionally, according to an IU estimate[1033], only 78% of the population has access to the internet. Factors such as accessibility, usability, and the range of services provided online do contribute to this ranking. Thanks to initiatives like the USAID-funded **ConnectED Activity**[1034] (led by World Education), significant progress has been made in this area. This framework, informed by the needs of youth and the private sector, ensures that the digital skills being taught are relevant and in-demand. It's crucial for bridging the gap between education and the job market. I think it's fantastic that ConnectED trained 175 teachers in digital skills[1035] integration. By empowering educators with the tools and knowledge to incorporate digital skills into their teaching, the quality of education can improve significantly. Also, the pilot youth digital skills internship program[1036] is another brilliant idea. Placing 55 students in internships and businesses across Saint

Lucia not only provides valuable hands-on experience but also helps them develop essential skills for the future job market.

Empowering blind and low-vision children with digital skills is another important step forward made a reality with the help of the Caribbean Digital Transformation Project[1037]. This is a collaborative effort by the Dominica, Grenada, Saint Lucia, St. Vincent and the Grenadines and the Organization of Eastern Caribbean States, that seeks to increase access to digital services, technologies and skills.

Where to focus?

Saint Lucia has great potential to expand its online services and invest in the right technology to benefit its citizens. To achieve this, it can and should do more to offer a wider range of services online.

21. SAINT VINCENT AND THE GRENADINES

Digital government of Saint Vincent and the Grenadines

Having a high Technological Infrastructure Index (TII)[1038] and Human Capital Index (HCI) means that the digital government of Saint Vincent and the Grenadines has good resources and skilled people to support its digital development. With the launch of initiatives like online government portals and digital ID systems, the government is modernising public services, making them more accessible and efficient for citizens. However, despite these advantages, Saint Vincent and the Grenadines still needs to improve its Online Service Index (OSI). This is important because it reflects how effectively the government provides services to its citizens through digital platforms. A high TII suggests that the country has strong digital infrastructure. Meanwhile, a high HCI indicates that there is a welleducated and skilled workforce ready to embrace digital technologies.

One thing's for sure, the digital government of Saint Vincent and the Grenadines has shown improvement over the past few years. Its EGDI value decreased slightly, placing it 117th out of 193 countries[1039](down from the 107th place in 2022). Along with this, the country's e-participation score also went down. It dropped by 20 spots, which means that in terms of how citizens are involved in e-government, Saint Vincent and the Grenadines is now ranked where it was back in 2020. This shows that, over the past couple of years, the country hasn't made much progress in these areas and has even fallen behind in some rankings.

Saint Vincent is planning to pilot its national digital ID system in 2024 with help from MOSIP.

Finance Minister Camilo Gonsalves' announcement[1040] regarding the pilot's use of this platform and integration with the country's Vital Statistics System is promising. This indicates a great approach to digital identity management, ensuring accuracy and reliability from birth to death. Funding for the digital ID system is partly sourced from the Caribbean Regional Digital Transformation Project (CARDTP)[1041]. This financial support not only facilitates the implementation of the digital identity system but also enables enhancements to other critical digital infrastructure, such as the civil registry and digital payments platform.

Where to focus?

While having high TII and HCI is a *good* start, focusing on improving the Online Service Index further will help the digital government of Saint Vincent and the Grenadines maximise the benefits of its digital infrastructure and human capital for the well-being of its citizens.

22. TRINIDAD AND TOBAGO

Among the top 5 Small Island Developing States of the world

Digital Trinidad and Tobago boasts high values in the E-Government Development Index (EGDI), indicating a somewhat strong performance in digital governance. Also, It's worth noting that Trinidad and Tobago ranks 5th among 37 Small Island Developing States (SIDS)[1042] meaning that it has EGDI values above the global average, showcasing its leadership in digital government among similar nations. Also it has made great progress in improving its e-participation, which was a major issue in the 2022 report. Back then, its E-Participation Index (EPI) was quite low. However, in just two years, the country has moved up 23 places in this area. Now, it ranks 120th out of 193 countries..huge step forward for the country. I'd like to add that one of digital Trinidad and Tobago's strengths lies in its extensive (digital) footprint. The widespread use of mobile phones[1043], robust internet consumption, and large numbers of social media users contribute to its advanced digital infrastructure compared to other Caribbean countries. These factors provide a solid foundation for *continued* progress, too.

Digital Trinidad and Tobago is receiving significant international support, particularly from organisations like the Inter-American Development Bank (IDB) and the European Commission. So, for example, the Inter-American Development Bank (IDB) has approved a substantial investment of US$90 million[1044], with an initial loan of US$42 million, aimed at facilitating the country's digital transformation. On the other hand, the European Commission has approved a blending operation with CAF (Development Bank of Latin

America and the Caribbean), amounting to 3 million Euros, to support Trinidad and Tobago's digital transformation program[1045]. What's more, Trinidad and Tobago has demonstrated a growing recognition of the potential of big data for driving digital innovation in the public sector. Efforts in this direction began in 2020 with the country's inaugural Big Data Forum[1046], organised by the UN. Since then, the country has been *actively* using big data analytics for different initiatives. For example, there have been efforts focused on crime prediction[1047] aimed at enhancing public safety and security in the country. They are also harnessing big data for public health purposes, particularly tracking and managing mosquitoborne disease outbreaks[1048]. By using data-driven insights, authorities can better understand disease patterns, allocate resources effectively, and implement *targeted* interventions to mitigate health risks.

Where to focus?

Ensuring inclusive access to digital technologies and addressing potential challenges related to e-participation will help maximise the benefits of its digital governance.

23. THE UNITED STATES OF AMERICA

Digital US government's long overdue wake-up call: Solid frameworks?

When people (or governments) think about digitalisation it's easy to get swept up in the latest technology and cutting-edge software. Forgetting that these innovations are only as good as the framework supporting them. I like to explain frameworks as the invisible backbone of a digital government, much like the strong core of a building. It's what holds everything together, ensuring that government services and interactions with citizens run smoothly, efficiently, and securely. So, it's not just about the technology itself or the number of services available online...a dependable framework is what makes it all work seamlessly. Despite the remarkable technological progress we've witnessed, many countries still struggle with inadequate or outdated frameworks. Citizens face frustration when accessing government services online, and security risks and data breaches become all too common. Ultimately, the digital experience and user-centricity[1049] fall short of its potential.

The digital US sets out the framework to improve the user experience. For 2024 they published their Delivering a Digital-First Public Experience[1050] policy guidance, which sets out "the pillars of government-wide digital experience". It's a bold step. And an important one as well. Why? Shockingly, only 2% of government firms have embraced digitisation, and around 45% of federal websites are still not mobile-friendly. Additionally, 60% of federal websites have potential accessibility issues, and a whopping 80% do not use the US Web Design System code. Many digital US federal government agencies are at different stages of their modernisation/transformation journey. With the new policy guidance in place, the government can track each agency's progress. This will help them make the right investments to support digital services, retire old websites and systems, and make the most of taxpayer money. The goal is to create a government that's secure from the ground up and accessible to everyone.

Where to focus?

The US is undoubtedly the digital leader in two American continents. But the real test lies in whether they can effectively harness the power of technology to deliver a modern, secure digital government that truly caters to the needs and expectations of their citizens. The journey ahead is bound to be a bumpy one, and the ultimate verdict on its success or failure will rest in the hands of time and the collective efforts of those involved.

SOUTH AMERICA

Digital governance
SUMMARY

The continent itself is vast, with countries that vary widely not just in size but in their digital maturity and governance strategies. We have the "giants" like Uruguay or Chile, which have made some really huge progress in digital governance, setting an example for other countries in the region. But then, we also have countries like Venezuela and Guyana, which are still in their early stages.

For clarity purposes I've added a list of countries that constitute South America (the continent) alphabetically:

1. Argentina
2. Bolivia
3. Brazil
4. Chile
5. Colombia
6. Ecuador
7. Guyana
8. Paraguay
9. Peru
10. Suriname
11. Uruguay

12. Venezuela

A snapshot of the continent

When I think about the state of digital governance in South America, I see a continent that has made progress yet still faces some challenges. Most countries here have established organisations dedicated to driving digital government initiatives, usually housed within a central or federal government structure.

These organisations are typically found within line ministries or special agencies, and in some cases, they are part of a coordinating ministry or even the centre of government. This setup might sound like a solid foundation for digital governance, but it's not without its flaws. However, I think it's important to point out that while these organisations exist, not all of them have the full scope of responsibilities and mandates they need to effectively drive and harmonise digital government reforms across the public sector. Even though I might add that this is an issue in many countries as well, not isolated to this continent. On a broader scale, there's a strong link between a country's economic development and its digital infrastructure. The positive correlation between per capita income levels and access to and use of the internet is a clear indicator of this.

Now, when we look at the UN's E-Government Development Index (EGDI), it's interesting to see that all the South American countries fall into either the very high or high EGDI categories. This is significant because it means that these nations are, for the most part, keeping pace with global digital governance standards. However, it's also worth noting that there's still variation within these groups. Some countries have really stood out in recent years due to their significant improvements in digital governance. Take Uruguay, Chile, and Colombia for example. These countries have made some of the most notable leaps in their EGDI rankings along the years. But, of course, not every country has seen the same level of progress. Some have experienced ups and downs along the way.

What's holding South America back?

A few key issues come to mind. First, there's a noticeable gap between the progress made in education and skills (what the Human Capital Index measures) and the development of infrastructure, like internet access (measured by the Telecommunication Infrastructure Index). When looking at the reports from 2022, South American countries were mainly focused on building up their human capital, like improving education and skills. But this year, I noticed a shift. There's been a lot more progress in improving telecommunication infrastructure, and it's clear when you look at the TII index. The growth in this area has been huge this year, showing a real improvement in how these countries are developing their digital networks and services. It's great to see this progress in the infrastructure area, but there's also something concerning. Some countries actually had lower HCI values this year compared to 2022, which suggests that while infrastructure is improving, there are still gaps in other areas that need attention...especially in the people and their skills.

Another issue that stands out to me is the uneven progress in online services across the continent. Some countries have developed fairly advanced e-government platforms, but others are still just getting started. This creates a digital divide, not only between South America and other continents but also within the continent itself. This uneven progress is due to different factors, like varying levels of government commitment, economic stability, and the ability of public sectors to push forward with digital projects. Having the technology and the skills is important, but without a strong effort to drive digital transformation, things don't move as quickly as they could.

Digital governance in South America: Regional leaders & laggards

To make it easier to understand, I've decided to rank all 12 countries in the region from best to worst in terms of digital governance. This ranking helps us see where each country stands and what challenges and opportunities they face.

Top and bottom performers in terms of digital governance

1. Uruguay
2. Chile
3. Argentina
4. Brazil
5. Peru
6. Ecuador
7. Colombia
8. Paraguay
9. Bolivia
10. Suriname
11. Guyana
12. Venezuela

Before I mention anything else, I just want to point out that this list hasn't changed much since the 2022 report. The only difference I noticed is that Ecuador has moved ahead of Colombia this year in terms of its digital government progress. Other than that, the rankings are mostly the same as they were in 2022. At the top of the list is Uruguay. I believe Uruguay's success in digital governance isn't just by chance. The country has consistently invested in its digital infrastructure, making sure that online services are available to everyone.

The government's commitment to using technology to improve services and be more transparent is impressive. Their focus on education and digital skills has really paid off, as people are more likely to use and benefit from these digital services.

I want to add that if we would see both Americas as one, this would be the top 5 rankings.

1. United States of America (North America)
2. Uruguay (South America)
3. Chile (South America)
4. Argentina (South America)
5. Canada (North America)
6. Brazil (South America)

Uruguay and Chile, in particular, stand out for their consistent efforts to improve online services and expand digital access. Meanwhile, Argentina and Brazil, with their vast and diverse populations, are have been making huge progress in integrating digital solutions into government operations. This is no small feat, especially when you consider the differences in resources and infrastructure between the two regions. I would also add that these South American South American countries are really setting a strong example for their neighbours. They're showing that with the right strategies, it's possible to create digital systems that work for everyone, even when there are challenges. What's even more impressive is that many of these countries have managed to surpass Canada, which had been the second-best in digital governance for many years, all the way back since 2003. The only time Canada wasn't in second place was in 2020, when Uruguay stepped up and took the spot, pushing Canada to third place.

This shows how much progress these countries have made in such a short time!

Opportunities for moving forward

The region has made some progress, but there are key areas that I believe need more attention to create lasting and effective results.

First, I think it's essential to focus on developing digital skills within the public sector.

Right now, many South American countries don't fully appreciate how important it is to invest in their government workers' digital skills. They do need a workforce that understands both technology and how government works. These are the people who can lead the way in making digital government a reality. This kind of talent (the right kind of talent) can bridge the gap between what technology can offer and what the government needs to achieve.

Another big area that needs improvement is how government services are designed and delivered. There's often a lack of consistency between the different levels of government—local, regional, and national. This can lead to confusion and inefficiency, which ultimately makes the government less effective. This would make things easier and more straightforward for citizens.

I also believe that South American governments need to build better capacities to invest in digital government. Governments need clear roles and strategies for handling data. Without a solid plan, it's hard to keep up with the fast pace of technology and the growing demands from citizens. Data is the foundation of digital governance, and without a clear strategy, governments might struggle to make the most of it.

This isn't just about finding the money—though that's important—but also about creating the structures and roles within government that can manage and drive these investments effectively. I think formalising roles, functions, and strategies for government data is a key step in this direction. Without clear accountability and strategic oversight, investments in digital government can become disjointed and less effective. In short, I think South America has a lot of opportunities to improve its digital governance, but it requires a shift in focus. The region needs to prioritise developing digital skills, creating more consistent service delivery, and building strong data management strategies. These steps are key to building a digital government that works well and serves everyone better. It needs the right focus.

1. ARGENTINA

Did digital Argentina find a faster path to its transformation?

The use of ICTs in the public sector in digital Argentina has only recently become a reality, particularly as compared with Latin American countries that have made significant strides in this area. All countries face challenges in bringing about the digital transformation of the public sector. However, the challenges Argentina has had to overcome to begin its digital transformation journey have been especially acute. Located in the southern part of South America, Argentina is the eighth-largest country in the world and the fourth-largest country in the Americas in terms of mainland area. It is also one of the largest economies in Latin America. However, when it comes to digital Argentina has had to build much of its infrastructure and legislation from the ground up. Until several years ago, coordination between different government agencies was limited, as was the use of digital technologies. Modernisation efforts were ad hoc and sectorfocused. By the end of 2015, only *three* cross-government information systems had been established and even those had limited coverage for their respective focus areas across government. In 2019, the government launched the Federal Digitalisation Plan. This plan established a strategy to use open source solutions for all government agencies and similar institutions. The e-filing system supported business continuity during the COVID-19 pandemic, allowing the public sector to operate smoothly[1051]. From 2020 to 2021, e-filing registered users increased by 73%

The single governmental website argentina.gob.ar[1052] is a platform for citizen and business digital services which provided safe and timely access to government services during the pandemic. **MiArgentina**[1053] is a citizen dashboard that has become the single starting point of any interaction with the government. In 2021, digital Argentina's new Open Government Federal Program (Programa Federal de Transformación Pública Digital)[1054] aims to promote the implementation of open government projects at the local level, strengthen capacity-building, diversify the open government community, and promote collaborative public policy design. In the 2024 EGDI report, Argentina is mentioned among the leaders of both American continents (4th to be exact), even surpassing Canada. Meanwhile in the global scene it ranks 42nd among 193 countries. Huge progress in just 2 years.

Where to focus?

Argentina needs to focus on the long-term sustainability of the results achieved so far. A more thorough digital government strategy and a complementary national data strategy will definitely improve policy accountability, ownership and sustainability.

2. BOLIVIA

Digital Bolivia has no clear strategy to promote gov innovation

Digital Bolivia, despite being a landlocked developing nation, holds significant potential for growth in its information and communications technology (ICT) sector. With a vast land area (exceeding 1 million square kilometres if I'm correct) and a population of over 12 million[1055], the country's low population density poses both challenges and opportunities for digital development. Despite being a lower-middle-income country, Bolivia demonstrates a noteworthy performance in certain aspects of e-government, as indicated by its high scores in the EGDI report[1056]. In 2024, Bolivia was classified in the high EGDI (E-Government Development Index) group, indicating significant progress in digital governance with a score of 0.6651[1057]. However, its EPI (E-Participation Index) value of 0.4247 suggests there's still room for improvement in engaging citizens digitally. Interestingly, Bolivia ranks among the top 17 landlocked countries in terms of EGDI. This indicates that geographical constraints don't necessarily hinder e-government advancement.

Nevertheless, there exists a noticeable disparity in e-government development within the Latin American and Caribbean (LAC) region. While Bolivia focuses on closing accessibility gaps and building digital infrastructure, neighbours like Brazil have achieved higher digital maturity by integrating service design into their strategic digital government goals. Moreover, the fact that only 73% of the population[1058] has access to the internet is concerning, especially considering the growing importance of digital connectivity in today's world. Nevertheless, it's interesting to note the increase in digital payments and e-commerce transactions, indicating a shift towards digital channels *despite* limited internet access. One significant barrier seems to be the high cost of internet services, largely attributed to the lack of sophistication among telecom companies.

Where to focus?

Its data and technology infrastructure remain underdeveloped compared to more advanced nations - despite introducing a new data protection bill back in 2023[1059]. Issues such as the shortage of digital talent, weak technology infrastructure, and the absence of clear government innovation strategies pose hurdles to the progress of digital Bolivia.

3. BRAZIL

Digital Brazil is in the top 30 global leaders in e-participation

Digital Brazil has been a leader in digital governance in both Americas for some time now.

With a strong(er) emphasis on e-participation, the country has achieved notable success, showing very high levels on the Open Society Index (OSI). This progress can be attributed to Brazil's significant investment in human capital development and infrastructure, which have provided a solid foundation for its digital initiatives.

In the 2024 EGDI report, Brazil ranked 50th out of 193 countries[1060] assessed, reflecting its commitment to advancing digital services and engagement. Moreover, even at the local level, Brazil demonstrates its digital prowess, with São Paulo securing the 19th position among 193 cities surveyed for the Local Online Service Index (LOSI).

One notable aspect of Brazil's digital governance framework is the presence of a coordinating ministry responsible for overseeing digital government initiatives. Comparatively, its stands out as one of the few countries in Latin America[1061] where such a coordinating ministry exists. This setup, as observed in other countries like Chile, where the Digital Government Division operates under the Ministry General Secretariat of the Presidency, shows and proves a proactive approach towards driving digital transformation at the *national* level. One standout feature is how Brazil's Digital Government Law[1062] is connecting open data with digital government initiatives. So, it's not just about transparency anymore... it's about using data to co-develop public services.

Regarding policies, Brazil has published the Brazilian Strategy for Digital Transformation (E-Digital) for the 2022-2026 cycle[1063], which includes a “Digital Transformation: citizenship and government” axis. They are seeking to make the government more accessible to the population and more efficient in offering services (in line with the Digital Government Strategy.) The fact that a 2023 OECD report[1064] ranks Brazil as one of the best countries i

n the region in terms of legislative coverage across these areas speaks volumes about their progress and dedication to digital governance. Training programs are really important for teaching digital skills to public officials in Brazil. But sometimes, it’s hard for these programs to be super effective because we’re not always clear on exactly what skills people need. To address this challenge, the National School of Public Administration in Brazil[1065] has taken proactive steps by offering dedicated courses focused on various aspects of digital capabilities. Also, the allocation of talent and skills within the public sector is very important for ensuring that institutions have access to the right people for the *right* roles. In response to this need, the Secretary of Digital Government has implemented the startup.gov.br project[1066].

Where to focus?

Brazil is really setting the bar high when it comes to digital government (and especially laws and regulations in the region) but it needs to pay a little more attention to the right infrastructure and to close the digital divide.

4. CHILE

The 3rd top performer in the Americas in 2024

The digital government in Chile has massively advanced in recent years. The government has always had a proactive attitude. The government decided to deregulate the telecom industry in the early 1990s to foster development. Chile has now become a leader in the region behind the US and Uruguay, even surpassing Argentina and Canada, according to the EDGI Index 2024[1067]. Its achievements in digital government have helped the country better manage and maintain its bureaucracy and administrative procedures while expanding access to information and contributing to governmental transparency and accountability. That's why finally in 2024 it is part of the very high EGDI group.

In the 2024 UN E-Government Survey[1068], Chile (along with some other countries as well) was applauded for significantly improving its EGDI values in just 2 years (ranking 31st up from the 42nd spot in 2022). The progress made reflects sustained efforts to create and implement comprehensive national e-government strategies, the evolution of supportive legal frameworks, and high levels of cooperation with regional and international actors in relevant digital fields. Like many countries, the digital government in Chile has consolidated its services into one integrated service system - ChileAtiende[1069]. The platform puts its users in touch with the local offices to attend face-to-face appointments or ask for documents to be delivered by mail or email. It provides services for 25 government institutions and reached a 57% net user satisfaction rate[1070] in the standardised measurement in 2020. However, the country's achievements have not gone unnoticed despite some hiccups along the way. Among the factors driving e-government development in Chile are improved telecommunications infrastructure and high penetration of mobile devices and the Internet. The digital government in Chile is also fully committed to supporting international and regional cooperation in digital government development. For instance, in 2019, Chile participated in the OECD E-Leaders Network and contributed to the Digital Agenda for Latin America and the Caribbean (eLAC)[1071].

Where to focus?

Lack of promotion and awareness of online services is a key barrier to adopting digital services in Chile. Moreover, concepts such as" digital by design", "Government as a Platform", and a "data-driven public sector"[1072] need to be embedded for achieving better internal efficiencies, delivering better value to all citizens, and avoiding discrimination.

5. COLOMBIA

Has been steadily moving forward

For much of the last two decades, the digital Colombia government has been looking for ways to increase transparency and public participation in a way that can be easily scaled at a low cost. Ministry of Information and Communications Technologies (MinTIC)[1073] is one of the pillars of the information society in digital Colombia. It was established in 2009, and now it aims to develop a competitive, innovative and prosperous information society that is fully integrated into the global information society. It wasn't until 2008 that then-President Alvaro Uribe Vélez made it one of the country's top priorities…helping it get to the 31st place 2 years later in e-governance (the best ranking it's ever had.) Then, the National Development Plan 2018-2022 (NDP)[1074] responded to the challenges of adapting the country's economy and society to the digital transformation. It aims to connect all nine sub-national territories in the country by focusing on digital inclusion and blockchain, IoT and AI.

Among other OECD countries, Colombia currently has the lowest fixed broadband dispersion[1075]. That's why it is looking to connect 80% of the population and 70% of households by 2022. The achievements the government has made over the years have not gone unnoticed. According to the EDGI index 2024[1076], digital Colombia has improved its ranking by 2 places compared to 2020. Also, according to a recent OECD report[1077], the government must create sustainable connections within the digital ecosystem. Digital Colombia currently has many digital government projects in motion, that are moving forward, but many of them are independent of one another. A lack of cross-agency collaboration makes these initiatives far less efficient than possible. To get things moving faster, agencies need to link up and work together.

Where to focus?

The government must demonstrate the impact of citizen engagement by increasing transparency and accountability. The administration needs to provide frequent updates on issues such as how much is being invested in technology projects, where they are taking place, their status and any delays they may be experiencing. This would instil confidence among its citizens in the government's commitment to digital government services.

6. ECUADOR

South America's leader in e-participation in 2024

Despite being the second smallest country in South America, Ecuador sits in the upper-middle-income bracket. And, it's commendable how it has managed to achieve very high levels in the Online Service Index (OSI) by leveraging its human capital development.

The one area where Ecuador is still falling behind is in infrastructure development, which continues to be a challenge even now. But that hasn't stopped the country from standing out. Ecuador has become a leader in the Americas for its efforts and investments in e-governance, showing how far determination and innovation can go, even with some obstacles in the way.

However, one are of future focus should be the portion of Ecuador's population (especially those residing in rural areas) that still faces barriers to accessing the digital economy. Ecuador has shown a strong political commitment to reducing inequalities through digital transformation, as outlined in its 2021-2025 Opportunity Plan[1078].

The fact that the internet penetration rate is 83.6% in 2024[1079] highlights the existing gaps in internet connectivity that need urgent attention. Also, digital skills remain an issue, too, especially between public sector officials and employees. For that reason, the Ministry of Telecommunications and Information Society (MINTEL) has collaborated with COURSERA to provide training[1080] to over 7,000 public sector officials. These training programs are very important for improving digital skills among government employees so they can deliver improved services to citizens.

In its region, it now ranks 10th, showing solid progress. Globally, it has moved up to the 67th spot on the UN's Electronic Government Development Index (EGDI) for 2024[1081]. That's a big jump from the 84th place it held back in 2022. This shows real progress in just two years, especially in areas like digital services and digital skills. It EPI values saw an improvement too, by 20 places to be exact (ranking 21st in the world.)

All this progress helped Ecuador surpass Colombia this year, taking the 6th place among the leaders of Southern America. Initiatives like Puntos del Encuentro[1082] promoting online government service usage, have been helpful in this direction (even though adoption rates remain *relatively* low.)

For instance, according to a World Bank report[1083] from 2024, less than 1% of internet users engage in procedures with public entities or government agencies online. Also, issues such as low app ratings and high bounce rates on government websites like www.gob.ec[1084] suggest challenges in user experience and functionality. For instance, the Gob. EC app has a rating of 2.2/5[1085] in the app store. This, coupled with high bounce rates, could possibly increase future dissatisfaction and potential usability issues.

Where to focus?

Issues like affordability, uneven infrastructure distribution, and gaps in digital skills are holding back millions of Ecuadorians from fully participating...digitally.

7. GUYANA

Becoming digitally driven by 2030 (with the help of global organisations)

With a profile of the high Telecommunication Infrastructure Index (TII), Human Capital Index (HCI) but a very Low E-Participation Index (EPI), digital Guyana presents a mixed picture. This suggests that while there's significant potential for digital growth, there are challenges in citizen engagement and participation. The sufficiently but unevenly developed infrastructure poses a constraint to e-government development in Guyana, as evidenced by the fact that only 65% of households have internet access, according to a recent ITU report[1086]. Since some parts of the country still lack access to the Internet, the gov. has launched the ICT Access and E-Services for Hinterland, Poor and Remote Communities initiative[1087]. This initiative aims to expand internet connectivity and improve information management systems, particularly in rural areas.One notable partnership Guyana has is with the United Nations Development Programme (UNDP) – working closely with the Office of the Prime Minister and over 200 Indigenous Communities to bridge the digital divide[1088]. This collaboration, supported by the Governments of Guyana and Norway under the Low Carbon Development Strategy (LCDS)[1089] and Guyana REDD+ Investment Fund (GRIF)[1090], focuses not only on adopting new technologies but also on modernising the public sector and providing e-government services. A key aspect of this partnership is the establishment of over 200 ICT hubs in the Hinterland, Poor, and Remote (HPR) communities mentioned before. These hubs will give residents access to essential e-government services and information, such as monitoring market prices for crops, receiving weather alerts, and facilitating remittances.

In recent years, the government of Digital Guyana has taken significant steps towards implementing a biometric national digital ID card initiative. So, in 2023, the government chose Veridos as the supplier for the ID cards[1091], which are compliant with the UN's International Civil Aviation Organization (ICAO) standards. The selection of Veridos to deliver an ICAO-compliant ID card aligns with international standards for travel documents, ensuring smooth international travel for Guyanese citizens. The contract value of $35.4 million[1092] indicates a substantial investment in building a solid digital identity infrastructure. Moreover, the Digital Identity Card Bill[1093] (once enacted) will establish a civil registry of identity data for citizens and non-citizens alike, managed by Guyana's Data Protection Commissioner.

Where to focus?

Citizen participation in digital governance is very very low in Guyana so that should be a main priority for this country.

8. PARAGUAY

Digital Paraguay improved its ranking by 14 places in 2 years

Despite its landlocked status digital Paraguay has abundant natural resources, a rich cultural heritage, diverse landscapes, and a unique history. But while it's working to improve its digital governance, it's still catching up compared to some other countries. Paraguay's high E-Government Development Index (EGDI)[1094] score indicates that it has made significant strides in digital governance, with strong performances in the Telecommunication Infrastructure Index (TII), Human Capital Index (HCI), and E-Participation Index (EPI). The city of Asuncion's website, which allows users to provide feedback on public services, is a positive step towards citizen engagement. Nonetheless, there are still areas that could be improved to further enhance the quality and accessibility of public services.

Looking at broader rankings, in the 2024 EGDI report, Paraguay is ranked 80th out of 193 countries. This is a big achievement, especially for a landlocked country. It's now the second landlocked nation, after Eswatini, to make such a big leap in the rankings. However, a 2023 OECD report[1095] highlights that Paraguay lags behind some of its Latin American and Caribbean counterparts like Argentina, Barbados, Chile, Costa Rica, and Uruguay in terms of e-governance development. Despite the progress it's below the region averages. The country has also faced challenges in effectively managing its natural resources, leading to missed opportunities and unmet water and sanitation needs. So, in 2023, Paraguay took a significant step forward by launching its first Water Information System (WIS)[1096]. This online portal serves as a central hub for data and information related to water quality, access, and sanitation levels. The WIS enables the government to monitor progress towards achieving Sustainable Development Goal 6 (SDG 6) on Clean Water and Sanitation, as outlined by the United Nations[1097]. Paraguay's Information Exchange System[1098] is a prime example of efforts to connect data registers across different areas, such as car registration, public safety, and civil registration. A significant regulatory framework guiding digital governance in Paraguay is Decree 8942, publishing the National ICT Plan 2022-2030[1099]. However, despite these efforts, there remains a gap in legal provisions and regulations[1100] concerning open government data in Paraguay.

Where to focus?

Using public-private collaboration is important to establish a healthy ecosystem that enables public service transformation. Paraguay understands that and that's why it has implemented the initiative *InnovandoPY*[1101] to attract the best technology solutions for citizens. However, despite all the efforts, it should focus more on improving its human capital base as well as its online services. So, moving forward, these should be the main points of focus for Paraguay.

9. PERU

Digital Peru has one of the best data law policies in the region

In the past few years digital Peru managed to improve its E-Government Development Index (EGDI)[1102] and E-Participation Index (EPI) values significantly, leading to a remarkable improvement in its international rankings. Moving from the high to the very high EGDI group back in 2022 was a notable achievement, especially considering that Peru was one of only four countries worldwide to make this jump. Also, in 2024, it is the 7th top country in the Americas and 58th in the world leading e-government…

Internationally, Peru's participation in projects like the Building the Europe Links with Latin America (BELLA)[1103] initiative shows its commitment to improving connectivity. Also, the Inter-American Development Bank (IDB) approved in 2023 a $50-million loan to Peru[1104] to improve and expand access to the government service of the Presidency of the Council of Ministers. This program seeks to expand digital citizenship opportunities in Peru, particularly for marginalised groups. At the regional level, Peru's collaboration with Colombia, Mexico, and Paraguay through the Better Than Cash Alliance[1105] is another great collaboration with a focus on transitioning towards digital payment systems. This initiative aligns with broader goals of reducing poverty and inclusive growth through digital innovation.

Moreover, its adoption of e-participation initiatives at both national and local levels, facilitated by platforms like *'Plataforma Participa Perú'* and Facilita Perú[1106], is another great achievement. These are well-designed and executed engagement portals, according to an OECD report[1107], even though the service catalogue could be broader. And, additionally, its exploration of Estonia's X-Road platform[1108] proves Peru's willingness to learn from international best practices and use such innovative solutions for its digital infrastructure.

Peru's Digital Government Law is a model in the region[1109] for using regulations to enhance data governance within the public sector and bridge gaps between different areas. The law provides a solid legal foundation for the development of a comprehensive *'Data Governance and Management Framework for the Peruvian State.'* This framework (once again) aligns with international best practices observed in countries like the Netherlands, the US, and Japan. In 2023, Peru took another significant step forward by issuing its national data strategy[1110] which is deeply rooted and connected to digitalisation efforts[1111] in the country and the digital government agenda.

Where to focus?

According to the OECD, Peru receives low scores for government effectiveness and the control of corruption. So, without strong government effectiveness and transparency, it can be difficult to implement digital solutions effectively and ensure accountability in their use. Also, one other area of important focus should be the development of the human capital base and their digital skills.

10. SURINAME

Strengthening its infrastructure for better government services

In just two years, Digital Suriname has made big improvements to its telecommunication infrastructure. Thanks to these changes, it earned a "very high" score in the 2024 EGDI report, showing how far it has come in a short amount of time. However, when it comes to the online service index (OSI) and e-participation index (EPI), Suriname ranks in the middle to low categories. In the UN's 2024 E-Government Development Index (EGDI)[1112] report, Suriname is positioned at 106th out of 193 countries assessed, improving its ranking by 2 places in 2 years.

Supported by the United Nations Development Programme (UNDP), Suriname has undertaken a thorough and participatory process to lay the groundwork for its digital transformation journey. This National Digital Strategy 2023-2030[1113] focuses on six strategic priorities, each addressing crucial aspects of digital transformation.

So, despite being the only country in the region with just one cable landing point, Suriname is taking proactive steps to enhance its digital connectivity. A substantial portion of Suriname's population is now online on a daily basis, with around 79% of citizens being daily internet users. But only 55% of households in the country have access to the internet[1114], reflecting the importance of investments in digital infrastructure. The planned Deep Blue One Cable[1115] initiative will connect Suriname with neighbouring countries like French Guiana, Guyana, and Trinidad & Tobago. Suriname's launch of its own Internet Exchange Point (SUR-IX)[1116] in November 2022 is another positive development that will facilitate more efficient and cost-effective internet traffic routing within the country. Also, the landing of the Suriname-Guyana Submarine Cable System[1117] in 2010 has further improved the affordability and accessibility of internet connectivity for Surinamese citizens.

Yet, Suriname's Online Service Index (OSI) score of 0.4814 in 2024[1118] falls below the global average of 0.6382, indicating some challenges in optimizing the user experience of government digital services.

And although digital Suriname has made progress with initiatives like the Gov.sr portal[1119], there's still more to be done. While there is a growing demand for digital products and services in Suriname, as evidenced by a respectable 'consumer readiness' score of 78.9% in the GSMA Mobile Connectivity Index (2023)[1120], more effort is needed. Why? Well, there's a gap in digital literacy compared to functional literacy, highlighting the need for targeted efforts to improve citizens' digital skills and cybersecurity knowledge.

Where to focus?

Expanding e-government functionalities (particularly self-service internet applications) can greatly enhance citizens' access to information and public services. Additionally, efforts to enhance digital literacy and promote digital entrepreneurship culture are essential.

11. URUGUAY

Ranking 2nd: A leader in digital governance after the US!

With very high scores across the board in e-government development, digital Uruguay stands out as one of the top performers in the region and in both American continents. Its exceptional performance is evident in its very high E-Government Development Index (EGDI) values[1121], placing it among the top countries in the Americas, just behind the US (it surpassed Canada.) However, Uruguay still faces challenges in e-participation, lagging behind Ecuador (which leads the sub-region in this aspect.) Despite that it has shown great progress in both dimensions; moving up by 10 spots in e-gov and 39 spots in e-participation rankings[1122] in just two years.

The government's focus on developing the AGESIC Interoperability Platform[1123] has been instrumental in shaping Uruguay's digital government strategy. It's also worth noting that its efforts in data protection have been recognised by the European Commission, along with Argentina, as meeting adequate levels of data protection in line with EU regulations[1124].In recent years, the country has demonstrated greater digital maturity than other countries in the region by prioritising the redesign of government services to meet user needs. The Digital Government Plan 2025[1125], issued by the Agency for Electronic Governance and Information and Knowledge Society (AGESIC), outlines clear objectives for streamlining, integrating, and offering proactive services to users. Moreover, Uruguay's Integrated Service Delivery System[1126] (managed by AGESIC) further facilitates the omnichannel approach by integrating online and offline delivery channels. A noteworthy aspect is its national portal, gub.uy/tramites/[1127], which hosts a comprehensive service catalogue covering 100% of government services (both informational and transactional.) This centralised platform ensures accessibility and convenience for citizens seeking government services. Another thing worth mentioning is that among all the countries in the region, Uruguay stands out with the most advanced digital identity system[1128]. What's more, its *firma.gub.uy* platform makes it easy for individuals and businesses to use and validate advanced electronic signatures, recognised across Argentina, Brazil, and Paraguay. This first-of-its-kind regional solution ensures secure, efficient cross-border transactions, saving time, reducing costs, and boosting business productivity.

Where to focus?

Overall, I see a country with a huge progress and a bright future ahead in the digital and innovation governance. With continued investment in talent, services and technology, I believe digital Uruguay will continue to lead the way in innovation and set an example for others to follow.

12. VENEZUELA

Digital Venezuela needs targeted investment toward service delivery

According to the IMF(2024), Venezuela ranks as the second country with the highest inflation rate[1129] in the world, right after Zimbabwe. This means prices are skyrocketing, making it tough for people to afford basic necessities. The country's high inflation rate poses severe economic difficulties that likely impact its ability to invest in digital infrastructure and government services. However, I've tried focusing on the information available to create a general panoramic view of digital Venezuela.

One thing that is easily analysed is that when it comes to e-participation[1130] Venezuela's performance continues to be notably low compared to other countries in Latin America. Even though I must add that their e-participation ranking has improved coming in at 1152nd in 2022 compared to 178th in 2022. This suggests that government efforts to engage citizens in collaborative governance have seen some progress but are still limited. Looking at their e-governance rankings, Venezuela has seen a decline in their scores over the past couple of years. In the 2024 EGDI report[1131], they keep dropping, ranking 131st globally, dropping from 128th place in 2022.

If you look at Venezuela's situation with its telecommunication infrastructure, it's pretty clear that things have been tough. The economic crisis they're facing, with years of recession and hyperinflation, has really taken a toll on their electrical and telecommunications systems[1132].

This has led to frequent blackouts and slow internet speeds, making it hard for people to stay connected and access information. Looking at the numbers, it's clear that internet access is a challenge for many Venezuelans. According to statistics from the International Telecommunication Union[1133] (ITU) the mobilebroadband penetration rate is only 52%, and fixed-line penetration is even lower at 10%. Moreover, Venezuela's median mobile broadband speeds rank among the slowest in the world, according to Ookla's Speedtest Global Index[1134].

For many Venezuelans, especially those in rural or low-income areas, internet services remain out of reach due to affordability issues. In fact, a large majority— more than 74%—can't even afford a basic mobile internet package, according to the 2023 Internet Poverty Index[1135].

Those who can afford reliable internet often have to pay in US dollars, further widening the gap between the haves and the have-nots. Higher rates of internet usage are concentrated in urban areas[1136], particularly in the Capital District and states on the more developed northern coast.

Where to focus?

Venezuela scores low in open data and GovTech readiness, according to an OECD report[1137]. So, the country needs to work on more basic digital government efforts before diving into more advanced GovTech initiatives. Without a strong foundation in place, it's challenging for digital Venezuela to implement effective digital governance strategies.

OCEANIA

Digital governance SUMMARY

Oceania's digital governance efforts and results are quite telling of the challenges faced by small island developing states (SIDS) in this region. When we compare it with other continents, Oceania is among the least developed in digital government, only slightly ahead of Africa. (Mind you, for e.g., Asia and America only have a slight difference between the two continents.)

A snapshot into Oceania

All 12 Small Island Developing States (SIDS) in Oceania have E-Government Development Index (EGDI) values substantially lower the global average. That's a striking statistic, showing how far behind many of these countries are in terms of digital governance.

It's important to note that only two countries in Oceania fall into the "very high" EGDI group. This alone tells us that digital governance isn't a widespread strength in the region. The majority, about 58% of the 14 countries, are in the middle EGDI group. These are mainly upper-middle-income countries, which is a crucial point to consider. There's an interesting exception in Nauru, which, despite being a high-income country, doesn't quite reach the top ranks of digital governance. This points to a broader issue: economic status doesn't always equate to digital advancement. Just because a country is wealthier doesn't automatically mean it has a strong digital government. It requires more than just money—it takes strategic planning, investment in technology, and the political will to drive digital initiatives.

The variation in EGDI scores within Oceania is another thing that can easily catch your eye if you know where to look. The scores have always ranged from as low as 0.3076 to as high as 0.9577. This wide range suggests that while some countries do make progress, most are lagging, with EGDI values well below the global average. This situation, once again, is comparable to that of Africa, where a few countries pull ahead while the majority struggle to keep up.

In 2024, it's particularly telling that Oceania has only 4 countries in the high EGDI group[1138] compared to Africa which has 17. This stagnation suggests that not much progress is being made, and I believe this could be due to several factors, including limited resources, a focus on other priorities, or perhaps even a lack of awareness about the benefits of digital governance. On average, countries in Oceania offer 12 services online. However, it's worth pointing out that all countries offering fewer than 12 services are SIDS with either middle or low Online Service Index (OSI) levels. Obviously, smaller nations have more challenges in developing AND maintaining digital services.

What's holding Oceania back?

The region faces some significant obstacles in advancing digital governance, and I think the root of the issue lies in a couple of key areas. First, the least developed Small Island Developing States (SIDS) in Oceania have some of the lowest EGDI values, and I believe this is primarily due to their poorly developed telecommunications infrastructure. In these small island nations, basic connectivity is still a major challenge. It's hard to talk about digital governance when so many people lack reliable internet access or even the basic infrastructure to support it. Without this foundation, any efforts to push forward with digital government services are bound to struggle. Many of these island nations are isolated, making it difficult to build and maintain the kind of infrastructure needed for robust digital governance. The costs associated with upgrading telecommunications infrastructure in these remote areas can be prohibitive, and I think this has contributed to the slow pace of progress.

But it's not just about infrastructure; I would also argue that there's a deeper issue at play here. Oceania has some impressive human capital, yet it hasn't been able to translate this into significant progress in e-government development. This is puzzling because, with such a strong base of educated and skilled individuals, you would expect to see more rapid advancements in digital governance. I think part of the problem might be a lack of strategic focus or perhaps even a disconnect between the available talent and the opportunities to apply it effectively in the public sector.

Top and bottom performers in Oceania

If you're wondering which regions are the most developed (or the least developed) here's the ranking

1. Australia New Zealand
2. Melanesia
3. Polynesia
4. Micronesia

It's clear that Australia and New Zealand are the front-runners in the region. They've set a high bar for the rest of Oceania..and the rest of the world actually. They stand out not just in Oceania but globally, with robust digital infrastructure and well-established e-government services. I believe this isn't just because of their advanced economies but also due to their strong commitment to integrating digital solutions into public services.

From online government services that make interacting with the state more efficient, to advanced telecommunication systems that ensure widespread internet access, they've created a digital environment that others in the region aspire to replicate. I think their success can be attributed to a combination of factors, including strong leadership, clear digital strategies, and a well-educated populace that is ready to engage with digital tools.

On the other hand, when we look at Melanesia, Polynesia, and Micronesia, the picture is quite different. These regions, while culturally rich and diverse, face significant challenges in their digital governance journey. Melanesia, which includes Fiji, Vanuatu, Solomon

Islands and Papua New Guinea, is making progress but still has a long way to go. The digital divide is more pronounced here, with many remote areas lacking reliable internet access, which hampers efforts to roll out comprehensive e-government services.

Polynesia and Micronesia also struggle with similar issues, though to varying degrees. In Polynesia, countries like Samoa and Tonga are pushing forward with digital initiatives, but they're often constrained by limited resources and the vast geographic spread of their populations...falling below world averages. Micronesia, comprising some of the smallest and most isolated nations in the world, faces perhaps the toughest challenges. However, it's important to recognise the efforts being made. For instance, mobile technology is gradually becoming a game-changer in some of these smaller nations. In places where traditional infrastructure is lacking, mobile phones are helping to bridge the gap, providing access to basic digital services that were previously unavailable.

The ranking of Oceania countries in terms of digital governance are:

Since there are only 14 (main) countries, here's the total ranking

1. Australia
2. New Zealand
3. Fiji
4. Vanuatu
5. Tonga
6. Palau
7. Samoa
8. Marshall Islands
9. Kiribati

10. Nauru

11. Tuvalu

12. Solomon Islands

13. Micronesia

14. Papua New Guinea

(Part of the continent are also the 'Cook Island' and "Niue" which despite having great deal of autonomy are in free association with New Zealand and are not included in the UN survey or in this report)

I want to note that there's a massive gap between the top two leaders—New Zealand and Australia—and the rest of the region. New Zealand and Australia consistently rank among the top 10 or 20 (sometimes even the top 5 to be fair) *globally* for e-governance. Their success is no surprise. The third-best country in this region (Fiji) doesn't even come close; it ranks 93rd in the world. Of course, the countries that rank lower aren't lacking in ambition or effort; they're often constrained by factors outside their control, such as geography, climate change issues, size, and resource availability.

Opportunities moving forward

While Oceania has some standout performers, the region as a whole faces significant disparities that need to be addressed. For true progress to be made (in the entirety of the region), there needs to be a concerted effort to share knowledge, resources, and best practices across the region. Only then can the less developed countries in Oceania start to close the gap and improve their digital governance capabilities.

From limited internet access to low levels of digital literacy, the challenges are multifaceted. But I would also add that there's potential for growth here. With targeted investments and international support, these countries could start to close the gap. However, it's going to require a lot of effort, both from within these nations and from external partners willing to help them leapfrog over some of the barriers they currently face.

1. AUSTRALIA

Australia - one of the world's most digitally capable governments

The Australian digital transformation agenda in earnest began in 2014 with an audit of the ICT projects, which led to the formation of the Digital Transformation Office in 2015, or what is known today as the Digital Transformation Agency (DTA). This agency was responsible for managing new and existing ICT projects and developing digital government services that are; *"easy to deal with, informed by users, and fit for the digital age."* These are currently the three priorities of the Australian Government's Digital Transformation Strategy[1139].

Over the last decade or so, Australia has managed to stay ahead of the curve by taking comprehensive steps towards a total digital transformation. Today, in 2024 it's the 8th country in the world leading in e-government. Australians can access their medical record, submit their tax returns, and apply for income support online from the comfort of their home or via their smartphones on the go. Australia has been making big moves to improve its digital services. Two key projects leading the way are the Data and Digital Government Strategy and the updated Digital Service Standard. These plans are focused on making government services more efficient and easier for people to use. One great example of this is the myGov platform. This online portal lets Australians access many government services in one secure place. Whether it's managing taxes, health, or benefits, it's all in one spot, which makes things so much simpler. By 2023, myGov had over 25 million accounts. That's a huge number, showing just how important it has become for people across the country. It's clear that myGov is playing a big role in shaping Australia's digital future and making everyday tasks much more convenient for everyone.

Have you heard about the Albanese government's 2023 Digital ID legislation[1140]? With this digital ID in Australia, citizens may no longer need to rely on their passports or driver's licences when applying for leases or phone plans. This move signals a significant step toward the establishment of a comprehensive *NATIONAL* Digital ID in Australia. It's worth noting that the groundwork for this system was laid as far back as 2015, and the current voluntary framework has already seen more than 10.5 million Australians adopting Digital IDs for government service access.

But, is the Albanese government's current system not enough? The fact that it isn't national in scope is a significant drawback. They can ONLY biometrically verify people against their passports. A driver's licence or any other ID document issued by state and territory governments is not usable. The current success of MyGovID[1141], used by millions of Australians for accessing government services, demonstrates the appetite for such solutions. But there's also one fact I forgot to mention - MyGovId is primarily confined to government services only. The fact that private sector providers currently cannot biometrically verify individuals against government-issued ID documents falls short of the grand vision of a truly national, economy-wide system.

Where to focus?

This system also needs to enable the hassle-free pre-filling of forms and automatic notifications for vital services and not only focus on cybersecurity like many countries (Australia included) are focusing on.

2. MICRONESIA (FEDERATED STATES)

Among the least developed countries in Oceania

The Federated States of Micronesia (FSM), faces unique challenges due to its geographical spread and remote location. This geographic dispersion of digital Micronesia poses significant limitations in connecting the population and integrating e-governance initiatives *effectively*. According to the latest UN report on e-government[1142], Micronesia leaves much room for improvement. Ranking 167th in e-governance[1143] and 172nd in e-participation, it falls below both regional and subregional averages. This highlights the gap in digital governance capabilities compared to neighbouring countries. Also, the World Bank's GovTech Maturity Index[1144] places Micronesia in the *D group*, indicating a low score in adopting and leveraging government technology solutions.

As of early 2024, internet usage in the Federated States of Micronesia remains relatively modest, with 46.9 thousand individuals actively using the internet[1145]. This accounts for approximately 40.5% of the population, indicating a gradual increase in digital connectivity over recent years. From January 2023 to January 2024, there was a slight uptick of 433 internet users, marking a 0.9 % growth. A substantial portion of the population—approximately 68.8 thousand people, or 59.5% —remains offline as of the beginning of 2024. This suggests persistent challenges in expanding digital access and bridging the digital divide in a geographically dispersed region like Micronesia.

Where to focus?

To address all these challenges, Micronesia must prioritise strategic investments in telecommunications infrastructure, digital literacy programs, and capacity building. Collaborative efforts with international partners and regional alliances could also provide crucial support in navigating these complex digital landscapes. I believe enhancing e-governance could streamline administrative processes and improve public service delivery, which is crucial for a geographically dispersed nation like Micronesia.

3. FIJI

Digital Fiji needs to focus more on citizen participation

Ranking 93rd out of 193 countries in the latest UN e-governance assessment[1146], Fiji stands above many of its global peers. However, it's worth noting that in terms of e-participation[1147], Fiji is positioned at 143rd, indicating a gap that needs to be addressed. Fiji's EGDI values are above the global average of 0.6754, which is commendable especially since it moved up into the high EGDI group in the 2024 report.. This shows that the country has made much progress in digital governance, placing it third in Oceania after New Zealand and Australia for some years now. What's more Fiji has made a big jump in its e-participation ranking over the last two years, climbing 31 spots. Now, it's ranked 112th out of 193 countries. That's a solid improvement and shows the country is moving forward. While Fiji is now ahead of the regional average, it still has some work to do to catch up to the world average. It's a step in the right direction, but there's more room for growth.

The digitalFIJI website[1148] is *OK*, although there's still a long way to go. Right now, the website allows users to register births, apply for and retrieve birth certificates, and register companies or businesses. These are the only e-services available online from the government. It's a start, but clearly, there's room for growth. Also, as of January 2024, there were about 800.8 thousand internet users in Fiji[1149]. That's quite significant because it means the internet penetration rate stood at 85%. Yet, despite this impressive penetration rate, it's important to remember that 138.9 thousand people in Fiji were still not using the internet at the start of 2024. This means 14.8 percent of the population remains offline. For a country striving towards digital inclusivity, that's a significant chunk of people who are missing out on the benefits of connectivity.

From a practical standpoint, this gap can impact various aspects of life, from accessing educational resources and health information to engaging in economic opportunities. What I'd like to add here is that addressing this offline population requires targeted efforts. Maybe focusing on improving infrastructure in remote areas or launching digital literacy programs could help bridge this gap.

Where to focus?

The high rankings in TII and HCI, coupled with a strong EGDI, showcase the country's potential. However, to fully realise this potential, there must be a concerted effort to further bridge the gap in e-participation.

4. KIRIBATI

Kiribati saw huge progress in a short time thanks to its human capital base

As an island nation in Oceania and classified as a Least Developed Country (LDC) and a Small Island Developing State (SIDS), the efforts of digital Kiribati are significantly impacted by its status. With a total land area of less than 800 square kilometres, nearly half of which is Kiritimati (Christmas) Island, Kiribati is one of the world's most remote and geographically dispersed nations and faces unique challenges in its digital journey.

According to the UN Knowledge Database[1150], the e-governance and e-participation scores for digital Kiribati are still below the regional average. But there's a bright side—it has actually managed to go above the average for the Micronesia region. This is a big deal when you think about how much New Zealand and Australia raise the region's overall average. Considering the competition, this is definitely a step in the right direction for Kiribati. What's more Kiribati boasts highly developed human capital.... which is a *significant* asset.

However, the nation has struggled to capitalize on this strength due to inadequate infrastructure. For instance, it tends to have middle Telecommunication Infrastructure Index (TII) and Online Service Index (OSI) values. This pattern is common among LDCs and SIDS, which often lack the necessary resources to invest in critical areas for e-government development. The costs associated with developing such infrastructure are often prohibitively high for a country with limited economic resources.

At the start of 2024, there were 73.3 thousand internet users in the country[1151], which means internet penetration stood at 54.4%. To put it in perspective, this means that out of Kiribati's total population, 61.4 thousand people did not use the internet. That's a substantial 45.6% of the population remaining offline. On the other hand, over 55,000 mobile subscribers are primarily 3G or 4G users in digital Kiribati[1152], showing a strong inclination towards mobile internet usage. However, increasing the availability and capacity of high-speed internet remains a challenge, especially for the Outer Islands.

The GovTech Maturity Index (GTMI) categorises Kiribati as *"Low – with minimal focus on GovTech."* In 2022, Kiribati was placed in group D[1153], which indicates substantial room for improvement. One of the most striking issues highlighted by the World Bank report is Kiribati's inability to maintain open data platforms. This lack of open data infrastructure hampers transparency and limits the ability of citizens to access and utilise government information, which is a crucial component of a robust digital governance framework.

Where to focus?

In my view, while Kiribati faces significant obstacles, there are also promising developments that signal a potential for progress. The key lies in building *upon* these initiatives → expanding digital infrastructure, and prioritising open data and citizen engagement.

5. MARSHALL ISLANDS

Digital Marshall Islands keeps improving its human capital base

With a population of around 43,000 people, the country is geographically isolated in the Pacific Ocean, far removed from its neighbours. In the World Bank's GMTI 2022 report[1154], the Marshall Islands is classified among the least developed in terms of GovTech in the East Asia and Pacific region. This categorisation indicates a significant gap between the Marshall Islands and other nations actively advancing their digital governance capabilities. According to the report, while 11 countries are making notable strides in groups A and B, the Marshall Islands, along with 13 others in groups C and D, show a medium to low focus on GovTech initiatives overall. Also, the United Nations' E-Government Development Index (EGDI)[1155] paints a similar picture. The Marshall Islands currently ranks 143rd[1156] in e-governance and 120th in e-participation, marking an improvement of 17 and 12 places over the past two years. Regarding connectivity, in early 2024, there were 30.9 thousand internet users[1157], which means that internet penetration stood at an impressive 73.2%. This translates to 11.3 thousand individuals who *did not use* the internet.

Did you know that Marshall Island made headlines back in 2018 by becoming the first nation to issue its own cryptocurrency? This move suggests a forwardthinking approach towards integrating digital solutions into its financial ecosystem. What's more, in 2023, it signed a memorandum of understanding (MOU) with Bitt, aiming to roll out a National Digital Payments System (NDPS) using the US Dollar. *(Bitt provides central bank digital currency and stablecoin solutions for central banks and governments - among other financial ecosystem participants.)* The rollout of the National Digital Payments System promises to reduce reliance on physical cash by offering viable alternatives that complement traditional banking methods.

Where to focus?

In these conditions, regional cooperation and seeking international partnerships *could* play a crucial role in accelerating digital development. By learning from the successes of other nations and adapting best practices to fit their unique context, the Marshall Islands could make significant progress in their GovTech initiatives.

6. NAURU

Digital Nauru lags behind its peers in using GovTech

Digital Nauru, despite being classified as a high-income country in Oceania, has below-average EGDI values for the region. This is primarily due to its underdeveloped infrastructure, which is a common characteristic among Small Island Developing States (SIDS) like Nauru is. I'd say this underdevelopment is particularly evident in its low *Online Service Index values,* as highlighted in the United Nations' E-Government Development Index (EGDI) report[1158]. There is clearly still room for improvement in this area. Also, according to the UN's E-government Knowledgebase[1159], Nauru ranked 151st in e-governance and 148th in e-participation in 2024 among 193 countries assessed. It has seen some decline in the past two years, moving down by 12 spots in e-governance and 13 places in e-participation. This signals a growing need to focus effort and investments in areas that truly matter so as to enhance digital engagement AND service delivery within the country.

The World Bank's GovTech Maturity Index (GTMI) provides a clear picture of how countries are advancing in several key areas: supporting core government systems, enhancing service delivery, mainstreaming citizen engagement, and fostering the necessary enablers for GovTech. For Nauru, there's significant room for improvement, especially in Digital Citizen Engagement[1160]. This aspect measures how well the government is doing in creating platforms for public participation, setting up mechanisms for citizen feedback, and maintaining open data and government portals. At the start of 2024, there were about 10.6 thousand internet users in Nauru[1161], with an internet penetration rate of 82.7%. That's quite significant when you consider the small population. Despite the "high" penetration rates, internet access in

Nauru is relatively expensive. For instance, a mobile contract with 2 GB of data at a minimum of 3G speed costs around $20.40 per month. This amount is equivalent to 1.5% of income, which is higher compared to the 1.1% of income in Emerging Market economies.

Where to focus?

Continued investment in digital infrastructure, capacity building, and regulatory frameworks will be essential to sustain momentum and further enhance Nauru's digital ecosystem so that it reaches up to its peers. Obviously...Addressing the online services gaps and expanding digital literacy initiatives will empower more citizens to participate actively in digital governance processes.

7. NEW ZEALAND

In the very high EGDI group: Ranked among the top 20 countries

New Zealand started to make big moves toward digital government about ten+ years ago. The country is small enough to potentially be considered an island, but is definitely punching above its weight when it comes to technological advancements. With the help of New Zealand's GDS (global digital solutions), the National Government started to transition their processes from a paper-based model to a digital one. Today, more than 1 million citizens interact with the government online each week through the Common Web Platform (CWP)[1162]. This is a platform-as-a-service used to create and host government and public sector websites utilising hundreds of digital services.

Meanwhile, the government website govt.nz[1163] allows citizens to apply for citizenship or renew their driver's licence from home or work instead of waiting in line at a post office and much more. The country has had some significant accomplishments to celebrate...even though lately it seems to have lost some of its momentum. According to the 2024 UN EGDI[1164], New Zealand is ranked 16th out of 193 countries, down from the 4th place it held in 2022 while the e-participation index puts it in the 12th place globally, showing a general decline from the 6th place it held in 2022.

Nowadays, it's almost impossible for New Zealand residents not to use an app or online portal to access government services. Even during the 2016 Summer Olympics, the country pioneered mobile ticketing, ranking it one of the first countries in the world for mobile infrastructure. The government is largely transparent about its digital operations, including collecting and using citizen data. It also has an online complaints system in place that allows citizens to voice their concerns regarding public service quality. Also they presented the Strategy for a Digital Public Service[1165], which sets the direction for modernising public service, putting people and businesses at the centre of government services.

Where to focus?

The focus should not only be on using new technologies but also on ensuring that the workforce has the right digital skills to succeed in the new world so as to gain some of the momentum it lost.

8. PALAU

The world's first Web3 digital ID platform

Nestled in the western Pacific Ocean, digital Palau is a high-income island nation, comprising hundreds of islands (some of them uninhabited). But, despite being high-income, Palau's e-governance values are below the region's average. This discrepancy is not uncommon among Small Island Developing States, where underdeveloped infrastructure can pose significant barriers to technological advancement.

According to the UN report, Palau is characterised by a middle telecommunication infrastructure index (TII) and a very high human capital index (HCI)[1166]. This means that while the country has a well-educated population capable of engaging with digital services, the actual infrastructure to support these services is lacking.

According to the UN's E-government Knowledgebase[1167], Palau ranked 137th in e-governance and 130th in e-participation out of 193 countries assessed. This translates into a pressing need for the country to enhance its digital services and citizen engagement strategies. The rankings reflect a gap between potential and actual performance. Also... the World Bank's GovTech Maturity Index (GTMI)[1168] places Palau in the D category, *"Minimal focus on GovTech."* This means that the country has not yet prioritised the integration of technology into government operations and service delivery.

Looking at connectivity in Palau, it's evident that there's been gradual progress in internet adoption, yet significant challenges remain for digital governance efforts. As of early 2024, Palau reported 12.3 thousand internet users[1169], with an internet penetration rate of 67.9%.

This indicates that a substantial portion of the population—about 32.1%—still lacks access to the internet.

Back in 2022, Palau launched a pioneering digital residency program in collaboration with Cryptic Labs, leveraging blockchain technology. This initiative, known as the Root Name System (RNS)[1170], introduced the *Palau ID* — a significant leap in digital identity solutions. What sets Palau's approach apart is its focus on sovereignty-based IDs, offering both physical and digital identity documents that can be obtained *remotely* from anywhere in the world.

Actually, it was the world's first Web3 digital identity platform to support the application and issuance of sovereignty-based IDs. For a fee individuals can acquire digital residency in Palau for one year without the need to physically visit the country.

Comparatively, Palau's approach echoes Estonia's pioneering efforts[1171] in e-residency but differs in its requirement for less disclosed information needed. While this flexibility may seem advantageous for privacy, it has raised concerns about regulatory standards of identity verification processes.

Where to focus?

For digital Palau to advance its e-governance agenda effectively, several key strategies could be considered. Such as: enhancing broadband infrastructure in rural and remote areas and investing in its online services provision.

9. PAPUA NEW GUINEA

The least developed digital govt in Oceania (again)

Papua New Guinea, as a lower middle-income country in Oceania, faces significant challenges in developing its digital governance capabilities. It ranked 171st in e-governance and 163rd in e-participation according to the UN's E-government Knowledgebase[1172]. Between 2022 and 2024, the country dropped one spot in its overall rankings (e-gov). While it's a small change, it shows there's still room for improvement to keep up with global progress. However, according to the World Bank's GTMI report[1173], Papua New Guinea falls into the C category with "*Some focus on GovTech.*" This classification highlights a measured approach to leveraging technology for governance, with efforts focusing on specific areas rather than comprehensive digital integration.

Yet the country has minimal internet and telecommunications coverage[1174], which is currently provided through "a rather inadequate patchwork of fixed lines, mobile wireless, satellite systems, and microwave band services." This situation is quite ironic, considering that PNG is the largest telecommunications market in the Pacific region. Yet, it remains one of the most poorly developed in terms of infrastructure. Also, at the start of 2024, there were 2.81 million internet users in Papua New Guinea[1175], representing an internet penetration rate of just 27.0%. This is quite low compared to global standards, and I believe it highlights the considerable gap that needs to be addressed. To put things in perspective.... these user figures reveal that *7.61 million people* in Papua New Guinea did not use the internet at the beginning of 2024. Which is one of the lowest internet penetration rates in the world[1176]. The country also lags behind the region and the worldwide average in both urban and rural settings when it comes to electricity access. This further complicates efforts to improve ICT infrastructure and expand internet coverage.

Despite all that, I have to mention that PNG is one of the few in the region with online payment! In 2011, Digicel PNG launched a mobile money service called Cellmoni in Papua New Guinea. Developed in partnership with the United Nations Development Programme's Pacific Financial Inclusion Programme[1177], Cellmoni allowed users to store money on their mobile devices.

Where to focus?

Investing heavily in ICT infrastructure, promoting digital literacy programs, and strengthening institutional frameworks for digital governance are all very important steps.

10. SAMOA

Digital Samoa is driven significantly by its human capital

Digital Samoa is an intriguing case when it comes to government efforts for digital transformation. Samoa (not to be confused with American Samoa - the unincorporated territory of the United States) is a Polynesian island country consisting of many inhabited and uninhabited islands. Despite all the efforts and international support, Samoa has had its own set of challenges and progress. According to a World Bank report[1178], in 2022, Samoa advanced to a higher GTMI group, specifically the C group, indicating a growing emphasis on GovTech. What's more Samoa has high *Human Capital Index (HCI)* values, indicating a well-educated and skilled population as the UN report concludes[1179].

One key issue impeding Samoa's progress in EGDI is its insufficient infrastructure development, because even the most skilled and educated workforce can struggle to fully engage in and benefit from digital advancements. According to the UN's E-government Knowledgebase[1180], Samoa ranks 140th in e-governance and 130th in e-participation out of 193 countries assessed. These rankings show that there has been some considerable improvement in the overall ranking for EGDI. According to DataReportal's report[1181] on digital adoption and use in Samoa in early 2024, there were 171.1 thousand internet users in the country, with an internet penetration rate of 75.3%. Also, the issue of digital literacy in Samoa[1182] is deeply intertwined with age, region, educational attainment, and socio-economic status. Samoans aged 25 to 44 years, residents of the 'Apia Urban' region, and those with higher education and income levels tend to perform better on several measures of digital literacy.

Where to focus?

The nation has a strong foundation in its skilled human capital, but to truly elevate its e-governance standing, there needs to be a concerted effort to enhance digital infrastructure and focus more on greater citizen participation. With the right investments Samoa can continue its upward trajectory and unlock new opportunities for digital transformation and inclusive growth.

11. SOLOMON ISLANDS

A pioneer in assessing its digital economy

When analysing the Solomon Islands, a lower middle-income country in Oceania, a few things come to mind. As a Small Island Developing State (SIDS) and a Least Developed Country (LDC)[1183], the Solomon Islands faces challenges that significantly impact its digital government progress. Additionally... the Solomon Islands (like many SIDS and LDCs) struggles with human capital development. While there is *no shortage of talent* and potential, there often isn't enough access to quality education and training in digital skills.

According to the UN E-government Knowledgebase[1184], the Solomon Islands ranked 164th in e-governance and 115th in e-participation in 2024. Yet, despite these incremental advancements (especially in e-participation), the Solomon Islands remains one of the least developed countries in Oceania regarding e-government progress, only surpassing Micronesia and Papua New Guinea[1185]. A World Bank report from 2023[1186] paints a similar picture. It categorises digital Solomon Islands as having *"some focus on GovTech,"* placing it in group strategy C (with D being the lowest) within the East Asia and Pacific region. This classification shows the ongoing challenges and the *relatively* low prioritisation of digital government technologies in the national strategy. Regarding connectivity, at the start of 2024 there were 336.5 thousand internet users[1187], representing an internet penetration rate of 45.0%. While nearly half of the population had access to the internet, this figure also starkly highlighted the digital divide, as 55.0% of the population... equivalent to 412.0 thousand people... remained offline.

What's more, back in 2020, the country made a strategic decision to leverage data by using UNCDF's Inclusive Digital Economy Scorecard[1188] (IDES) to gain a better understanding of its digital economy's development and inclusiveness. As the first country in the Pacific to adopt this tool, the Solomon Islands demonstrated a pioneering spirit in assessing and driving its digital economy. At the end of 2020[1189], the Digital Economy Score (DES) was 39%, firmly placing the Solomon Islands in the Start-Up stage[1190] (of a digital economy.) By the end of 2022[1191], they saw a slight increase to 42%. This incremental progress, though modest, signifies a continued effort and determination to build a digital economy.

Where to focus?

The Solomon Islands should continue to build on this momentum by focusing on targeted interventions that address specific areas of need. Enhancing digital literacy and infrastructure, improving internet accessibility and (consequently) bridging this digital divide should be the top priorities for the government.

12. TONGA

Digital Tonga is among top 5 Oceania countries

Tonga, along with Fiji, Vanutau and Palau, stands out in Oceania for being in the high EGDI (E-Government Development Index) group according to the UN survey[1192]. This is a notable achievement, considering the unique challenges faced by small island nations. According to the UN E-Government Knowledgebase[1193], Tonga ranked 134th in e-governance and 120th in e-participation out of 193 countries assessed in 2024. This ranking means that there's a considerable journey ahead in terms of digital governance and involving its citizens in e-participation initiatives. Moreover, according to the World Bank report on East Asia and Pacific countries[1194], Tonga (along with six other nations) shows *"some focus on GovTech."* This means that Tonga is beginning to recognise the importance of leveraging technology to enhance government operations and service delivery. However, "some focus" is a far cry from a strong, strategic commitment. As of the start of 2024, there were 62.2 thousand internet users in digital Tonga[1195]. This means that internet penetration stood at 57.5%. Now...that's more than half of the population, which is quite significant for a small island nation. But it also means that 46.0 thousand people in Tonga were not using the internet at the start of the year. In 2021, the United Nations Capital Development Fund (UNCDF) initiated its first Inclusive Digital Economy Scorecard (IDES) data collection in Tonga, making it the second country in the Pacific to participate in this effort. The Digital Economy Score (DES) in 2022 in Tonga[1196], which indicates the level of development of the digital economy, stood at 53%.

The government policy and regulation component scored 61%. For the infrastructure, Tonga scored 59%. Another notable aspect of Tonga's digital economy is its focus on education. The country's score of 63%

on the *Skills* component highlights just that. With free education provided for the first 12 years of a child's life, coupled with appropriate curriculums at primary and secondary schooling levels, digital Tonga is laying a solid foundation for a digitally literate population.

Where to focus?

The nation's strong educational infrastructure, as highlighted by the High HCI, provides a solid base to build upon. However, the moderate telecommunication infrastructure and online services continue to need significant investment and development.

13. TUVALU

Digital Tuvalu is threatened by rising sea levels

According to the UN E-government survey from 2024[1197]while the people of Tuvalu have the education and skills needed for digital engagement, the infrastructure simply isn't there to support comprehensive online services. It's a classic case of having the human resources but lacking the digital foundation to fully utilise them. In 2024, Tuvalu ranks 158th in e-governance[1198] with no change from the 2022 report. These rankings highlight how the country is struggling to keep up with the global push towards digital governance... As of the start of 2024, there were 9,285 internet users in Tuvalu[1199], which translates to an impressive internet penetration rate of 81.2%. This indicates that a significant majority of Tuvalu's population is online. The World Bank's report[1200] on East Asia and Pacific countries emphasises that Tuvalu (along with six other nations in this region) has a *"minimal focus on GovTech."* This means that the government's attention and resources are not sufficiently directed towards leveraging technology for governance and public service delivery.

Did you know that Tuvalu is projected to be one of the first countries to be completely lost to climate change?[1201] Actually, rising sea levels are slowly eroding its land, threatening to submerge the entire country. In response to this dire situation, Tuvalu has launched the Future Now Project[1202], an ambitious plan with three major initiatives aimed at preserving its nationhood, governance, and culture, even in the worst-case scenario. By transferring access to government and consular services into the cloud, Tuvalu hopes to ensure the continuity of its governance structures. This means that, even if the physical land is lost, elections can still be held, and government bodies can continue to function virtually. It's a really forward-thinking approach that uses technology to preserve sovereignty AND governance.

By the way, Australia has offered Tuvalu land for relocation, but they want maritime and fisheries rights in exchange, which the Tuvaluan government has rejected. Seeing as there aren't any other choices, Tuvaluans have been looking for solutions that don't come with such significant trade-offs. Hence...the digital twin. (Fun fact: Singapore, which is also vulnerable to the rising sea levels, has already created its digital twin.)[1203]

Where to focus?

Seeing the increasing risk of climate change, it's clear that the *Future Now Project* is a bold and necessary step for digital Tuvalu. The digitisation of government services is a critical part of ensuring the nation's continuity. Yet, the challenges are immense.

14. VANUATU

Digital Vanuatu is the only country in Oceania moving to a higher EGDI group in 2024

Vanuatu is a country in the South Pacific Ocean nation made up of roughly 80 islands that stretch for thousands of kilometres. Just like many island nations, digital Vanuatu used to be one of those least developed countries, but it "graduated" from this status in 2020. Vanuatu has a high TII[1204] (Telecommunication Infrastructure Index), which signifies a high (sufficient) level of infrastructure to support digital communication. As of early 2024, the country had 236.5 thousand internet users[1205], translating to a penetration rate of 69.9%. Social media usage stood at 121.1 thousand users, accounting for 35.8% of the population. Also, there were 260.7 thousand active mobile connections, covering 77.0% of the total population. However, it's the high HCI (Human Capital Index) that really stands out. This high HCI indicates a well-educated and skilled population, which is very important for effectively using digital tools and technologies.

According to the UN e-government Knowledgebase[1206], Vanuatu ranked 129th in e-governance and 94th in e-participation out of 193 countries assessed in 2024. These rankings reflect progress, with Vanuatu improving its position by 6 places in e-governance and 16 places in e-participation. This upward trajectory is quite encouraging and points to the effectiveness of recent initiatives and policies. But, the World Bank's report[1207] on East Asia and Pacific countries highlights that digital Vanuatu has only "*some* focus on GovTech" alongside six other countries in the region. This focus on GovTech, which refers to the use of technology to enhance public sector services, means that Vanuatu is seeking to modernise its government operations and service delivery through digital means, but hasn't had much result.

Digital divide is also an issue. In the southern region of Malekula (which is Vanuatu's second-largest island)villagers face profound limitations in accessing *essential* services first.... like quality healthcare, banking facilities, and reliable utilities such as power and clean water. E-services are even more difficult to access (if available.)

Where to focus?

Digital connectivity and technology not only helps manage disaster risks (for which digital Vanuatu is highly vulnerable) but also connect the unconnected remote islands and extend the reach of public services. So, there's still work to be done to ensure that all its citizens, regardless of their location, can reap the benefits of the digital age.

CHAPTER 4

Key Takeaways

As we come to the end of this exploration of digital governance across 198 countries, it's important to reflect on the key takeaways and the overarching themes that have emerged throughout the book. In this conclusion, I'll summarize the main points that I believe readers should take away, highlighting the leading regions and countries, as well as those that are still in the early stages.

The leaders in digital governance: A view into continents

This is the ranking

1. Europe
2. Asia
3. North America
4. South America
5. Oceania
6. Africa

Europe undeniably stands at the forefront. The continent has set the benchmark for digital government systems. Obviously, Europe's leadership in this area is not just a result of financial resources but also a deep-seated belief in the power of technology to enhance governance. The continent's focus on transparency (especially), citizen engagement, and data-driven decision-making have really helped it stay on top. Asia follows Europe as the second most developed region in terms of digital governance. The continent's rapid economic growth and technological innovation have played a key role in its advancement. Countries like Singapore, Estonia, UAE and Saudi Arabia have been trailblazers.

North America, led by the United States, has been a pioneer in adopting digital technologies for government use. The region's focus on innovation and entrepreneurship has spurred the development of sophisticated e-government platforms. However, the disparity between North and South America is notable, with countries in South America generally lagging behind. Oceania, a region with a smaller number of countries, ranks fourth. The subregion of Australia and New Zealand stands out as the leader here, with both countries consistently performing extremely well in global digital governance rankings. However, other subregions within Oceania, are among the least developed in terms of digital governance, highlighting the significant variation within the region.

Africa, despite being the least developed region in terms of digital governance, is a continent of immense potential. The challenges are substantial—ranging from limited infrastructure to political instability—but there are also incredible opportunities.

Subregional analysis: A closer look

While the overall rankings by continent provide a broad overview, it's also valuable to consider the performance of specific subregions.

If I had to choose the best subregions, the ranking would look like this:

1. **Australia and New Zealand:** This subregion tops the list, but it's important to note that it consists of only two countries. Both Australia and New Zealand have high scores in digital governance, thanks to their strong economies, advanced infrastructure, and proactive digital policies. The limited number of countries in this subregion means that the overall score is not dragged down by less developed nations, making it easier for this region to maintain its top position.

2. **Northern Europe:** Northern Europe is another high-performing subregion, with countries like Denmark, Estonia, Iceland, Finland leading the way. Northern Europe's success can be attributed to a combination of factors, including high levels of education, technological infrastructure, and a culture that values public participation in governance.

3. **North America:** North America, particularly the United States, has been a leader in digital governance for years. The region's focus on technological innovation and its strong private sector have driven the development of sophisticated e-government services.

4. **Western Europe:** Western Europe is home to some of the most developed digital governance systems globally. Countries like the Netherlands and Germany ave invested heavily in digital infrastructure and have implemented comprehensive e-government strategies. Western Europe's success is closely tied to its strong economies.

5. **Eastern Europe:** Eastern Europe may not be as advanced as its Western counterpart, but it's a region is rapidly catching up. Countries like Ukraine or Poland have become global leaders in digital governance thanks to their innovative approaches and willingness to embrace new technologies, and it has helped "carry" the region to the top.

6. **Southern Europe:** Spain is the only country in the subregion with a "Very High" rating, thanks to its advanced digital systems and strong focus on modernizing public services. Malta and Croatia are also doing well as part of the 3 top leaders in this sub region. Malta has been a standout for its work in e-governance and blockchain, even if it slipped a bit this year.

7. **Eastern Asia:** Eastern Asia ranks 7th globally in digital governance, with countries like South Korea, Singapore, Japan, and China leading the way and Mongolia and North Korea staying behind. South Korea was once the top performer

but was overtaken by Singapore in 2024 due to its strong focus on innovation and citizen engagement. Japan uses technology to improve public services, especially for its aging population, while China's approach centers on control through AI and big data.

The least developed subregions

On the other end of the spectrum, we have the subregions that are still in the early stages of developing their digital governance capabilities. These regions face significant challenges, including limited infrastructure, political instability, and economic constraints. The least developed subregions are (ranked from best to the worst):

1. **Polynesia (Oceania):** Polynesia, part of the broader Oceania region, faces significant challenges in digital governance. The region's geographic isolation, small population sizes, and limited resources make it difficult to develop and maintain digital infrastructure.

2. **Micronesia (Oceania):** Like Polynesia, Micronesia is also struggling with the challenges of isolation and limited resources.

3. **Western Africa:** Western Africa faces a range of challenges, from political instability to limited technological infrastructure. However, there are signs of progress, with some countries in the region beginning to adopt mobile technologies and other innovative solutions to improve governance.

4. **Eastern Africa:** Eastern Africa shares many of the same challenges as Western Africa, including limited infrastructure and political instability. While there are pockets of innovation the region as a whole still lags behind in digital governance compared to the rest of the world.

5. **Middle Africa:** Middle Africa is the least developed subregion in terms of digital governance in the entire world. The region's

challenges are significant, including widespread poverty, political instability, and a lack of infrastructure.

Top countries in digital governance

At the country level, the leaders in digital governance are predominantly from Europe, with a few notable exceptions from Asia and Oceania.

The top-ranked countries are:

1. **Denmark:** Denmark consistently ranks as the top country in digital governance. The country's success can be attributed to its strong technological infrastructure, high levels of internet penetration, and a culture that values transparency and citizen participation.

2. **Estonia:** Estonia is a standout performer in digital governance, particularly given its small size and recent history. The country's success is due to its innovative approach to e-governance, which is way ahead of many other countries and even helps them with its tried and tested roadmaps.

3. **Singapore:** For the first time, it is the top EGDI performer in Asia and it holds the third place in the world; setting high standards by offering seamless, secure and efficient services. Its main focus has been advancing digital infrastructures from which Government on Commercial Cloud (GCC) platform was born.

4. **South Korea:** South Korea is the highest-ranking country in Eastern Asia and among global leaders in digital governance. The country's success is due to its advanced technological infrastructure, high levels of internet penetration, and a government that is committed to innovation.

5. **Iceland:** Iceland is another high-ranking country in digital governance. The country's small population and strong technological infrastructure have allowed it to implement

innovative digital solutions that enhance public administration and citizen engagement.

6. **Saudi Arabia:** Guided by Saudi Vision 2030, launched in 2016, Saudi Arabia has achieved remarkable digital transformation with 99% internet penetration and 98% of government services online. Innovative projects like a carbon-free 5G network with solar-powered, 3D-printed towers and the Sehhaty platform, serving over 30 million users, highlight its progress in healthcare and technology.

7. **The UK:** Since 2015, the UK's Government Digital Service (GDS) has used the "Government as a Platform" approach to drive digital transformation and improve public services. This strategy focuses on creating user-centred services that meet people's needs, as highlighted by a former GDS executive. Additionally, the UK plays an active role in shaping international digital government standards, contributing to best practices and global norms.

8. **Australia:** Australia, part of the top-ranked subregion of Australia and New Zealand, is a global leader in digital governance.

9. **Finland:** Finland is another top performer, known for its innovation and strong focus on digitalisation and transparency

10. **Netherlands:** The Netherlands is another high-ranking country in digital governance with a huge focus on governmental AI.

The least developed countries in digital governance

On the other end of the spectrum, we have the countries that are still in the early stages of developing their digital governance capabilities.

- **Burundi:** The country is in the early stages of adopting digital tools, with most services still reliant on manual systems, hindering efficiency and transparency.

- **North Korea:** North Korea's digital governance is extremely restricted, with limited internet access controlled by the state. The government focuses on internal surveillance rather than public services.

- **Yemen:** Yemen's digital governance is severely impacted by ongoing conflict and a lack of resources. Basic digital infrastructure is either underdeveloped or destroyed, making it difficult for the government to provide online services to its citizens.

- **Haiti:** Haiti faces significant challenges in digital governance, including economic constraints and a lack of infrastructure. The country's digital capabilities are among the lowest in the world.

- **Niger:** Again significant challenges, including widespread poverty and political instability.

- **Afghanistan:** Afghanistan's digital governance capabilities are severely limited by ongoing conflict, political instability, and a lack of effort/focus.

- **Chad:** Repression and delayed legislative election have shifted the focus elsewhere

- **Eritrea:** The country's challenges include political isolation and poverty as it's a militarized authoritarian state.

- **Somalia:** Somalia's digital governance capabilities are severely limited by ongoing conflict as it struggles to reestablish a functioning state.

- **South Sudan:** South Sudan is the least developed country in terms of digital governance in the entire world. The country suffers from uncontrolled corruption and threatening economic circumstances.

- **Central African Republic:** Ongoing conflict has plagued the Central African Republic with the absence of state authority in much of the country.

If there's one thing I hope you take away from this book, it's that digital governance is not just about technology—it's about people, policies, laws, regulations, business and operating models and the future of how we live together as societies. The road ahead is long and filled with challenges, but it's also full of possibilities.

I believe that by learning from each other and sharing our successes and failures, we can create a more connected, transparent, and just world.

In writing this book, I've had the privilege of diving deep into the stories of 198 countries, each with its own unique path. I've been struck by the creativity and resilience shown by governments in adapting fast so as to better serve their citizens. Whether we're talking about the most advanced digital nations or those just beginning their journey, there is a common thread: a desire to use technology to make life better for everyone.

ENDNOTES

1. https://www.vfsglobal.com/en/governments/about.html
2. https://www.globalinnovationexchange.org/innovation/mobilized-construction 3.Ibid
3. https://www.engineeringforchange.org/news/fixing-the-worlds-rural-roadswith-a-shovel-and-a-phone-app/
4. https://www.eesti.ee/en/traffic/vehicles-and-right-to-drive/driving-licence
5. https://u.ae/en/about-the-uae/strategies-initiatives-and-awards/federalgovernments-strategies-and-plans/emirates-blockchain-strategy-2021 Ibid
6. https://www.rijksictdashboard.nl/
7. https://www.classcentral.com/report/moocwatch-23-moocs-backin-the spotlight/#:~:text=The%20ongoing%20pandemic%20has%20 increased, increase%20compared%20to%20last%20year.
8. https://fedtechmagazine.com/article/2020/04/air-force-turns-vr-ar-trainingand-maintenance
9. "Smart Nation Sensor Platform", GovTech,
10. https://www.tech.gov.sg/productsand-services/smart-nation-sensor-platform/, accessed 25 Oct 2019
11. https://publicadministration.un.org/egovkb/en-us/Data-Center
12. https://desapublications.un.org/sites/default/files/publications/2022-09/
13. Web%20version%20E-Government%202022.pdf
14. https://www.itu.int/hub/publication/d-ind-ict_mdd-2023-1/
15. https://www.itu.int/en/ITU-D/Statistics/Pages/facts/default.aspx
16. https://www.ptsecurity.com/ww-en/analytics/africa-cybersecuritythreatscape-2022-2023/
17. https://data.worldbank.org/indicator/SP.POP.TOTL?locations=DZ

18. https://www.gsmaintelligence.com/?utm_source=DataReportal &utm_medium=article&utm_campaign=State_Internet_Conne ctivity
19. https://datareportal.com/reports/digital-2023-algeria#:~:text=Algeria's%20 internet%20penetration%20rate%20stood,percent)%20between %202022%20 and%202023.
20. https://datareportal.com/reports/digital-2024-algeria
21. https://blogs.worldbank.org/arabvoices/how-digital-financial-services-canprovide-path-toward-economic-recovery-algeria
22. https://publicadministration.un.org/egovkb/en-us/Data/Country-Information/ id/3-Algeria
23. https://desapublications.un.org/sites/default/files/publications/2022-09/ Web%20version%20E-Government%202022.pdf
24. https://publicadministration.un.org/egovkb/en-us/Data/Country-Information/ id/5-Angola
25. https://observatoriotic.gov.ao/data/marketplace/internet_1669367534948
26. https://datareportal.com/reports/digital-2024-angola
27. https://www.sepe.gov.ao/ao/
28. https://agt.minfin.gov.ao/PortalAGT/#!/servicos-eletronicos/
29. https://simuladortributario.minfin.gov.ao/simulador
30. https://www.economiaemercado.co.ao/artigo/governo-prepara-condicoes-para-assegurar-a-identificacao-digital
31. https://desapublications.un.org/sites/default/files/publications/2024-09/%28Web%20version%29%20E-Government%20Survey%20 2024%201392024.pdf
32. https://www.worldbank.org/en/programs/govtech/2022-gtmi
33. https://www.ictworks.org/wp-content/uploads/2024/01/benin-e-government-services.pdf
34. https://cyber.ee/resources/news/benin-uxp/
35. https://service-public.bj/
36. https://intracen.org/news-and-events/news/benin-paves-the-way-for-aiand-big-data-with-senia

37. https://numerique.gouv.bj/assets/documents/national-artificial-intelligence-and-big-data-strategy-1682673348.pdf
38. https://www.wearetech.africa/en/fils-uk/news/public-management/benin-and-canada-explore-ai-collaboration-to-boost-digital-economy
39. https://desapublications.un.org/sites/default/files/publications/2024-09/%28Web%20version%29%20E-Government%20Survey%20 2024%201392024.pdf
40. https://www.nbfira.org.bw/bofinet%E2%80%99s-stakeholder-engagement-data-protection-act-and-digital-data-centre
41. https://www.speedtest.net/global-index
42. https://www.wipo.int/edocs/pubdocs/en/wipo-pub-2000-2023/bw.pdf
43. https://desapublications.un.org/sites/default/files/publications/2024-09/%28Web%20version%29%20E-Government%20Survey%20 2024%201392024.pdf
44. https://ida.worldbank.org/
45. https://www.worldbank.org/en/results/2023/06/26/from-connectivity-to-services-digital-transformation-in-africa
46. https://www.ookla.com/?utm_source=DataReportal
47. https://datareportal.com/reports/digital-2024-burkina-faso
48. https://desapublications.un.org/sites/default/files/publications/2024-09/%28Web%20version%29%20E-Government%20Survey%20 2024%201392024.pdf
49. https://worldinvestmentforum.unctad.org/session/gala-reception-and-global-digital-government-awards
50. https://www.un.org/sustainabledevelopment/
51. https://www-iwacu--burundi-org.translate.goog/bujumbura-collecte-donnees-carte-didentite-biometrique/?_x_tr_sl=auto&_x_tr_tl=en&_x_tr_hl=en
52. https://www.biometricupdate.com/202211/nearly-half-of-african-countries-lack-proper-safeguards-for-biometric-data-collection

53. https://desapublications.un.org/sites/default/files/publications/2024-09/%28Web%20version%29%20E-Government%20Survey%20 2024%201392024.pdf
54. https://thedocs.worldbank.org/en/doc/379941605627277587-0090022020/original/DE4ACameroonCountryDiagnosticJun26.pdf
55. https://publicadministration.un.org/egovkb/en-us/Data/Country-Information/id/30-Cameroon
56. https://www.guichetunique.org/
57. https://www.wearetech.africa/en/fils-uk/news/public-management/cameroon-officializes-the-e-visa
58. https://idl-bnc-idrc.dspacedirect.org/bitstream/handle/10625/60372/IDL%20-%2060372.pdf?sequence=2&isAllowed=y
59. https://openknowledge.worldbank.org/server/api/core/bitstreams/5e157ee3e97a-5e42-bfc0-f1416f3de4de/content
60. https://www.biometricupdate.com/202306/cameroon-partners-with-frenchdevt-agency-to-ramp-up-birth-registration
61. https://datareportal.com/reports/digital-2024-cameroon
62. https://desapublications.un.org/sites/default/files/publications/2024-09/%28Web%20version%29%20E-Government%20Survey%20 2024%201392024.pdf
63. https://nosi.cv/en/e-gov
64. https://portalconsular.mnec.gov.cv/
65. https://www.techpark.cv/
66. https://ella.link/
67. https://datareportal.com/reports/digital-2024-cabo-verde
68. https://www.itu.int/hub/publication/D-IND-ICT_MDD-2023-2/
69. https://international-partnerships.ec.europa.eu/policies/global-gateway_en
70. https://international-partnerships.ec.europa.eu/countries/cabo-verde_en

71. https://desapublications.un.org/sites/default/files/publications/2024-09/%28Web%20version%29%20E-Government%20Survey%20 2024%201392024.pdf
72. https://freedomhouse.org/country/central-african-republic/freedom-world/2023
73. https://datareportal.com/reports/digital-2024-central-african-republic?rq=central%20african%20republic
74. https://www.oecd-ilibrary.org/content/component/f2e7ffb6-en
75. https://www.cnbc.com/2022/04/28/central-african-republic-adopts-bitcoin-as-legal-tender.html
76. https://sango.org/
77. https://www.itu.int/epublications/publication/D-STR-GCI.01-2021-HTM-E
78. https://freedomhouse.org/country/chad/freedom-world/2023
79. https://publicadministration.un.org/egovkb/en-us/Data-Center
80. https://publicadministration.un.org/egovkb/en-us/Data/Country-Information/id/34-Chad
81. https://publicadministration.un.org/egovkb/en-us/Data/Country-Information/id/38-Comoros
82. https://publicadministration.un.org/egovkb/en-us/Data/Country-Information/id/38-Comoros
83. http://www.tourisme.gouv.km/index.php
84. https://www.agid.gouv.km/cgi-sys/suspendedpage.cgi
85. http://mpt.gouv.km/
86. https://anaden.org/
87. https://www.anaden.org/uploads/media/5e3969272d9f8/strat-comores-numerique-v2-3-compresse.pdf
88. https://unsdg.un.org/sites/default/files/2021-06/Comoros_Cooperation_Framework_%202022-2026.FR_.pdf
89. https://datareportal.com/reports/digital-2024-comoros
90. https://www.worldbank.org/en/country/congo/overview
91. https://desapublications.un.org/sites/default/files/publications/2024-09/%28Web%20version%29%20E-Government%20Survey%20 2024%201392024.pdf

92. https://publicadministration.un.org/egovkb/en-us/Data/Country-Information/id/47-Democratic-Republic-of-the-Congo
93. https://openknowledge.worldbank.org/server/api/core/bitstreams/5e157ee3e97a-5e42-bfc0-f1416f3de4de/content
94. https://www.numerique.cd/pnn/
95. https://marchepublic.cd/
96. https://techcabal.com/2024/03/22/congo-fintechs/
97. https://emploi.gouv.cd/inspection-travail/
98. https://republique.cd/e-gov/
99. https://desapublications.un.org/sites/default/files/publications/2024-09/%28Web%20version%29%20E-Government%20Survey%20 2024%201392024.pdf
100. https://datareportal.com/reports/digital-2024-republic-of-the-congo?rq=congo
101. https://projects.worldbank.org/en/projects-operations/procurement-detail/ OP00209946
102. https://www.eib.org/en/press/all/2023-222-together-towards-digitalization-in-the-republic-of-congo-89-4-billion-cfa-francs-mobilized-for-the-acceleration-of-digital-transformation-in-congo
103. https://publicadministration.un.org/egovkb/en-us/Data/Country-Information/id/49-Djibouti
104. https://douanes.gouv.dj/
105. https://projects.worldbank.org/en/projects-operations/project-detail/ P162904
106. https://djiboutiembassykuwait.net/assets/files/djibouti-2035-en.pdf
107. https://e-estonia.com/solutions/interoperability-services/x-road/
108. https://www.biometricupdate.com/202401/ethiopia-digital-id-project-getswb-push-as-govt-solicits-more-private-sector-support
109. https://mcit.gov.eg/

110. https://www.un.org/sites/un2.un.org/files/2020_un_e-government_survey_full_report.pdf
111. https://publicadministration.un.org/egovkb/en-us/Data/Country-Information/id/53-Egypt
112. https://desapublications.un.org/sites/default/files/publications/2024-09/%28Web%20version%29%20E-Government%20Survey%20 2024%201392024.pdf
113. https://blogs.worldbank.org/arabvoices/digital-transformation-time-covid-19-case-mena
114. https://desapublications.un.org/sites/default/files/publications/2022-09/Web%20version%20E-Government%202022.pdf
115. https://publicadministration.un.org/egovkb/en-us/Data/Country-Information/id/55-Equatorial-Guinea
116. https://datareportal.com/reports/digital-2024-equatorial-guinea
117. https://thedocs.worldbank.org/en/doc/61714f214ed04bcd6e9623ad0e215897-0400012021/related/P1793391f4a4c800219f00014c68aefed3c8.pdf
118. https://freedomhouse.org/country/eritrea/freedom-world/2024
119. https://desapublications.un.org/sites/default/files/publications/2024-09/%28Web%20version%29%20E-Government%20Survey%20 2024%201392024.pdf
120. https://publicadministration.un.org/egovkb/en-us/Data/Country-Information/id/56-Eritrea
121. https://datareportal.com/reports/digital-2024-eritrea?rq=eritrea
122. https://publicadministration.un.org/egovkb/en-us/Data/Country-Information/id/164-Eswatini
123. https://desapublications.un.org/sites/default/files/publications/2024-09/%28Web%20version%29%20E-Government%20Survey%20 2024%201392024.pdf
124. https://www.worldbank.org/en/country/eswatini/overview
125. https://www.itu.int/en/ITU-D/Statistics/Documents/DDD/ddd_SWZ.pdf

126. https://datareportal.com/?utm_source=DataReportal&utm_medium=Country_Article_Hyperlink&utm_campaign=Digital_2024&utm_term=Eswatini&utm_content=Home_Page_Link

127. https://documents1.worldbank.org/curated/en/099074503132323149/pdf/P17281301a0e1c01c0b32f093ce7cb40366.pdf

128. https://publicadministration.un.org/egovkb/en-us/Data/Country-Information/id/58-Ethiopia

129. https://desapublications.un.org/sites/default/files/publications/2024-09/%28Web%20version%29%20E-Government%20Survey%20 2024%201392024.pdf

130. https://datareportal.com/reports/digital-2024-ethiopia

131. https://www.itu.int/en/ITUD/Statistics/Documents/DDD/ddd_ETH.pdf

132. https://www.hrw.org/tag/tigray-conflict

133. https://faolex.fao.org/docs/pdf/eth215804.pdf

134. https://www.biometricupdate.com/202404/ethiopian-pm-hails-digital-id-as-driver-of-digital-ethiopia-2025-strategy

135. https://www.biometricupdate.com/202404/ethiopia-announces-procurement-process-for-digital-id-support-hardware

136. https://www.biometricupdate.com/202403/ethiopia-begins-issuing-refugees-digital-id-cards-to-facilitate-service-access

137. https://desapublications.un.org/sites/default/files/publications/2024-09/%28Web%20version%29%20E-Government%20Survey%20 2024%201392024.pdf

138. https://www.worldbank.org/en/news/press-release/2024/01/02/gabon-the-world-bank-boost-its-support-to-accelerate-digital-transformation

139. https://www.biometricupdate.com/202305/gabon-hopes-to-deliver-on-itslingering-national-id-card-promise-this-year

140. https://www.linkedin.com/posts/pr%C3%A9sidence-de-la-r%C3%A9publique-gabonaise_re%C3%A7u-en-audience-par-le-chef-de-l%C3%A9tat-le-activity-7162935913445101569-i7yz/

141. https://desapublications.un.org/sites/default/files/publications/2024-09/%28Web%20version%29%20E Government%20Survey%20 2024%201392024.pdf
142. https://publicadministration.un.org/egovkb/en-us/Data/Country-Information/id/63-Gambia
143. https://www.uneca.org/sites/default/files/TCND/Digital%20ID%20Transformation%20Strategy%20_Gambia%20V_9.pdf
144. https://www.uneca.org/stories/validation-of-the-gambia%E2%80%99s-national-digital-id-and-digital-transformation-strategy
145. https://datareportal.com/reports/digital-2024-gambia
146. https://www.itu.int/en/ITUD/Statistics/Documents/DDD/ddd_AFG.pdf
147. https://desapublications.un.org/sites/default/files/publications/2024-09/%28Web%20version%29%20E-Government%20Survey%20 2024%201392024.pdf
148. https://openknowledge.worldbank.org/handle/10986/34366
149. https://publicadministration.un.org/egovkb/en-us/Data/Country-Information/id/66-Ghana
150. https://www.ghana.gov.gh/
151. https://www.ghanapostgps.com/
152. https://gcnet.com.gh/
153. https://passport.mfa.gov.gh/
154. https://www.ghipss.net/index.php/publications/ghqr-customer
155. https://presidency.gov.gh/index.php/briefing-room/news-style-2/1181time-for-a-digital-roadmap-for-ghana-vp-bawumia
156. https://www.worldbank.org/en/news/press-release/2022/04/28/afw-worldbank-provides-200-million-to-accelerate-ghana-digital-transformation-agendafor-better-jobs
157. https://publicadministration.un.org/egovkb/en-us/Data/Country-Information/id/70-Guinea
158. https://desapublications.un.org/sites/default/files/publications/2022-09/ Report%20without%20annexes.pdf
159. https://datareportal.com/reports/digital-2024-guinea
160. https://www.aguipe.gov.gn/page-aguipe

161. https://blogs.worldbank.org/digital-development/digitalizing-guinea-bissau-future-starts-now
162. https://documents1.worldbank.org/curated/en/0997450062622 16743/pdf/P177016084979202b08dd501a5690c82506.pdf
163. https://www.itu.int/en/ITU-D/Statistics/Pages/stat/default.aspx
164. https://publicadministration.un.org/egovkb/en-us/Data/Country-Information/id/71-Guinea-Bissau
165. https://documents1.worldbank.org/curated/en/0997450062622 16743/pdf/P177016084979202b08dd501a5690c82506.pdf
166. https://projects.worldbank.org/en/projects-operations/project-detail/ P176932
167. https://desapublications.un.org/sites/default/files/publications/2022-09/Web%20version%20E-Government%202022.pdf
168. https://desapublications.un.org/sites/default/files/publications/2024-09/%28Web%20version%29%20E-Government%20Survey%20 2024%201392024.pdf
169. https://publicadministration.un.org/egovkb/en-us/Data/Country-Information/id/41-Cte-dIvoire
170. https://www.worldbank.org/en/results/2022/07/11/afw-advancing-digital-entrepreneurship-and-financial-inclusion-in-cote-divoire 171. https://datareportal.com/reports/digital-2024-cote-divoire
171. https://www.itu.int/en/ITUD/Statistics/Documents/DDD/ddd_CIV.pdf
172. https://desapublications.un.org/sites/default/files/publications/2024-09/%28Web%20version%29%20E-Government%20Survey%20 2024%201392024.pdf
173. https://publicadministration.un.org/egovkb/en-us/Data/Country-Information/id/88-Kenya
174. https://www.techinafrica.com/kenya-to-earn-1-4-trillion-from-the-digitaleconomy-by-2025/
175. https://www.undp.org/kenya/press-releases/undp-unveils-digital-public-infrastructure-portfolio-and-signs-mou-drive-inclusive-digital-transformation

176. https://www.hudumakenya.go.ke/HUDUMAKENYADIGITALIZATIONPLAN-V1.5.1.pdf
177. https://ecdpm.org/application/files/5517/0254/4789/Digital-ID-systems-in-Africa-ECDPM-Discussion-Paper-360-2023.pdf
178. https://cms.icta.go.ke/sites/default/files/2022-04/Kenya%20Digital%20 Masterplan%202022-2032%20Online%20Version.pdf
179. https://desapublications.un.org/sites/default/files/publications/2024-09/%28Web%20version%29%20E-Government%20Survey%20 2024%201392024.pdf
180. https://publicadministration.un.org/egovkb/en-us/Data/Country-Information/id/95-Lesotho
181. https://kepios.com/?utm_source=DataReportal&utm_medium=Country_Article_Hyperlink&utm_campaign=Digital_2024&utm_term=Lesotho&utm_ content=Kepios_Home_Link
182. https://www.itu.int/en/ITUD/Statistics/Documents/DDD/ddd_LSO.pdf
183. https://desapublications.un.org/sites/default/files/publications/2024-09/%28Web%20version%29%20E-Government%20Survey%20 2024%201392024.pdf
184. https://publicadministration.un.org/egovkb/en-us/Data/Country-Information/id/96-Liberia
185. https://data.worldbank.org/indicator/SP.REG.BRTH.ZS?locations=LR
186. https://eliberia.gov.lr/services/
187. https://www.undp.org/liberia/stories/decentralizing-liberia-one-stop-service-shops
188. https://www.worldbank.org/en/programs/govtech/gtmi
189. https://publicadministration.un.org/egovkb/en-us/Data/Country-Information/id/97-Libya
190. https://desapublications.un.org/sites/default/files/publications/2024-09/%28Web%20version%29%20E-Government%20Survey%20 2024%201392024.pdf
191. https://www.budde.com.au/Research/Libya-Telecoms-Mobile-and-Broadband-Statistics-and-Analyses ibid

192. https://www.itu.int/en/ITUD/Statistics/Documents/DDD/ddd_LBY.pdf
193. https://datareportal.com/reports/digital-2024-libya
194. https://desapublications.un.org/sites/default/files/publications/2022-09/Web%20version%20E-Government%202022.pdf
195. https://desapublications.un.org/sites/default/files/publications/2024-09/%28Web%20version%29%20E-Government%20Survey%20 2024%201392024.pdf
196. https://publicadministration.un.org/egovkb/en-us/Data/Country-Information/id/101-Madagascar
197. https://www.itu.int/en/ITUD/Statistics/Documents/DDD/ddd_MDG.pdf
198. https://torolalana.gov.mg/fr/
199. https://datareportal.com/reports/digital-2021-madagascar?rq=madagascar
200. https://public.digital/pd-insights/blog/2023/07/transforming-access-to-public-services-for-madagascars-citizens
201. https://blogs.worldbank.org/en/nasikiliza/legal-identity-all-what-can-madagascar-learn-namibia
202. https://projects.worldbank.org/en/projects-operations/project-detail/P169413
203. https://x-road.global/
204. https://blogs.worldbank.org/en/governance/madagascars-digital-transformation-helping-deliver-better-and-faster-services
205. https://desapublications.un.org/sites/default/files/publica-
206. tions/2024-09/%28Web%20version%29%20E-Government%20Survey%20 2024%201392024.pdf
207. https://publicadministration.un.org/egovkb/en-us/Data/Country-Information/id/102-Malawi
208. https://www.itu.int/en/ITUD/Statistics/Documents/DDD/ddd_MWI.pdf
209. https://datareportal.com/reports/digital-2024-malawi
210. https://www.uncdf.org/admin/editors/ArticleItem/Index/8255?articleTitle=ides-report-malawi

211. https://www.undp.org/malawi/press-releases/breaking-barriers-malawis-idt4m-project-paves-way-inclusive-digital-futures
212. https://desapublications.un.org/sites/default/files/publications/2024-09/%28Web%20version%29%20E-Government%20Survey%20 2024%201392024.pdf
213. https://publicadministration.un.org/egovkb/en-us/Data/Country-Information/id/105-Mali
214. https://datareportal.com/reports/digital-2024-mali
215. https://www.ecofinagency.com/telecom/0801-45142-mali-govt-invests-117-3bn-to-improve-fiber-optic-network
216. https://desapublications.un.org/sites/default/files/publications/2022-09/Web%20version%20E-Government%202022.pdf
217. https://publicadministration.un.org/egovkb/en-us/Data/Country-Information/id/108-Mauritania
218. https://mtnima.gov.mr/sites/default/files/Agenda%20Num%C3%A9rique%202022-25%20MTNIMA.pdf
219. https://www.itu.int/en/ITUD/Statistics/Documents/DDD/ddd_MRT.pdf
220. https://datareportal.com/reports/digital-2024-mauritania
221. https://datareportal.com/reports/digital-2024-mauritania
222. https://international-partnerships.ec.europa.eu/countries/mauritania_en
223. https://desapublications.un.org/sites/default/files/publications/2024-09/%28Web%20version%29%20E-Government%20Survey%20 2024%201392024.pdf
224. https://publicadministration.un.org/egovkb/en-us/Data/Country-Information/id/109-Mauritius
225. https://desapublications.un.org/sites/default/files/publications/2024-09/%28Web%20version%29%20E-Government%20Survey%20 2024%201392024.pdf
226. https://publicadministration.un.org/egovkb/en-us/Data/Country-Information/id/115-Morocco
227. https://identityreview.com/moroccan-digital-identity-expanding-accessibility/

228. https://www.oecd.org/en/publications/digital-government-review-of-morocco_9789264298729-en.html
229. https://desapublications.un.org/sites/default/files/publications/2024-09/%28Web%20version%29%20E-Government%20Survey%20 2024%201392024.pdf
230. https://publicadministration.un.org/egovkb/en-us/Data/Country-Information/id/116-Mozambique
231. https://datareportal.com/reports/digital-2024-mozambique?rq=mozambique
232. https://www.imf.org/en/Publications/CR/Issues/2023/07/13/Republic-of-Mozambique-Second-Review-Under-the-Three-Year-Arrangement-Under-the-Extended-536309
233. https://desapublications.un.org/sites/default/files/publications/2024-09/%28Web%20version%29%20E-Government%20Survey%20 2024%201392024.pdf
234. https://publicadministration.un.org/egovkb/en-us/Data/Country-Information/id/118-Namibia
235. https://www.undp.org/acceleratorlabs/undp-namibia-accelerator-lab
236. https://www.governance4id.org/
237. https://www.npc.gov.na/wp-content/uploads/2021/11/vision_2030.pdf
238. https://d4dhub.eu/au-eu-project
239. https://www.worldometers.info/world-population/niger-population/
240. https://openknowledge.worldbank.org/server/api/core/bitstreams/08e3d677-cd68-400d-b7c2-7f3f8197864c/content
241. https://desapublications.un.org/sites/default/files/publications/2024-09/%28Web%20version%29%20E-Government%20Survey%20 2024%201392024.pdf
242. https://publicadministration.un.org/egovkb/en-us/Data/Country-Information/id/124-Niger
243. https://datareportal.com/reports/digital-2024-niger?rq=niger

244. https://desapublications.un.org/sites/default/files/publications/2024-09/%28Web%20version%29%20E-Government%20Survey%20 2024%201392024.pdf
245. https://publicadministration.un.org/egovkb/en-us/Data/Country-Information/id/125-Nigeria
246. https://desapublications.un.org/sites/default/files/publications/2022-09/Web%20version%20E-Government%202022.pdf
247. https://a4ai.org/report/2021-affordability-report/
248. https://ncc.gov.ng/documents/880-nigerian-national-broadband-plan-2020-2025/file
249. https://www.biometricupdate.com/202310/nigerian-govt-minister-stresses-need-for-data-harmonization-single-biometric-database
250. https://www.biometricupdate.com/202404/nigerians-decry-duplicative-biometric-capture-for-sim-registration-id-cards-sim-nin-linkage
251. https://www.biometricupdate.com/202301/mosip-registrations-pass-76mburkina-faso-partners-for-pilot-with-more-in-pipeline
252. https://desapublications.un.org/sites/default/files/publications/2024-09/%28Web%20version%29%20E-Government%20Survey%20 2024%201392024.pdf
253. https://irembo.gov.rw/home/citizen/all_services
254. https://www.worldbank.org/en/country/rwanda/publication/rwanda-economic-update-leveraging-digital-transformation-for-sustainable-growth 256. ibid.
255. https://publicadministration.un.org/egovkb/en-us/Data/Country-Information/id/142-Rwanda
256. https://international-partnerships.ec.europa.eu/countries/sao-tome-andprincipe_en
257. https://desapublications.un.org/sites/default/files/publications/2024-09/%28Web%20version%29%20E-Government%20Survey%20 2024%201392024.pdf
258. https://publicadministration.un.org/egovkb/en-us/Data/Country-Information/id/148-Sao-Tome-and-Principe

259. https://openknowledge.worldbank.org/server/api/core/bitstreams/ff1c2057-9dd3-4021-8a30-957e371d97a9/content

260. https://datareportal.com/reports/digital-2024-sao-tome-and-principe?rq=sao

261. https://blogs.unicef.org/evidence-for-action/reimagining-education-through-digital-learning-in-sao-tome-and-principe/

262. https://www.worldbank.org/en/country/saotome/overview

263. https://desapublications.un.org/sites/default/files/publications/2022-09/Web%20version%20E-Government%202022.pdf

264. https://publicadministration.un.org/egovkb/en-us/Data/Country-Information/id/150-Senegal

265. https://www.worldbank.org/en/data/interactive/2022/10/21/govtech-maturity-index-gtmi-data-dashboard

266. https://datareportal.com/reports/digital-2024-senegal?rq=senegal

267. https://www.itu.int/en/ITUD/Statistics/Documents/DDD/ddd SEN.pdf

268. https://www.worldbank.org/en/news/press-release/2023/06/29/higher-education-in-senegal-over-150-million-to-ensure-rapid-integration-into-the-job-market

269. https://www.afdb.org/en/news-and-events/press-releases/senegal-african-development-bank-provides-additional-eu501-million-diamniadio-digital-technology-park-57642#:~:text=The%20Board%20of%20Directors%20of,Technology%20Park%20in%20Diamniadio%2C%20Senegal.

270. https://guardian.ng/apo-press-releases/senegal-develops-its-national-data-strategy-in-partnership-with-smart-africa-and-giz/ 273. https://desapublications.un.org/sites/default/files/publications/2024-09/%28Web%20version%29%20E-Government%20Survey%20 2024%201392024.pdf

271. https://publicadministration.un.org/egovkb/en-us/Data/Country-Information/id/152-Seychelles

272. https://datareportal.com/reports/digital-2024-seychelles?rq=Seychelles

273. https://www.biometricupdate.com/companies/wisekey
274. https://www.biometricupdate.com/202211/seychelles-launches-digital-id-platform-from-wisekey-for-government-private-sector
275. https://thedocs.worldbank.org/en/doc/290341604360934635-0090022020/ original/seychellesdesigndecv4.pdf
276. https://www.dsti.gov.sl/wp-content/uploads/2023/07/Sierra-Leone-National-Innovation-and-Digital-Strategy.pdf
277. https://publicadministration.un.org/egovkb/en-us/Data/Country-Information/id/153-Sierra-Leone
278. https://ace-submarinecable.com/en/submarine-cable/
279. https://datareportal.com/reports/digital-2024-sierra-leone?rq=sierra%20 leone
280. https://www.itu.int/en/IT-D/Statistics/Documents/DDD/ddd_SLE.pdf
281. https://www.speedtest.net/global-index
282. https://www.reuters.com/world/africa/sierra-leone-energy-minister-resigns-over-electricity-crisis-power-returns-2024-04-26/
283. https://desapublications.un.org/sites/default/files/publications/2024-09/%28Web%20version%29%20E-Government%20Survey%20 2024%201392024.pdf
284. https://datareportal.com/reports/digital-2024-somalia
285. https://publicadministration.un.org/egovkb/en-us/Data/Country-Information/id/159-South-Africa
286. https://desapublications.un.org/sites/default/files/publications/2024-09/%28Web%20version%29%20E-Government%20Survey%20 2024%201392024.pdf
287. https://datareportal.com/reports/digital-2024-south-africa?rq=south%20 africa
288. https://www.dcdt.gov.za/sa-connect-document.html
289. https://www.treasury.gov.za/documents/National%20Budget/2023/ene/ FullENE.pdf
290. https://www.itweb.co.za/article/r3bn-budget-boost-for-sa-connect-phasetwo/Gb3Bw7WagoWq2k6V

291. https://www.speedtest.net/global-index/south-africa#mobile
292. https://www.gov.za/sites/default/files/gcis_document/201409/ndp-2030our-future-make-it-workr.pdf
293. https://www.gov.za/sites/default/files/gcis_document/201711/41241gen886.pdf
294. https://www.eservices.gov.za/
295. https://www.bizportal.gov.za/default.aspx
296. https://documents1.worldbank.org/curated/en/460341563539588094/ pdf/Mobile-Money-Ecosystem-Survey-in-South-Sudan-Exploring-the-Current-and-Future-Potential-of-Using-Mobile-Money-for-Effective-Humanitarian-and-Development-Cash-Programming-Executive-Summary.pdf
297. https://desapublications.un.org/sites/default/files/publications/2024-09/%28Web%20version%29%20E-Government%20Survey%20 2024%201392024.pdf
298. https://publicadministration.un.org/egovkb/en-us/Data/Country-Information/id/193-South-Sudan
299. https://desapublications.un.org/sites/default/files/publications/2024-09/%28Web%20version%29%20E-Government%20Survey%20 2024%201392024.pdf
300. https://desapublications.un.org/sites/default/files/publications/2024-09/%28Web%20version%29%20E-Government%20Survey%20 2024%201392024.pdf
301. https://publicadministration.un.org/egovkb/en-us/Data/Country-Information/id/183-United-Republic-of-Tanzania
302. https://www.submarinecablemap.com/landing-point/dar-es-salaam-tanzania
303. https://datareportal.com/reports/digital-2024-tanzania?rq=tanzania
304. https://www.itu.int/itu-d/reports/statistics/2022/11/24/ff22-internet-usein-urban-and-rural-areas/
305. https://www.gsma.com/solutions-and-impact/connectivity-for-good/mobile-for-development/blog/limited-usage-women-and-mobile-money-in-tanzania/

306. https://publicadministration.un.org/egovkb/en-us/Data/Country-Information/id/172-Togo
307. https://desapublications.un.org/sites/default/files/publications/2024-09/%28Web%20version%29%20E-Government%20Survey%20 2024%201392024.pdf
308. https://www.npr.org/sections/goatsandsoda/2021/02/15/966848542/thepandemic-pushed-this-farmer-into-deep-poverty-then-something-amazinghappene
309. https://novissi.gouv.tg/en/home-new-en/
310. https://www.weforum.org/agenda/2023/09/togo-digital-inclusion-journey-to-equitable-access/
311. https://www.edisonalliance.org/home
312. https://datareportal.com/reports/digital-2024-togo?rq=togo
313. https://www.speedtest.net/global-index/togo#fixed
314. https://publicadministration.un.org/egovkb/en-us/Data/Country-Information/id/175-Tunisia
315. https://desapublications.un.org/sites/default/files/publications/2024-09/%28Web%20version%29%20E-Government%20Survey%20 2024%201392024.pdf
316. https://documents1.worldbank.org/curated/en/099040723102586165/pdf/P1694820e047c901008b7e04cb6ee11fa9f.pdf
317. https://datareportal.com/reports/digital-2024-tunisia?rq=tunisia
318. https://www.speedtest.net/global-index/tunisia#fixed
319. https://www.worldbank.org/en/programs/teri/overview
320. https://desapublications.un.org/sites/default/files/publications/2024-09/%28Web%20version%29%20E-Government%20Survey%20 2024%201392024.pdf
321. https://publicadministration.un.org/egovkb/en-us/Data/Country-Information/id/179-Uganda
322. https://datareportal.com/reports/digital-2024-uganda?rq=uganda
323. https://www.worldbank.org/en/news/press-release/2021/06/02/uganda-secures-200-million-to-accelerate-digital-transformation-and-inclusiveness

324. https://ict.go.ug/programmes/digital-transformation-roadmap/
325. https://news.trust.org/item/20220513155511-l53t0/?utm_source=twitter&utm_medium=social&utm_campaign=trf-corro&utm_content=thread
326. https://desapublications.un.org/sites/default/files/publications/2022-09/Web%20version%20E-Government%202022.pdf
327. https://desapublications.un.org/sites/default/files/publications/2024-09/%28Web%20version%29%20E-Government%20Survey%20 2024%201392024.pdf
328. https://publicadministration.un.org/egovkb/en-us/Data/Country-Information/id/191-Zambia
329. https://datareportal.com/reports/digital-2024-zambia?rq=zambia
330. https://www.biometricupdate.com/202312/bangladesh-philippines-sri-lanka-zambia-advance-with-digital-credentials-projects
331. https://news.sky.com/story/zimbabwe-declares-state-of-disaster-overdrought-sweeping-across-southern-africa-13107431
332. https://www.linkedin.com/posts/tariqmalik1_zambia-digitizing-id-activity-7194733492256063488-JHlA/
333. https://www.macrotrends.net/global-metrics/countries/ZWE/zimbabwe/ population
334. https://publicadministration.un.org/egovkb/en-us/Data/Country-Information/id/192-Zimbabwe
335. https://openknowledge.worldbank.org/server/api/core/bitstreams/ ff1c2057-9dd3-4021-8a30-957e371d97a9/content
336. https://www.enca.com/news/misery-zimbabwe-over-19-hour-power-cuts
337. https://datareportal.com/reports/digital-2024-zimbabwe?rq=zimba
338. https://www.worldbank.org/en/country/zimbabwe/publication/digitaltransformation-a-key-enabler-of-long-term-resilient-growth-in-zimbabwe

339. https://documents1.worldbank.org/curated/en/982981621880260112/pdf/Digital-Economy-for-Zimbabwe-Country-Diagnostic-Report.pdf
340. https://www.bloomberg.com/news/articles/2024-05-13/zig-usd-zimbabwe-to-revive-mobile-money-service-once-blamed-for-currency-crash
341. https://desapublications.un.org/sites/default/files/publications/2024-09/%28Web%20version%29%20E-Government%20Survey%20 2024%201392024.pdf
342. https://publicadministration.un.org/egovkb/en-us/Data/Country-Information/id/1-Afghanistan
343. https://desapublications.un.org/sites/default/files/publications/2024-09/%28Web%20version%29%20E-Government%20Survey%20 2024%201392024.pdf
344. https://www.itu.int/en/ITU-D/Statistics/Documents/DDD/ddd_AFG.pdf
345. https://datareportal.com/reports/digital-2023-afghanistan
346. https://www.kentik.com/blog/whats-next-for-the-internet-in-afghanistan/
347. https://mcit.gov.af/en/nixa-national-internet-exchange-afghanistan-8
348. https://desapublications.un.org/sites/default/files/publications/2024-09/%28Web%20version%29%20E-Government%20Survey%20 2024%201392024.pdf
349. https://publicadministration.un.org/egovkb/en-us/Data/Country-Information/id/8-Armenia
350. https://sdgs.un.org/goals
351. https://www.worldbank.org/en/news/press-release/2022/03/03/armeniato-improve-public-sector-performance-through-digital-solutions-with-worldbank-support
352. https://www.gov.am/en/news/item/9211/
353. https://corporate.armed.am/en/about-system/ehealth-in-armenia
354. https://eu4armenia.eu/projects/eu-project-page/?id=1645

355. https://www.worldbank.org/en/news/press-release/2023/10/31/improving-the-digital-service-delivery-in-armenia

356. https://ereforms.gov.az/en/media/meqale-ve-musahibeler/azerbaijan-pursues-strategic-digital-transformation-oriented-policies-towards-regional-digital-hub-425

357. https://jamestown.org/program/azerbaijans-latest-steps-toward-becoming-a-regional-digital-hub/

358. https://desapublications.un.org/sites/default/files/publications/2024-09/%28Web%20version%29%20E-Government%20Survey%20 2024%201392024.pdf

359. https://publicadministration.un.org/egovkb/en-us/Data/Country-Information/id/11-Azerbaijan

360. https://desapublications.un.org/sites/default/files/publications/2024-09/%28Web%20version%29%20E-Government%20Survey%20 2024%201392024.pdf

361. https://www.itu.int/en/ITU-D/Statistics/Documents/DDD/ddd_BHR.pdf

362. https://www.bahrain.bh/wps/portal/!ut/p/a1/rZFBT4NAEIX_Cj1wJDuwhYUjEqwSaU0rWvbSbGFpsbBA3Tb67wuiiRekJs5tku9N3puHKFojKtg53zGZV4IV3U6tzd0CLN2wjcDGEQZ3YXlLxwd9BmYLxD8BwNjvAPJInh3DsuE6PRihp99PW30YArj2zfLh6dYDmOEx_QuiiCZC1nKPYr6rznV1lKzYcKHCviq5Cs0pTw5KkYvDmwpsW52k0nH8KEoupAriK6vSK7t7dZKnKE7TzDSdDDQHb7E2BYdpzNaJZhKmZyzLjEQn3_4Hxh3Nv-KizzDyxU_gtzf1wLCPuDVKBp20F1Z_TB5cUW3-2jTUbQuqhOTvEq3_paG6jKLSxh9a4GfzuUZjdzK5AMpBg1A!/dl5/d5/L2dBISEvZ0FBIS9nQSEh/

363. https://www.go-globe.com/bahrains-digital-transformation-vision-2030/

364. https://www.moic.gov.bh/en/eServices

365. https://www.sehati.gov.bh/

366. https://www.nea.gov.bh/Attachments/iGA_Cloud-First_Policy_V1.0.pdf

367. https://play.google.com/store/apps/details?id=bh.bahrain.corona.tracker&hl=en&gl=US
368. https://www.bna.bh/en/Bahrainthe1stinregiontoimplementmulticloudandhybridcloudsystemingovernmentsector.aspx?cms=q8FmFJgiscL2fwIzON1%2BDuifwoHe0Fmxa66okKjOXz0%3D
369. https://www.bna.bh/en/Bahrainthe1stinregiontoimplementmulticloudandhybridcloudsystemingovernmentsector.aspx?cms=q8FmFJgiscL2fwIzON1%2BDuifwoHe0Fmxa66okKjOXz0%3D
370. https://info.undp.org/docs/pdc/Documents/BGD/UNDP%20a2i-II%20 closing%20report_Final.pdf
371. https://a2i.gov.bd/
372. https://projects.worldbank.org/en/projects-operations/project-detail/ P161086
373. https://www.un.org/sites/un2.un.org/files/2020_un_e-government_survey_full_report.pdf
374. https://publicadministration.un.org/egovkb/en-us/Data/Country-Information/id/14-Bangladesh
375. https://desapublications.un.org/sites/default/files/publications/2024-09/%28Web%20version%29%20E-Government%20Survey%20 2024%201392024.pdf
376. https://blogs.worldbank.org/endpovertyinsouthasia/how-can-digital-technology-transform-lives-and-improve-opportunities-bhutan
377. https://desapublications.un.org/sites/default/files/publications/2024-09/%28Web%20version%29%20E-Government%20Survey%20 2024%201392024.pdf
378. https://publicadministration.un.org/egovkb/en-us/Data/Country-Information/id/25-Brunei-Darussalam
379. https://www.mtic.gov.bn/DE2025/documents/Digital%20Economy%20 Masterplan%202025.pdf
380. https://www.data.gov.bn/Pages/index.aspx
381. https://www.gov.bn/SitePages/Home.aspx
382. https://www.itu.int/itu-d/reports/statistics/idi2023/
383. https://publicadministration.un.org/egovkb/en-us/Data/Country-Information/id/29-Cambodia

384. https://asset.cambodia.gov.kh/mptc/media/Cambodia_Digital_Government_Policy_2022_2035_English.pdf
385. https://digitaleconomy.gov.kh/index?lang=en
386. https://www.undp.org/cambodia
387. https://datareportal.com/reports/digital-2024-cambodia?rq=cambodia
388. https://desapublications.un.org/sites/default/files/publications/2024-09/%28Web%20version%29%20E-Government%20Survey%20 2024%201392024.pdf
389. https://publicadministration.un.org/egovkb/en-us/Data/Country-Information/id/36-China
390. https://english.www.gov.cn/policies/latestreleases/202302/28/content_WS63fd33a8c6d0a757729e752c.html
391. https://www.fmprc.gov.cn/eng/wjb_663304/zzjg_663340/jks_665232/kjlc_665236/qtwt_665250/202305/t20230525_11083607.html?utm_source=substack&utm_medium=email
392. https://www.fmprc.gov.cn/mfa_eng/wjdt_665385/2649_665393/202009/ t20200908_679637.html
393. https://datareportal.com/reports/digital-2024-china?rq=china
394. https://www.itu.int/en/ITU-D/Statistics/Dashboards/Pages/Digital-Development.aspx
395. https://publicadministration.un.org/egovkb/en-us/Data/Country-Information/id/36-China
396. https://www.china-briefing.com/news/china-data-centers-new-cross-regional-plan-to-boost-computing-power-across-regions/
397. https://datacommons.org/place?utm_medium=explore&dcid=country/IN-D&mprop=count&popt=Person&hl=en
398. https://www.oecd.org/gov/innovative-government/India-case-study-UAEreport-2018.pdf
399. https://www.npci.org.in/what-we-do/upi/product-overview
400. https://www.mygov.in/
401. https://www.indiatoday.in/india/story/data-leak-cyber-attack-hacking-cybersecurity-internet-threat-crime-top-trends-2023-2478994-2023-12-

21#:~:text=One%20of%20the%20most%20significant,data%20c ould%20not%20be%20 verified.

402. https://ycpsolidiance.com/article/indonesia-government-digital-transformation

403. https://govinsider.asia/intl-en/article/is-indonesia-on-track-to-a-fully-digital-government-by-2025

404. https://publicadministration.un.org/egovkb/en-us/Data/Country-Information/id/78-Indonesia

405. https://desapublications.un.org/sites/default/files/publications/2022-09/Web%20version%20E-Government%202022.pdf

406. https://therecord.media/iran-linked-hackers-claim-attack-on-albania-census-org

407. https://www.latimes.com/world-nation/story/2024-01-03/states-congress-wrestle-with-cybersecurity-after-iran-hacks-small-town-water-utilities

408. https://www.theguardian.com/technology/2024/feb/08/iran-backed-hackers-interrupt-uae-tv-streaming-services-with-deepfake-news

409. https://publicadministration.un.org/egovkb/en-us/Data/Country-Information/id/79-Iran-Islamic-Republic-of

410. https://datareportal.com/reports/digital-2024-iran?rq=iran

411. https://www.speedtest.net/global-index/iran

412. https://publicadministration.un.org/egovkb/en-us/Data/Country-Information/id/80-Iraq

413. https://desapublications.un.org/sites/default/files/publications/2024-09/%28Web%20version%29%20E-Government%20Survey%20 2024%201392024.pdf

414. https://www.undp.org/sites/g/files/zskgke326/files/2023-06/undp_iq_digital_landscape_assessment_en.pdf

415. https://desapublications.un.org/sites/default/files/publications/2024-09/%28Web%20version%29%20E-Government%20Survey%20 2024%201392024.pdf

416. https://www.leadingdigitalgovs.org/organization

417. https://www.consumers.org.il/category/en-consumers

418. https://www.trade.gov/market-intelligence/israel-artificial-intelligence-partnering-opportunities#:~:text=Israel%20launches%20the%20national%20AI%20program%20to%20enhance%20government%20services
419. https://www.ey.com/en_ca/government-public-sector/how-can-digital-government-connect-citizens-without-leaving-the-disconnected-behind#:~:text=Investment%20in%20high%2Dspeed%20digital%20infrastructure%2C%20 including%20broadband%20and%205G%20networks%2C%20 must%20provide%20connectivity%20in%20all%20parts%20of%20a%20country
420. https://www.itu.int/en/ITUD/Statistics/Dashboards/Pages/Digital-Development.aspx
421. https://www.biometricupdate.com/202311/israel-shows-what-biometricdata-control-looks-like-during-war
422. https://desapublications.un.org/sites/default/files/publications/2024-09/%28Web%20version%29%20E-Government%20Survey%20 2024%201392024.pdf
423. https://publicadministration.un.org/egovkb/en-us/Data/Country-Information/id/85-Japan
424. https://asia.nikkei.com/Spotlight/Asia-Insight/COVID-gives-Japan-lastchance-to-reverse-digital-defeat
425. https://www.youtube.com/watch?v=Szs2qeSeR6Q
426. https://digital-gov.note.jp/n/nce6537f3ba02
427. https://digital-gov.note.jp/n/nce6537f3ba02
428. https://portal.jordan.gov.jo/wps/portal/Home
429. https://publicadministration.un.org/egovkb/en-us/Data/Country-Information/id/86-Jordan
430. https://desapublications.un.org/sites/default/files/publications/2022-09/Web%20version%20E-Government%202022.pdf
431. https://desapublications.un.org/sites/default/files/publications/2024-09/%28Web%20version%29%20E-Government%20Survey%20 2024%201392024.pdf

432. https://datareportal.com/reports/digital-2023-kazakhstan

433. https://publicadministration.un.org/egovkb/en-us/Data/Country-Information/id/87-Kazakhstan

434. https://www.undp.org/kazakhstan/stories/digitalisation-sustainable-development-and-social-well-being-society

435. https://datahub.itu.int/data/?e=KAZ

436. https://desapublications.un.org/sites/default/files/publications/2024-09/%28Web%20version%29%20E-Government%20Survey%20 2024%201392024.pdf

437. https://publicadministration.un.org/egovkb/en-us/Data/Country-Information/id/46-Democratic-Peoples-Republic-of-Korea

438. https://www.jstor.org/stable/27160576?read-now=1&seq=5

439. https://datareportal.com/reports/digital-2024-north-korea?rq=korea 442. https://www.oecd.org/governance/2023-oecd-digital-government-index-1a89ed5e-en.htm

440. https://publicadministration.un.org/egovkb/en-us/Data/Country-Information/id/90-Kuwait

441. https://gulfnews.com/world/gulf/kuwait/covid-19-kuwait-launches-homedelivery-service-of-civil-id-cards-1.75233209

442. https://www.arabtimesonline.com/news/suspending-home-delivery-service-of-civil-id-cards/

443. https://fastcompanyme.com/news/kuwait-forges-strategic-alliance-with-google-cloud-for-digital-transformation-roadmap/

444. https://www.intelligentcio.com/me/2024/07/11/goo-gle-cloud-opens-new-offices-in-kuwait-to-accelerate-digital-transformation/

445. https://publicadministration.un.org/egovkb/en-us/Data/Country-Information/id/91-Kyrgyzstan

446. https://desapublications.un.org/sites/default/files/publications/2024-09/%28Web%20version%29%20E-Government%20Survey%20 2024%201392024.pdf

447. https://nas.gov.kg/dp/ezhegodnye-otchety-agenstva/

448. https://datareportal.com/reports/digital-2024-kyrgyzstan?rq=kyrgy
449. https://www.speedtest.net/global-index/kyrgyzstan
450. https://projects.worldbank.org/en/projects-operations/project-detail/ P181416
451. https://projects.worldbank.org/en/projects-operations/project-detail/ P160230
452. https://desapublications.un.org/sites/default/files/publications/2024-09/%28Web%20version%29%20E-Government%20Survey%20 2024%201392024.pdf
453. https://publicadministration.un.org/egovkb/en-us/Data/Country-Information/id/92-Lao-Peoples-Democratic-Republic
454. https://www.itu.int/en/ITUD/Statistics/Dashboards/Pages/Digital-Development.aspx
455. https://www.reuters.com/markets/rates-bonds/lebanons-financial-crisis-how-it-happened-2022-01-23/
456. https://desapublications.un.org/sites/default/files/publications/2022-09/ Web%20version%20E-Government%202022.pdf
457. https://publicadministration.un.org/egovkb/en-us/Data/Country-Information/id/94-Lebanon
458. https://www.libandata.org/en/article/administrative-distribution-lebanese-municipalities-may-2016
459. https://merip.org/2016/10/municipal-politics-in-lebanon/
460. https://www.thenationalnews.com/world/mena/lebanon-s-municipalfund-runs-over-2-billion-deficit-as-waste-expenses-multiply-1.778968
461. https://www.budde.com.au/Research/Lebanon-Telecoms-Mobile-and-Broadband-Statistics-and-Analyses
462. https://datareportal.com/reports/digital-2024-lebanon?rq=lebanon
463. https://www.adb.org/sites/default/files/publication/518351/government-glance-southeast-asia-2019.pdf
464. https://www.statista.com/statistics/249562/number-of-worldwide-internet-users-by-region/

465. https://mydigital.gov.my/

466. https://www.malaysia.gov.my/portal/content/30901?language=my

467. https://rmke12.epu.gov.my/en

468. https://www.adb.org/sites/default/files/publication/518351/government-glance-southeast-asia-2019.pdf

469. https://www.mydigital.gov.my/centre4ir/

470. https://www.marketing-interactive.com/Malaysia-surpasses-RM70-billion-digital-investments-target-MDEC

471. https://www.ipsos.com/en-my/do-malaysians-lack-trust-government-and-institutions

472. https://desapublications.un.org/sites/default/files/publications/2024-09/%28Web%20version%29%20E-Government%20Survey%20 2024%201392024.pdf

473. https://www.biometricupdate.com/202306/maldives-launches-efaas-digital-id-app-for-public-preview

474. https://one.gov.mv/entities

475. https://datareportal.com/reports/digital-2024-maldives

476. https://www.itu.int/en/ITUD/Statistics/Documents/DDD/ddd_MDV.pdf

477. https://desapublications.un.org/sites/default/files/publications/2024-09/%28Web%20version%29%20E-Government%20Survey%20 2024%201392024.pdf

478. https://publicadministration.un.org/egovkb/en-us/Data/Country-Information/id/113-Mongolia

479. https://www.itu.int/en/ITUD/Statistics/Documents/DDD/ddd_MNG.pdf

480. https://desapublications.un.org/sites/default/files/publications/2024-09/%28Web%20version%29%20E-Government%20Survey%20 2024%201392024.pdf

481. https://publicadministration.un.org/egovkb/en-us/Data/Country-Information/id/117-Myanmarhttps://publicadministration.un.org/egovkb/en-us/Data/ Country-Information/id/117-Myanmar

482. https://datareportal.com/reports/digital-2024-myanmar?rq=myanmar
483. https://www.itu.int/en/ITU-D/Statistics/Documents/DDD/ddd_MMR.pdf
484. https://asia.nikkei.com/Spotlight/Myanmar-Crisis/Myanmar-citizens-oppose-military-takeover-on-social-media
485. https://mizzima.com/article/daily-power-outages-yangon-lasting-morefive-hours-time
486. https://www.itu.int/en/ITUD/Statistics/Dashboards/Pages/Digital-Development.aspx
487. http://www.mip.gov.mm/%E1%80%94%E1%80%AD%E1%80%AF%E1%80%84%E1%80%BA%E1%80%84%E1%80%B6%E1%80%90%E1%80%B1%E1%80%AC%E1%80%BA%E1%80%85%E1%80%AE%E1%80%99%E1%80%B6%E1%80%A1%E1%80%AF%E1%80%95%E1%80%BA%E1%80%81%E1%80%BB%E1%80%AF-3/
488. http://www.mip.gov.mm/%E1%80%95%E1%80%BC%E1%80%8A%E1%80%BA%E1%80%91%E1%80%B1%E1%80%AC%E1%80%84%E1%80%BA%E1%80%85%E1%80%AF%E1%80%9D%E1%80%94%E1%80%BA%E1%80%80%E1%80%BC%E1%80%AE%E1%80%B8-%E1%80%99%E1%80%B-C%E1%80%84%E1%80%B7/
489. http://www.mip.gov.mm/national-database-%E1%80%85%E1%80%94%E1%80%85%E1%80%BA%E1%80%90%E1%80%8A%E1%80%BA%E1%80%86%E1%80%B1%E1%80%AC%E1%80%80%E1%80%BA%E1%80%9B%E1%80%B1%E1%80%B8%E1%80%A6%E1%80%B8%E1%80%86%E1%80%B1%E1%8 0%AC/
490. https://asiapacific.unfpa.org/en/news/unfpa-we-reaffirm-our-commitment-stay-and-deliver-women-and-girls-across-myanmar
491. http://www.mip.gov.mm/%E1%80%95%E1%80%BC%E1%80%8A%E1%80%BA%E1%80%91%E1%80%B1%E1%80%AC%E1%80%84%E1%80%BA%E1%80%85%E1%80%AF%E1%80%9D%E1%80%94%E1%80%BA%E1%

80%80%E1%80%BC%E1%80%AE%E1%80%B8-
%E1%80%A6%E1%80%B8%E1%80%99-93/
492. https://desapublications.un.org/sites/default/files/publications/2022-09/Web%20version%20E-Government%202022.pdf
493. https://datareportal.com/reports/digital-2024-nepal?rq=nepal
494. https://thehrmnepal.com/report/nepali-universities-reelunder-falling-studentenrollment/
495. https://www.adb.org/where-we-work/nepal/poverty
496. https://desapublications.un.org/sites/default/files/publications/2022-09/Report%20without%20annexes.pdf
497. https://publicadministration.un.org/egovkb/en-us/Data/Country-Information/id/127-Oman
498. https://www.oman2040.om/?lang=en
499. https://anwaar.squ.edu.om/Post/Post-Detail/ArticleID/388/IoT-LabOpened-at-SQU
500. https://www.omanobserver.om/article/1105289/business/energy/dedicated-zone-for-ai-activities-in-duqm-sez
501. https://oman.om/en/home-top-level/whole-of-government/central-initiative/oman-national-cert#:~:text=The%20Oman%20National%20Computer%20Emergency,security%20incidents%20in%20the%20Sultanate.
502. https://publicadministration.un.org/egovkb/Portals/egovkb/Documents/un/2020-Survey/2020%20UN%20E-Government%20Survey%20(Full%20Report).pdf
503. https://publicadministration.un.org/egovkb/en-us/Data/Country-Information/id/128-Pakistan
504. https://desapublications.un.org/sites/default/files/publications/2024-09/%28Web%20version%29%20E-Government%20Survey%20 2024%201392024.pdf
505. https://www.undp.org/policy-centre/singapore/blog/celebrating-future-digital-government
509. https://philsys.gov.ph/
506. https://desapublications.un.org/sites/default/files/publications/2024-09/%28Web%20version%29%20E-Government%20Survey%20 2024%201392024.pdf

507. https://publicadministration.un.org/egovkb/en-us/Data/Country-Information/id/134-Philippines/dataYear/2024
508. https://desapublications.un.org/sites/default/files/publications/2024-09/%28Web%20version%29%20E-Government%20Survey%20 2024%201392024.pdf
509. https://www.psa.gov.qa/en/nds1/nds3/Documents/QNDS3_EN.pdf
510. https://digitalcenterofexcellence.qa/#:~:text=The%20Qatar%20Digital%20Center%20of,Intelligence%20and%20Cybersecurity%20among%20others.
511. https://www.mcit.gov.qa/en/media-center/news/mcit-launches-e-paymentgateway-partnership-qnb
512. https://www.unescwa.org/publications/government-electronic-mobile-services-gems-maturity-index-2023
513. https://www.unescwa.org/publications/government-electronic-mobile-services-gems-maturity-index-2022
514. https://openknowledge.worldbank.org/server/api/core/bitstreams/5e157ee3-e97a-5e42-bfc0-f1416f3de4de/content 519. https://desapublications.un.org/sites/default/files/publications/2024-09/%28Web%20version%29%20E-Government%20Survey%20 2024%201392024.pdf
515. https://ictandhealth.com/saudi-arabia-brings-worlds-first-virtual-hospitalto-life/news/
516. https://www.worldbank.org/en/events/2023/09/21/digitalization-of-public-services-for-an-inclusive-and-prosperous-future-in-the-kingdom-of-saudi-arabia#3
517. https://www.moj.gov.sa/English/Ministry/Pages/NajizCenter.aspx
518. https://www.worldbank.org/en/events/2023/09/21/digitalization-of-public-services-for-an-inclusive-and-prosperous-future-in-the-kingdom-of-saudi-arabia#3
519. https://www.nytimes.com/2024/03/19/business/saudi-arabia-investment-artificial-intelligence.html

520. https://www.iproov.com/wp-content/uploads/2021/03/Case-Studies-in-Government-Digital-Identity-2021.pdf

521. https://datareportal.com/reports/digital-2021-singapore

522. https://www.smartnation.gov.sg/

523. https://publicadministration.un.org/egovkb/en-us/Data/Country-Information/id/154-Singapore

524. https://statescoop.com/three-things-the-u-s-can-learn-from-singaporessmart-city-crusade/

525. https://www.zdnet.com/article/cloud-data-amongst-apac-digital-skillsmost-needed/ 531. ibid.

526. https://www.trc.gov.lk/content/files/statistics/SORQ4202331012024745.pdf

527. https://datareportal.com/reports/digital-2024-sri-lanka?rq=sri%20lanka

528. https://www.adaderana.lk/news/84723/trcsl-approves-tariff-hike-for-mobile-fixed-broadband-pay-tv-services

529. https://www.parliament.lk/news-en/view/3660

530. https://desapublications.un.org/sites/default/files/publications/2024-09/%28Web%20version%29%20E-Government%20Survey%20 2024%201392024.pdf

531. https://publicadministration.un.org/egovkb/en-us/Data/Country-Information/id/167-Syrian-Arab-Republic

532. https://openknowledge.worldbank.org/server/api/core/bitstreams/7a58a34b-ead6-4cb0-a90b-0ddd386666e5/content

533. https://documents1.worldbank.org/curated/en/099515505222471242/pdf/ IDU12e419274142fc14ff31baf411ef0c0aef81c.pdf

534. https://datareportal.com/reports/digital-2024-syria?rq=syria

535. https://www.unicef.org/syria/stories/digital-learning-helps-children-al-hasakeh-continue-their-education

536. https://education-profiles.org/northern-africa-and-western-asia/syrian-arab-republic/~technology

537. https://publicadministration.un.org/egovkb/en-us/Data/Country-Information/id/168-Tajikistan

538. https://www.worldbank.org/en/events/2024/03/01/elevating-global-access-through-e-commerce-in-tajikistan

539. https://eabr.org/en/about/states-participants/tadzhikistan/
540. https://www.itu.int/en/ITUD/Statistics/Dashboards/Pages/Digital-Development.aspx
541. https://eurasianet.org/tajikistan-communications-regulator-loosening-monopoly
542. https://unctad.org/system/files/official-document/der2019_en.pdf
543. https://digi.taiwan.gov.tw/
544. https://join.gov.tw/
545. https://info.vtaiwan.tw/
546. https://www.bdigital.asia/en/insights/common-web-platform-taiwan/#:~:text=The%20main%20issues%20facing%20these%20sites%20are%20accessibility%20issues
547. https://publicadministration.un.org/egovkb/en-us/Data/Country-Information/id/169-Thailand
548. https://www.imd.org/centers/wcc/world-competitiveness-center/rankings/ world-digital-competitiveness-ranking/
549. https://www.itu.int/en/ITU-D/Cybersecurity/Pages/global-cybersecurity-index.aspx
550. https://www.bangkokpost.com/business/general/2744996/eec-id-systemset-for-september-launch
551. https://asia.nikkei.com/Business/Technology/Thailand-s-cybersecurity-negligence-causes-personal-data-breaches
552. https://www.bangkokpost.com/thailand/general/2545164/sergeant-whohacked-data-of-55-million-thais-identified
553. https://www.databreaches.net/major-data-breach-in-thailand-exposes-personal-data-of-20-million-elderly-citizens/
554. https://desapublications.un.org/sites/default/files/publications/2024-09/%28Web%20version%29%20E-Government%20Survey%20 2024%201392024.pdf
555. https://publicadministration.un.org/egovkb/en-us/Data/Country-Information/id/171-Timor-Leste
556. https://openknowledge.worldbank.org/server/api/core/bitstreams/5412b8b6-0db6-4bf8-ad3b-043755f8fa61/content

557. https://datareportal.com/reports/digital-2024-timor-leste?rq=timor-leste
558. https://www.uncdf.org/article/8606/assessing-digital-and-financial-literacy-in-timor-leste-a-survey-on-knowledge-skills-and-access
559. https://digital-strategy.ec.europa.eu/en/library/egovernment-benchmark-2023
560. https://publicadministration.un.org/egovkb/en-us/Data/Country-Information/id/176-Trkiye
561. https://www.sbb.gov.tr/wp-content/uploads/2022/07/Eleventh_Development_Plan_2019-2023.pdf
562. https://desapublications.un.org/sites/default/files/publications/2024-09/%28Web%20version%29%20E-Government%20Survey%20 2024%201392024.pdf
563. https://desapublications.un.org/sites/default/files/publications/2022-09/Report%20without%20annexes.pdf
564. https://publicadministration.un.org/egovkb/en-us/Data/Country-Information/id/177-Turkmenistan
565. http://www.e.gov.tm/
566. https://e-estonia.com/solutions/interoperability-services/x-road/
567. https://www.undp.org/turkmenistan/press-releases/undp-and-government-turkmenistan-expand-cooperation-digital-transformation
568. https://desapublications.un.org/sites/default/files/publications/2024-09/%28Web%20version%29%20E-Government%20Survey%20 2024%201392024.pdf
569. https://mori-m-foundation.or.jp/pdf/GPCI2023_summary.pdf
570. https://www.uaecabinet.ae/en/details/news/uae-cabinet-adopts-national-artificial-intelligence-strategy-2031
571. https://ai.gov.ae/strategy/
572. https://www.pwc.com/m1/en/media-centre/2023/uae-government-intends-launch-of-digital-excellence-centre-to-enhance-best-practice.html

573. https://selfcare.uaepass.ae/
574. https://identityreview.com/uae-invests-early-in-digital-identity-and-blockchain/
575. https://www.singpass.gov.sg/main/singpass-our-ndi/
576. https://www.mediaoffice.ae/en/news/2023/November/19-11/Mohammedbin-Rashid-announces-star-ratings-of-124-federal-govt-services-channels
577. https://twitter.com/HHShkMohd/status/1726147973040549905?ref_src=twsrc%5Etfw%7Ctwcamp%5Etweetembed%7Ctwterm%5E1726147973040549905%7Ctwgr%5Ee85286e00c64e20828d8471a15c7a983437f165e%7Ctwcon%5Es1_&ref_url=https%3A%2F%2Fgulfnews.com%2Fuae%2Fgovernment%2Fuae-sheikh-mohammed-bin-rashid-approves-results-of-star-rating-system-for-124-government-service-centres-1.99486103
578. https://gsr.ae/
579. https://desapublications.un.org/sites/default/files/publications/2024-09/%28Web%20version%29%20E-Government%20Survey%20 2024%201392024.pdf
580. https://mori-m-foundation.or.jp/pdf/GPCI2023_summary.pdf
581. https://www.uaecabinet.ae/en/details/news/uae-cabinet-adopts-national-artificial-intelligence-strategy-2031
582. https://ai.gov.ae/strategy/
583. https://www.pwc.com/m1/en/media-centre/2023/uae-government-intends-launch-of-digital-excellence-centre-to-enhance-best-practice.html
584. https://selfcare.uaepass.ae/
585. https://identityreview.com/uae-invests-early-in-digital-identity-and-blockchain/
586. https://www.singpass.gov.sg/main/singpass-our-ndi/
587. https://www.mediaoffice.ae/en/news/2023/November/19-11/Mohammedbin-Rashid-announces-star-ratings-of-124-federal-govt-services-channels
588. https://twitter.com/HHShkMohd/status/1726147973040549905?ref_src=twsrc%5Etfw%7Ctwcamp%5Etweetembed%7Ctwterm%5E1726147973040549905%7Ctwgr%5Ee85286e00c64e20828d

8471a15c7a983437f165e%7Ctwcon%5Es1_&ref_url=https%3A%2F%2Fgulfnews.com%2Fuae%2Fgovernment%2Fuae-sheikh-mohammed-bin-rashid-approves-results-of-star-rating-system-for-124-government-service-centres-1.99486103

589. https://gsr.ae/

590. https://desapublications.un.org/sites/default/files/publica-

591. tions/2024-09/%28Web%20version%29%20E-Government%20Survey%20 2024%201392024.pdf

592. https://publicadministration.un.org/egovkb/en-us/Data/Country-Information/id/189-Viet-Nam

593. https://www.vietnam-briefing.com/news/information-communication-infrastructure-master-plan-approved.html/

594. https://en.sggp.org.vn/hcmc-striving-to-effectively-implement-project-06-on-digital-transformation-post108280.html

595. https://publicadministration.un.org/egovkb/en-us/Data/Country-Information/id/190-Yemen

596. https://publicadministration.un.org/egovkb/en-us/Data/Country-Information/id/190-Yemen

597. https://openknowledge.worldbank.org/server/api/core/bitstreams/7a58a34b-ead6-4cb0-a90b-0ddd386666e5/content

598. https://datareportal.com/reports/digital-2024-yemen?rq=yemen

599. https://desapublications.un.org/sites/default/files/publications/2024-09/%28Web%20version%29%20E-Government%20Survey%20 2024%201392024.pdf

600. https://digital-strategy.ec.europa.eu/en/library/egovernment-benchmark-2023

601. https://publicadministration.un.org/egovkb/en-us/Data/Country-Information/id/2-Albania

602. https://aspa.gov.al/en/

603. https://www.dw.com/en/albania-once-again-the-target-of-cyberattacks-after-cutting-diplomatic-ties-with-iran-and-expelling-diplomats/a-63146285

604. https://publicadministration.un.org/egovkb/en-us/Data/Country-Information/id/4-Andorra

605. https://desapublications.un.org/sites/default/files/publications/2024-09/%28Web%20version%29%20E-Government%20Survey%20 2024%201392024.pdf
606. https://andorralive.com/en/blog/law-42-2022-on-digital-economy-in-andorra-opportunities-for-investors-and-entrepreneurs/
607. https://bopadocuments.blob.core.windows.net/bopa-documents/035065/ pdf/GR20230515_11_02_39.pdf
608. https://www.bmaw.gv.at/
609. https://digital-strategy.ec.europa.eu/en/policies/desi
610. https://datareportal.com/reports/digital-2022-austria
611. https://www.oecd-ilibrary.org/docserver/9989e95c-en.pdf?expires=1-661941868&id=id&accname=guest&checksum=C15E5701B2DD9B7BCE77099844C84A3C
612. https://www.ris.bka.gv.at/Dokument.wxe?Abfrage=BgblAuth&Dokumentnummer=BGBLA_2004_I_10
613. https://www.digitalaustria.gv.at/
614. https://www.oesterreich.gv.at/public.html
615. https://www.usp.gv.at/Portal.Node/usp/public/content/en/startpage.html?template=microsite
616. http://www.digital.austria.gv.at/
617. http://www.egiz.gv.at/en/
618. https://publicadministration.un.org/egovkb/en-us/Data/Country-Information/id/10-Austria
619. https://digital-strategy.ec.europa.eu/en/policies/desi
620. https://smartcity.wien.gv.at/en/
621. https://www.govlabaustria.gv.at/
622. https://publicadministration.un.org/egovkb/en-us/Data/Country-Information/id/16-Belarus
623. https://www.epam.com/about/who-we-are/history
624. https://netherlands.mfa.gov.by/en/bilateral_relations/trade_economic/htp/
625. https://www.voiceofbelarus.org/belarus-news/do-belarusian-cyber-partisans-cause-damage-to-the-lukashenko-regime/

626. https://publicadministration.un.org/egovkb/en-us/Data/Country-Information/id/16-Belarus
627. https://digital-strategy.ec.europa.eu/en/policies/desi-belgium
628. https://www.vlaanderen.be/
629. https://www.wallonie.be/fr
630. https://ostbelgienlive.be/
631. https://michel.belgium.be/fr/premiere-reunion-des-digital-minds-smartnation
632. https://ec.europa.eu/info/strategy/priorities-2019-2024/europe-fit-digital-age/europes-digital-decade-digital-targets-2030_en
633. https://etno.eu/library/reports/103-investment-vhcn-2022.html
634. https://www.agoria.be/en/human-capital-education/education-labour-market/agoria-8-out-of-10-in-work-means-600000-extra-jobs
635. https://dt.bosa.be/fr/digital_belgium_skills_fund
636. https://publicadministration.un.org/egovkb/en-us/Data/Country-Information/id/22-Bosnia-and-Herzegovina
637. https://digitalstorm.ba/bs/dih-forum-2023-bos?fbclid=IwAR1K-u1j7Y92mMEYaGyhJBIg10yuFx_L0cIeMsiy11puU8ZwnC35f8J-g64
638. https://ec.europa.eu/commission/presscorner/detail/es/IP_18_4242
639. https://digital-strategy.ec.europa.eu/en/policies/desi-bulgaria
640. https://publicadministration.un.org/egovkb/en-us/Data/Country-Information/id/26-Bulgaria
641. https://www.mtc.government.bg/sites/default/files/uploads/it/09-12-2019_ programa_-cifrova_bulgariya_2025.pdf
642. https://www.mtc.government.bg/sites/default/files/uploads/it/09-12-2019_ putna_karta_cifrova_bulgariya_2025.pdf
643. https://digital-strategy.ec.europa.eu/en/library/country-reports-digital-decade-report-2023
644. https://commission.europa.eu/strategy-and-policy/priorities-2019-2024/ europe-fit-digital-age/europes-digital-decade-digital-targets-2030_en

645. https://www.zakon.hr/z/736/Zakon-o-dr%C5%BEavnoj-informacijskoj-infrastrukturi
646. https://narodne-novine.nn.hr/clanci/sluzbeni/2017_06_60_1362.html
647. https://narodne-novine.nn.hr/clanci/sluzbeni/2019_06_60_1150.html
648. https://openknowledge.worldbank.org/handle/10986/35541
649. https://digital-skills-jobs.europa.eu/en/actions/national-initiatives/national-strategies/croatia-national-development-strategy-2030#:~:text=The%20 National%20Development%20Strategy%20of,the%20Croatian% 20society%20 and%20economy.
650. https://gov.hr/en/using-and-activating-the-electronic-identity-card-eoi/368
651. http://www.cezih.hr/
652. https://digital-strategy.ec.europa.eu/en/policies/desi-croatia
653. https://openknowledge.worldbank.org/handle/10986/35541
654. https://digital-strategy.ec.europa.eu/en/policies/desi-croatia
655. https://publicadministration.un.org/egovkb/en-us/Data/Country-Information/id/42-Croatia
656. https://digital-strategy.ec.europa.eu/en/policies/desi-czech-republic
657. https://digital-strategy.ec.europa.eu/en/policies/desi-czech-republic
658. https://www.mpo.cz/en/guidepost/for-the-media/press-releases/ road-to-digital-economy--government-approved-document-for-the-implementation-and-development-of-5g-networks--252109/
659. https://www.mpo.cz/cz/e-komunikace-a-posta/elektronicke-komunikace/ koncepce-a-strategie/narodni-plan-rozvoje-siti-nga/narodni-plan-rozvoje-siti-s-velmi-vysokou-kapacitou--259858/
660. https://ec.europa.eu/eurostat/statistics-explained/index.php?title=ICT_ specialists_-

_statistics_on_hard-to-fill_vacancies_in_enterprises&oldid=534531

661. https://www.digitalnicesko.cz/koncepcni-materialy/
662. https://www.msmt.cz/vzdelavani/skolstvi-v-cr/strategie-2030
663. https://digikoalice.cz/
664. https://ec.europa.eu/info/strategy/priorities-2019-2024/europe-fit-digital-age/europes-digital-decade-digital-targets-2030_en
665. http://www.mcw.gov.cy/mcw/dec/digital_cyprus/ict.nsf/ict_02_gr/ict_02_ gr?opendocument
666. https://www.europarl.europa.eu/factsheets/en/sheet/64/digital-agenda-for-europe
667. http://www.mlsi.gov.cy/mlsi/kepa/kepa_new.nsf/index_en/index_en
668. https://dec.dmrid.gov.cy/dmrid/dec/ws_dec.nsf/home_en/home_en?openform
669. https://www.research.org.cy/wp-content/uploads/InnovateCyprusCYRIStrategyFramework2019-2023NBRIMay2019.pdf
670. https://mof.gov.cy/assets/modules/wnp/articles/201907/480/docs/blockchain_strategy_english_final.pdf
671. https://digital-strategy.ec.europa.eu/en/policies/desi-cyprus
672. https://digital-strategy.ec.europa.eu/en/library/country-reports-digital-decade-report-2023
673. https://joinup.ec.europa.eu/collection/nifo-national-interoperability-framework-observatory/digital-public-administration-factsheets-2021
674. https://publicadministration.un.org/egovkb/en-us/Data/Country-Information/id/48-Denmark
675. https://impact.economist.com/projects/digital-cities/2022-executive-summary/
676. https://en.digst.dk/
677. https://digital-strategy.ec.europa.eu/en/policies/desi-denmark
678. https://digital-strategy.ec.europa.eu/en/library/egovernment-benchmark-2022 684. ibid.

679. https://www.linkedin.com/pulse/why-estonia-far-ahead-digital-government-advancement-mohammad-j-sear/?trackingId=gZ%2BJF2vHQ0GqkfKv68Xvlg%3D%3D
680. http://www.virtualschoolsandcolleges.eu/index.php/Tiger_Leap_Foundation
681. https://technews180.com/estonians-unicorns-and-soonicorns/
682. https://startupestonia.ee/why-estonia/value-for-startups#:~:text=So%20far%2C%20Estonia%20has%20produced,reputation%20as%20a%20startup%20 miracle.
683. https://e-estonia.com/wp-content/uploads/green_digital_analysis_english. pdf
684. https://e-estonia.com/facts-and-figures/
685. https://www.mkm.ee/en/e-state-and-connectivity/digital-agenda-2030
686. https://www.kratid.ee/en/ai-use-cases
687. https://govinsider.asia/intl-en/article/privacy-enhancing-tools-may-offera-way-out-of-a-difficult-digital-dilemma
688. https://e-estonia.com/
689. https://www.euractiv.com/section/digital/news/finland-seeks-to-becomemetaverse-global-leader-by-2035/
690. https://www.digitalfinland.org/
691. https://ec.europa.eu/newsroom/dae/redirection/document/88764
692. https://julkaisut.valtioneuvosto.fi/bitstream/handle/10024/165248/ OKM_2023_48.pdf?sequence=1&isAllowed=y
693. https://digital-decade-desi.digital-strategy.ec.europa.eu/datasets/desi-2022/ charts
694. https://www.itu.int/net/itunews/issues/2011/04/pdf/201104_10.pdf
695. https://commission.europa.eu/strategy-and-policy/priorities-2019-2024/ europe-fit-digital-age/europes-digital-decade-digital-targets-2030_en
696. https://digital-decade-desi.digital-strategy.ec.europa.eu/datasets/desi-2022/ charts
697. https://digital-strategy.ec.europa.eu/en/policies/desi-france

698. https://publicadministration.un.org/egovkb/en-us/Data/Country-Information/id/61-France
699. https://www.modernisation.gouv.fr/transformer-laction-publique/transformer-laction-publique
700. https://societenumerique.gouv.fr/plannational/
701. https://ec.europa.eu/info/strategy/priorities-2019-2024/europe-fit-digital-age/europes-digital-decade-digital-targets-2030_en
702. https://digital-strategy.ec.europa.eu/en/policies/desi-france
703. https://desapublications.un.org/sites/default/files/publications/2024-09/%28Web%20version%29%20E-Government%20Survey%20 2024%201392024.pdf
704. https://publicadministration.un.org/egovkb/en-us/Data/Country-Information/id/64-Georgia-Country
705. https://eufordigital.eu/georgia-approves-broadband-development-strategy-2020-2025/
706. https://www.gov.ge/files/41_78149_280277_GP.pdf
707. https://www.itu.int/en/ITUD/Statistics/Documents/DDD/ddd_GEO.pdf
708. https://www.economy.ge/?page=news&nw=1854&lang=en
709. https://publicadministration.un.org/egovkb/en-us/Data/Country-Information/id/64-Georgia-Country
710. https://www.de.digital/DIGITAL/Redaktion/EN/Publikation/digital-strategy-2025.pdf?__blob=publicationFile&v=9
711. https://digital-strategy.ec.europa.eu/en/policies/desi-germany
712. https://commission.europa.eu/strategy-and-policy/priorities-2019-2024/ europe-fit-digital-age/europes-digital-decade-digital-targets-2030_en
713. https://joinup.ec.europa.eu/sites/default/files/inline-files/Digital_Government_Factsheets_Germany_2019.pdf
714. https://digital-strategy.ec.europa.eu/en/policies/countries-digitisation-performance
715. https://publicadministration.un.org/egovkb/en-us/Data/Country-Information/id/67-Greece
716. https://digital-strategy.ec.europa.eu/en/policies/desi-greece

717. https://digital-strategy.ec.europa.eu/en/policies/countries-digitisation-performance
718. https://www.gov.gr/
719. https://digitalstrategy.gov.gr/
720. https://5gventures.gr/wp-content/uploads/2021/07/Law-4727_2020-Art92-93-94-as-adopted-by-Parliament-EN_05.05.2021.pdfhttps://www.ey.com/ en_gr/tax/tax-alerts/electronic-communications-law-4727-2020
721. https://digital-strategy.ec.europa.eu/en/policies/countries-digitisation-performance
722. https://digital-strategy.ec.europa.eu/en/policies/desi-hungary
723. https://digital-strategy.ec.europa.eu/en/library/country-reports-digital-decade-report-2023
724. https://datareportal.com/reports/digital-2024-hungary?rq=hungary
725. https://ec.europa.eu/info/strategy/priorities-2019-2024/europe-fit-digital-age/europes-digital-decade-digital-targets-2030_en
726. https://2015-2019.kormany.hu/download/f/58/d1000/NDS.pdf
727. https://digital-strategy.ec.europa.eu/en/policies/desi-hungary
728. https://publicadministration.un.org/egovkb/en-us/Data-Centerhttps://publicadministration.un.org/egovkb/en-us/Data/Country-Information/id/76-Iceland
729. https://digital-strategy.ec.europa.eu/en/library/egovernment-benchmark-2022 ibid.
730. https://digital-strategy.ec.europa.eu/en/library/egovernment-benchmark-2022
731. https://digital-strategy.ec.europa.eu/en/policies/desi-ireland
732. https://www.gov.ie/en
733. https://digital-strategy.ec.europa.eu/en/library/country-reports-digital-decade-report-2023
734. https://www.businesspost.ie/news/state-on-track-to-outstrip-eu-targetson-use-of-electronic-id/ 742. https://www.mygovid.ie/
735. https://www.europarl.europa.eu/RegData/etudes/BRIE/2021/698772/EPRS_BRI(2021)698772_EN.pdf

736. https://www.irishstatutebook.ie/eli/2019/act/5/enacted/en/html 745. https://www.gov.ie/en/policy-information/72309-data-governance-board/#:~:text=The%20Data%20Governance%20Board%20was, way%20 to%20deliver%20public%20services.
737. https://www.gov.ie/en/publication/adf42-harnessing-digital-the-digital-ireland-framework/
738. https://www.gov.ie/en/publication/136b9-connecting-government-2030-a-digital-and-ict-strategy-for-irelands-public-service/
739. https://www.agid.gov.it/it/agenzia/piano-triennale
740. http://www.pongovernance1420.gov.it/it/progetto/italia-login/
741. https://docs.italia.it/italia/mid/piano-nazionale-innovazione-2025-docs/it/ stabile/index.html
742. https://digital-strategy.ec.europa.eu/en/policies/desi
743. https://publicadministration.un.org/egovkb/en-us/Data/Country-Information/id/83-Italy
744. https://documents.worldbank.org/en/publication/documents-reports/documentdetail/249951531020771941/kosovo-kosovo-digital-economy-kode-project
745. https://www.undp.org/kosovo/digital
746. http://eparticipimi.opendatakosovo.org/issues
747. https://ekosova.rks-gov.net/#
748. https://www.undp.org/kosovo/digital
749. https://www.undp.org/kosovo/news/launch-digital-skills-programme-bootcamps
750. https://opendatakosovo.org/wp-content/uploads/2022/07/Kosovo-Country-Report-2022.pdf
751. https://publicadministration.un.org/egovkb/en-us/Data/Country-Information/id/93-Latvia
752. https://tap.mk.gov.lv/mk/tap/?pid=40496916
753. https://digital-strategy.ec.europa.eu/en/library/country-reports-digital-decade-report-2023
754. https://digital-strategy.ec.europa.eu/en/library/egovernment-benchmark-2023

755. https://ec.europa.eu/info/funding-tenders/opportunities/portal/screen/ how-to-participate/org-details/921298047
756. https://publicadministration.un.org/egovkb/en-us/Data/Country-Information/id/98-Liechtenstein
757. https://www.llv.li/de/landesverwaltung/amt-fuer-informatik/ueber-uns/ strategie
758. https://www.digital-liechtenstein.li/initiative
759. https://desapublications.un.org/sites/default/files/publications/2024-09/%28Web%20version%29%20E-Government%20Survey%20 2024%201392024.pdf
760. https://digital-strategy.ec.europa.eu/en/library/egovernment-benchmark-2023
761. https://www.epaslaugos.lt/
762. https://govtechlab.lt/
763. https://govtechlab.lt/govtech-challenge-series/
764. https://govinsider.asia/intl-en/article/arune-matelyte-manager-govtech-lab-lithuania-agency-for-science-innovation-and-technology-lithuania-women-in-govtech-2020
765. https://publicadministration.un.org/egovkb/en-us/Data/Country-Information/id/99-Lithuania
766. https://www.worldbank.org/en/programs/govtech/gtmi
767. https://digital-strategy.ec.europa.eu/en/library/egovernment-benchmark-2022
768. https://www.oecd.org/publication/government-at-a-glance/2023/country-notes/luxembourg-0106cf78#chapter-d1e22
769. https://digital-strategy.ec.europa.eu/en/policies/desi-luxembourg
770. https://digital-strategy.ec.europa.eu/en/library/egovernment-benchmark-2023
771. https://digital-strategy.ec.europa.eu/en/library/egovernment-benchmark-2023
772. https://publicadministration.un.org/egovkb/en-us/Data/Country-Information/id/106-Malta

773. https://digital-strategy.ec.europa.eu/en/library/country-reports-digital-decade-report-2023
774. https://www.maltadigitali.mt/
775. https://desapublications.un.org/sites/default/files/publications/2024-09/%28Web%20version%29%20E-Government%20Survey%20 2024%201392024.pdf
776. https://ec.europa.eu/commission/presscorner/detail/en/qanda 23_5629
777. https://www.oecd-ilibrary.org/sites/9d35a60f-en/index.html?itemId=/content/publication/9d35a60f-en
778. https://www.undp.org/moldova/digitaltransformation
779. https://mded.gov.md/en/a-100-digital-state-the-digital-transformationstrategy-of-the-republic-of-moldova-for-the-years-2023-2030-approved-by-theexecutive/
780. https://eufordigital.eu/new-digital-transformation-strategy-to-guide-moldova-in-european-integration/
781. https://desapublications.un.org/sites/default/files/publications/2024-09/%28Web%20version%29%20E-Government%20Survey%20 2024%201392024.pdf ibid.
782. https://monaconow.com/extended-monaco-the-principality-in-the-digital-world/
783. https://www.itu.int/en/ITU-D/Regional-Presence/Europe/Documents/Events/2020/5G_EUR_CIS/5G_Monaco-final.pdf
784. https://monaconow.com/monaco-cloud-the-first-operational-sovereign-cloud-in-europe/
785. https://news.vmware.com/releases/government-of-monaco-vmware-sovereign-cloud
786. https://lagazettedemonaco.com/en/news/technologie/le-jumeau-numerique-cet-autre-monaco-daide-a-la-decision-en
787. https://publicadministration.un.org/egovkb/en-us/Data/Country-Information/id/112-Monaco
788. https://publicadministration.un.org/egovkb/en-us/Data/Country-Information/id/114-Montenegro

789. https://desapublications.un.org/sites/default/files/publications/2022-09/Web%20version%20E-Government%202022.pdf

790. https://digital-strategy.ec.europa.eu/en/library/egovernment-benchmark-2023

791. https://www.gov.me/dokumenta/0c802520-e016-41ee-a6e4-7af6eb66e19d

792. http://www.sluzbenilist.me/pregled-dokumenta-2/?id=%7b5580F3CE-BB54-46F0-9CFC-46ED5D5A7B58%7d

793. https://www.undp.org/montenegro/projects/digital-governance-acceleration

794. https://publicadministration.un.org/egovkb/en-us/Data/Country-Information/id/121-Netherlands

795. https://investinholland.com/news/netherlands-digital-economy-society-index-2022/

796. https://www.rijksoverheid.nl/documenten/kamerstukken/2022/03/08/kamerbrief-hoofdlijnen-beleid-voor-digitalisering

797. https://www.government.nl/documents/reports/2022/11/30/value-driven-digitalisation-work-agenda

798. https://www.rijksoverheid.nl/documenten/kamerstukken/2022/08/29/ kamerbrief-rijksbreed-cloudbeleid-2022

799. https://english.nctv.nl/topics/netherlands-cybersecurity-strategy-2022-2028/documents/publications/2022/12/06/the-netherlands-cybersecurity-strategy-2022-2028

800. https://www.linkedin.com/posts/undp-mk_loges-digital-software-activity-7051577765652742144-sObJ/

801. https://northmacedonia.un.org/en/213011-empowering-municipal-councils

802. https://digital-strategy.ec.europa.eu/en/library/egovernment-benchmark-2023

803. https://publicadministration.un.org/egovkb/en-us/Data/Country-Information/id/126-Norway

804. https://www.oecd-ilibrary.org/sites/864f5673-en/index.html?itemId=/content/component/864f5673-en#section-d1e8721

805. https://digital-strategy.ec.europa.eu/en/policies/desi-norway

806. https://eid.difi.no/en/minid
807. https://digital-strategy.ec.europa.eu/en/library/egovernment-benchmark-2023
808. https://www.regjeringen.no/no/dokumenter/nasjonal-strategi-for-eid-i-offentlig-sektor/id2973307/
809. https://www.regjeringen.no/en/dokumenter/one-digital-public-sector/ id2653874/
810. https://www.gov.pl/web/digitalization
811. https://dane.gov.pl/en
812. https://epuap.gov.pl/wps/portal/english
813. https://obywatel.gov.pl/
814. https://publicadministration.un.org/egovkb/en-us/Data/Country-Information/id/135-Poland
815. https://digital-strategy.ec.europa.eu/en/policies/desi
816. https://eportugal.gov.pt/en/servicos/pedir-o-cartao-de-cidadao
817. https://eportugal.gov.pt/en/servicos/ativar-a-chave-movel-digital
818. https://joinup.ec.europa.eu/collection/egovernment/document/zero-licensing-and-entrepreneurs-desk-united-simplify-business-procedures
819. https://eportugal.gov.pt/en/inicio
820. https://www.simplex.gov.pt/
821. https://labx.gov.pt/
822. https://www.ama.gov.pt/web/english/citizen-spothttps://www.ama.gov.pt/ web/english/assistence
823. https://portugaldigital.gov.pt/wp-content/uploads/2022/01/Portugal_Action_Plan_for_Digital_Transition.pdf
824. https://portugaldigital.gov.pt/en/about-us/
825. https://ec.europa.eu/eurostat/databrowser/view/tin00093/default/table 836. https://publicadministration.un.org/egovkb/en-us/Data/Country-Information/id/136-Portugal
826. https://digital-strategy.ec.europa.eu/en/policies/desi-romania
827. https://www.opengovpartnership.org/members/romania/commitments/RO0018/

828. https://edirect.e-guvernare.ro/SitePages/landingpage.aspx
829. https://www.ghiseul.ro/ghiseul/public/
830. https://rm.coe.int/16809e375d
831. https://www.adr.gov.ro/
832. https://www.gov.ro/en/government/cabinet-meeting/national-strategy-on-the-digital-agenda-for-romania-2020
833. https://www.statista.com/statistics/1059093/share-of-russians-using-online-public-services/
834. https://desapublications.un.org/sites/default/files/publications/2024-09/%28Web%20version%29%20E-Government%20Survey%20 2024%201392024.pdf
835. https://publicadministration.un.org/egovkb/en-us/Data/Country-Information/id/141-Russian-Federation
836. https://www.statista.com/statistics/262966/number-of-internet-users-in-selected-countries/
837. https://publicadministration.un.org/egovkb/en-us/Data/Country-Information/id/147-San-Marino
838. https://www.srbija.gov.rs/vest/en/157415/digital-transformation-changes-serbias-economy-fast.php
839. https://www.itu.int/en/myitu/News/2020/06/08/14/29/How-broadband-fuels-growth-in-Serbia
840. https://hbr.org/2020/12/which-economies-showed-the-most-digital-progress-in-2020
841. https://www.google.com/search?q=slovakia+population&oq=slovakia+po&gs_lcrp=EgZjaHJvbWUqBwgBEAAYgAQyBggAEEUYOTIHCAEQABiABDINCAIQLhjHARjRAxiABDIHCAMQABiABDIHCAQQABiABDIHCAUQABiABDIHCAYQABiABDIGCAcQRRg80gEINDE1MWowajeoAg-CwAgA&sourceid=chrome&ie=UTF-8
842. https://publicadministration.un.org/egovkb/en-us/Data/Country-Information/id/155-Slovakia
843. https://digital-strategy.ec.europa.eu/en/library/egovernment-benchmark-2023
844. https://ec.europa.eu/commission/presscorner/detail/en/ip_23_5651

845. https://digital-decade-desi.digital-strategy.ec.europa.eu/datasets/desi/charts/desi-indicators?indicator=desi_1a2&breakdown=ind_total&period=desi_2023&unit=pc_ind&country=AT,BE,BG,HR,CY,CZ,DK,EE,EU,FI,FR,DE,EL,HU,IE,IT,LV,LT,LU,MT,NL,PL,PT,RO,SK,SI,ES,SE

846. https://digital-decade-desi.digital-strategy.ec.europa.eu/datasets/desi/ charts/compare-countries-progress?indicator=desi_1b1&breakdown=total&unit=pc_ind_emp&country=EU,SK

847. https://mirri.gov.sk/wp-content/uploads/2019/10/SDT-English-Version-FINAL.pdf

848. https://publicadministration.un.org/egovkb/en-us/Data/Country-Information/id/156-Slovenia

849. https://e-uprava.gov.si/en

850. http://appsso.eurostat.ec.europa.eu/nui/show.do?dataset=isoc_bde15ei&lang=en

851. http://www.stopbirokraciji.si/en/home/

852. https://www.gov.si/en/topics/digitalisation-of-society/

853. https://digital-strategy.ec.europa.eu/en/policies/desi

854. https://digital-strategy.ec.europa.eu/en/policies/countries-digitisation-performance

855. http://www.mju.gov.si/en/

856. https://www.oecd-ilibrary.org/governance/digital-government-review-of-slovenia_954b0e74-en

857. https://www.lamoncloa.gob.es/serviciosdeprensa/notasprensa/asuntos-economicos/Documents/2021/270121-%20Agenda_Digital_2025.pdf

858. https://portal.mineco.gob.es/RecursosNoticia/mineco/prensa/noticias/2021/210127_np_pyme.pdf

859. https://portal.mineco.gob.es/RecursosNoticia/mineco/prensa/noticias/2020/201201_np_conectivid.pdf,

860. https://portal.mineco.gob.es/RecursosNoticia/mineco/prensa/noticias/2020/201201_np_impulso5G.pdf

861. https://www.lamoncloa.gob.es/presidente/actividades/Documents/2020/ ENIAResumen2B.pdf

862. https://digital-strategy.ec.europa.eu/en/policies/desi-spain

863. https://publicadministration.un.org/egovkb/en-us/Data/Country-Information/id/160-Spain

864. https://publicadministration.un.org/egovkb/en-us/Data/Country-Information/id/165-Sweden

865. https://commission.europa.eu/strategy-and-policy/priorities-2019-2024/ europe-fit-digital-age/europes-digital-decade-digital-targets-2030_en#:~:text=to%20digital%20ID-,The%20Path%20to%20the%20Digital%20Decade,the%20 Commission%20and%20Member%20States.&text=The%20Commission%20 has%20developed%20EU%2Dlevel%20trajectories.

866. https://www.digg.se/en

867. https://www.digg.se/globalassets/framja-den-offentliga-forvaltningens-formaga-att-anvanda-ai-1.1.pdf

868. https://www.norden.org/en/project/nordic-baltic-eid-project-nobid

869. https://rib.msb.se/filer/pdf/28898.pdf

870. https://www.ey.com/en_fi/government-public-sector/how-can-nordic-governments-successfully-bridge-the-digital-divid

871. https://www.oecd-ilibrary.org/sites/48cb8829-en/index.html?itemId=/content/component/48cb8829-en

872. https://publicadministration.un.org/egovkb/en-us/Data/Country-Information/id/166-Switzerland

873. https://desapublications.un.org/sites/default/files/publications/2024-09/%28Web%20version%29%20E-Government%20Survey%20 2024%201392024.pdf

874. https://www.oecd.org/publication/government-at-a-glance/2023/country-notes/switzerland-8f88ce47/#chapter-d1e22

875. https://www2.deloitte.com/ch/en/pages/public-sector/articles/study-digital-government.html

876. https://publicadministration.un.org/egovkb/en-us/Data/Country-Information/id/180-Ukraine
877. https://ukraine.ua/invest-trade/digitalization/
878. https://www.usaid.gov/news-information/press-releases/jan-18-2023-ussupported-e-government-app-accelerated-digital-transformation-ukraine-nowukraine-working-scale-solution-more-countries
879. https://e-estonia.com/estonia-to-pilot-a-national-mobile-app-based-onthe-ukrainian-diia-application/
880. https://www.devex.com/organizations/foreign-commonwealth-development-office-fcdo-158082
881. https://www.itu.int/en/mediacentre/Pages/PR-2023-09-12-universal-and-meaningful-connectivity-by-2030.aspx
882. https://assets.publishing.service.gov.uk/media/65fc540965ca2f00117da813/ FCDO-Digital-Development-Strategy-2024-2030.pdf
883. https://www.gov.uk/government/publications/dfid-digital-strategy-2018to-2020-doing-development-in-a-digital-world
884. https://publicadministration.un.org/egovkb/en-us/Data/Country-Information/id/182-United-Kingdom-of-Great-Britain-and-Northern-Ireland
885. https://www.oecd.org/development-cooperation-learning/practices/leaving-no-one-behind-in-a-digital-world-the-united-kingdom-s-digital-accessprogramme-e8b15982/
886. https://mdr-maa.org/resource/digital-vatican-library-dvl/#:~:text=DigiVatLib%20is%20a%20digital%20library%20service
887. https://digi.vatlib.it/mss/
888. https://www.vatican.va/content/vatican/en/info.html#:~:text=visit%20 the%20Vatican%20Necropolis%20%28write%20to%20the%20Excavations%20
889. Office%20by%20e%2DMail%20scavi%40fsp.va%20or%20by%20fax%20%2B39%2006%2069873017%29

890. https://www.dell.com/en-us/perspectives/spreading-a-message-of-kindness-why-and-how-the-vatican-revamped-its-technology/#:~:text=Vatican%20 Internet%20Service%E2%80%94the%20telecommunications%20department%20behind%20the%20Vatican%E2%80%99s%20web%20service
891. https://www.comunicazione.va/en.html
892. https://www.vatican.va/roman_curia/dpc/documents/20230528_dpc-verso-piena-presenza_en.html#:~:text=of%20young%20people%E2%80%99s%20identity%20and%20way%20of%20life
893. https://www.iubilaeum2025.va/en.html
894. https://desapublications.un.org/sites/default/files/publications/2022-09/Web%20version%20E-Government%202022.pdf
895. https://www.oecd-ilibrary.org/docserver/29f32e64-en.pdf?expires=1724247278&id=id&accname=guest&checksum=E33A83832273094B216A9A1F2FD0DED2
896. https://www.itu.int/en/ITUD/Statistics/Pages/facts/default.aspx
897. https://ab.gov.ag/
898. https://www.undp.org/sites/g/files/zskgke326/files/migration/ks/Factsheet_ DRA_final.pdf
899. https://caribbean.un.org/en/238290-antigua-and-barbuda-holds-digital-readiness-assessment-workshop
900. https://sdgs.un.org/conferences/sids2024
901. https://desapublications.un.org/sites/default/files/publications/2024-09/%28Web%20version%29%20E-Government%20Survey%20 2024%201392024.pdf
902. https://publicadministration.un.org/egovkb/en-us/Data/Country Information/id/6-Antigua-and-Barbuda
903. https://desapublications.un.org/sites/default/files/publications/2024-09/%28Web%20version%29%20E-Government%20Survey%20 2024%201392024.pdf
904. https://www.oecd-ilibrary.org/governance/digital-government-review-of-latin-america-and-the-caribbean_29f32e64-en
905. https://www.iadb.org/en/whats-our-impact/BA-L1046

906. https://nationnews.com/2024/01/05/digital-id-coming-this-year/
907. https://desapublications.un.org/sites/default/files/publications/2022-09/ Report%20without%20annexes.pdf
908. https://www.belize.gov.bz/
909. https://www.pressoffice.gov.bz/e-governance-and-digitalization-unit-supports-belize-motor-vehicle-registration-and-licensing-system/
910. https://belize.com/news/belize-government-moves-to-digital-transformation-of-judiciary/
911. https://www.unicef.org/innovation/giga
912. https://www.moecst.gov.bz/wp-content/uploads/2022/02/The-Belize-Education-Sector-Plan-2021-2025_MoECST.pdf
913. https://digitalagenda.gov.bz/
914. https://www.timescolonist.com/technology/canada-will-need-250000-digital-workers-by-2025-are-we-ready-6518645
915. https://canadianinnovators.medium.com/ccis-talent-skills-strategy36dba791a4dd
916. https://www.canadim.com/blog/tech-talent-strategy-open-work-permit/
917. https://www.canada.ca/en/immigration-refugees-citizenship/news/2023/06/canadas-tech-talent-strategy.html
918. https://www.linkedin.com/in/mohammad-j-sear/recent-activity/articles/
919. https://policyoptions.irpp.org/magazines/october-2022/ottawa-needs-thousands-of-tech-workers-to-serve-canadians-properly/#:~:text=Luelo%20said%20estimates%20reached%20as,programs%20today%20depend%20on%20technology.
920. https://publicadministration.un.org/egovkb/en-us/Data/Country-Information/id/31-Canada
921. https://www.accenture.com/ca-en/insights/public-service/chro-change-accelerator?c=acn_glb_hr-driventransfmediarelations_13677056&n=mrl_0523
922. https://publicadministration.un.org/egovkb/en-us/Data/Country-Information/id/40-Costa-Rica

923. https://desapublications.un.org/sites/default/files/publications/2022-09/ Report%20without%20annexes.pdf

924. https://ec.europa.eu/isa2/eif_en/

925. https://www.oecd-ilibrary.org/governance/digital-government-review-of-latin-america-and-the-caribbean_29f32e64-en

926. https://www.pgrweb.go.cr/scij/Busqueda/Normativa/utilitarios/PagError. aspx?nError=5

927. http://www.pgrweb.go.cr/scij/Busqueda/Normativa/Normas/nrm_tex-to_completo.aspx?param1= NRTC&nValor1=1&nValor2=86815&nValor3=112831&strTipM=TC

928. http://www.pgrweb.go.cr/scij/Busqueda/Normativa/Normas/nrm_texto_completo.aspx?param1=NRTC&nValor1 =1&nValor2=84166&n-Valor3=108486&strTipM=TC

929. http://www.pgrweb.go.cr/scij/Busqueda/Normativa/normas/nrm_texto_ completo.aspx?nValor1=1&nValor2=84004

930. http://www.pgrweb.go.cr/scij/Busqueda/Normativa/Normas/nrm_texto_ completo.aspx?nValor1=1&nValor2=74352

931. http://www.pgrweb.go.cr/scij/Busqueda/ Normativa/Normas/nrm_texto_completo.aspx?param1=NRTC &nValor1=1&nV alor2=70975&nValor3=85989#:~:text=Ninguna%20persona%20estar%C3%A1%20obligada%20a,la%20orientaci%C3%B3n%20sexual%2C%20entre%20otros

932. http://gob.go.cr/

933. https://desapublications.un.org/sites/default/files/publications/2022-09/ Report%20without%20annexes.pdf

934. https://publicadministration.un.org/egovkb/en-us/Data/Country-Information/id/43-Cuba

935. https://eltoque.com/los-memes-estallan-con-las-pruebas-de-internet-pordatos-moviles-en-cuba

936. https://desapublications.un.org/sites/default/files/publications/2024-09/%28Web%20version%29%20E-Government%20Survey%20 2024%201392024.pdf

937. https://data.worldbank.org/indicator/SP.POP.TOTL?locations=DM
938. https://desapublications.un.org/sites/default/files/publications/2024-09/%28Web%20version%29%20E-Government%20Survey%20 2024%201392024.pdf
939. https://tron.network/
940. https://publicadministration.un.org/egovkb/en-us/Data/Country-Information/id/50-Dominica
941. https://www.facebook.com/workonlinedominica
942. https://projects.worldbank.org/en/projects-operations/project-detail/ P171528
943. https://easterncaribbean.un.org/en/134830-dominicans-shape-their-digital-future-support-undp
944. https://desapublications.un.org/sites/default/files/publications/2024-09/%28Web%20version%29%20E-Government%20Survey%20 2024%201392024.pdf
945. https://publicadministration.un.org/egovkb/en-us/Data/Country-Information/id/51-Dominican-Republic
946. https://sustainabledevelopment.un.org/content/documents/20170Executive_Summary_Domincan_RepublicEn_.pdf
947. https://play.google.com/store/apps/details?id=com.map.servicios_publicos&hl=en&gl=US
948. https://www.oecd-ilibrary.org/governance/digital-government-review-of-latin-america-and-the-caribbean_29f32e64-en
949. https://observatorioserviciospublicos.gob.do/publicaciones/encuestas/institucionales/resolucion_03_2019.pdf
950. https://e-estonia.com/solutions/interoperability-services/x-road/
951. http://www.gobiernoelectronico.gob.sv/?page_id=21
952. https://www.innovacion.gob.sv/
953. https://sdgs.un.org/goals
954. https://datareportal.com/reports/digital-2023-el-salvador
955. https://www.gsmaintelligence.com/?utm_source=DataReportal&utm_medium=article&utm_campaign=State_Internet_Connectivity

956. https://datareportal.com/reports/digital-2024-el-salvador
957. https://www.globalcitizen.org/es/content/el-salvador-education-digital-revolution/
958. https://openknowledge.worldbank.org/bitstream/handle/10986/35080/Digital-Skills-Frameworks-and-Programs.pdf?sequence=1
959. https://www.mined.gob.sv/category/emtt/sedes-megatec/
960. https://www.macrotrends.net/countries/GRD/grenada/population#:~:text=The%20population%20of%20Grenada%20in,a%200.77%25%20increase%20 from%202020.
961. https://publicadministration.un.org/egovkb/en-us/Data/Country-Information/id/68-Grenada
962. https://desapublications.un.org/sites/default/files/publications/2024-09/%28Web%20version%29%20E-Government%20Survey%20 2024%201392024.pdf
963. https://www.undp.org/barbados/publications/grenada-smart-small-state-developing-vision
964. https://theblueallliance.org/project-bluebot/
965. https://www.undp.org/barbados/publications/grenada-smart-small-state-developing-vision
966. https://www.undp.org/barbados/climate-resilient-agriculture-integrated-landscape-management
967. https://www.undp.org/barbados/carisecure
968. https://desapublications.un.org/sites/default/files/publications/2024-09/%28Web%20version%29%20E-Government%20Survey%20 2024%201392024.pdf
969. https://transparencia.gob.gt/wp-content/uploads/Plan-de-Gobierno-Digital_M-1.pdf
970. https://www.itu.int/cn/ITUD/Statistics/Dashboards/Pages/Digital-Development.aspx
971. https://www.usaid.gov/sites/default/files/2023-05/Guatemala%20 DECA%20Report.pdf
972. https://www.usaid.gov/sites/default/files/2023-05/Guatemala%20 DECA%20Report.pdf

973. https://www.itu.int/en/ITUD/Statistics/Dashboards/Pages/Digital-Development.aspx
974. https://desapublications.un.org/sites/default/files/publications/2024-09/%28Web%20version%29%20E-Government%20Survey%20 2024%201392024.pdf
975. https://publicadministration.un.org/egovkb/en-us/Data/Country-Information/id/73-Haiti
976. https://www.usaid.gov/haiti/fact-sheet/jan-05-2024-haiti-national-id-cardprogram
977. https://documents1.worldbank.org/curated/en/099005006212227622/pdf/ P17411109a9dce07b0b6bf0e5389ab9ceac.pdf
978. https://www.wfp.org/publications/digital-financial-inclusion-practice-haiti-brief
979. https://publicadministration.un.org/egovkb/en-us/Data/Country-Information/id/74-Honduras
980. https://www.diger.gob.hn/republica
981. https://www.diger.gob.hn/republica
982. https://www.sanpedrosula.hn/
983. https://ampuertocortes.hn/
984. https://www.oecd-ilibrary.org/sites/e7a00fd6-en/index.html?itemId=/content/component/e7a00fd6-en#annex-3.A1
985. https://www.worldbank.org/en/news/press-release/2023/12/18/honduras-fortalecera-registro-civil-identificacion-personas-y-facilita-acceso-servicios-apoyo-banco-mundial
986. https://publicadministration.un.org/egovkb/en-us/Data/Country-Information/id/84-Jamaica
987. https://desapublications.un.org/sites/default/files/publications/2022-09/ Report%20without%20annexes.pdf
988. https://international-partnerships.ec.europa.eu/news-and-events/news/global-gateway-eu-launches-digital-jamaica-connect-schools-universities-andhomes-high-speed-2023-10-10_en

989. https://www.biometricupdate.com/202212/cayman-islands-pass-digital-idand-id-card-bills-jamaica-begins-zero-fail-pilot

990. https://www.biometricupdate.com/202308/face-biometrics-planned-forjamaica-airport-may-replace-passport-checks-in-singapore

991. https://jis.gov.jm/pica-acquiring-new-border-security-management-system/

992. https://jis.gov.jm/one-jamaica-app-being-proposed-for-accessing-multiple-govt-services/

993. https://jis.gov.jm/data-protection-act-takes-effect-today/

994. https://jis.gov.jm/ict-council-established-to-spearhead-re-organisation-of-government-operations/

995. https://www.oecd-ilibrary.org/governance/digital-government-review-of-latin-america-and-the-caribbean_29f32e64-en

996. https://www.mckinsey.com/industries/public-and-social-sector/our-insights/the-opportunity-in-government-productivity

997. https://desapublications.un.org/sites/default/files/publications/2024-09/%28Web%20version%29%20E-Government%20Survey%20 2024%201392024.pdf

998. https://www.mexicox.gob.mx/

999. https://aprende.gob.mx

1000. https://www.gob.mx/epn/es/articulos/interoperamx 1011.
https://openknowledge.worldbank.org/server/api/core/bitstreams/62c7b526-3a67-4557-9942-74a2697c67d9/content

1001. https://desapublications.un.org/sites/default/files/publica-

1002. tions/2024-09/%28Web%20version%29%20E-Government%20Survey%20 2024%201392024.pdf

1003. https://publicadministration.un.org/egovkb/en-us/Data/Country-Information/id/123-Nicaragua

1004. https://datareportal.com/reports/digital-2024-nicaragua?rq=nicaragua

1005. https://www.reuters.com/world/americas/economic-cost-central-america-power-outage-seen-18-mln-2021-07-08/

1006. https://www.swissinfo.ch/spa/nicaragua-apag%C3%B3n_fallo-provoca-un-apag%C3%B3n-total-en-nicaragua-y-parcial-en-centroam%C3%A9rica/46692528
1007. https://www.antai.gob.pa/
1008. https://www.doingbusiness.org/content/dam/doingBusiness/country/p/ panama/PAN.pdf
1009. https://publicadministration.un.org/egovkb/en-us/Data/Country-Information/id/130-Panama
1010. https://aig.gob.pa/
1011. https://www.internetparatodos.gob.pa/nosotros
1012. https://www.panamacompra.gob.pa/Inicio/
1013. https://panamahub.digital/es/panama-hub-digital/acerca-de
1014. https://www.panamasolidario.gob.pa/
1015. https://publicadministration.un.org/egovkb/en-us/Data/Country-Information/id/143-Saint-Kitts-and-Nevis
1016. https://desapublications.un.org/sites/default/files/publications/2024-09/%28Web%20version%29%20E-Government%20Survey%20 2024%201392024.pdf
1017. https://www.socialdevelopment.gov.kn/
1018. https://www.socialdevelopment.gov.kn/forms/
1019. https://www.itu.int/en/ITU-D/Statistics/Documents/DDD/ddd_KNA.pdf
1020. https://www.ilo.org/caribbean/projects/WCMS_872172/lang--en/index. htm
1021. https://publicadministration.un.org/egovkb/en-us/Data/Country-Information/id/144-Saint-Lucia
1022. https://desapublications.un.org/sites/default/files/publica-
1023. tions/2024-09/%28Web%20version%29%20E-Government%20Survey%20 2024%201392024.pdf
1024. https://www.itu.int/en/ITUD/Statistics/Documents/DDD/ddd_LCA.pdf
1025. https://worlded.org/project/saint-lucia-connected-activity/
1026. https://worlded.org/a-youth-led-and-youth-centered-approach-to-building-digital-resilience/

1027. https://worlded.org/st-lucia-connected-activity-launches-innovative-digital-literacy-skills-youth-internship-program/
1028. https://projects.worldbank.org/en/projects-operations/project-detail/P171528
1029. https://desapublications.un.org/sites/default/files/publications/2024-09/%28Web%20version%29%20E-Government%20Survey%20 2024%201392024.pdf
1030. https://publicadministration.un.org/egovkb/en-us/Data/Country-Information/id/145-Saint-Vincent-and-the-Grenadines
1031. https://www.stvincenttimes.com/st-vincent-to-launch-digital-identification-pilot-project-in-2024/
1032. https://www.oecs.org/en/our-work/knowledge/library/projects/caribbean-digital-transformation-project-cardtp
1033. https://desapublications.un.org/sites/default/files/publications/2024-09/%28Web%20version%29%20E-Government%20Survey%20 2024%201392024.pdf
1034. https://datareportal.com/reports/digital-2023-trinidad-and-tobago
1035. https://www.iadb.org/en/news/trinidad-and-tobago-will-advance-digital-transformation-idb-support-0
1036. https://www.caf.com/en/currently/news/2024/01/caf-and-the-eu-willpromote-digitization-in-trinidad-and-tobago-with-the-first-global-gatewayproject-in-the-country/
1037. https://www.untrinidadandtobago.org/bigdataforumtt2020/
1038. https://link.springer.com/article/10.1007/s41060-023-00386-9
1039. https://www.finance.gov.tt/wpcontent/uploads/2021/12/Keynote-Address-by-the-Hon.-Colm-Imbert-Minister-of-Financc-at-the-UN-Big-Data-Forum-2021.pdf
1040. https://www.linkedin.com/pulse/neglected-user-centricity-oversight-government-platform-sear-odjpf?trackingId=BgHeZ2jrQ2u06sjogBgYVA%3D%3D&lipi=urn%3Ali%3Apage%3Ad flagship3 profile view base recent a

ctivity_content_view%3B51me6v6PTVu%2BGLCHtvk5Xg%3D%3D

1041. https://www.whitehouse.gov/omb/briefing-room/2023/09/22/why-the-american-people-deserve-a-digital-government/#:~:text=Every%20 day%2C%20Americans%20use%20their,make%20it%20easy%20for%20you.

1042. https://www.worldbank.org/en/results/2022/05/27/delivering-efficient-high-quality-digital-government-services-in-argentina

1043. https://www.argentina.gob.ar/jefatura/innovacion-tecnologica/servicios-y-pais-digital

1044. https://id.argentina.gob.ar/ingresar/?next=/authorize/%3Fclient_id%3D613410%26response_type%3Dcode%26scope%3Dopenid%2Bprofile%2Bemail%2Boptional%26redirect_uri%3Dhttps%3A//mi.argentina.gob.ar/_oauth/oidc%26state%3DeyJsb2dpblN0eWxlIjoicmVkaXJlY3QiLCJjcmVkZW50aWFsVG9rZW4iOiI5WWY3ZFdHSGNQTmFUem83ayIsImlzQ29yZG92YSI6ZmFsc2UsInJlZGlyZWN0VXJsIjoiaHR0cHM6Ly9taS5hcmdlbnRpbmEuZ29iLmFyLyJ9

1045. https://www.argentina.gob.ar/noticias/programa-federal-de-transformacion-publica-digital

1046. https://www.worldometers.info/world-population/bolivia-population/#:~:text=Bolivia%202023%20population%20is%20estimated,of%20the%20 total%20world%20population.

1047. https://desapublications.un.org/sites/default/files/publica-

1048. tions/2024-09/%28Web%20version%29%20E-Government%20Survey%20 2024%201392024.pdf

1049. https://publicadministration.un.org/egovkb/en-us/Data/Country-Information/id/21-Bolivia

1050. https://www.itu.int/en/ITUD/Statistics/Documents/DDD/ddd_AFG.pdf

1051. https://www.dataguidance.com/sites/default/files/agetic.pdf

1052. https://publicadministration.un.org/egovkb/en-us/Data/Country-Information/id/24-Brazil

1053. https://www.oecd.org/publications/digital-government-review-of-latin-america-and-the-caribbean-29f32e64-en.htm

1054. https://www.oecd-ilibrary.org/governance/open-government-review-ofbrazil_3f9009d4-en

1055. https://www.gov.br/mcti/pt-br/acompanhe-o-mcti/transformacaodigital/arquivosestrategiadigital/e-digital_ciclo_2022-2026.pdf

1056. https://www.oecd-ilibrary.org/sites/29f32e64-en/1/3/2/index.html?itemId=/content/publication/29f32e64-en&_csp_=ece5ecf893144f8e281b1ad4b465ae8d&itemIGO=oecd&itemContentType=book#endnote974d61c79723

1057. https://www.escolavirtual.gov.br/programas

1058. http://startup.gov.br/

1059. https://desapublications.un.org/sites/default/files/publications/2024-09/%28Web%20version%29%20E-Government%20Survey%20 2024%201392024.pdf

1060. https://publicadministration.un.org/egovkb/Portals/egovkb/Documents/un/2020-Survey/2020%20UN%20E-Government%20Survey%20(Full%20Report).pdf

1061. https://www.chileatiende.gob.cl/

1062. https://www.satisfaccion.gob.cl/

1063. https://www.elac.edu/

1064. https://www.oecd-ilibrary.org/sites/b94582e8-en/1/3/1/index.html?itemId=/content/publication/b94582e8-en&_csp_=864d08acdfdb1985bef8f2d 586727be5&itemIGO=oecd&itemContentType=book

1065. https://mintic.gov.co/portal/inicio/Micrositios/English-overview/Ministry-of-ICT/

1066. https://www.oecd.org/dev/americas/Colombia-Country-Note-Leo-2019.pdf

1067. https://www.oecd-ilibrary.org/sites/781185b1-en/1/1/1/index.html?itemId=/content/publication/781185b1-en&mimeType=text/html&_ csp_=2e55b885b2f1f6b5f49b8e209518fce4&itemIGO=oecd&itemContent-Type=book

1068. https://publicadministration.un.org/egovkb/en-us/Data/Country-Information/id/37-Colombia
1069. http://www.businessgoing.digital/digital-transformation-in-colombiastate-of-play-in-the-public-and-private-sectors/
1070. http://observatorioplanificacion.cepal.org/es/planes/plan-de-creacion-deoportunidades-2021-2025-de-ecuador
1071. https://datareportal.com/reports/digital-2024-ecuador
1072. https://www.telecomunicaciones.gob.ec/el-mintel-y-coursera-ofrecencursos-en-linea-para-la-reactivacion-de-la-fuerza-laboral-en-ecuador/
1073. https://desapublications.un.org/sites/default/files/publications/2024-09/%28Web%20version%29%20E-Government%20Survey%20 2024%201392024.pdf
1074. https://puntosdigitalesgratuitos.mintel.gob.ec/
1075. https://openknowledge.worldbank.org/entities/publication/522ef03f-7ccd-4f39-ac03-f6c85ba33102
1076. http://www.gob.ec/
1077. https://play.google.com/store/apps/details?id=ec.gob.gobiernoelectronico. gobec&hl=sq&gl=US
1078. https://datahub.itu.int/dashboards/umc/indicator/?e=GUY&i=12047
1079. https://lcds.gov.gy/timeline/ict-access-and-e-services-for-hinterlandpoor-and-remote-communities/
1080. https://www.undp.org/latin-america/blog/bridging-digital-divide-empowering-indigenous-regions-through-internet-connectivity-guyana-0
1081. https://lcds.gov.gy/
1082. https://www.guyanareddfund.org/
1083. https://www.biometricupdate.com/202303/contracts-for-national-bio-metric-travel-ids-won-by-hid-in-bahrain-veridos-in-guyana
1084. https://guyanatimesgy.com/digital-id-card-with-high-security-featuresto-shield-against-fraud/
1085. https://www.parliament.gov.gy/chamber-business/bill-status/digitalidentitycardbill2023

1086. https://desapublications.un.org/sites/default/files/publications/2024-09/%28Web%20version%29%20E-Government%20Survey%20 2024%201392024.pdf
1087. https://www.oecd.org/publications/digital-government-review-of-latin-america-and-the-caribbean-29f32e64-en.htm
1088. https://www.data4sdgs.org/towards-water-information-system-paraguay#:~:text=The%20result%20of%20this%20process,sanitation%20services%20 across%20the%20country.
1089. https://www.un.org/sustainabledevelopment/water-and-sanitation/
1090. https://www.mitic.gov.py/viceministerios/tecnologias-de-la-informacion-y-comunicacion/servicios/sistema-de-intercambio-de-informacion
1091. https://www.mitic.gov.py/viceministerios/tecnologias-de-la-informacion-y-comunicacion/servicios/sistema-de-intercambio-de-informacion
1092. https://www.oecd-ilibrary.org/sites/29f32e64-en/1/3/4/index.html?itemId=/content/publication/29f32e64-en&_csp_=ece5ecf893144f8e281b1ad4b465ae8d&itemIGO=oecd&itemContentType=book#endnotee5342ee08210
1093. https://www.innovando.gov.py/
1094. https://desapublications.un.org/sites/default/files/publications/2022-09/Web%20version%20E-Government%202022.pdf
1095. https://international-partnerships.ec.europa.eu/policies/programming/programmes/bella-building-europe-link-latin-america_en
1096. https://www.iadb.org/en/news/peru-advance-its-digital-transformation-idb-support
1097. https://www.betterthancash.org/
1098. https://www.gob.pe/participa
1099. https://www.oecd-ilibrary.org/sites/29f32e64-en/1/3/6/index.html?itemId=/content/publication/29f32e64-en&_csp_=ece5ecf893144f8e281b1ad4b465ae8d&itemIGO=oecd&itemContentType=book

1100. https://e-estonia.com/solutions/interoperability-services/x-road/
1101. https://www.oecd.org/publications/digital-government-review-of-latin-america-and-the-caribbean-29f32e64-en.htm
1102. https://www.gob.pe/15777-estrategia-nacional-de-gobierno-de-datos
1103. https://www.gob.pe/15777-estrategia-nacional-de-gobierno-de-datos 1112. https://publicadministration.un.org/egovkb/en-us/Data/Country-Information/id/163-Suriname
1104. https://gov.sr/wp-content/uploads/2023/09/Suriname-National-Digital-Strategy-2023-2030.pdf
1105. https://www.itu.int/en/ITUD/Statistics/Documents/DDD/ddd_SUR.pdf
1106. https://www.submarinenetworks.com/en/systems/brazil-us/deep-blue-one 1116. https://www.sur-ix.sr/
1107. https://www.submarinecablemap.com/submarine-cable/suriname-guyana-submarine-cable-system-sg-scs
1108. https://desapublications.un.org/sites/default/files/publications/2022-09/Web%20version%20E-Government%202022.pdf
1109. http://gov.sr/
1110. https://www.mobileconnectivityindex.com/index.html#year=2022&zoneIsocode=SUR
1111. https://desapublications.un.org/sites/default/files/publications/2024-09/%28Web%20version%29%20E-Government%20Survey%20 2024%201392024.pdf
1112. https://publicadministration.un.org/egovkb/en-us/Data/Country-Information/id/185-Uruguay
1113. https://www.gub.uy/agencia-gobierno-electronico-sociedad-informacion-conocimiento/que-es-la-plataforma-de-interoperabilidad
1114. https://commission.europa.eu/law/law-topic/data-protection/international-dimension-data-protection/adequacy-decisions_en

1115. https://www.gub.uy/agencia-gobierno-electronico-sociedad-informacion-conocimiento/politicas-y-gestion/plan-gobierno-digital-2025

1116. https://www.gub.uy/agencia-gobierno-electronico-sociedad-informacion-conocimiento/comunicacion/publicaciones/modelo-atencion-ciudadania/ componentes-del-modelo/sistema-integrado

1117. https://www.gub.uy/tramites/

1118. https://www.oecd-ilibrary.org/sites/29f32e64-en/1/3/6/index.html?itemId=/content/publication/29f32e64-en&_csp_=ece5ecf893144f8e281b1ad4b465ae8d&itemIGO=oecd&itemContentType=book#endnote01cb09578920

1119. https://www.imf.org/external/datamapper/PCPIPCH@WEO/OEMDC/ADVEC/WEOWORLD/PIQ/SMQ

1120. https://publicadministration.un.org/egovkb/en-us/Data/Country-Information/id/188-Venezuela

1121. https://desapublications.un.org/sites/default/files/publications/2022-09/Web%20version%20E-Government%202022.pdf

1122. https://www.elimpulso.com/2021/03/18/cedice-libertad-en-febrero-2021el-100-de-los-hogares-venezolanos-tuvo-fallas-con-las-telecomunicaciones-18mar/

1123. https://www.itu.int/en/ITUD/Statistics/Documents/DDD/ddd VEN.pdf

1124. https://web.archive.org/web/20230619205748/https://www.speedtest.net/ global-index

1125. https://www.isocfoundation.org/2023/05/internet-poverty-index-more-than-1-billion-people-live-in-internet-poverty-worldwide/ 1136. http://www.conatel.gob.ve/informe-cifras-del-sector-primer-trimestre-2022/

1126. https://www.oecd.org/publications/digital-government-review-of-latin-america-and-the-caribbean-29f32e64-en.htm

1127. https://desapublications.un.org/sites/default/files/publications/2024-09/%28Web%20version%29%20E-Government%20Survey%20 2024%201392024.pdf

1128. https://www.dta.gov.au/digital-transformation-strategy/3-strategic-priorities/government-thats-fit-digital-age
1129. https://www.digitalidentity.gov.au/have-your-say/2023-digital-id-legislation-quick-and-simple-survey
1130. https://www.mygovid.gov.au/
1131. https://desapublications.un.org/sites/default/files/publications/2024-09/%28Web%20version%29%20E-Government%20Survey%20 2024%201392024.pdf
1132. https://publicadministration.un.org/egovkb/en-us/Data/Country-Information/id/111-Micronesia-Federated-States-of
1133. https://openknowledge.worldbank.org/server/api/core/bitstreams/5412b8b6-0db6-4bf8-ad3b-043755f8fa61/content
1134. https://datareportal.com/reports/digital-2024-federated-states-of-micronesia?rq=micronesia
1135. https://desapublications.un.org/sites/default/files/publica-tions/2024-09/%28Web%20version%29%20E-Government%20Survey%20 2024%201392024.pdf
1136. https://publicadministration.un.org/egovkb/en-us/Data/Country-Infor-mation/id/59-Fiji
1137. https://mobile.digital.gov.fj/EServices/Index
1138. https://datareportal.com/reports/digital-2024-fiji?rq=fiji
1139. https://publicadministration.un.org/egovkb/en-us/Data/Country-Information/id/89-Kiribati
1140. https://datareportal.com/reports/digital-2024-kiribati?rq=Kiribati
1141. https://www.itu.int/en/ITU-D/Statistics/Documents/DDD/ddd_KIR.pdf
1142. https://openknowledge.worldbank.org/server/api/core/bitstreams/5412b8b6-0db6-4bf8-ad3b-043755f8fa61/content
1143. https://openknowledge.worldbank.org/server/api/core/bitstreams/5412b8b6-0db6-4bf8-ad3b-043755f8fa61/content
1144. https://desapublications.un.org/sites/default/files/publications/2022-09/Report%20without%20annexes.pdf

1145. https://publicadministration.un.org/egovkb/en-us/Data/Country-Information/id/107-Marshall-Islands
1146. https://datareportal.com/reports/digital-2024-marshall-islands?rq=marshall
1147. https://desapublications.un.org/sites/default/files/publications/2022-09/Report%20without%20annexes.pdf
1148. https://publicadministration.un.org/egovkb/en-us/Data/Country-Information/id/119-Nauru
1149. https://openknowledge.worldbank.org/server/api/core/bitstreams/5412b8b6-0db6-4bf8-ad3b-043755f8fa61/content
1150. https://datareportal.com/reports/digital-2024-nauru?rq=nauru
1151. https://www.cwp.govt.nz/
1152. https://www.govt.nz/
1153. https://publicadministration.un.org/egovkb/en-us/Data/Country-Information/id/122-New-Zealand
1154. https://www.digital.govt.nz/digital-government/strategy/strategy-summary/strategy-for-a-digital-public-service/
1155. https://desapublications.un.org/sites/default/files/publications/2024-09/%28Web%20version%29%20E-Government%20Survey%20 2024%201392024.pdf
1156. https://publicadministration.un.org/egovkb/en-us/Data/Country-Information/id/129-Palau
1157. https://openknowledge.worldbank.org/server/api/core/bitstreams/5412b8b6-0db6-4bf8-ad3b-043755f8fa61/content
1158. https://datareportal.com/reports/digital-2024-palau?rq=palau
1159. https://rns.id/?rc_by=hTLbTE3v
1160. https://www.e-resident.gov.ee/
1161. https://publicadministration.un.org/egovkb/en-us/Data/Country-Information/id/131-Papua-New-Guinea
1162. https://openknowledge.worldbank.org/server/api/core/bitstreams/5412b8b6-0db6-4bf8-ad3b-043755f8fa61/content
1163. https://www.cipe.org/resources/papua-new-guineas-digital-transformation-understanding-legal-and-regulatory-challenges/

1164. https://datareportal.com/reports/digital-2024-papua-new-guinea?rq=papua%20new%20guinea
1165. https://unctad.org/publication/digital-economy-report-pacific-edition-2022
1166. http://mptf.undp.org/fund/jxb00#:~:text=The%20Pacific%20Financial%20Inclusion%20Joint%20Programme%20expands%20inclusive%20access%20to,assistance%20to%20policy%20makers%20and
1167. https://openknowledge.worldbank.org/server/api/core/bitstreams/5412b8b6-0db6-4bf8-ad3b-043755f8fa61/content
1168. https://desapublications.un.org/sites/default/files/publications/2024-09/%28Web%20version%29%20E-Government%20Survey%20 2024%201392024.pdf
1169. https://publicadministration.un.org/egovkb/en-us/Data/Country-Information/id/146-Samoa
1170. https://datareportal.com/reports/digital-2024-samoa?rq=samoa
1171. https://www.uncdf.org/article/8489/assessing-digital-and-financial-literacy-in-samoa
1172. https://desapublications.un.org/sites/default/files/publications/2022-09/Web%20version%20E-Government%202022.pdf
1173. https://publicadministration.un.org/egovkb/en-us/Data/Country-Information/id/157-Solomon-Islands
1174. https://desapublications.un.org/sites/default/files/publications/2024-09/%28Web%20version%29%20E-Government%20Survey%20 2024%201392024.pdf
1175. https://openknowledge.worldbank.org/server/api/core/bitstreams/5412b8b6-0db6-4bf8-ad3b-043755f8fa61/content
1176. https://datareportal.com/reports/digital-2024-solomon-islands?rq=solomon
1177. https://ides.uncdf.org/
1178. https://ides.uncdf.org/2020/SLB
1179. https://ides.uncdf.org/about/market-development-stages
1180. https://ides.uncdf.org/2022/SLB
1181. https://desapublications.un.org/sites/default/files/publications/2022-09/Web%20version%20E-Government%202022.pdf

1182. https://publicadministration.un.org/egovkb/en-us/Data/Country-Information/id/173-Tonga
1183. https://openknowledge.worldbank.org/server/api/core/bitstreams/5412b8b6-0db6-4bf8-ad3b-043755f8fa61/content
1184. https://datareportal.com/reports/digital-2024-tonga?rq=tonga
1185. https://ides.uncdf.org/2022/TON
1186. https://desapublications.un.org/sites/default/files/publications/2024-09/%28Web%20version%29%20E-Government%20Survey%20 2024%201392024.pdf
1187. https://publicadministration.un.org/egovkb/en-us/Data/Country-Information/id/178-Tuvalu
1188. https://datareportal.com/reports/digital-2024-tuvalu?rq=tuvalu 1200.
1189. https://openknowledge.worldbank.org/server/api/core/bitstreams/5412b8b6-0db6-4bf8-ad3b-043755f8fa61/content
1190. https://www.theguardian.com/world/2023/jun/27/tuvalu-climate-crisis-rising-sea-levels-pacific-island-nation-country-digital-clone
1191. https://dfa.gov.tv/index.php/future-now-project/
1192. https://www.straitstimes.com/singapore/researchers-build-digital-twinof-singapore-to-assess-urban-heat-find-ways-to-cool-city
1193. https://desapublications.un.org/sites/default/files/publications/2024-09/%28Web%20version%29%20E-Government%20Survey%202024%201392024.pdf
1194. https://datareportal.com/reports/digital-2024-vanuatu?rq=vanuatu
1195. https://publicadministration.un.org/egovkb/en-us/Data/Country-Information/id/187-Vanuatu
1196. https://openknowledge.worldbank.org/server/api/core/bitstreams/5412b8b6-0db6-4bf8-ad3b-043755f8fa61/content

www.ingramcontent.com/pod-product-compliance
Lightning Source LLC
Chambersburg PA
CBHW071407230926
51846CB00001B/32
* 9 7 8 9 6 9 6 3 9 2 6 7 5 *